I0801821

Research & Design
Textile Tectonics

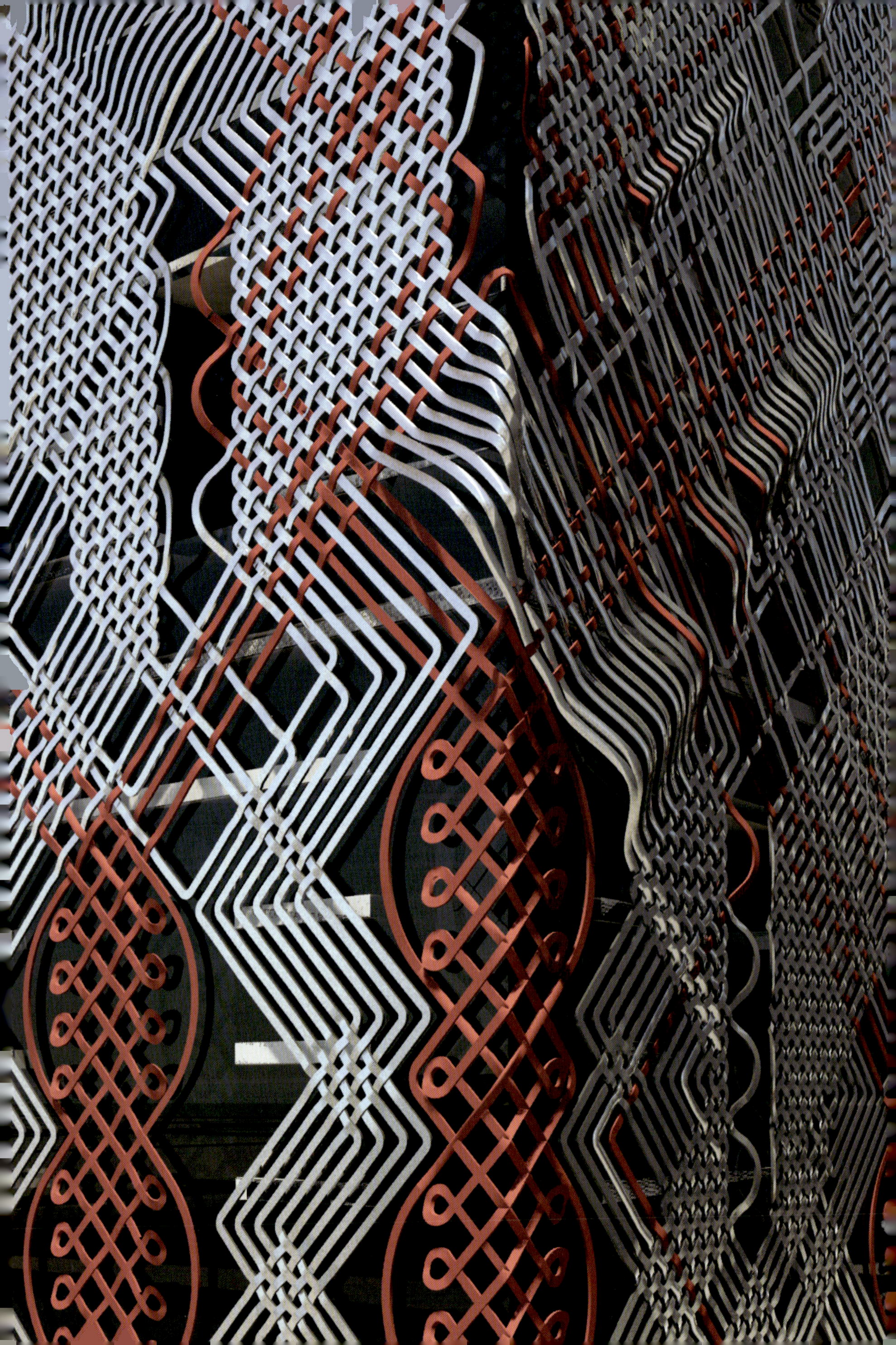

Research & Design

Textile Tectonics

Edited by Lars Spuybroek

Georgia Institute of Technology
School of Architecture

NAi Publishers

Contents

Introduction: Textile Tectonics

Before you is the second book in the Research & Design series. *Textile Tectonics* follows *The Architecture of Variation* and has a similar background, drawing on the same notions of history as an active provider of pattern and variation and of digital design not as a playing field for happy-go-lucky formalism but as a source for an architecture of precision and rigor.

I am becoming more and more convinced that digital design techniques have no business making references to the twentieth century, the age of standardization, minimalism and the sublime, but should instead look to the nineteenth, the century of Ruskin and Darwin, when variation began to claim a leading role in aesthetics and science. Today, digital design is still considered a platform for free-form architecture, streamlining and swooshism, while the nineteenth century's architectural forms – the Picturesque, the Gothic Revival, Arts & Crafts – form a much more stable foundation for developing a digital notion of architecture. To elaborate this concept further, I have rewritten John Ruskin's *The Nature of Gothic* from a contemporary perspective. Ruskin is much too infrequently read today, yet I cannot imagine anyone more necessary at a time when one Shanghai after the other is rising from the ground and architecture continues to resemble nothing so much as a drunk rambling down a badly lit street: all directions are possible, but we don't seem to be heading anywhere.

The theme of this volume in the series, *Textile Tectonics,* however, is only tangentially connected to Ruskin's thought – understandably, since it is a direct descendant of Gottfried Semper's *The Four Elements of Architecture,* famed for its idea that textile was the driving force behind the birth of architectonic form. Although textile is only one of the four elements (the others are the earth mound, timber frame and hearth fire), it is far and away the most important for Semper, chiefly because woven structures changed from physical space dividers into symbolic impressions visible in the stone of buildings. In short, his theory is one of ornamentation. But – because textile consists of flexible elements connected by means of specific techniques to form stable elements – it is also inherently one of tectonics. Semper's theory of *Bekleidung* is often seen as one in which the facade becomes drapery, but this view fails to take account of the fact that textile has its own structure, and hence also its own tectonics. The construction aspect of this theme is developed extensively in the Textile Towers section of the book, while the ornamentation aspect is explored in the Textile Façades section.

This second book, like the first, is the work of my department and my students at the Georgia Institute of Technology in Atlanta, where we are setting up a digital curriculum with the aim of prizing digital design techniques out of their technological straitjacket while preventing them from subsequently rushing into the arms of academic formalism. We believe that bridging that vast historic, but still very existent gap between the Polytechnique and the Beaux-Arts is one of digital design's most important tasks.

Lars Spuybroek

The Digital Nature of Gothic

Lars Spuybroek

Ruskin's *The Nature of Gothic* is inarguably the best-known book on Gothic architecture ever published; argumentative, persuasive, passionate, it's a text influential enough to have empowered a whole movement, which Ruskin distanced himself from on more than one occasion. Strangely enough, given that the chapter we are speaking of is the most important in the second volume of *The Stones of Venice,* it has nothing to do with the Venetian Gothic at all. Rather, it discusses a northern Gothic with which Ruskin himself had an ambiguous relationship all his life, sometimes calling it the noblest form of Gothic, sometimes the lowest, depending on which detail, transept or portal he was looking at. These are some of the reasons why this chapter has so often been published separately in book form, becoming a mini-bible for all true believers, among them William Morris, who wrote the introduction for the book when he published it with his own Kelmscott Press. It is a precious little book, made with so much love and care that one hardly dares read it.

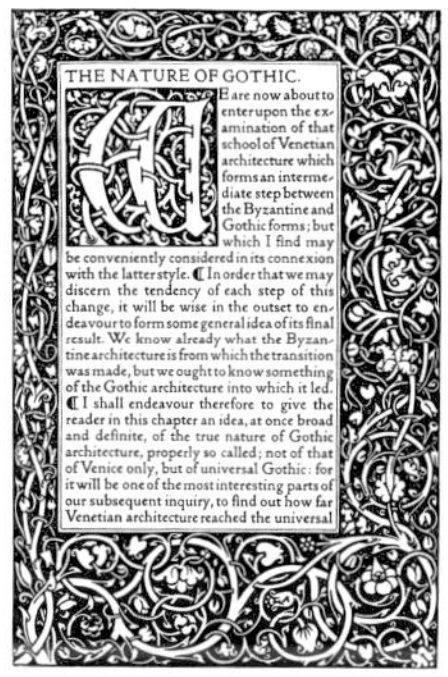
THE NATURE OF GOTHIC.
WE are now about to enter upon the examination of that school of Venetian architecture which forms an intermediate step between the Byzantine and Gothic forms; but which I find may be conveniently considered in its connexion with the latter style. ¶ In order that we may discern the tendency of each step of this change, it will be wise in the outset to endeavour to form some general idea of its final result. We know already what the Byzantine architecture is from which the transition was made, but we ought to know something of the Gothic architecture into which it led. ¶ I shall endeavour therefore to give the reader in this chapter an idea, at once broad and definite, of the true nature of Gothic architecture, properly so called; not of that of Venice only, but of universal Gothic: for it will be one of the most interesting parts of our subsequent inquiry, to find out how far Venetian architecture reached the universal

First Page of John Ruskin's "The Nature of Gothic: a chapter of The Stones of Venice" (Kelmscott Press, 1892).

Like its theoretical number-one enemy, classicism, the Gothic has protagonists who write like partisans in an especially ferocious army. They are not your usual historians – the Gothic hasn't been able to attract a significant number of the best historians; it has no Gombrich, Wölfflin or Wittkower, nobody of such caliber – but a series of hybrid and atypical historians such as Pugin and Worringer who have tried again and again, like Ruskin, to create a Gothic for the present, in whatever form: revivalist, expressionist, or, as in my case, digitalist, if that is a word. Each of them bends, distorts, and plunders the history of the Gothic, but invariably uses it as a weapon against that other architecture of the south. Pugin, in *Contrasts,* rescued the Gothic from its phase of folly, the phase of the *Gothick* (which was nothing but a dark Rococo), took it into the top league and pitted it against classicism, calling the latter "pagan" on page after page, denigrating it as a white, marbleized ghost of an essentially wooden architecture. Ruskin, no less subtly, kept calling classicism "Greek," meaning not-English or worse, not-from-the-North. Another nationalist from the other side of the North Sea, Wilhelm Worringer, preferred to label the Gothic as "Nordic"; Nordicism then wasn't as bad as its 1920s variant (with aviator Charles Lindbergh as one of its chief straight-nosed, high-foreheaded champions), but this nonetheless signaled a serious disqualification of Mediterranean architecture. Gilles Deleuze, who is known as a vitalist, was the most watered-down proponent of the Gothic, never giving it any serious historical attention save for making a repeated reference to Worringer's Gothic line and borrowing from him the concept of nonorganic life, in which free, proliferating curves are equated with deterritorializing barbarians, nomads and vagabonds breaking away from the state, whether Greek or Egyptian.

A. W. N. Pugin. "Revival of Christian Architecture" (1843).

We – for I have joined that partisan army now too, so from here on it is "we" – do not need to designate Gothicism as a stylistic entity like classicism, which keeps throwing the same columns, the same Corinthian or Ionic orders, the same universal whiteness in our faces age after age, and in its latest postmodern version has shown its true nature by jumping directly into the laps of all the world's developers and dressing up modernist skyscrapers and building fake Arcadias on top of five-story underground parking garages (I am writing this in Atlanta, itself currently trying to become a resurrected Atlantis). The Gothic, by contrast, is like a barbarian guerrilla force, constantly changing its face and adapting – fitting itself into a bourgeois niche, as in Art Nouveau; becoming historically self-evident, as in the Victorian revival; taking the form of the metallic, magnetic storm of its digital incarnation.

Hundreds, if not thousands, of books have been written about John Ruskin, a man to whom an entire library containing all his manuscripts is now dedicated, but one searches in vain for any reference to *The Nature of Gothic* in any scholarly book on the Gothic. There is none in Focillon, nor in Jantzen, nor in Frankl, except for a single degrading remark calling him a "dilettantist" – though thousands, if not hundreds of thousands, more people have read Ruskin's book than Frankl's own. Clearly, it is unnecessary to read Ruskin as if he is a historian of the Gothic; he is an advocate of it: of which Gothic exactly, neither he nor we know. He argues a case for his time, terrified by the state of the empire as he watches it slowly being engulfed in iron and shrouded in smoke. His way of working certainly should have stimulated more historians, who undeniably would have profited from its empiricism: lying on scaffolds for days drawing a detail high up in some forgotten corner, sketching capitals bathed in shadow, painting watercolors of inlaid marble baking in the sun, taking exact measurements, drawing up tables – things we do not get from the Frankls and Focillons. Ruskin is a hero of architecture, feeling it, smelling it, noting it down in its every detail, drawing its minutest part for us. In *Stones*, we get a complete archaeology, the actual stones of Venice dug out from reality, drawn, measured and categorized: not a single plan, not a single section of a building, only stones and members. We get them as they were carved and as we see them, nothing bigger, no system, no "metaphysics."

John Ruskin. Entrance to the South Transept of Rouen Cathedral (1854).

In *The Nature of Gothic*, Ruskin sets up a grand rhetoric to state his case, with a cascading list of "characteristics," all of them exclusively anti-classical, dramatically building one argument on top of the other. Since there have been so many books on Ruskin, books on every aspect of him, and books comparing every aspect of him and every other Victorian, it will suffice here to briefly summarize the six characteristics before I begin mobilizing the most important ones for my own case.

The first one, a close relative of the Picturesque, is savageness – a delightful term in itself, which Ruskin does not use in the same way as Owen Jones in his reference to "savage tribes" but nonetheless equates with a form of primitivism. "Savage" describes the workmen, the rough northern laborers, with their hands freezing, their heads in the mist and their feet in the mud, inevitably making "mistakes" in their carving because of their "rude" nature but also because of the open design system of the Gothic, which at certain points leaves them to decide what to do, hesitate suddenly, and ultimately present us with "failed, clumsy" ornament. All the same, it is the more beautiful because such savage details are markers of who the workers are, where they live and what they do:

"Imperfection is in some sort essential to all that we know of life. It is the sign of life in a mortal body, that is to say, of a state of progress and change. Nothing that lives is, or can be, rigidly perfect; part of it is decaying, part of it is nascent" (X, 203).

If there ever was a vitalist, it was John Ruskin. Some might be inclined to contest this statement and argue that he was a Christian (long periods of doubt notwithstanding), and a pious one at that. This is true, but he was usually a Christian at the *end* of an argument, never at the start: that is, after all thoughts had been thought. With Ruskin, a line of reasoning never relies on his Christianity, but it does heavily rely on his vitalism. He sincerely despises everything about Greek and Renaissance architecture: the form, the structure, the details – it is "an architecture invented, as it seems, to make plagiarists of its architects and slaves of its workmen" (XI, 227), who are forced merely to copy and repeat a single detail, one curve after another, without ever adding anything of their own, clumsy or otherwise.

The second characteristic, changefulness, if not a more admirable term than the first, does not, like savageness, indicate anything about the nature of the stonemason's execution of his craft but rather signifies a broader sense of variety in *design*, that is, the work of the architect, the master mason: "The vital principle is not the love of Knowledge, but the love of *Change*" (X, 214). Such variety – not too distinct from Hogarth's notion of it, especially the Hogarth of the *serpentine line* – is demonstrated in the curvature of the moldings, the bundled grouping of the shafts, the tracery of the windows, the pointedness of each arch, and the meshing of the ribbed vaults. The third characteristic, naturalism, is an index of the "intense affection" of the Gothic workmen for living foliage. Previously, Ruskin had called the Gothic a "foliated architecture" (X, 260) that "has been derived from vegetation," which gives it a natural component. This is a category we might expect from the author of *Modern Painters,* who taught us to draw every twig, every cloud and rock as unique and filled with personality. The fourth, grotesqueness, occurs in extension of savageness, taking imagination into the realm of fancy, humor, and often the burlesque. It is the best-known feature of the Gothic, with its pagan gargoyles, and Ruskin covers it in just three sentences. The fifth, rigidity, is especially interesting because Ruskin has been accused more than once of not appreciating structural notions of architecture. In this section, he explains in detail how we should understand the Gothic as an active form of support and transfer of loads rather than a simple form of resisting forces. The sixth characteristic, "redundance," relates to "an accumulation of ornament" that expresses "a profound sympathy with the fullness and wealth of the material universe," a logical final category since redundancy directly opposes the classical reductionism Ruskin so despises.

All six are closely related – redundance to naturalism, naturalism to changefulness, grotesqueness to savageness – and all intersect at the point of rigidity, but for us the relationship between savageness and changefulness is the most relevant since it raises the main question: How does the Gothic succeed in converging all existing forces into form? If there are forces of perception and of social organization alongside the forces of gravity, how are all these channeled into form? Ruskin's deeply philosophical answer is "through variation": the Gothic takes variation as its main formative drive by acting changeful at the level of design and savage at the level of execution. In alignment with Ruskin, we must first ask ourselves what exactly constitutes each quality, and second, how the two relate to each other. How does changefulness contain, permit or give rise to savageness, or vice versa? In the course of this essay, we will find that each produces different types of variation, one smooth and delicate, the other rough and incremental, but we will also find that together they aggregate not only into an amalgam of forms but also one of manners of organization of work. We will find that fields of changeful smoothness contain not only hard little bits of savageness but themselves develop hard edges that allow the structure to grow, to transform or even to be broken off.

During this essay, we will encounter various types of hands, which turn up one after the other – not only Ruskin's workman's hands chiseling stone and the craftman's hands of Sennett's Chinese butcher Chuang Tzu, but angels' ethereal hands, and little girls holding hands during a dance, and a master mason's hands scissoring compasses, and robot hands operating with magical dexterity, and even objects taking matters into their own hands, literally self-assembling. We'll see activity and work take on an abstraction, either occurring in small chunks distributed over all the stages of the process or concentrated into a single phase. In whatever form, work cannot be isolated or definitively located: even when done by a group, it is activity to be passed on. The notion is one of physical work being as much part of the design as drawing and tracing are part of cutting and carving: in short, *work is in design, and design is in work* – and thus savageness is in changefulness, and vice versa. This makes our argument specifically one of the digital, since the digital constitutes the realm of self-generating and self-drawing form.

Let us now start to investigate Ruskin's characteristics of the nature of Gothic more closely, while concentrating in particular on savageness, changefulness and rigidity – not because the other three are of no importance, but because they fall outside the scope of this essay.

Savageness

Not surprisingly, the argument for savageness has met with vehement ridicule. Take one look at the cathedral in Reims and you will immediately understand that savageness cannot be called a main characteristic of the Gothic. The building is completely designed, and with a precision that continues to baffle us today. For some reason, there is still a widespread misconception that the Gothic was an era without architects. In fact, the inverse is true: it was the time of their definitive ascent after a millennium's absence. Architects, mostly from northern France – men who had exchanged their hammers and chisels for compasses and rulers – traveled around Europe from one project to the next. The eleventh and twelfth centuries saw the emergence of master masons who no longer concerned themselves with personally carving the stone but with drawing it, a practice that was not always met with equal acceptance. According to a sermon from 1261:

"In these huge buildings there is an architect who directs by word alone and who seldom or never dirties his hands; however he receives much higher recompense than the others. (Nicolas de Biard)"

What is most important for us, however, is to understand the distance and the stages between the drawing and its executed form. When an architect today makes a drawing, it has all the details worked out; it is *prescriptive*: drawings of different scales, front and side views, and cross-sections together geometrically determine the whole object. The architects of the Gothic, however, had only recently said farewell to pure craft, and hence we see drawings not only marked on paper but also cut into wood and carved into stone floors. Most drawings were made (in so-called trasuras – tracing houses or drawing offices) on paper that perished fairly quickly, but some have been preserved on parchment, and one can see that in the main they were overall designs. Not everything that was ultimately built would have been included in a drawing: drawings were mostly *descriptive* in nature. In the stone floors of a few Gothic buildings, so-called tracings have been found: deeply scratched full-scale schematic drawings of parts such as window traceries in the form of a horizontal *plan*. In addition, there were so-called templates that provided information about the *cross-section* of an object; these wooden models were mainly used by stonecutters to determine the profile of a molding, base or rib. Dozens of these templates can be found in the famous remaining books of Villard de Honnecourt. Thus we find drawings on paper, but in a way also in wood and stone, and each of these techniques is embodied by a group, a guild with its own laws and opinions; and neither these groups nor their techniques fit hierarchically together.

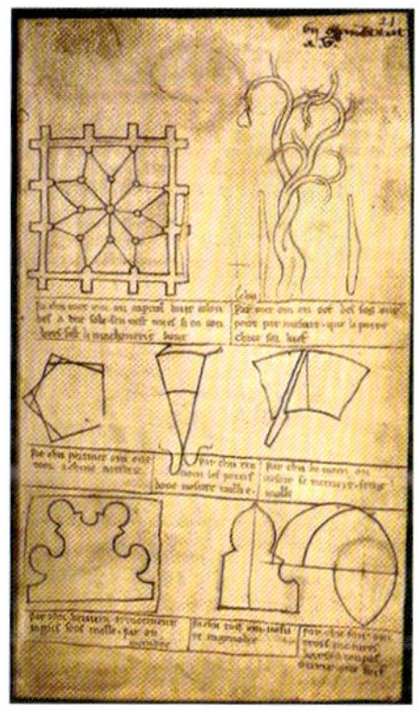

Page showing various wooden templates (below) from: Sketchbook of Villard de Honnecourt, folio 41 (13th century).

It is in no way true that the higher group only actively performed and the lower receptively and passively executed; there was some space between drawing and execution, enough for individual details, though not as much as Ruskin hoped. For him, architecture chiefly belonged to the realm of ornament, and ornament was small, so it was mainly in the capitals and added images, such as the famous gargoyles, that his savageness appeared. Of course, a project's success depended on a continuous flow of information supported by the necessary legal remedies and financing – in short, by a high level of organization – but this is not to say there was no room for invention and imperfection. Later in this essay, we will see that savageness appears to a much more significant degree on the collective scale.

Changefulness

Variability's greatest influence in the Gothic, however, was determined by something else: not incomplete execution but changefulness, the second characteristic on Ruskin's list – the idea of variety, in which the wide applicability of the rib as the driving design principle leads to an incredible multitude of solutions. Variation thus lies much more in design technique than in manual labor. Here again, Ruskin's argument is much closer to Hogarth's (although he never says this in so many words), which thereby takes on a specific aesthetic meaning. Ruskin devotes a wonderful long paragraph to the principle:

"[...] they were capable of *perpetual novelty*. The pointed arch was not merely a bold variation from the round, but it admitted of millions of variations in itself; for the proportions of a pointed arch are changeable to infinity, while a circular arch is always the same. The grouped shaft was not merely a bold variation from the single one, but it admitted of millions of variations in its grouping, and in the proportions resultant from its grouping. The introduction of tracery was not only a startling change in the treatment of window lights, but admitted endless changes in the interlacement of the tracery bars themselves" (X, 208).

Ruskin is always cited at length, but nowhere do we come across this section, a paragraph that makes clear the penetrating insight with which he analyses the Gothic. He always writes of "millions" as opposed to "a few," and variation as opposed to uniformity. In the third part of *Stones*, entitled *The Fall*, he expounds at length on why the Gothic differs so strongly from the Renaissance, which knows no variation, or at least only *proportional variation*: an element remains constant when the whole is scaled up or down, so that the proportions are changed but not the element itself. In the Gothic, the element is changed through the ever-shifting combination of the subelements, the ribs: we will call this *configurational variation*. Ruskin tells us exactly which configurations are those of variation: the grouped shaft (generally known as the compound pier), the webbed or net vault, the pointed arch, the traceried window, and a bit later savage massing – none of which are in fact elements but rather combinations in context, configurations, collective patterns of figures. Each has its own variations, its own way of putting ribs together to yield new results, new designs, again and again, with a variation of "perpetual novelty." On this point Ruskin's observation is critical: to keep getting new configurations, one needs both different figures and different combinations of figures. It is this relationship between figure and configuration that makes the Gothic unique. While other architectural styles often revolve around elements and form, the Gothic is much more about relationships, and how they are expressed in members. Most theories of the Gothic are still elementarist, though, infected as they are by classical analysis, and concern themselves solely with the resulting members, sometimes so much so that they get called "membrology," as by Rickman and Willis, early historians of the Gothic. Such element-focused analysis completely disregards the fact that in the Gothic all those relationships are formed by something that moves through all the members: the linear rib.

Every rib is formed by linear figures in which every point on the line is active. In the Middle Ages, these were always combinations of straight lines and arches, exactly as Aristotle had prescribed – third-degree curves did not yet exist, so everything was linear or quadratic, and every curve was an interplay of the two. In the Gothic we can distinguish a number of curves or motifs, which from now on we will call *figures*. At the beginning of this analysis, it is important to establish that the underlying circles we often see in diagrams of the Gothic (cf. Billings, *The Power of Form*, 1851) are not properly figures. Such circles merely help to organize the figures and are not themselves visible. Figures are the combinations of lines that move over such circles and straights, and thus take on something of both. We see S-curves, J-curves, C-curves – not the ogives, pinnacles, tiercerons, liernes, ogees, crockets and trefoil of typical Gothic nomenclature – for the figures we distinguish are more fundamental within Gothic grammar, because they are relatively independent of the member embodying them. Crucial in the concept of changefulness is that the variation of the individual figure is linked to the possible configurations that can be formed of multiple figures. In short, the line is active and shows *behavior*. It can stretch and contract, not merely changing in scale but altering while still remaining itself; in short, it can be modulated.

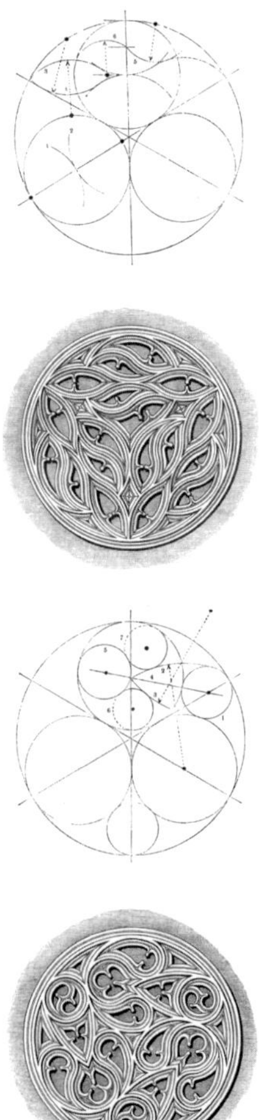

Two rose windows from: Robert Billings. "The Power of Form" (London, 1851)

It can be a J-figure with a long or short shaft, with a wide or narrow arch; or a C-figure with various sizes of opening, which together form the familiar cusps of the trefoil; or an S-figure, which we know in the arch as the ogee – a curve that can be flattened but can also appear as a deep wave, such as we encounter in many traceries.

In fact, this is the first argument for why Gothic patterns are essentially digital: the fundamental variability of all figures. Secondly, though, the fact that all figures are relational makes the Gothic even more digital. Every change in a figure always occurs in relation to another figure with which it crosses, merges or collides; a wide spectrum of effects flows from this collective behavior of figures. This dynamic, interactive relationship between figure and configuration is at the conceptual heart of Ruskin's remark about "millions" and the "infinite number" of variations. Every figure is a formal organization of variable points, not a fixed form. The organization is fixed, but not the form; figures vary in degree, not in kind, as we say since Bergson. And each of these figures is willing to be a part of large populations, which in turn have features of their own. This is not almost but exactly how the digital is defined today. Fairly simple behavior by individual members resulting in complex and irreducible collective behavior is a form of computation, which finds its most fundamental form in the digital, though not necessarily electronically. We often understand "digital" as meaning "electronically computed," but the speed of those electrons is actually irrelevant to the notion of computing, which refers solely to the method of calculation, a stepwise procedure of iterative adjustments. Some might argue (after pointing out that there weren't any computers in 1280) that while these relationships are indeed mathematical in nature, comparably to Arabic patterns, they are not specifically digital. Of course geometry does play a role in both, but with Arabic patterns the effect never contributes to the pattern on a larger scale. Of course they are also configurations, but they lack hierarchy and thus more often have the character of wallpaper: pattern independent of form. They do not *form* a column, window or vault but are applied to it later.

By contrast, Gothic patterns are very efficient at filling large geometric frames. The curves usually form smaller groups of five or six, resulting in a leaflike contour, a kind of mini-configuration, which then often, through different proliferation techniques such as translations and rotations, forms larger configurations bound together by a heavy frame. These might consist of high, pointed gables such as we see in portals, or the big, round circles of rose windows, or the ogive of a pointed arch. Though framed, all are constructed out of mini-configurations without any overly complicated additional figures becoming necessary. Each of these combinations gives a specific expression to each of these elements; thus, a rose window can be completely static like a spoked wheel, or floral like a chrysanthemum, or radiant like a flaming sun, or winding like a yin-yang design. The figures' movability on a small scale results in a stable tracery structure, but the configuration's expression on the larger scale is also one of movement, which in turn relates to other loci of action.

As I argued earlier, Ruskin's concept of changefulness evokes Hogarth's "serpentine line," but in fact it relates even more strongly to Worringer's concept of the "Northern line," with its "ceaseless melody": linear figures that seem to have come to life, connect to each other, and form patterns. For Worringer, an even more extreme expressionist than Ruskin, the Northern line is a line that both possesses abstraction and arouses empathy. In *Abstraction and Empathy* (1908), the famous thesis he wrote at the age of twenty-five (which had enormous influence on people as diverse as Franz Marc, T.E. Hulme and Herbert Read), he develops this distinction as a fundamental one, in which abstraction identifies with the mechanical forces in the world, with structure, while empathy identifies with organic form and ornament. According to Worringer, the Gothic occupies an in-between position, which makes the world of forces palpable:

Some examples of German Illuminated initials, from: "Initial-Ornamentik des VIII. bis XIII. Jahrhunderts" by Karl Lamprecht (Leipzig, 1882).

"Here they run parallel, then entwined, now latticed, now knotted, now plaited, then again brought through one another in a symmetrical checker of knotting and plaiting. Fantastically confused patterns are thus evolved, whose puzzle asks to be unravelled, whose convolutions seem alternately to seek and avoid each other, whose component parts, endowed as it were with sensibility, captivate sight and sense in passionately vital movement."

He is referring to Karl Lamprecht's *Initial-Ornamentik,* a late-nineteenth-century book on the aesthetics of illumination and interlaced decoration. According to Worringer, the lines seem to possess a life of their own, and an inclination to constantly keep copying and proliferating, without forming a closed organic body,

"...far outstripping any possibilities of organic movement. The pathos of movement which lies in this vitalized geometry – a prelude to the vitalized mathematics of Gothic architecture – forces our sensibility to an effort unnatural to it. When once the barriers of organic movement have been overthrown, there is no more holding back: again and again the line is broken, again and again checked in the natural direction of its movement; again and again it is forcibly prevented from peacefully ending its course, again and again diverted into fresh complications of expression, so that, tempered by all these restraints, it exerts its energy of expression to the uttermost until at last, bereft of all possibilities of natural pacification, it ends in confused, spasmodic movements, breaks off unappeased into the void or flows senselessly back upon itself" (*Form in Gothic,* 41).

And here, on the same page, he is even more clear:

"In short, the Northern line doesn't get its life from any impress which we willingly give it, but appears to have an expression of its own, which is stronger than our life."

This life is not corporeal, and hence it is nonorganic, and "of a spiritual vitality." It is no longer the classical interplay between element and form that is operating here but one of figure-relationship and configuration-expression. In short, it is not the case that the theories of Ruskin and Worringer apply only to ornament (although they seldom articulate this themselves); on the contrary, the behavior of the lines, however small and thin they are, displays a structural and connective logic. The division between structure and ornament we know from classicism is eliminated in Gothic architecture. When there is no fundamental distinction between mechanical laws and organic curves, because, for example, all the curves can interweave with each other into a straight, strong braid, or straight ribs shoot out of a column and subsequently transform into arched fans, or curves spring from the straight mullions of windows, we suddenly find ourselves in an in-between world, one David Channell calls the world of the "vital machine," where the one is merely a gradation of the other.

Looking up at the web vault of the Lady Chapel in Wells Cathedral.

It is not only a changefulness of columns, vaults, or traceries in themselves, but also one in which *columns transform into vaults into traceries.* Variation frees the column not only from the classical formal canon but also from its own definition, thus making it possible for it to change into a fan, and from a fan into a vault, of which no two are the same. Variability *within* an element thus also determines variability *between* elements. This makes the Gothic more radical than any other architectural style up to the present day. The Gothic has movement, but it does not result in either an image of movement or a vague amorphic mass, because it converts this physical movement into abstract structure. It does so with the most precise articulation, by counting, grouping, unraveling, regrouping, precisely in the manner of textile techniques that previously had been normally found only in ornament.

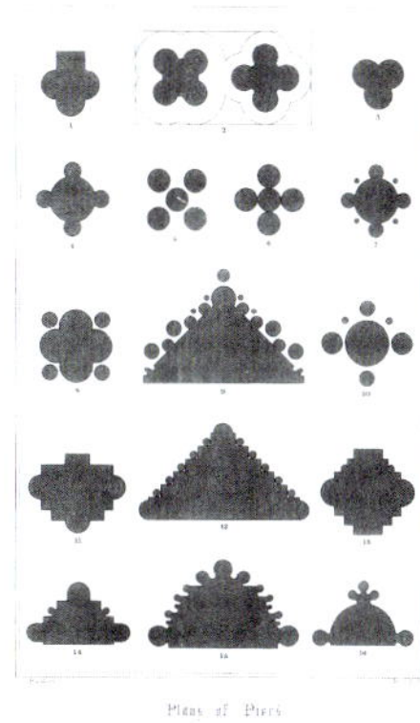

"Plans of Piers," from: John Ruskin. The Stones of Venice, Vol.I: Foundations (IX, 130).

In *The Stones of Venice, I: The Foundations,* Ruskin does nothing more or less than look very closely at these column-bundling techniques, which he calls "grouped shafts." Actually, in imitation of him, we can look just as precisely at window traceries or networks of vaults, because these too are morphologies specifically consisting of configurations of ribs. And these ribs are flexible – not literally, *after* they have been carved from stone, but *before,* during the design phase, when changefulness is in charge.

Let us look a bit more precisely at the intriguing plates that deal with the grouped shafts. We see pages of a kind we are only accustomed to seeing in natural history books, filled with various kinds of flowers or insects, something like the famous plates of Ernst Haeckel, who grouped radiolaria taxonomically with all the varieties on a single sheet. Not entirely unexpectedly, I was also put in mind of Hogarth's plates with thirty or forty faces *en profil,* and Bentley and Humphreys´ beautiful photo books exposing the morphological richness of snowflakes. The grouped shaft is a splendid discovery, in the same category as the tracery window, rose window or net vault (a complex variation of the earlier "rib vault"). Instead of understanding it as a single column with ornament, like the Doric fluted type, we can see it as a column articulated in a way that allows it to do much more than merely shoot straight upward. The column is freed from its constructional unequivocalness, since the grouping makes the shaft immediately related and gives it a context. All members exist only in context, never in advance. On either side of the main shaft there is usually a lower arch, and since in the Gothic the arch is continuous with the column, two smaller columns are needed on either side of the main one. In addition, the main shaft has to split into two or even three again at the top, by the main vault, since the cross vault consists of multiple ribs. So we already need three rib columns at the front and two on both sides, and behind, two or three more that also comprise part of the lower cross vault in the aisle. This already makes eight rib columns, which, although they require a cross-shaped distribution over the shaft, do not have a fixed morphology. This results not in a fixed circle on which eight smaller ones are distributed but in a free grouping, in

Example of plate showing various snowflakes, from: W. A. Bentley and W. J. Humphreys. Snow Crystals (Dover, 1962).

which the eight – or, often, as many as twelve or even more – thinner rib columns can merge but also break free again of the main group. Like the braiding of hair, it's simply a rearrangement of material into strands, in which one is continually able to decide whether to combine the strands into a single heavy line, i.e., a thick braid, or to let them fan out over the head and then make them into smaller braids further on. None of the Gothic members are elements that can be shown separately and in isolation on the page; they exist only in context, are created out of relationships with each other, which is precisely why Ruskin's plates became taxonomies.

We can make a similar argument, with plates of variations, for window traceries, net vaults and pointed arches – though Ruskin does not do so for any of these three in *Stones I* – and for moldings, which he does elaborate, following Pugin, for whom the direction in which rain drips is just as important as the beholder's viewing angle. They are directions, mechanical and organic forces that find their nexus in a morphology (we will not call it a typology), which has its hallmarks and is constructed according to certain rules but has no fixed form. These hallmarks are operational and procedural; they include bundling in columns, interweaving in tracery, meshing in vaults, and, in moldings, a protruding, a flaring out from and rejoining with the wall. And these are the sources of Ruskin's "perpetual novelty" born of the "millions of variations" the Gothic has for each morphology, as an "expression of life."

By this reasoning, we understand better and better what the role of work is and how, in the process of forces concentrating at a nexus, it ultimately finds expression in stone, in a specifically surfaced stone. Very early, in 1848, Ruskin wrote:

"Now I think that Form, properly so called, may be considered as a function or exponent either of Growth or of Force, inherent or impressed; and that one of the steps to admiring it or understanding it must be a comprehension of the laws of formation and of the forces to be resisted; that all forms are thus either indicative of lines of energy, or pressure, or motion, variously impressed or resisted, and are therefore exquisitely abstract and precise" (VIII, 178-9).

So we proceed stepwise, from kneading, constitutive natural forces to human action and work, first design work and then execution work, towards a sociocultural form-expression, a long string of mapping and passing on of forces toward a form, with an indexing at each level that expresses itself on the next. Design is work too, since it consists of the handling and processing of forces, and the realm of changefulness channels life as much as savageness does. Every stage receives templates from the previous one, and some of those templates are more rigid than others. When an architect designs a column, it will take on the morphology of a column and nothing else, but therein lies his freedom, because he takes the column for granted, since it will not materialize as such anyway; he is merely interested in an expression of the bundling. So, in his "fancy," as Ruskin always calls it, the architect conceives a specific form of bundling but does not decide on the capitals, the grooves in the column or the figures that will sit on top. And so a wooden template of the column's profile is made, with some room for the mason to carve his own pattern behind the template. In this sense, the wooden templates used in Gothic building should not be confused with, say, the molds we use in prefab; the Gothic mold is not filled with inert matter but elaborated to a subsequent, more detailed level. We should try to understand this as a savageness that runs through all stages of changefulness, becoming more intense at each, and leaving more and more room for mistakes, fancy, and grotesquerie. But let us now study savageness again in another context.

The movement that Worringer describes in such flowery style is that of a living line, it is true; but this does not mean it gives rise to an architecture of proliferation, frayed on all sides, stopping only at the point of exhaustion. All the movements are choreographically related in such a way that together they form a system, and although implicitly restless and unending, it (almost) always results in balanced, symmetrical forms. The movement that endlessly swarms over some capitals is in no sense the same movement as that of window traceries, which always move in mirror image, very precisely coordinated with each other, and fit within the heavy framework of the ogive. But this does not do Worringer's analysis an injustice; the variation of the *Nordische Linie* is still the agent of all variability in design; moreover, the fact that such complex choreographies yield such an infinite variation in traceries and net vaults is actually evidence of its productivity. Life always mirrors and segments its endless variation, and this makes it not vague but precise. The mirroring and segmenting of the body plan actually ensures that variation continues to function and does not merely lead to shapeless piles of flesh. *First there is variation, then there is differentiation* – and then there is more variation, and again differentiation.

It is no accident that when biologists are explaining these principles of body plans and their phyla, they often reach for Gothic floor plans and not Greek or modernist ones. First there is the nave, then the transept, and if the nave is long enough a second transept if necessary, then a Lady Chapel, and the Cloisters, and then an octagonal Chapter House (always with that splendid single column in the middle). They extend and stretch, yes, but only *to a certain point*; then they sprout off sideways, on either side of the nave, and stretch again, once more *to a certain point*; then more additions are made perpendicular to the transepts, a chapel here and another one there, hexagonal or octagonal, single or multiple, but again *to a certain point*; and then it grows some more, vertically, once again *to a certain point*.

The Gothic body is what these days we would call a fractal body, a body of splittings, extensions and continuous breaks. Of course, the Gothic *Trieb* is nonorganic, an unstoppable *flow* and irrepressible urge to multiply, but its expression is not simply nonorganic and certainly not antiorganic; it segments, and keeps *tending* toward the making of a body. It has all the instruments necessary for doing so, but the result need not be the body of Christ; the *nave* can become as long as a snake, and even bend and twist if desired, zigzagging over the field; but then you get more than one transept, and multiple spires of different heights at every crossing – not a problem, but it will always subdivide and segment. Gothic logic is like that of an ice crystal branching out to propagate itself over a cold windowpane, reorganizing water vapor by giving it form.

In light of this, it does not make much sense to radically oppose the organic and nonorganic, as Deleuze does; this is as pointless as placing water vapor and ice crystals in opposition to each other, because the rules that lead toward the making of a body in no way imply that that body will always be finished, as if it were to run up against the wall of an invisible mold and find itself unable to keep mutating. And although the existing Gothic cathedrals do not feature examples as extreme as those described in the previous paragraph ("zigzagging over the field" with "multiple spires"), great variation is still present. The well-known historical fact that construction was constantly being halted, delayed and interrupted cannot account for this. Gothic architecture always has the urge to mutate, and even when a floor plan is completely symmetrical, the spires need not follow that symmetry. This picture, which we know from Chartres, seems an all-too-familiar one, and when we are confronted with two unmatched spires, which may not even share the same composition, we all too quickly blame it on some medieval lack of organization, funds, or political will. But if we assume that such a thing was done relatively willfully, that the cathedral was deliberately designed that way by a collective, not an individual, then it suddenly no longer makes sense to us, as if the Baroque Vierzehnheiligen suddenly had two different spires, even if a few hundred years stood between them. But this is the way it was, or if not, mismatched spires were at least acceptable to the late medievals, which is enough for me. Of course, an entire community that has invested an amount of time, money and labor beyond our comprehension does not decide at a certain point to simply halt construction or change its mind – that the steeple may as well be left off, or one tower may as well be this way and the other one that way. Rather, something totally different lies behind it: namely, self-segmentation and limb formation. Here we see Ruskin's primary argument, savageness, returning on a different scale, not the scale of individual labor but the largest scale of collective execution, in which all the groups and guilds together, along with the patron and possibly his successors, allow imperfection.

Front view of Chartres Cathedral

We may as well get used to it: the concept of symmetry in the Gothic is completely opposed to the Greek one. It is a symmetry that guides and channels growth rather than checking it. The process is filled with obstacles ("problems," as Worringer fittingly calls them), but they do not block things, only structure them, not unlike a system of locks, which is dynamic and functions on different levels using thresholds and channels. Each reservoir can hold only a certain amount of variation. Growth never works when there is a lack of differentiation; it is absolutely impossible for a system to increase in scale without segmenting, because, as Galileo demonstrated, simply enlarging the same form leads to something that very quickly collapses under its own weight. No, growth is the redistribution of material, not blind excrescence; it is continual reorganization, not continual enlargement of the same form of organization.

Here, we seem to arrive at some essential point. Whereas before, we observed the complex relationship between changefulness – smooth variation of design – and savageness – rough variation of execution – proceeding downward in scale, we now see that it proceeds upward as well. Changefulness needs savageness in all directions; nothing can grow or shrink without cracks in the fields of smoothness. The Gothic requires smooth variations of woven tracery and bundled columns together with as much crudeness in the capitals as in the massing of the whole building.

To imply that multiplication and growth are the opposite of organization and constitute a nonorganic force is a gross misconception of life and movement. It is to confuse organization with finalism, because life thrives on organization, which is not what stops growth but what actually encourages it, and encourages change, if not outright mutation. We must emphasize, though, that Worringer's and Ruskin's understanding of the Gothic as fundamentally non-classical, as an architecture that denies finalism, is completely correct. From this perspective, Alberti's organicism seems fatally flawed, a misconception of matter if not a complete misconception of nature. What we see in nature is a continuity of elements and a discontinuity of bodies. What we find in Classicism is a discontinuity of elements and a continuity of bodies.

When we keep in mind that Worringer makes his theory of the Gothic a racial one (I wouldn't say racist just yet), constantly referring to "das Nordische," the *Nordic*, not "the Northern" – the word that always pops up in the mellowed English translations of his books – we can understand why his conception of the Gothic is so influenced by Norse and Nordic ornament, the most twisted and serpentine (often literally featuring snakes and dragons) ribbon decoration in history, which runs over door frames, rune stones and capitals alike. Granted, the notion is rather an uncomfortable one, but viewing the Gothic within a framework of migration and population politics can be taken unusually far. The classic theory is that Gothic patterns came about when holes were drilled in Romanesque arches (Robert Willis, 1835, ch. 6: "Tracery," cited by Ruskin in *The Seven Lamps of Architecture*). That may be, but the great disadvantage of such historical explanations in general is that the way something evolved is not the same as its concept; that is, the predecessor never serves as the content, much less the design method, of the successor. It explains how an idea arises, but not the idea itself. It may be obvious that the Gothic wall sprang from a Roman wall that was hollowed out step by step, but this does not at all mean that it is one. The drilled circles of the early trefoils and quatrefoils very quickly became virtual ones, drawn on paper, then on stone, and the circles touch at the tangents perpendicular to their diameters, and inevitably the figures begin moving over these virtual trajectories.

We should notice how the status of the lines keeps changing: a continuous line one day is a dashed line the next; what is physical one day is schematic the next. If you make the holes big enough, lines will remain between them, and these tangents turn all the previous completely upside down; suddenly, it no longer changes from a solid wall into a porous screen but begins immediately with fibers, with ribbons and stalks, and now it is these that are drawn as continuous, and the circles as dashed. This transition from what art historians call plate tracery to bar tracery (as it flourished during the French *Rayonnant* and the English *Decorated* style, the so-called mid-Pointed) is essential, for suddenly the holes in the wall, high in the spandrels between the arches, are able to forge links with the columns rising up from the wall below; two separate design problems are suddenly related, part of the same family, not through proportion but through form and methodology, through being made to share a part more fundamental than themselves, not even a part but a subpart: the rib. This is exactly the kind of thing biological evolution comes up with all the time: the invention of nonparts, or almost-parts, parts that are neither brick nor wall but kind of a bit of everything – which is why Stephen Jay Gould was so interested in the spandrel. This is how the Gothic should be understood: as the *genetic engineering* of architectural language. From the early twelfth century all the way to the late fourteenth, a recoding was constantly taking place, bringing all the elements into the same family: a northern invasion conducted not by the earlier methods of violence but via the much more effective means of cultural transmission, so that everything came to share the same DNA. All work – the concentration of forces in a column, the distribution of forces in a wall or vault – was done via the constant reorganization of ribs.

As they carved out the walls, the *Norsemen*, the Norman master masons of the Somme valley, must have recognized their own ancient weaving, their insanely complex knotwork, their leather belts and bronze clasps, their straw baskets and red braids, more clearly with every step. And their work is linked not only to Norman weaving techniques but also to the older Insular illuminations found in the Book of Kells and the Lindisfarne Gospels, in which spirals and cat-headed snakes fill the initials, gradually interweave and become long straight bands that clasp the text, only to explode again and swarm across the empty margins of the page. If one looks closely at illumination patterns, one sees that, just as in the Gothic, everything is continually subdivided into ribbons – straight bars and initials and tendrils – and all these ribbons can connect to each other again and again in new variations, solving new problems, such as variable amounts of white on the page, blocks of text of different widths, different numbers of columns, initials and subheads, and so on. Celtic knotwork, by contrast, is even more exact, more mathematically complex, and always symmetrical, with an intelligence far beyond that found in the Norse snake pit: braids not only run freely under and over each other but loop back to form increments, small woven units that can split off from each other, in a technique that makes it possible to fill the discontinuous figure of a cross in a continuous way, just as later in Gothic illumination it would be possible to fill a capital T or G with weaving as easily as an O. This does not, perhaps, mean there was a linear historical evolution from *knotwork* to *illumination* to *tracery*, but a meshed, conceptual relationship certainly exists. From a historical point of view, it is true that the Celts traveled from France to England centuries *earlier* and the Gothic arrived centuries *later* in England by way of French Normandy, but we are talking about similar styles, in which separate ribbons were woven together into complex configurations, in a decorative technique that could avail itself of individual tendrils on the one hand and tightly packed surfaces on the other, and in fact everything in between. In this sense, Norse weaving techniques are more closely related to the Gothic than the Gothic is to its predecessor the Romanesque. Worringer in effect expands Lamprecht's theory of northern ornament from the clasps and initials to the Gothic. Ruskin devotes a paragraph in *The Flamboyant Architecture of the Valley of the Somme* (XIX, 258–9) to the comparison but unfortunately does not elaborate it further:

Richard of Mediavilla's Commentary on the Sentences of Peter Lombard (Paris, early 14th century)

Book of Kells; Initial "T" from folio 124r, Insular Style (8th century).

"You are doubtless all aware that from the earliest times, a system of interwoven ornament has been peculiarly characteristic of northern design, reaching greatest intensity of fancy in the Irish manuscripts represented by the Book of Kells – and universal in Scandinavia and among the Norman race. But you may not have considered – that, disguised by other and more subtle qualities, the same instinct is manifest in the living art of the whole world. This delight in the embroidery, intricacy of involution – the labyrinthine wanderings of a clue, continually lost, continually recovered, belongs – though in a more chastised and delicate phase – as much to Indian, to Arabian, to

Egyptian, and to Byzantine work, as to that of Norway and Ireland – nay, it existed just as strongly in the Greek."

The last statement is true, though he forgets to add that the Greeks were limited to tiny, meager bands that could only move forward and backward.

What makes the comparison of the Gothic to knotwork so significant for us is that it enables a different kind of fusion of savageness and changefulness than the one Ruskin had in mind, something we have hinted at previously: when design technique is influenced by craft, a fundamental displacement occurs. Since design customarily retreats from the material into the abstract world of drawing, while craft maintains a one-on-one relationship with matter, bending every twig with its own hand, at first sight the two appear to lie as far apart as possible. But when the line of a drawing is directly informed by that pliable twig, and thus an entire design by the craft of weaving and knotting, then the argument gradually changes: in the Gothic, work, activity and craft were taking place at the design stage, rather than only appearing on the scene at the execution stage. This may not be labor as Ruskin imagined it, with bad Mondays, mistakes and earthy Gothic stonecutters, but his concept of labor was ultimately a strongly ideologically tinted one. The fact is that handicraft and design mingled because the drawing – later to be carved in stone – was informed by a world of interweaving twigs, leather handles and bundled hair. Although the whole logic is one of the assembly of flexible elements, this is not a case of *skeuomorphism* (as developed by Semper), in which stone often much too literally seems to weave, intertwine and knot. The fact that Gothic tracery, even Flamboyant tracery, treats mullions as if they are flexible does not mean the final pattern mimics fabric – which Ruskin, none too flatteringly, liked to call "cobwebs." No, the tracery's flexibility, though material, is abstract, not literal or imitative. In a way, this makes the twin phenomena of savageness and changefulness more reciprocal than his class-driven view of the draughtsman and stonemason suggests, since *the former draws as if he is weaving and the latter carves as if he is drawing*. Yet we should not brush aside Ruskin's vision of labor as obsolete, since for him, aesthetics is at all times related to work, and work to aesthetics; mountains and clouds are as much the result of construction as are paintings and buildings. In this sense, work is the gathering of forces, their collaboration, convergence or intersection, instigated not by a person or a deity but by the forces themselves, unanchored, turning work into an act of the mind as well as the body, into something Ruskin always calls "noble" – the same phenomenon that makes Worringer plead for the Gothic as spiritual and not sensuous, and the reason Focillon's description of the Flamboyant as "baroque" is so terribly off the mark. The French always consider the early High Gothic and Flamboyant to run in parallel to the Renaissance and Baroque, probably in an attempt to make the Gothic acceptable, but one which fails miserably time after time. There is nothing sensuous or baroque in the intertwining of mullions, because, as Worringer says, there is nothing organic – referring to the classical realm of imitative ornament and bodily, symmetrical wholes – about it. The Gothic whole is frayed, created by parts strangely both abstract and alive, by flexible ribbons that interlace, connect and bundle together: their labor is like that of ants, their behavior like that of bacteria, leading the simple life of immanence and intuition.

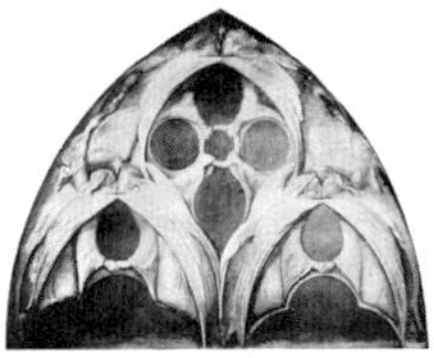

John Everett Millais. Design for a Gothic window (1853).

Here, we must recall the short-lived collaboration between Ruskin and Millais. Under striking (and rather humorous) circumstances during a vacation in Scotland, Millais was working on a portrait of Ruskin as well as *The Order of Release*, which featured Effie Gray, Ruskin's then-wife. Millais and Gray, whom Ruskin was completely ignoring, fell for each other, so much so that a marriage and eight children would eventually result. Amid this situation, the two men were trying to develop a "new style" together, for the only time in their lives – Ruskin by talking, Millais by drawing. Only one known sketch by Millais representing this episode exists, but it is a truly remarkable one, which had Ruskin "beside himself with pleasure," "slapping his hands together." In the positions of the two lancet arches and single quatrefoil that would form a Gothic window, ethereal beings join hands at the points where the ribs would come together to form the pattern's figures and switches. (And they kiss on the lips, and above each kiss, there flares a flame!) In other words, all the tracery is replaced by angels, in a seeming attempt not only to revitalize organic ornament within the realm of the Gothic by leaving vegetal and animal figuration behind but, moreover, to express the status of labor, to render stone carving equal to design and handicraft to thought, and to visualize lines and fibers that seem to have a life of their own.

Imagine, for a moment, a building made entirely of angels. All the material is animated, not by souls inhabiting matter but by flexible matter living within rigid matter, textile inhabiting stone, weaving inhabiting carving, carving inhabiting drawing. Again, labor is not located – not in a class, or a pair of hands, or even in human beings; work is continuously displaced, and boundaries blur; it is omnipresent, and therefore spiritual. And the angels and agents not only work, they collaborate. Agents make agency. The flexibility of elements in the Gothic is radically opposed to that found in the Baroque; there, structure comes first, and *then* movement is added. The relationship between columns, friezes and pedestals does not change at all; they only bend *afterward*. Baroque is just classicism on acid. It sticks to all the classicist elements but soaks them until they are bent and twisted, and however distorted they become, they remain simply capitals, pedestals, flutings, friezes, all dipped in the same eternal white of uniformity and universality. In the Gothic, the elements are free – free *beforehand*, not in the sense of being loose but in the sense of being free *to find each other* – and when they do, they build; they hold onto each other. We see the most complex relationships: mergings, splittings, crossings, branchings, overlappings; and these forms of collaboration lead us to the following unusual conclusion: in the Gothic, *ornament acts like structure and structure acts like ornament.*

The historicizing opinion still prevails that, because columns were chronologically first smooth and Romanesque and only later "covered" with ribs, structure and ornament are theoretically separate, à la Alberti. One does the work, the other provides the beauty; one is mechanical, the other organic. What a grave misconception. It may be true of Greek ornament, where the organic oozes out like marmalade from between rigid structural parts. But this theory fatally separates empathy from abstraction, and worse, *Werkform* from *Kunstform*; and even more fatally, it causes most historians – following Kenneth Frampton – to think of all ornament as an excrescence of the joint, the *knot* as a *Naht*, which is, of course, an opposing concept and not a related one.

Rigidity

In the Gothic, all ornament is vertical: ribs are fundamentally vertical, like the vegetal tendrils of Art Nouveau, and to make horizontal connections, these verticals need to bend, touch and interweave, creating a web spanning from one side to the other. Generally, structure is conceived as big and ornament as small, but in the Gothic, the ribs exist on an in-between scale, too thin to carry weight and too thick to be delicate. Pragmatically, it solves the former problem by bundling ribs and the latter by interweaving and splitting them, obtaining more and more vertical articulation through molding. It is a beauty that works. It is a flexible rigidity, which Ruskin, describing his fifth characteristic of the nature of Gothic, calls

"an *active* rigidity: the peculiar energy that gives tension to movement, and stiffness to resistance, which makes the fiercest lightning forked rather than curved" (X, 239).

And, probably thinking of Millais' angels, he writes:

"Egyptian and Greek buildings stand, for the most part, by their own weight and mass, one stone passively incumbent on another; but in the Gothic vaults and traceries there is a stiffness analogous to that of the bones of a limb, or the fibres of a tree; an elastic tension and communication of force from part to part, and also a studious expression of this throughout every visible line of the building" (X, 240).

Many have argued, as does Pol Abraham, that the Gothic rib vault is partly an illusion: the rib, he states, has no real structural properties. This reasoning is faulty, since the Gothic has never been concerned with the rationalism introduced by Viollet-le-Duc (who never made such accusations himself). Reading ribs as primary structure with secondary filling is thoroughly inaccurate (as if one is comparing them to modernist paneling!); the Gothic has nothing of the engineer's art, nor of some transparent pre-high-tech, because it treats structural forces as equal to perceptual and historical ones it regards as just as real and powerful. Again, the Gothic is *configurational, not simply structural,* and being configurational means it operates via interconnection, via patterning; all this is materiality, yes, though not solely for the transfer of loads. In a sense, the Gothic is even more materialist than the engineer's approach, since it extends the thinking in forces to the realm of the social, aesthetic and religious.

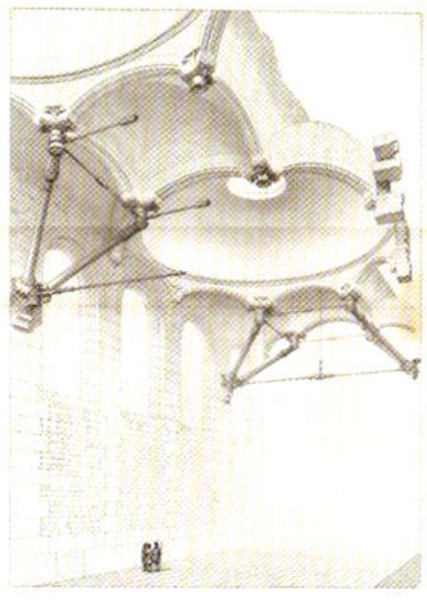

Eugène Viollet-le-Duc. Design for a brick vault supported by iron, replacing the need for an external stone buttress. From: Entretiens sur l'Architecture (Paris, 1863).

Viollet's addition of the iron rod to replace the flying buttress is nothing but a purification and cleansing of the Gothic, making all stone ribs into compression elements and all tie-rods into tension elements, replacing Worringer's vitalized geometry with a pure, crystalline, mechanical geometry. The weak, delicate elements interact and build structure, actively creating rigidity, and the final strength is the result of a collaborative effort, similar to what we nowadays call an emergent property. To say all Gothic vaults are "essentially the same," as the engineer Jacques Heyman does in *The Stone Skeleton,* contributes nothing, since the fact is that they are actually different, precisely because materiality already plays a role at the level of design and organization, not just in the structure. All the life and movement of the ribs is transferred to the structure, and this makes it beautiful. Life and beauty are not added to a column afterwards, like classical acanthus leaves; they are effectively what produces that column. The standard opinion on Ruskin's theoretical development has always been that he started out with aesthetics and proceeded to political economy and social criticism, but he never made such distinctions; for him, mountains, churches, factories were all one, and so should they be for us.

The truth is, *life is abstract*; it pervades organic things as much as inorganic ones. And it is this abstract life of agency that makes the nature of Gothic fundamentally digital.

Craft, Design and Code

Let us not get into a retrospective discussion of what John Ruskin – a man who hated the railways, every cast iron column, and basically every piece of machinery, steam-blowing or not – might have said to such a remark. But those machines were spitting out the same things over and over: the same profile over the length of a beam, the same ornament cast again and again, the same five million bricks or sugar cubes every day. They made the same thing every time they were operated, and worse, they operated in the same way over and over, turning their operators into machines too. Well, digital machines are different – they thrive on difference.

When you print out a piece of writing, is it your work? Was it written by you? I am sure that you are as proud of the page that comes out of the printer as if you had written it in longhand – even if we disregard the now not-very-useful metaphysics of tools, which separate the pen from the typewriter, and from the laptop computer, with its inherent notion of copy-paste.

Richard Sennett believes we should write in longhand first. In *The Craftsman*, he claims that Renzo Piano's architectural designs are proof of the hand's primacy over computing because Piano sketches them by hand first; which is absurd. Sennett's book is generally admirable: he elegantly lays out all the states of work, from the operation of dumb assembly-line machinery to the highly charged flashes of brilliance of artists like Cellini and Stradivarius, while gradually carving out a middle zone for craft and pragmatism. Disappointingly, though, in his conclusion he takes a position of moderation – not the radical middle of our radical Picturesque, *the middle as a way out*, but a middle that is stuck between extremes. Our preferred option of implanting craft into machinery is not the same as having little islands of craft surrounded by a vast ocean of machines. We come across the same erroneous idea time and time again, be it in Mumford, Schumacher, Ellul or Illich: the belief that we can humanize machines by slowing them down, refraining from their continuous use, alternating their use with authentic home- and handcrafting, or using them on a less massive scale. Finding a way to use them more slowly or less often is no good; such theories are always ones of abstinence, which propose a kind of technological diet. Believe me, diet is not the issue; the point is not to make the same machine *do the same thing more slowly*, at a human pace or in a friendlier way. The point is to make machines do things differently. The issue is not technology itself but how it relates to human perception and action, whether it renders them extinct or causes them to proliferate – life or death, as Ruskin would say. We should look carefully at how human action organizes itself around machinery, how machinery organizes and even institutionalizes action, and how it slowly takes away or enables freedom. And though the sociological aspects of technology are beyond the scope of my argument, I want to make clear that the machine-work relationship is never predetermined in any way; the extinction of one type of human activity can – and generally does – make another flourish, and must at all times be studied ecologically, not ideologically.

The oldest forms of technology are tools, like the hammer and the sword; they are operated by hand, and interwoven with complete ecologies of action, with a much wider network of activities than simple use. Tools have persistently been misrepresented through the notion of use, which defines action as fixed purpose. For example, let us observe how a butcher dismembers a carcass. See how he points his razor-sharp knife away from him, how he turns it with his elbow and not his wrist, and how he spins and flips the piece of meat simultaneously with the rotations of the knife. See how the knife slides into the unresisting layers of fat, between the layers of muscle, the joints; see how everything falls apart, with apparent effortlessness. Is this "use"? The gracefulness of the actions, the way the butcher's flowing attention accompanies them without interrupting: all this is something very different from following the instructions in a manual. The example, which originated with Chuang Tzu in the twelfth century and was used by Baudrillard and then by Sennett as an example of the path of least resistance, is a good illustration of how we work: with a complex *motor schema* in our heads – not a mental image of an end product (a tableful of sirloins, tenderloins, prime ribs) or a drawing but a series of actions we know by heart, which have a rhythm as much as an order. It is much more like a tune than an image. Cutting, slicing, paring: the work is always the same and yet always different, the same organization of actions under ever-changing circumstances. Work takes place in time, as a process, and the mental-motor schema determines its order; concentration accompanies action, to prevent it becoming a pensiveness that interrupts the flow.

Let us conduct a little experiment, much simpler than the one with the carcass. Take a sheet of paper and write ten separate *a*s in a row: *a a a a a a a a a a*. Unlike the printing in this book, your handwriting will contain no identical letters: many small differences will occur in various places, though with luck, all the *a*s will be legible. Bringing in the argument from the preceding paragraph, we could say they all have the same motor schema of an *a*: curve down, curve up, go down sharply, go sideways. Activated by the fingers and thumb, with a bit of wrist movement and a small amount of corrective feedback via the eyes, the schema turns out a different actual letter every time it is written. The execution or activation of the schema is based in variation; the loops can be thinner, wider, closed or open at the top, though there is a powerful constraint to this variation: legibility. It would be impossible to make every *a* the same, even if one wanted to; the schema is not like a mold, fixed and geometric, but flexible: it does contain points on lines, but those points are movable in the surrounding space to make the lines bend. The schema represents an organization and a procedure more than a description or drawing of an actual form. It is a guide for all the minute muscular forces involved, which works from the inside out (each letter must be "enacted" more than executed), not a negative form casting a positive one.

To extend the experiment somewhat, let's write another ten lines of ten *as* each. In my own handwriting, two out of a total of 110 *as* look like *us*, and two others look like *ds* (which would be rather embarrassing if this weren't being done in the name of science). While the ten *as* in the first line were all variations, these four new ones are mutations, what the reader would call "mistakes" and John Ruskin would probably deem "rude" or "savage," and certainly imperfect. Nonetheless, changefulness and savageness are completely continuous. We have seen how changefulness can never be fully isomorphic, and starts to break down on both the small and large scales. And, more importantly, we have also seen that savageness does not come out of the blue; it is not a streak of genius breaking through a system. Rather, it needs changefulness: it is variation pushed to the limit and beyond. A system not based on variation does not accept imperfection; a Greek, state-run controlling mechanism of elements that are preconfigured and of fixed proportions, and refer constantly to authorized examples, would never be able to absorb crudeness; it would be like a single handwritten *a* amid clones. Since changefulness is a highly coordinated system of movements, of figures channeling force and balancing with other figures, it tries to include everything, but *only up to a point,* when the pattern starts to crack, which does not mean the system is failing but that the pattern is reorganizing itself on another scale. When we step back, we see that another pattern has emerged, which contains the first. Here we arrive at a seemingly paradoxical conclusion: that systems based on joints, on elements, do not allow for imperfection and breaks, but continuous systems do.

Again: what did we conclude changefulness was? The coming to life of a motif via figuration: that is, a line with active points on it, a line that, when those points are moved, still runs through all of them, in a new expression. In his explanation of the expressionism of the figure, Worringer constantly refers back to the gesture, to the biomechanics of elbow, wrist and hand and how their collaboration gives us an infinite variety of expression:

"If we trace a line in beautiful, flowing curves, our inner feelings unconsciously accompany the movements of our wrist. We feel with a certain pleasant sensation how the line as it were grows out of the spontaneous play of the wrist. [...] If we meet such a line in another composition, we experience the same impression as if we ourselves had drawn it."

The Northern line has – or better, *is* – a motor schema, and just like the *a,* which is many *as* and becomes *ds* and *us*, it is nothing more or less than what today we would call a *script,* or a code, which in the case of handwriting cannot be exact, since we never write a letter by itself but always positioned within a word, meaning all letters must adapt to each other's variations. The code itself, then, needs to be flexible, the formula not of a single line but of many lines drawn simultaneously, by many hands acting likewise, coordinated like a flock of birds; and those lines – traceries and tracings – interact, find common points at which to link, merge, cross, form cusps, whatever, as long as the free action results in a structural entity, be it a bundle or a web, a fan or a rose. A computer is not an outgrowth of the hammer, like the four-stroke engine, amplifying the lever that is the human arm; it is not even a tool or an extension, in fact hardly even a medium – it is simply the conflation of design and work. A computer is not a machine that replaces hand-drawing or handicraft; it is *handicraft taking place at the level of drawing and design,* a way of positioning any possible motor schema inside matter itself.

Such a historically strenuous, if not impossible, merging of opposites brings us to an illuminating comparison between John Ruskin and one of his Victorian contemporaries, the two of whom were among no more than a dozen pillars holding up nineteenth-century culture, but positioned as far apart as possible. On the one hand, we have Ruskin's nonnegotiable repudiation of all machinery, accompanied by an acceptance only of things that were as natural as possible, in all their uniqueness, all their variation, each crafted by hand, on a certain day in a certain place, under a certain light. Then, at the other extreme, we find Charles Babbage, the inventor of the Difference Engine – no less than the first computer – but also a perceptive critic of Victorian economics. The two men were as antipodal as can be imagined. Whereas Ruskin was against all division of labor, Babbage was emphatically in favor of it, not only because he supported utilitarian laissez-faire economics but especially because he was a radical abstractionist. Instead of conceiving of machines as simply iron versions of human labor, Babbage understood the whole industrial revolution as a transformation of "making" into "manufacturing" – that is, the making of real things into the abstract organization of that making. Or, in the words of Henry Colebrooke, on awarding Babbage the Astronomical Society's gold medal in 1823: "In other cases, mechanical devices have substituted machines for simpler tools or for bodily labor. But the invention to which I am adverting comes in place of mental exertion: it substitutes mechanical performance for an intellectual process," therefore not just replacing human labor with mechanical power but mechanical power with the abstract processing of digits. I need not emphasize that this represents John Ruskin's worst nightmare: a world in which "working" becomes "tasking," the execution of labor not only by a machine but by a set of instructions, a code, a punched card read by the movable pins of a machine. The punched card had been invented a few decades earlier to program a Jacquard loom, which – recalling our own notion of changefulness being akin to weaving – directly informed Babbage's steam-powered Difference Engine and, later, his improved Analytical Engine, which he called "a manufactory of figures." As Ada Lovelace said: "We may say most aptly that the Analytical Engine weaves algebraic patterns just as the Jacquard loom weaves flowers and leaves." What makes Babbage's "contrivances" so useful for our thesis is that he saw his engines not simply as devices for doing calculations but as the foundation of a larger machinery for producing material forms, if not the whole material universe.

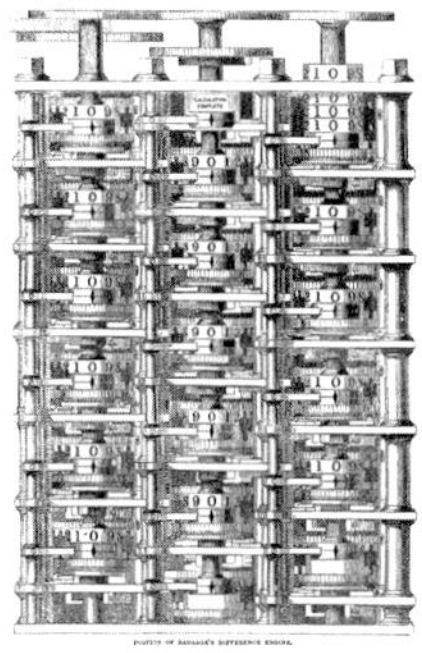

Charles Babbage. Design for a section of the Difference Engine (1833-53).

Firmly remaining on Ruskin's side, however, we should stress that Charles Babbage mistook such abstraction for the production of inevitably pristine objects, manufactured with "unerring precision" and thus without variation, perfectly uniform. Though the formative, organizational forces behind every shape are abstract, as Babbage correctly asserted, this does not mean the real object is not concrete, or lacks specific aspects or unique traits. He simply mistook his Difference Engine for a Platonic cave, in which "the industrial arts realize identity by the unbounded use of the principle of copying" (*The Exposition of 1851*, 49). To upgrade the Difference Engine with a capacity for variation, however, one would have to convert its singular, mechanical schema into a biomechanical, multiplied motor schema, to make its punched card flexible and soft, thus making the engine truly differential and allowing the abstraction to be concretized differently each time a product is created, so that the variation of handicraft would become part of the mechanical abstraction – which makes a good definition of digital computing.

This is precisely the point at which Sennett's examples run aground. With all due respect, Gehry and Piano are examples of how *not* to use computing. Piano takes a completely gridded, Greek, industrialized system and adds a swoosh by hand, just a single humanized stroke, a gesture that does not configure with anything (often simply resting on top of the structure, in the case of a roof, or wrapping around it, in the case of a wall), that does not result in pattern and becomes an unintentional sign of failing humanism and pragmatism. Gehry's designs consist of large, handmade models of curved surfaces, which are digitally scanned three-dimensionally by a free-moving robot arm. All these warped planes are smashed blindly into each other on every corner of the volume, light-years away from Gothic grace and coordination. The only thing Gehry and Piano have to offer us is quasi-variation, because their introduction of craft into design lasts for but a single, artistic moment, in opposition to the complex, elaborated methodology of Gothic interweaving and braiding. If instead we had such multi-handed craft working at the core of design today – and the digital is the first unified medium of our time to allow for it – it would mean a displacement not only of work but of the designer's relationship to matter. The equal relationship between craft and matter has always been challenged by the designer, who tries to control and impose form on matter but, even acting in good faith and in possession of the right techniques, cannot fully inhabit matter and must assume the position of the mold. If we view the situation in this way, our question becomes how to combine mold and craft in design, at a point when design technique and technology are converging.

Ruskin's strongest criticism of nineteenth-century industrialism concerning the relationship between aesthetics and work invariably focused on the casting of matter into molds, with its implied notion of Babbage's mechanical copying: the handwork of carving only occurs during the making of the mold and is undone by the subsequent repetition and "the unbounded use" of identical castings. Seen from this angle, Ruskin's criticism applies mostly to the problem of the copying, because of its intrinsic lack of variation, and not so much to the operation of carving in one material and casting in another, as is customary in the production of bronze sculpture, for instance. The act of casting in itself, according to Ruskin, only becomes questionable when it approaches a form of deceit, when one material is used to imitate a second. Hence, even in the notion of casting, some carving is still present: the carving of the original negative form (from a block into a designed shape), followed by the casting of the final material (transformation from liquid to solid) in the mold. In short, casting consists of two types of work, not one. Evidently, the creative, qualitative work, the carving, is completely "outnumbered" by the machine work, the casting-copying, which is pure quantity. To better understand this problem, we must pose the question of how work relates to the production of forms in terms of technology, and how such technology relates to matter and to activity.

Adrian Stokes, in his Ruskinian *The Stones of Rimini* (1934), distinguishes between two types of sculptural techniques: *carving*, which is stereotomic by nature and works from the outside, and *modeling*, which works from the inside out, building up form through adding material. Between the poured liquid state of cast materials and the solid state of carvable materials like marble and even wood, there is a third kind of material, soft and malleable, such as clay or wax, that can be modeled and elaborated during working. In both sculptural techniques, the statue's final contour is the end product of a process. In neither does a mold blindly create a form; in both cases, an active process of formation takes place. In the early eighteenth century, seeking to conceptualize the growth of an embryo, Comte de Buffon came up with a similar idea, a merging of the concepts of carving and modeling, so to speak, when he decided embryos were molded from the inside. Though seriously flawed scientifically, this idea of an internal mold should interest us, especially because it is so contradictory. While a negative form has to be positioned on the outside of the material, in Comte de Buffon's mind, it needed to nestle inside matter to facilitate the principle of a form growing over time rather than being cast in a single moment; therefore, the form needed to be cast in parts, internally, at different moments during a process of formation. Something was at work inside matter. Or, in Ruskinian terms, carving and casting operated on a more equal basis than had been thought. Buffon, though, reasoned that the observed biological variation in the world was a case of increasingly bad copies of that first mold, and was therefore gravely mistaken. We would need to understand such an internal mold as staying active during the time of formation, as a mold that is itself variable, undergoing what the French technology philosopher Simondon called "continuous temporal modulation." He reasoned that a triode, for instance, was continuously molding variable electrical information by inserting a third electrode between the cathode and anode. Simondon termed this variable molding "modulation." The in-between electrode "molds" and modulates a given flow of matter, which means all output always exists within a certain range, varying between minimum and maximum states.

Potentially, when seen from a broader perspective that does not only include electrically charged matter, variable modulation liberates the mold from the doom of identical copies, in which the design work is done once and execution is purely atemporal. Simondon's variable mold would combine a continuous supply of matter, such as we find in industrial casting, with the variable carving of handicraft. The action that is needed during every second of carving – whereas in casting, action is needed only for a single moment – is here called for again, to continuously instruct the mold how to vary. Such a set of instructions, which we characterized earlier as a motor schema, is what today we would call digital code, and also similar to what we know of genetic code, which is precisely such a temporal modulator in a flow of ever-replicating matter, running activation and inhibition scripts in a variable manner. We should keep in mind that in growth (or decay), there is copying going on; the creativity lies in the stopping and allowing of such copying at certain positions in certain modalities. Quality is the modulation of quantities. Again, with genetic code, the material activity of multiplication is a given; it doesn't need to be inserted or inspired, but it does need to be regulated, corrected and informed.

Theoretically, the dual relationship between drawing and carving is combined in the concept of digital code, in which each element is fed a coded motor schema, i.e., a set of instructions for how agents should behave in various situations. If we observe many elements behaving simultaneously, a general behavior emerges out of all the interactions. We call this generalized, collective behavior a pattern. Again, this does not take work out of the equation. Naturally, programming itself is a complex craft, but that is not what I mean. It is the operational, procedural logic of the Gothic which makes it code-dependent, its relational approach to problems of design – its manner of knitting its way through every question by separating the figural behavior of agents from configurational effects, and its rule-based consistency. Since the early 1990s, if not before, the most persistent misunderstanding about the digital has been that it is somehow "immaterial," even "gnostic." The fact that code is written doesn't make it immaterial or linguistic; on the contrary, the language we speak every day is descriptive, while programming language is instructive. Code talks to things just as things talk to things. If that, do this. If this, do that. Code is not immaterial; it speaks the language matter speaks. This means its instructions tell matter not just to do something but also to stop doing it at a certain point. But speaking a simple language does not result in a simple outcome – far from it. Babbage already grasped this fundamental trait of computing, proposing a transformation of skillful work by individuals into a complex "manufactory" of mindless computation by a large group of clerks, identical to the simple behavior of our changefully tracing angels, which through interaction creates myriad crystalline configurations of incredible beauty and complexity.

Within the framework of human design and production, such a shift means not only the transformation of design from hand-drawing to code-scripting but a move from hand-carving to the laser- and water-cutting of glass and metal sheets under the guidance of numerically controlled machines, and the milling by free-moving robot arms of volumetric blocks of foam and wood to be used as cores for panelwork or unique molds for casting liquids such as concrete. Just as digital code can bring life into elements, instructing them to self-assemble into patterned structures, it can also tell machinery to print, cut, or mill, i.e., to stereotomically carve any given shape at any moment, at the right speed and, more importantly, as a unique part. This technological argument brings us to the following, again seemingly contradictory conclusion: if we want to bring craft to design, that is, move design from the single-swoosh artistic approach to the complex interlacing and interweaving of craft – which is an aesthetics of the elaborated, if not the laborious – all actual manipulation of materials needs to be transferred into the hands of machines. Or, to use a subtle distinction: *as all craft moves toward design, all labor must move toward robotics.* All changefulness, all savageness and imperfection, evolves during the design stage; the final execution must be perfect – and done by slaves of steel. Our age can expect a totally unforeseen convergence of John Ruskin and Charles Babbage.

Crystals of Life

Now that we have refined our insight into the nature of digital, we can rephrase Ruskin's list of the characteristics of the nature of Gothic, keeping the same properties, but inevitably changing their order. Whereas his list was arranged ideologically, ours needs to have a more procedural, computational logic, in which each property is actively dependent on the one preceding it. Code often consists of a set of smaller coded packages of code, activated one by one at different moments during the procedure; again, instead of a single formula there is a strategy of incremental actions, and one package is always activated after another. In short, this code is an algorithmic, stepwise procedure that works over a period of time, in which certain actions are initiated, executed and then stopped, to be overtaken by the next set of actions, and so on, until completion – if any.

Let us observe how this works in the design of a Gothic cathedral according to a coded, digital methodology. Imagine lines on the screen, not stiff and dead but able to stretch, bend, interlock and connect, as if made from that malleable, vital, codified material, all according to Gothic rules, each line straight or circular. Step by step, we will try to describe how each level becomes responsible for tackling a set of design problems within the morphology of the structure:

1) Redundancy: Though Ruskin lists this characteristic last, it would be much more correct to start our Gothic operation with redundancy and abundance. Crucially, we will not define it as the extra ornament left over from all executed operations but as an initial indeterminacy of all available ribs. Redundancy in information theory is defined as a basic noise permeating all things, an overall relationality that after a program has been run results in effects (grouped shaft, traceried window, webbed vault), but also in-between effects (fan vault) and aftereffects (reticulated walls, pinnacles).

In Gothic digital design, redundancy means the availability of an enormous, but not infinite, number of ribs, organized at first in row-like fashion, which are willing to interact. Usually found in opposing pairs, they are initially straight verticals that start to copy two by two, in fixed increments, when we push the start button.

2) Changefulness: Every figure is variable in its own way; it consists of lines activated by points that can be moved sideways, up or down. All such movements – motifs – are limited, however, by the definition of the figure. In short, its variation is parametric, controlled by a continuous function.

Depending on how one sets up the operational systemacy to generate the Gothic cathedral, the bundles of lines will start copying in the longitudinal direction of the nave while at the same time growing upward and, as they bend inward, interlacing into a vault, while the column does the same at the opposite side of the nave. The nave will keep growing until a certain length is reached (checked by the surrounding buildings), when it will turn 90 degrees to create the transepts, though not always, and the nave will only be copied sideways to the aisles. Meanwhile, the spaces in between will be filled on the exterior with finer tracery movements.

3) Rigidity: All free movement of figures settles into configurational patterns; hence, the Gothic is characterized by a flexible rigidity, a concept not far removed from Ruskin's concepts of help and crystallization. Such rigidity has two modalities, one structural and one ornamental; the former relates rigidity to the actual transfer of loads to the earth, while the latter remains solely configurational, a patterned outcome of all line interaction.

In our digital procedure, we can observe three different stages on the screen: in the first, all the lines are straight and unbent; then they bend as they interact; and then they come to a stop after their interaction. They can only stop when ribs either cross diagonally, merge like railway switches, or bifurcate to form liernes and tiercerons. After the aisles have been formed, flying buttresses form as a function of the outer columns.

4) *Naturalism*: Though the figural movement and configurational pattern are not necessarily "natural," they are certainly not alien to us. Such behavior by figures does not mimic human or animal movement, nor does the pattern of configurations mimic crystalline or biological structures, yet there is a fundamental sympathy between the two.

Looking at our screen again, while we would not say our digital lines grow like trees, since they do not bifurcate as branches do, their movement looks familiar, or at least not unnatural. This is not the same as natural or representational, but it is not purely abstract either.

5) *Savageness*: Though Ruskin placed this at the top of his list, I think it is the result of all the other operations, not their basis. Yet imperfection is essential: it means that a system that nests figures in all kinds of configurations must meet its limit at several thresholds. Such points appear as heterogeneous breaks in fields of variation. Therefore, systems that don't allow for much changefulness have more breaks and cuts than ones that allow for more variability. These breaks occur on two levels: the smaller-scale level and the larger-scale level of massing. The latter, in particular, makes a Gothic building what it is, with its broken symmetries, sudden additions and unfinished parts.

In our digital "breeding box," we see thick lines emerging on the growing object, at right angles to the general movement of the figures. Sometimes new spires shoot up following the formation of savage ridges; sometimes they do not because the threshold value has not been met.

6) *Grotesqueness*: When savageness goes further over the limit, the result is a grotesqueness that can be either humorous or monstrous. Since it is a subset of savageness, one encounters it even less often than the previous category.

At the end of our digital Gothic experiment, very strange excrescences may appear at certain points. We do not remove these.

Surprisingly enough, we can thus manage remarkably well with Ruskin's list of characteristics when we look at it from a digital and operational perspective. I can imagine that a number of historically inclined readers will think that I am pushing reality over the limit here, but bringing a historic argument into our own age is impossible without recasting it as a purely conceptual and theoretical one. I am trying to revive Ruskin's argumentation, and to follow it as far as I can, though in another age it seems to lead us into another domain. Today, 150 years later, it would carry no weight to start advocating a return to handicraft; our world is covered with more ugly buildings every day, there are more unbearable DVDs, disaffected design and useless printed matter than ever. Would it help to start another Guild of St. George colony where we all – all thirty-seven of us – worked by hand, as the world around us was swamped in generic sameness? I don't think so; sharing the same ethics need not result in the same action. All Ruskin's morals are unfailingly valid today, although we need them for other reasons: just as he needed the Gothic to save his era from the division of labor, we need it in order to unify design, so architects can be anonymous again, designers can move away from product and commodity, and artists can leave the museums and start occupying real, everyday spaces. The return to variation, more precisely to configurational variation, including a material understanding of it, that I am commending necessarily implies another, more forward-looking Gothic, which probably won't even look Gothic to most of us but nonetheless will show the same rigor, the same changefulness and savageness: an art of digital, configurational variation. Handicraft, while offering variation, cannot provide us with nearly enough continuity; and inversely, industrial casting (prefab) offers continuity but no variation. By bringing the concept of handicraft into the very heart of molding technology, we can have both variability and continuity. Code and modulated fabrication give us exactly that, but let us not forget that code specifically demands an art of configurational variation (be it architecture, design, music or something else) – that is, *a digital Gothic,* not the digital swooshism of a Frank Gehry or the generations following him, which we are supposed to believe defines coded architecture today. We see nothing but a persistence of the same old Beaux-Arts, purely artistic modeling in digital plaster of Paris, merely a digital Arts without Crafts, the exertion of sheer technological control over a design that is itself out of control. Of course, it is possible to code anything; one can even code the design of a Greek temple or Miesian skyscraper (recommended only as a freshman assignment), but take a good look at what happens on the screen when you do. All the elements fly in as if from out of the blue, appearing on the screen as if popping out of hidden drawers, stiff and preformed, seemingly moved into position by some exterior force; nothing "forms," nothing bends or interlaces.

What a profound correlation between the vital machine of the Gothic and the vital machine of the digital! Coded properly, the digital could establish a type of formation that is neither completely abstract nor completely organic, because the two states collaborate without a direct, linear relationship. It is mechanical, all right, but only on the lower, molecular scale of the figure; it tends toward organic form on the larger, configurational scale. It is an abstraction that never fully retracts from the real, and an organicity that is never fully accomplished – never completely organic, never completely mechanical. "Then we really may believe that mountains are living?" asks one of the young girls in *The Ethics of the Dust*. "Things are not either wholly alive, or wholly dead. They are less or more alive," responds Ruskin's Lecturer, and he has the girls – not unlike Millais' angels fifteen years before – walk around and grasp each other's hands, as in a dance, creating "*crystals of life*," to empirically teach them the configurational nature of all things (XVIII, 346 and 233-40). Less or more alive! Nothing inanimate, no mountain or cloud, can be considered completely dead, and nothing organic can be described as being fully alive at every scale.

My earlier fantasy of a Gothic crystal with a nave proliferating across an open field, zigzagging and producing multiple spires and transepts, shows how such vitality depends both on the copying mechanism and the organic tendency toward form, though the final result always depends on context. Obviously, the edges have to tell the copying to halt. This is the sole reason why the English Gothic differs from the French: English cathedrals are exceptionally long because they were generated in open fields or on lawns, while French ones mostly occur in dense urban areas, where proportions were often inflexible. The two are definitely products of the same code. For instance, Salisbury has grown such a long nave that the transept has had to branch off twice, while Bourges has no transepts at all. Instead of making the structure grow into an elongated morphology, the same set of instructions can just as easily generate a short, fat volume; when a site has little depth but plenty of width, the algorithm simply starts adding more aisles instead of transepts. The whole secret is that the algorithm is coded in packages, incrementally, with each section containing a certain amount of variation. And if the content were something other than a church, and the urban environment was different, such a system could generate an endless number of forms most beautiful (as Darwin would have said), varying depending on which problems needed tackling. Ruskin, as well as Revivalist architects like George Edmund Street and George Gilbert Scott, stressed the fact that the Gothic dealt with problems in a relaxed way, which later historians confused with the methodology of functionalism. Obviously, the Gothic system allows for an extra spire, or an extra stair or turret, but not because it resorts to amorphism and simply aggregates accidents. Accident – though it is the motor of the Picturesque, according to Ruskin in *The Seven Lamps* (VIII, 236) – is here absorbed by a flexible, relaxed systemacy, which constantly adapts to change rather than exposing accidents as mishaps. When a system adapts to accident, that accident changes from the random to the variable.

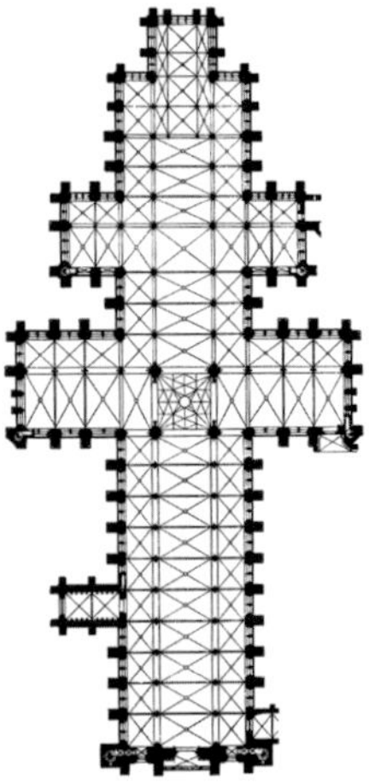

Plan of Salisbury Cathedral (1220-1320).

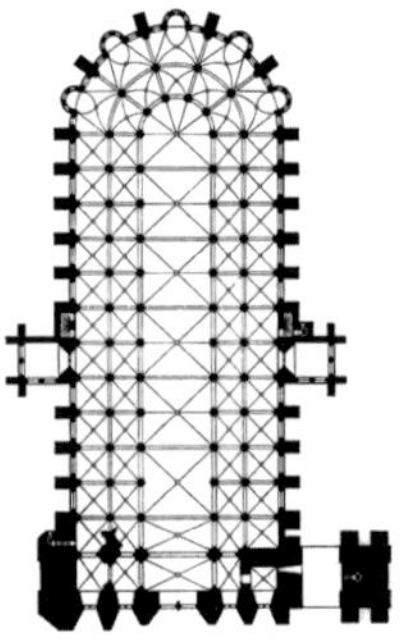

Plan of Bourges Cathedral (1190-1324).

Gottfried Semper was the first theoretician to remark that the Gothic was "Scholasticism in stone," and though he meant the comment to be derogatory, the idea was elaborated and transformed by Worringer in *Form Problems in Gothic* (slightly mistranslated by Read as *Form in Gothic*), and again by Erwin Panofsky – who fails to mention Worringer, by the way – in *Gothic Architecture and Scholasticism* forty years later, in 1951. It is no surprise that Worringer did the best job of making us understand how the parallel is developed. The well-known criticism that Scholastic thought only convolutes and never reaches a moment of knowledge, Worringer argued, is exactly what makes it so powerful, and Gothic. More methodological than epistemological, Scholasticism is a mechanical way of thinking that circumvents problems with a strict logic. Its understanding of form as a set of problems, ones not to be resolved but to be handled without contradiction, is precisely the logic of Gothic continuity and connectedness. It attacks the problem of the column, just as it attacks the problem of the vault with the invention of the continuous rib, but such problems must be reformulated over and over, until all the variations have run out. Is there a better way of explaining the digital? The digital is a totally scholastic, numerical, clickety-clack way of thinking. Not really even mental but much more material, it is a way of thinking akin to the way hands treat matter. The digital nature of Gothic should be taken literally: it not only offers a new way of rethinking the Gothic in our own time, but it also means the Gothic was already digital (and expressionist) in the twelfth and thirteenth centuries.

Why does the Gothic seem to be best understood in art and architectural history by "dilettantes" (Worringer and Ruskin, both expressionists) and so much less well by the official spokespeople (Frankl, Jantzen, Von Simson, Panofsky)? It seems to me that this is mainly owed to the structure of historiography. Much too often, architectural history is about that vague modernist concept, "space," or worse, "meaning," or, worst of all, "iconology"; such terms are wholly irrelevant to the Gothic. A cathedral is hardly interesting in spatial terms; iconologically, it is ridiculous (except for the statues, which are meant to be read) and in terms of meaning, incomprehensible. And the argument of the microcosm is also continually resurrected, the idea that Gothic "represents" the world, or the universe, and naturally God too. Of all the arguments, this is the worst – as if the world, and the universe, are anywhere other than where you are right now. I would rather hear Ruskin saying the Gothic embodies "a profound sympathy with the fullness and wealth of the material universe" than Panofsky explaining to me what it all means. There is no meaning, just building.

Why does architectural history not simply work with techniques, materiality and morphologies? By techniques, I mean those of design as well as building; materiality is what the two have in common, and the concept is thus a much broader one than structure or construction. The third, morphology, is the final effect, the result of the other two, and covers a much broader idea than the familiar term "typology" (but much narrower than the vague "form"), because typology is always fixed in advance and is not active on every scale of the building. Each of the three has its own history, and each of the three affects the others. This classification makes no a priori distinction between ornament and structure, nor between structure and form. Forms evolve, and consist of tendencies of continuous transformation, for none of the three elements are ever in balance. It is never the ideas that change; if there are ideas, they follow the above three. Language simply never precedes form, for it is not instrumental, and if it is, it is code, not language. Unfortunately, only a few biologists have ventured into art theory, but one of the best is Alfred Haddon, whose *Evolution in Art* simply looks at forms as forms, made by groups of people, using certain materials and techniques, and with a certain morphological history. One must look at forms as if one does not understand them, simply observe what they do and how they do it. Of course, Focillon's *The Life of Forms in Art* formulates a clear program for such an approach ("That our idea of matter should be intimately linked with our idea of technique is altogether unavoidable"), but not the method itself. And his *The Art of the West* (one of whose two volumes discusses the Gothic in full) does not follow such a program and is still full of references to meaning.

A zebra or a finch has no meaning either, does it? A finch is certainly an expression (of a genetic code), but that doesn't mean it has anything to tell us. The relationship among the dozens of different kinds of beaks on the Galápagos Islands shows us a complete relational history of the finches and their environment. What good to us are Sedlmayer's baldachin, Jantzen's diaphanous structure, and Panofsky's Scholasticism if we get to hear nothing about the techniques by which these effects come about? All of them surely exist, but they can be achieved just as well through other means besides the Gothic. It is the means and techniques that determine the idea, not the other way around. And then, when one thinks one has distilled an idea, one can be certain it is the wrong one. In the Gothic, the means are specific and unique, and it is these means, set in train by design and building techniques, that make the Gothic what it is.

The effect is "diaphanous," of course, but the word does not capture the true theoretical crux of the Gothic – namely, that *walls and windows are of the same order*. This can be done only through study of the connection between the design techniques (reticulation, articulation, interweaving, molding) and material building techniques (carving, stereotomy). The perfectly reasonable, everyday conclusion that windows are open and walls are not does not apply in the Gothic. In the Gothic design technique, the fact that the ribs weave the building is primary; how and with what (glass or stone) the holes are eventually filled is secondary. Its fabric doesn't make the cathedral "transparent" – certainly not "phenomenally transparent," in the modernist sense of an object penetrated by an exterior world – but it does make it delicate. This tendency in the Gothic is generally viewed as anti-wall or pro-window; neither notion draws attention to what is actually going on: all the elements are turning into relationships, threads and fibers. It is its overall delicacy, rather than light as a form of antimatter, that makes the Gothic so "spiritual," the word Worringer and many others after him have used to describe the Gothic. The term has some uncomfortable connotations, which shouldn't deter us from using it; on the contrary. In the first place, this spirituality has nothing to do with religion or Christianity. Gothic cathedrals are Christian churches, of course, but that doesn't mean the mental structure of Christianity automatically explains the Gothic in any way; even Ruskin knew that. Secondly, the notion of spirituality replaces that of "idea."

The Gothic is *an architecture of spirituality, not of ideas*. Idea stands in opposition to materiality, transcending it; spirituality stands on the same side, sympathizing with it. Or, to word it more strongly, idea exists outside materiality, in antithesis to it, while spirituality takes place within it, inhabiting it; this is why an architecture of heaviness suffices for the former while the latter requires that everything be thinned out, made delicate and movable. The act only looks like one of "dematerialization": that word is a major philosophical trap if ever I saw one. No such thing is taking place (how could it?). The fact that the building gets lighter does not mean it becomes less material; less material is merely needed to build it. The material becomes more active and less inert. The Gothic provides an *improved view of matter*, not an antimaterial one. But although material, the Gothic offers no direct bodily experience of materiality: again, it is no Baroque, no Rococo, not sensual and physical; it is not happiness, ecstasy or theater but a perfectly ordinary everyday relationship with... well, everything. It is not about forming an idea of the world (*Weltanschauung*) but about being connected to it. Hence, the Gothic is an architecture of *relationality*, of pattern, an architecture that constantly forges new relationships and expresses them in every possible form and shape.

This actually makes it ecological and topological rather than organic, as William Morris always thought. The Gothic makes this-place-here into every place, and this-moment-now into always. Maybe not everything-everything, but everything-enough, and maybe not always-always, but always-long enough. Enough so that other things concern you. As you see this thing here and now, in fact you are "seeing" all things, or, as Ruskin says, you are experiencing "a sympathy" with everything. But "seeing" is not the right word; it is not about an image. "Believing" is actually much better – another uncomfortable word, like "spirituality," although it too refers not to something transcendent but to things. *I believe in things*. Seeing becomes saturated with believing. How else can we orient ourselves in this Brotherhood of Things? Seeing one thing makes us believe in all things – and if that's not radical empiricism, I don't know what is. One might ask: Is that not a bit strange and unnecessary, believing when you can see things? Well, the issue is precisely that you cannot see them, for they lie hidden behind the horizon, or under your feet and behind your back, but you believe they are there – not as a collection of objects but in all their connectedness; that is, in their relatedness to this thing here. It is not that we imagine them but that we *feel* them: we stretch one thing out spiritually across all the others, by an act of sympathy. Seeing is a concrete experience in which we single out one object amid our basic relatedness to things. Yet this doesn't mean our background relatedness disappears: the selected thing is still tied in with the others. Between concrete experiences, we still experience abstractly; even without an object, we are still ready, so to speak. Even without content, experience is charged. We could see this readiness as belief or spirituality – not faith, hallucination or even imagination but more of an awareness; a basic, given involvement of ourselves with things. To believe in things is to be prepared to be involved.

And, by the way, belief in things stands in diametrical opposition to what today we call "the media." There, you see everything and believe nothing.

Monet's Rouen series. I keep looking at them all the time, one page after another. He has painted the same façade of Rouen Cathedral over and over – warming up in the morning light, ice-cold in December, on a grey afternoon, in a glorious summer sunset. Thirty-one amazing paintings, all from the same angle but all in different light, at various times of day, various times of year. Compare them to Ruskin's plates, his pages filled with moldings, and all the grouped shafts. Monet's paintings show a single Gothic thing over time, Ruskin's plates all the different variations of one Gothic thing; I see the two as reflections. Formation and experience mirror each other: first, time is reflected in form, then form in time. Monet's light immediately overwhelms us, of course; it is much thicker and more viscous than light as we know it. No southern sun brightens up this northern church; light is not cast on it. Rather, the stone itself seems to shine, completely reversing the notion of the Gothic as transparent, and also reversing the experience of the stained glass in the interior, making the whole building radiate light.

Monet's Rouen glows – which is perfect. There is no chiaroscuro in the Gothic, no white marble, no contours, except the fractal one of the roof, which is not a roof but a landscape of spires, pinnacles and buttresses that dissolves anything defining a volume, such as a cornice. The northern Gothic is one of deep grooves, ribs and moldings, the southern Gothic one of marble paneling. Why is the northern always viewed from the interior and the southern from the exterior? Why, furthermore, is the northern Gothic always treated as if it scarcely has an exterior at all (Semper considered it naked and uncovered), as something turned inside out? The

Claude Monet. Three of the 31 views of the front portal of Rouen Cathedral. From the top: Morning Light (1894); Facade 1 (1892); Full Sunlight (1893).

Gothic amalgam of stone, light and rain mixes dirt with design; just take another look at Pugin's diagrams, with all that water dripping off the moldings and intersecting with the eyes' gaze upward, as both enjoy the profile. It is the light that dresses the building, not the shadows; the numerous stone dressings cause it to nestle in the countless profiles; everything seems to absorb light and radiate it back. Again, wall and window are of the same order, both expelling light outward as much as they drink it in.

This light is decidedly different from that of the Mediterranean sun, which outlines things against a blue sky; this light is diffuse and opaque, mixed with clouds, with limestone, with the dirt in all the profiles. This is animism as opposed to metaphysics. All things Greek drop out of the blue, from a cloudless sky of idealism, finished, pure and polished; nothing is grown, no work or sweat required. In opposition to this, we find no metaphysics in the northern Gothic: the spirits enter from soaking wet ground, out of mud and dirt, not immaculate sky. It is sky against ground, beach against forest, and hence gods against spirits, or as we know them, ideas against things, ideas thought against things made.

All references to John Ruskin's works are from *The Works of John Ruskin*, Library Edition, edited by E. T. Cook and Alexander Wedderburn, 39 vols. (London, 1903–1912) and are noted parenthetically in the text.

References to Wilhelm Worringer's *Form in Gothic* are from the 1957 edition introduced by Herbert Read (London), the English translation of *Formprobleme der Gotik* published in Munich (1911).

The reference to the famous sermon of Nicolas de Briard comes from Alain Erlande-Brandenburg's *The Cathedral Builders of the Middle Ages* (London, 1995).

Other references sources:
Bizup, Joseph. *Manufacturing Culture: Vindications of Early Victorian Industry* (Charlottesville and London, 2003).
Frankl, Paul. *The Gothic: Literary Sources and Interpretations through Eight Centuries* (Princeton, 1960).
Heyman, Jacques. *The Stone Skeleton* (Cambridge, 1995).
Jantzen, Hans. *High Gothic: The Classical Cathedrals of Charteres, Reims, Amiens* (New York, 1962).
Panofsky, Erwin. *Gothic Architecture and Scholasticism* (New York, 1951).
Willis, Robert. *Remarks on the Architecture of the Middle Ages* (Cambridge, 1835).
Sennett, Richard. *The Craftsman* (Yale, 2008).

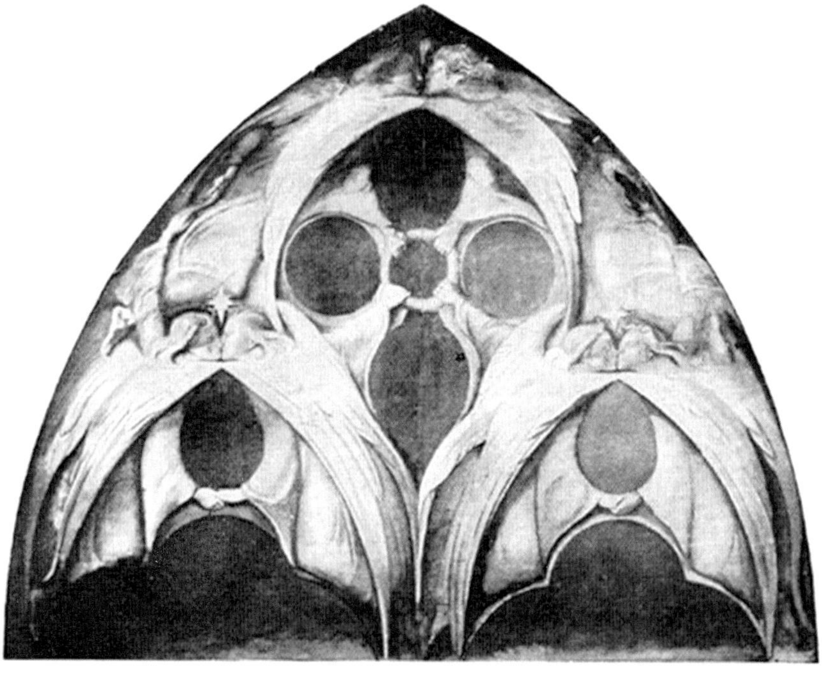

MAURISCH MORESQUE No 3 MAURESQUES

TAFEL XLI. PL. XLI.

Figure-Configuration Taxonomies

C-Curve

J-Curve

S-Curve

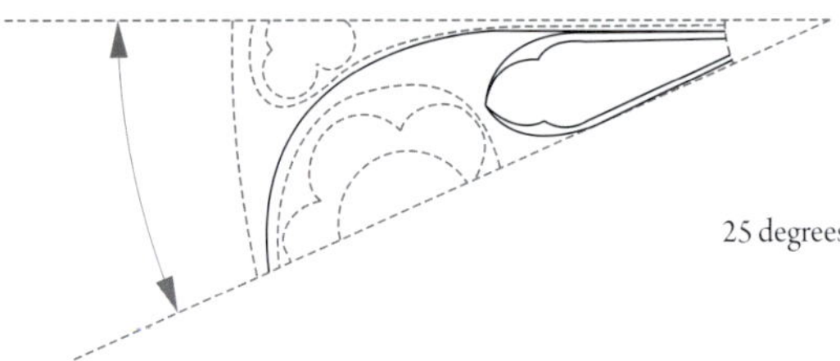
25 degrees

Rose Windows, Spoked
J-Curves

C-Curve

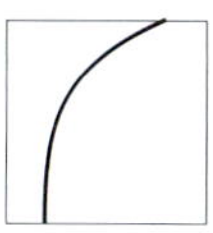

J-Curve

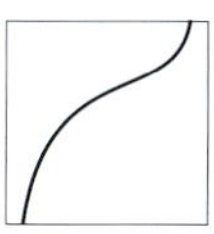

S-Curve

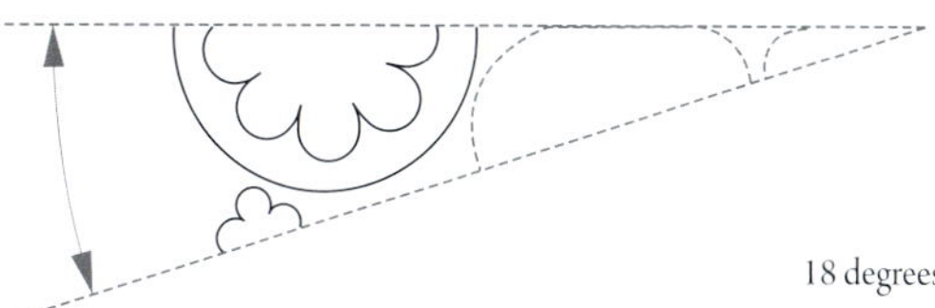

18 degrees

Rose Windows, Pitted
C-Curves

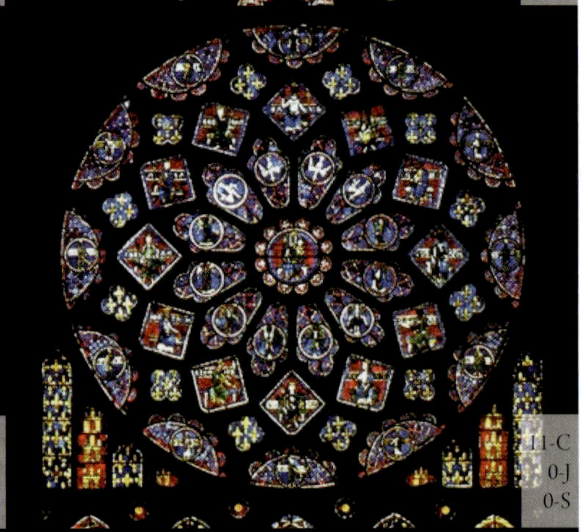

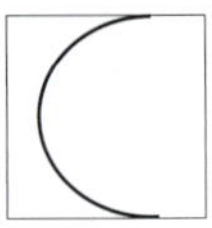

C-Curve

J-Curve

S-Curve

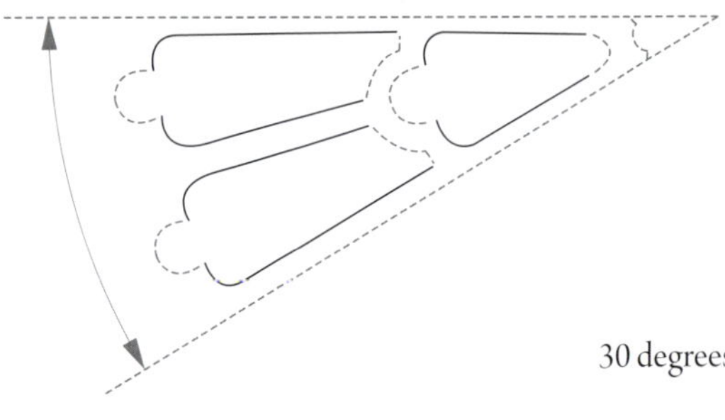

Rose Windows, Petaled
J-Curves

30 degrees

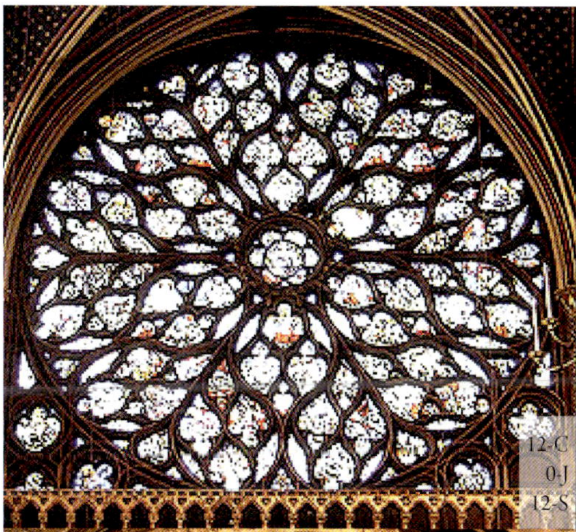

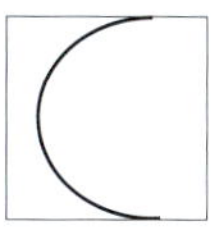

C-Curve

J-Curve

S-Curve

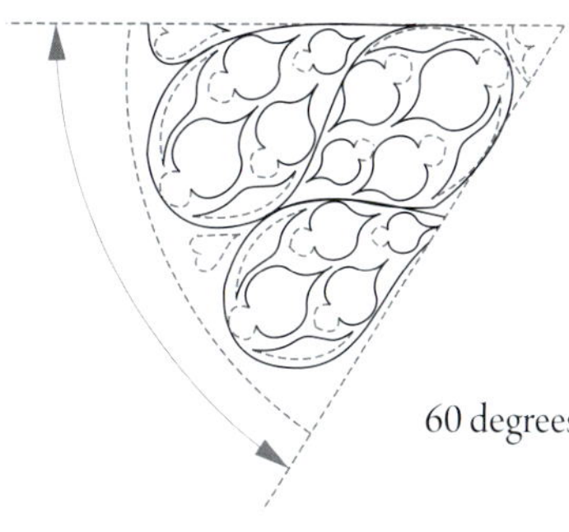

60 degrees

Rose Windows, Radiant
S-Curves

C-Curve

J-Curve

S-Curve

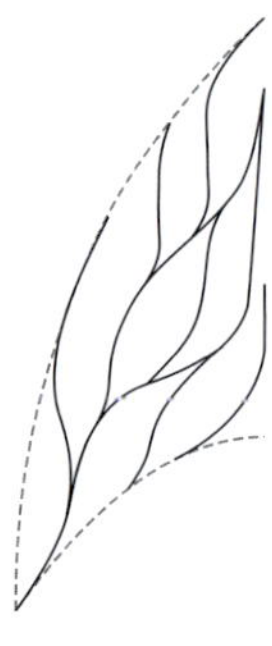

Traceries, Nested
S-Curves

C-Curve

J-Curve

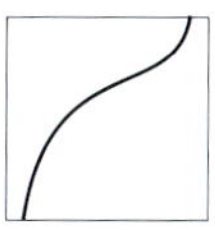
S-Curve

Traceries, Clustered
J-Curve

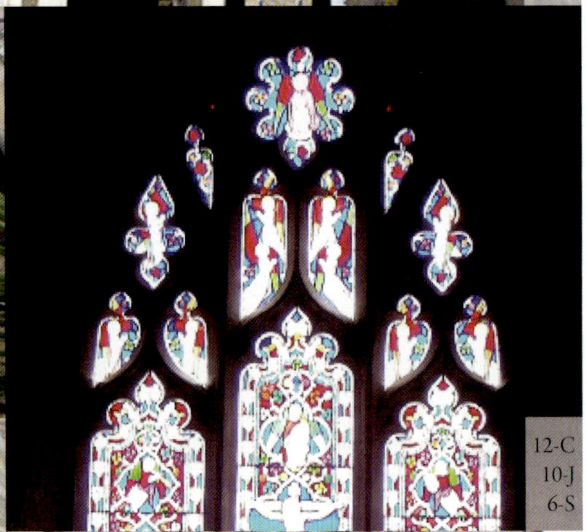

C-Curve

J-Curve

S-Curve

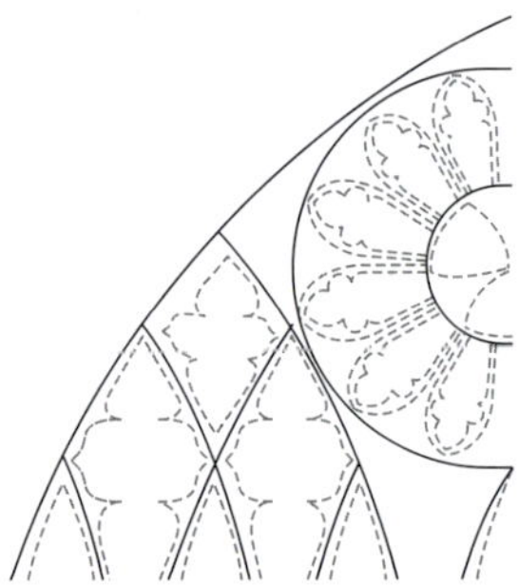

Traceries, Speared
J-Curve

C-Curve

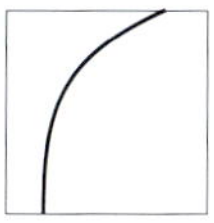

J-Curve

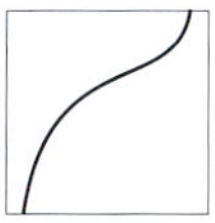

S-Curve

Traceries, Stacked
C-Curve

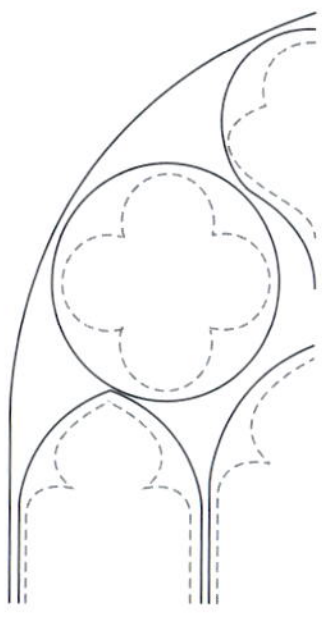

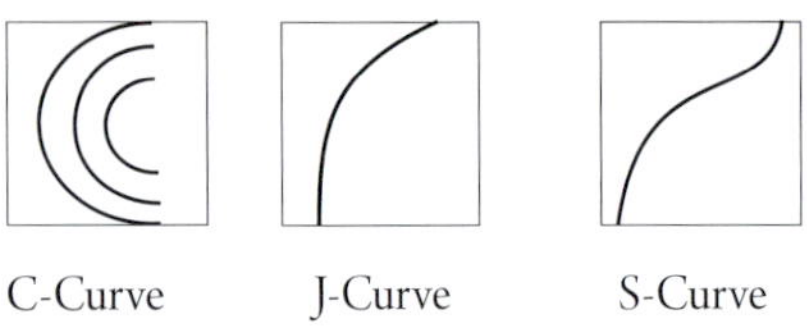

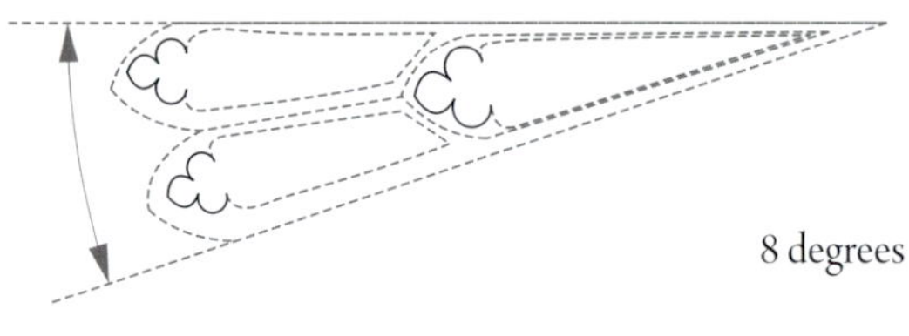

Fan Vaults, Swept
C-Curve

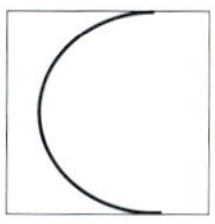

C-Curve

J-Curve

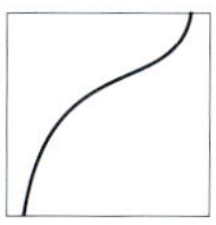

S-Curve

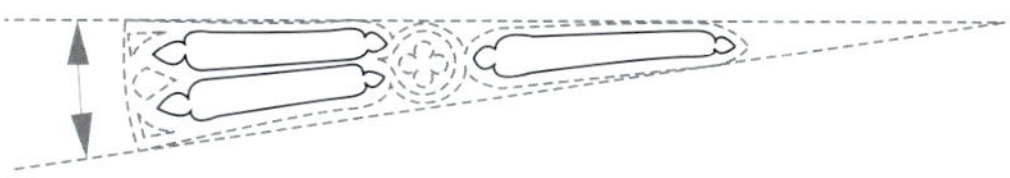

12 degrees

Fan Vaults, Splayed
J-Curve

C-Curve

J-Curve

S-Curve

90 degrees

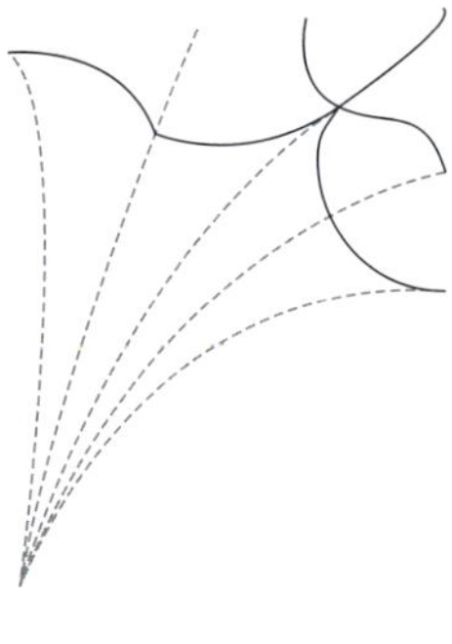

Rib Vaults, Interlaced
S-Curves

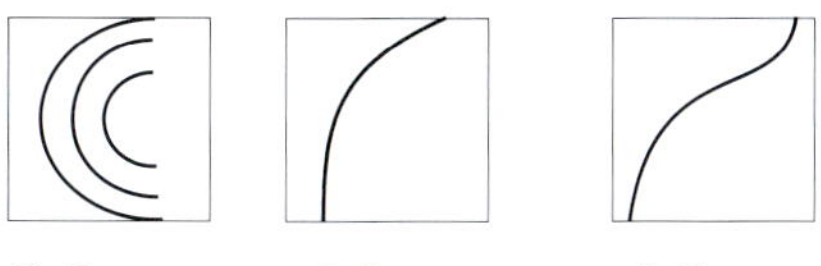

90 degrees

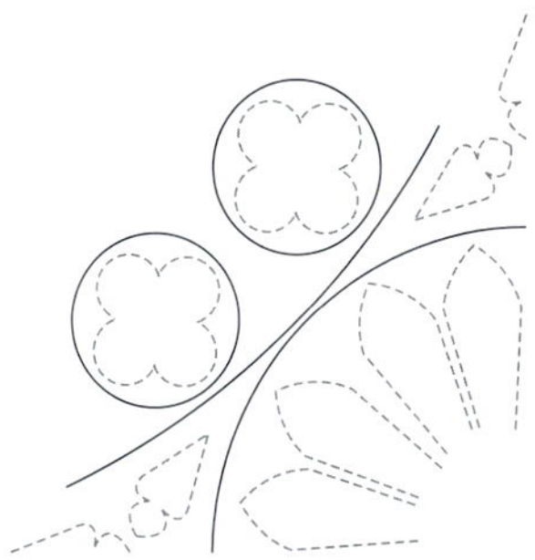

Ceiling Centers, Compressed
C-Curves

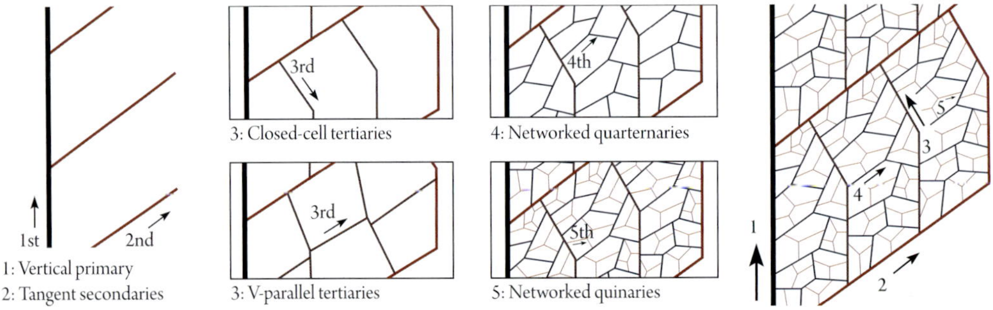

1: Vertical primary
2: Tangent secondaries

3: Closed-cell tertiaries

3: V-parallel tertiaries

4: Networked quarternaries

5: Networked quinaries

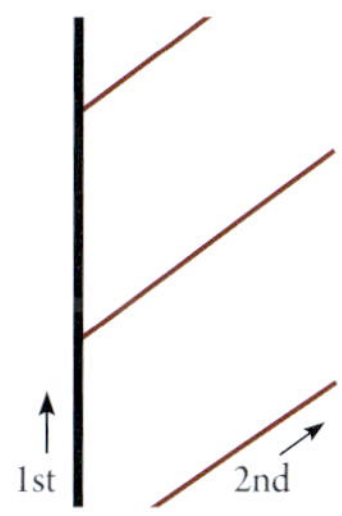

1: Vertical primary
2: Tangent secondaries

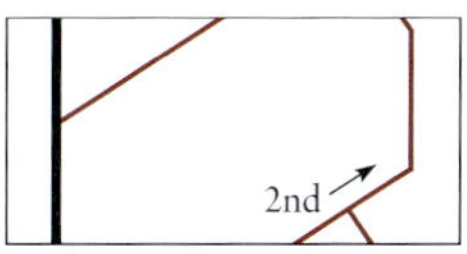

3: Closed-cell secondaries

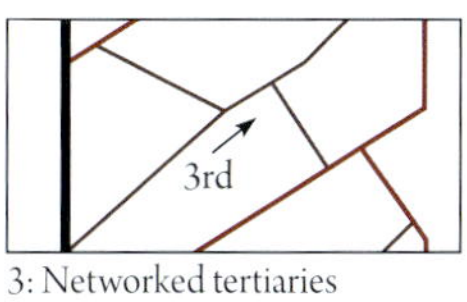

3: Networked tertiaries

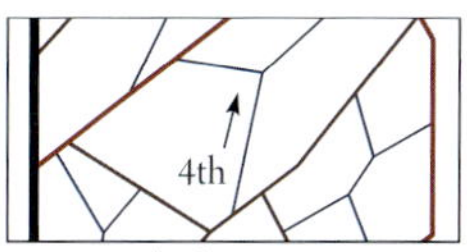

4: Networked quaternaries

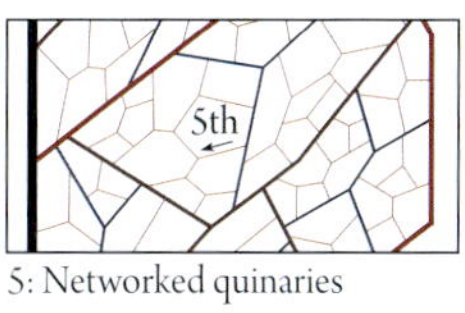

5: Networked quinaries

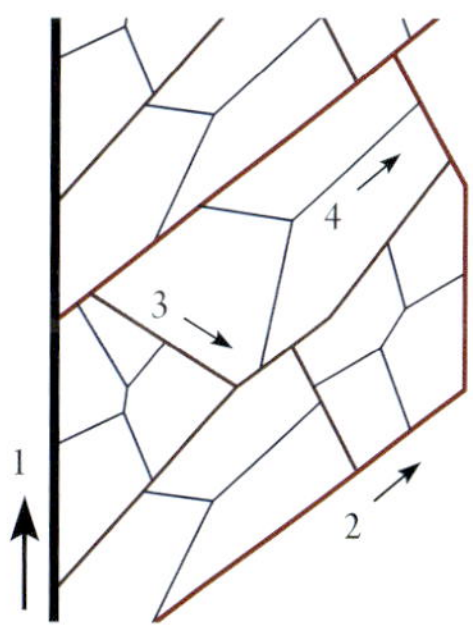

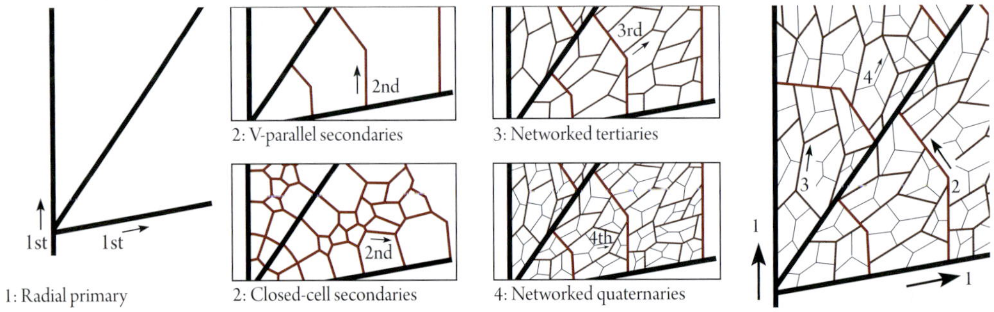
1st
1st
1: Radial primary
2nd
2: V-parallel secondaries
2nd
2: Closed-cell secondaries
3rd
3: Networked tertiaries
4th
4: Networked quaternaries
4
3
2
1
1

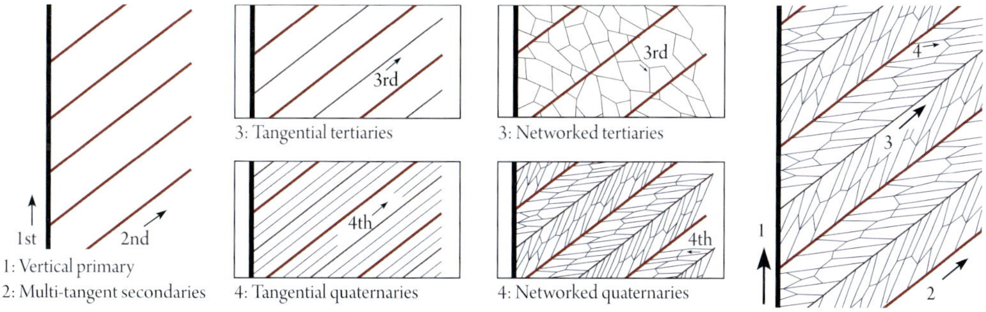

1: Vertical primary
2: Multi-tangent secondaries
3: Tangential tertiaries
4: Tangential quaternaries
3: Networked tertiaries
4: Networked quaternaries

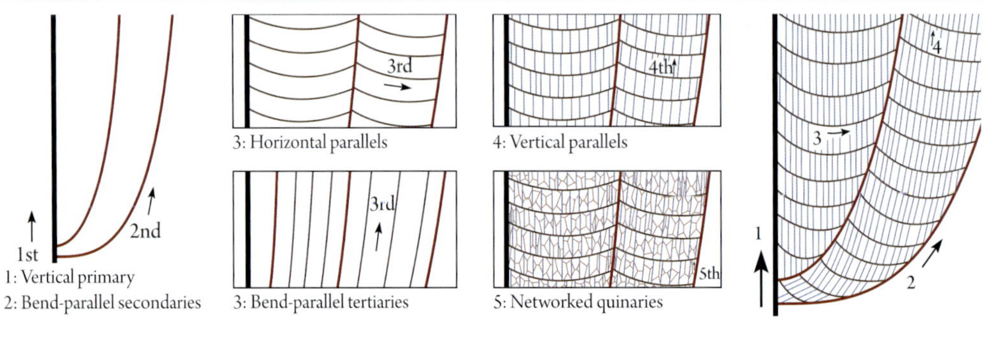

1: Vertical primary
2: Bend-parallel secondaries
3: Horizontal parallels
3: Bend-parallel tertiaries
4: Vertical parallels
5: Networked quinaries

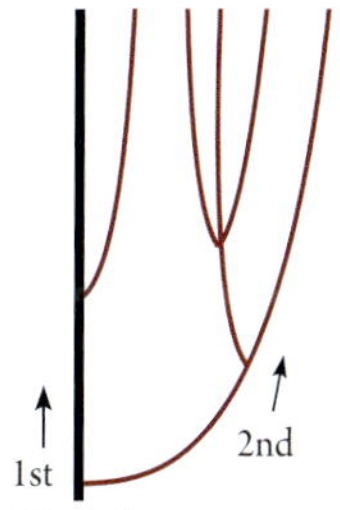

1: Vertical primary
2: Split & bend-parallel

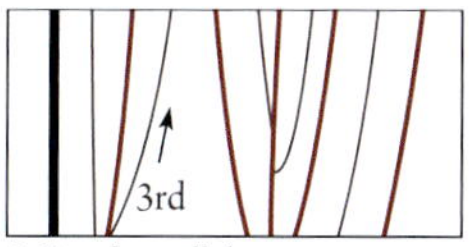

3: Bend-parallel tertiaries

3: Networked tertiaries

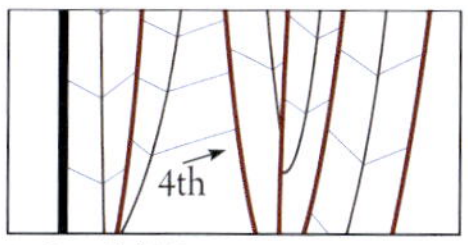

4: Parallel-V quaternaries

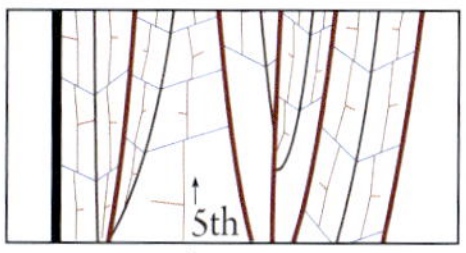

5: Horizontal-T quinaries

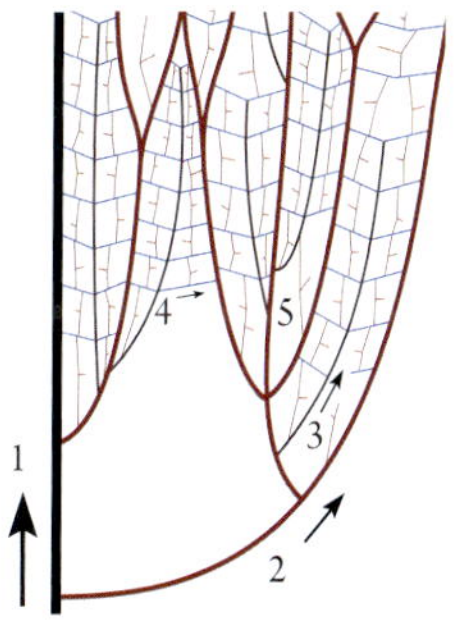

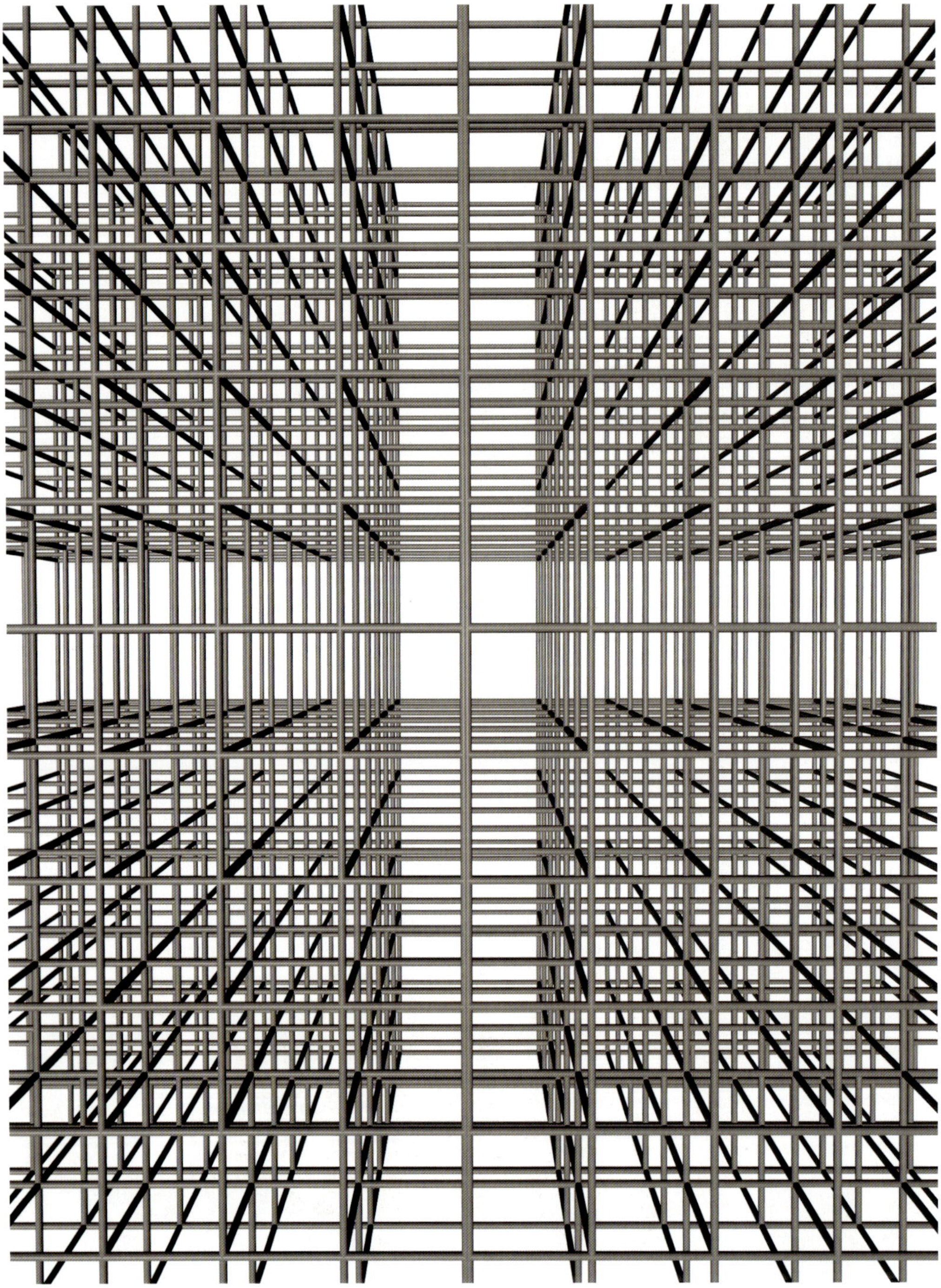

#S: 64
SV: 904.78
sV: 14.14
bV: 1728.67
# of sides: 6

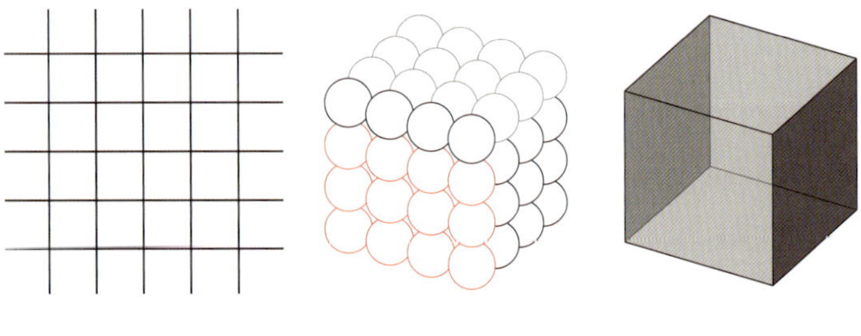

Regular Packing Networks:
Rectangular Stacking, Rectangular Packing

#S: 80
SV: 1130.97
sV: 14.14
bV: 2092.92
# of sides: 12

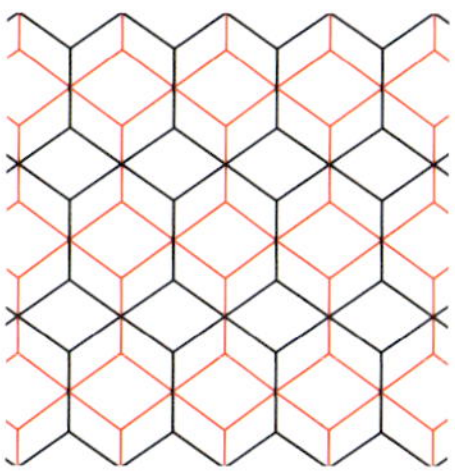

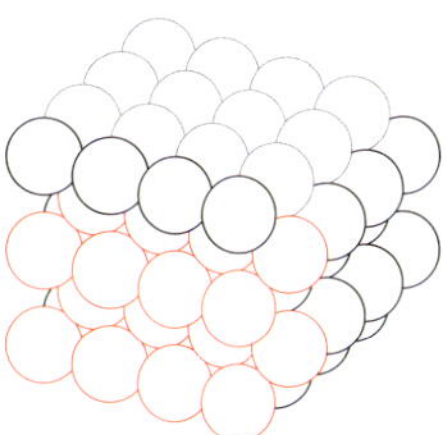

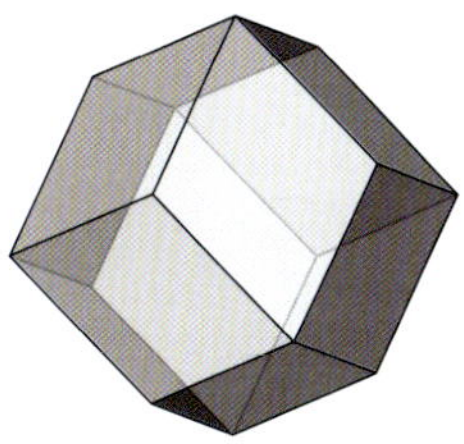

Regular Packing Networks:
Hexagonal Stacking, Rectangular Packing

#S: 64
SV: 904.78
sV: 14.14
bV: 1728.67
# of sides: 8

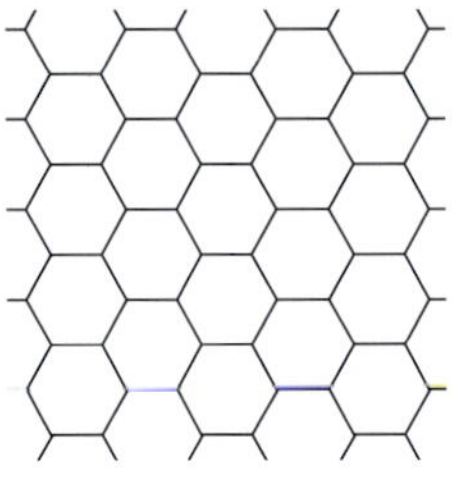

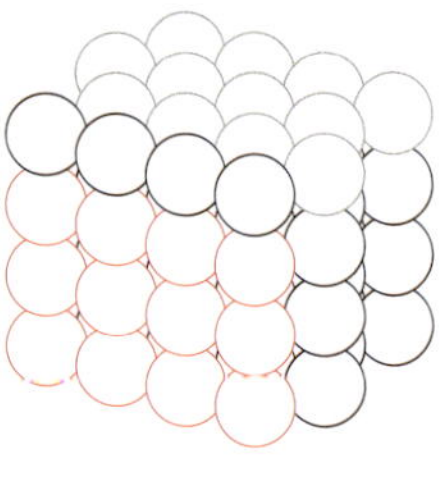

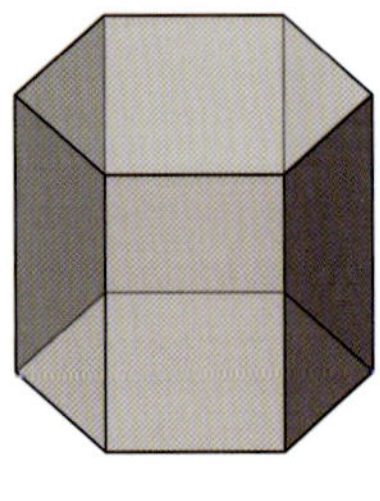

Regular Packing Networks:
Rectangular Stacking, Hexagonal Packing

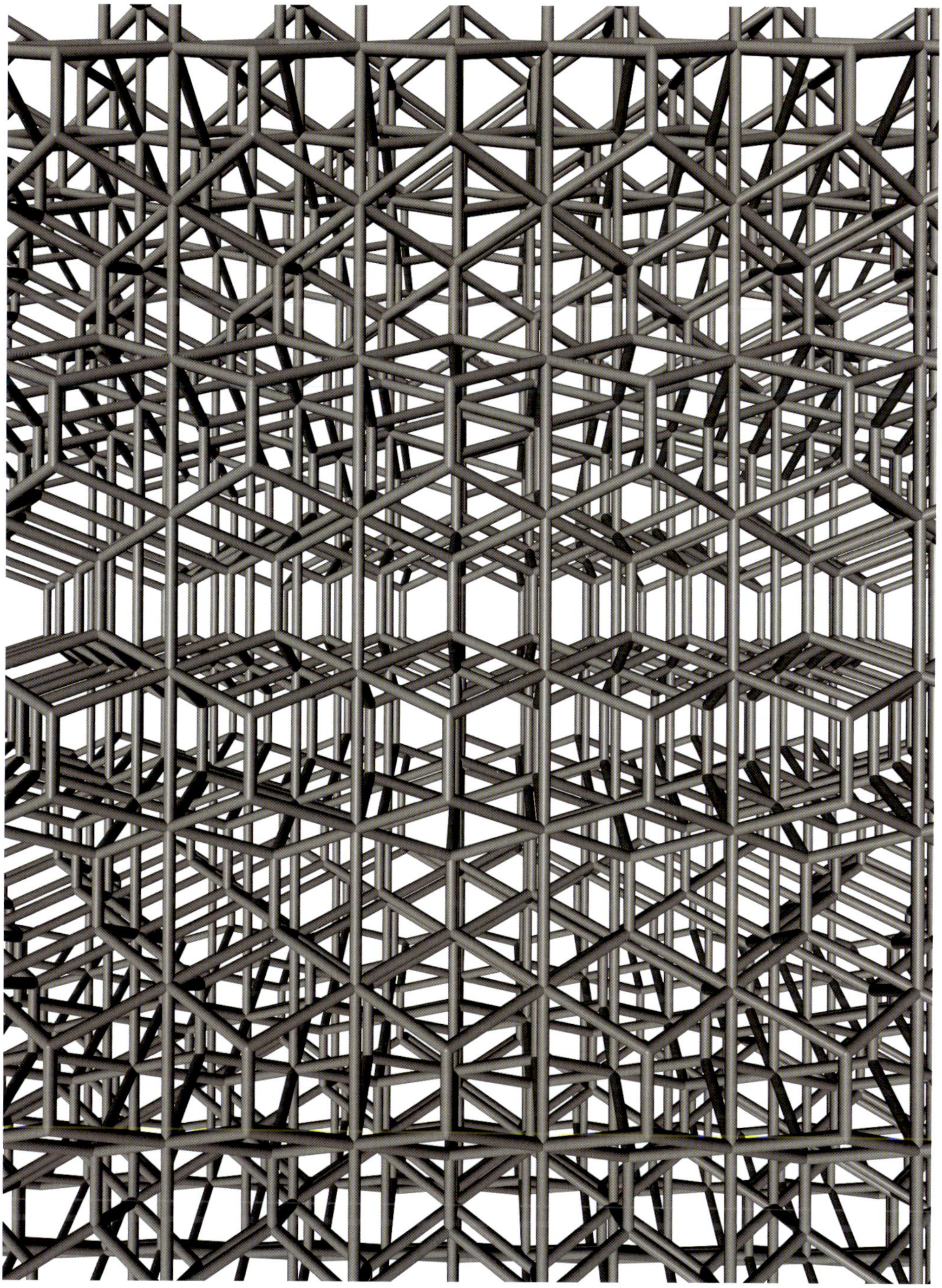

#S: 80
SV: 1130.97
sV: 14.14
bV: 2092.92
# of sides: 12

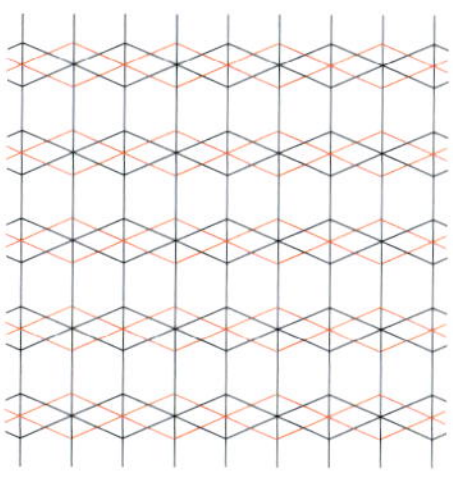

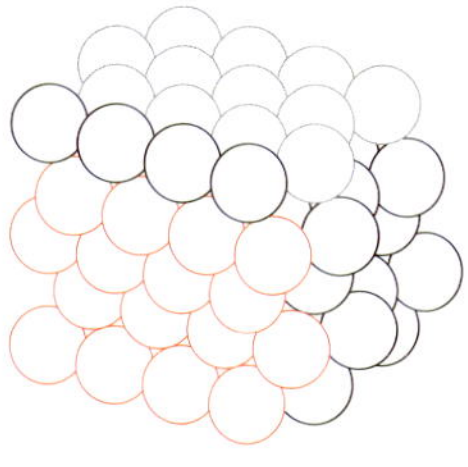

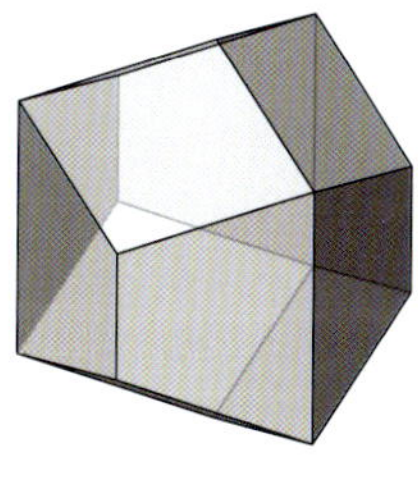

Regular Packing Networks:
Hexagonal Stacking, Hexagonal Packing

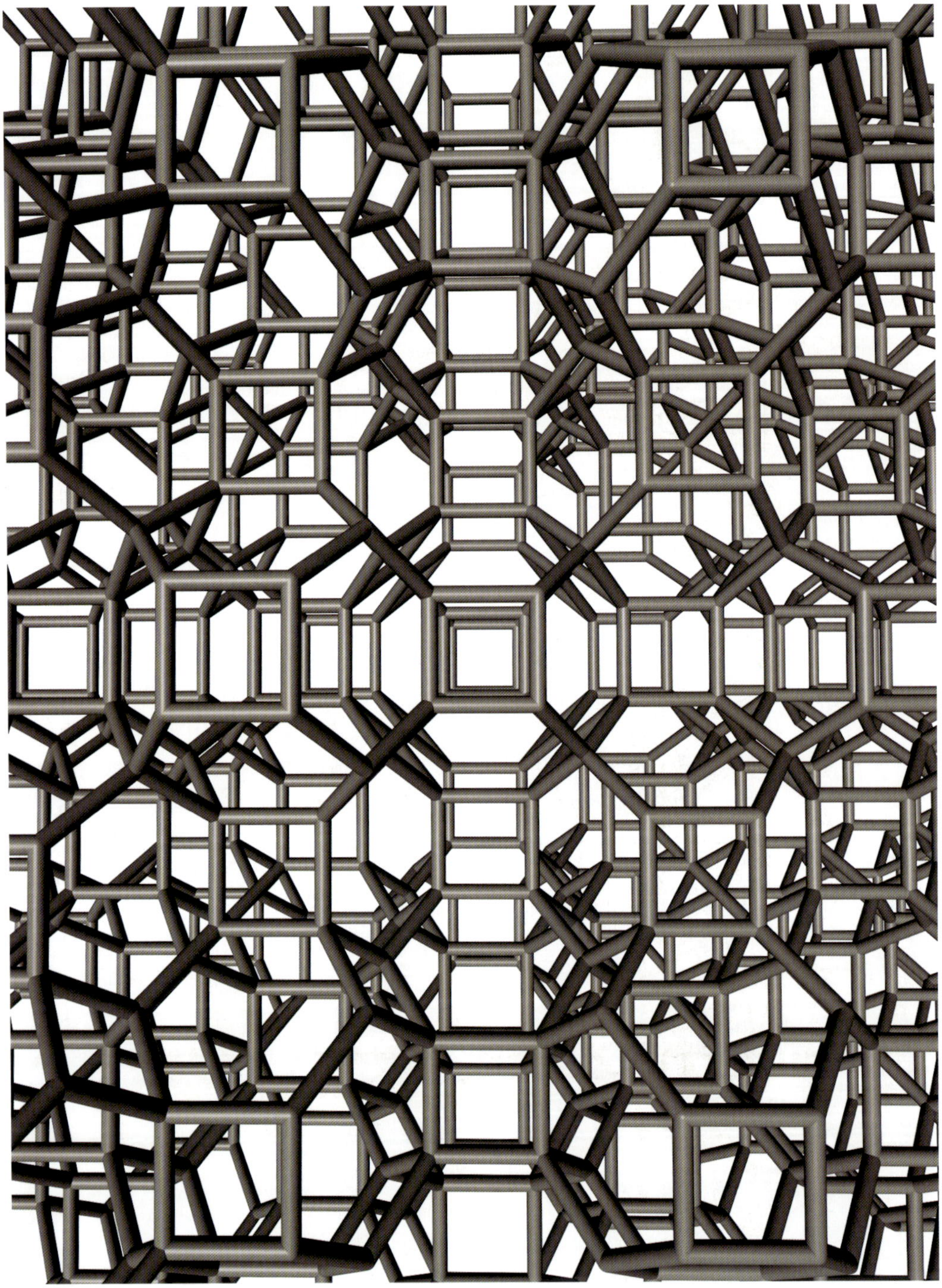

#S: 80
SV: 904.78
sV: 14.14
bV: 1728.67
# of sides: 14

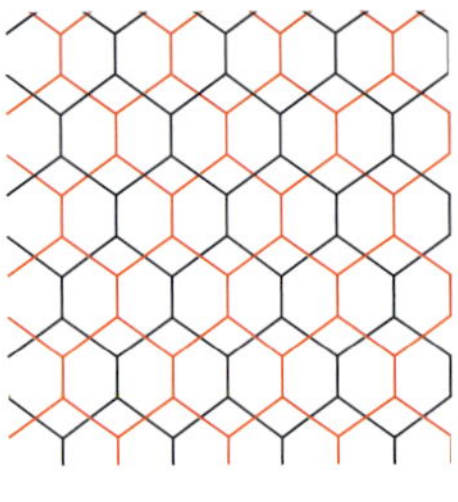

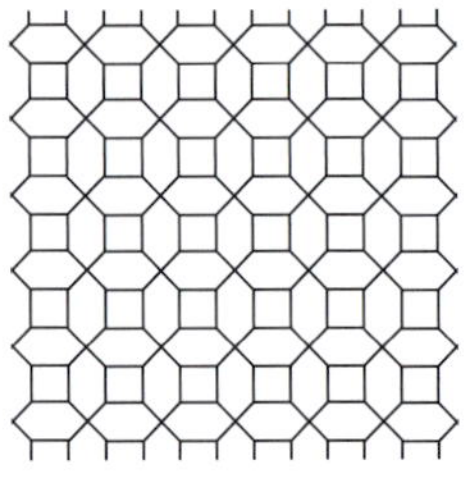

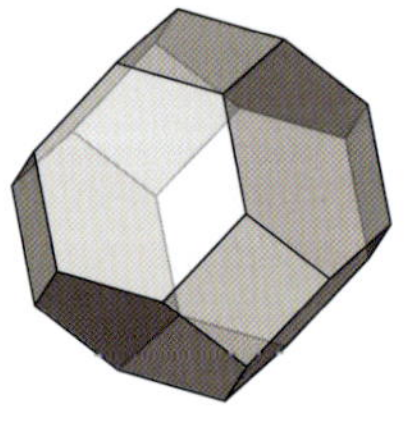

Special Packing Networks:
Truncated Octahedron

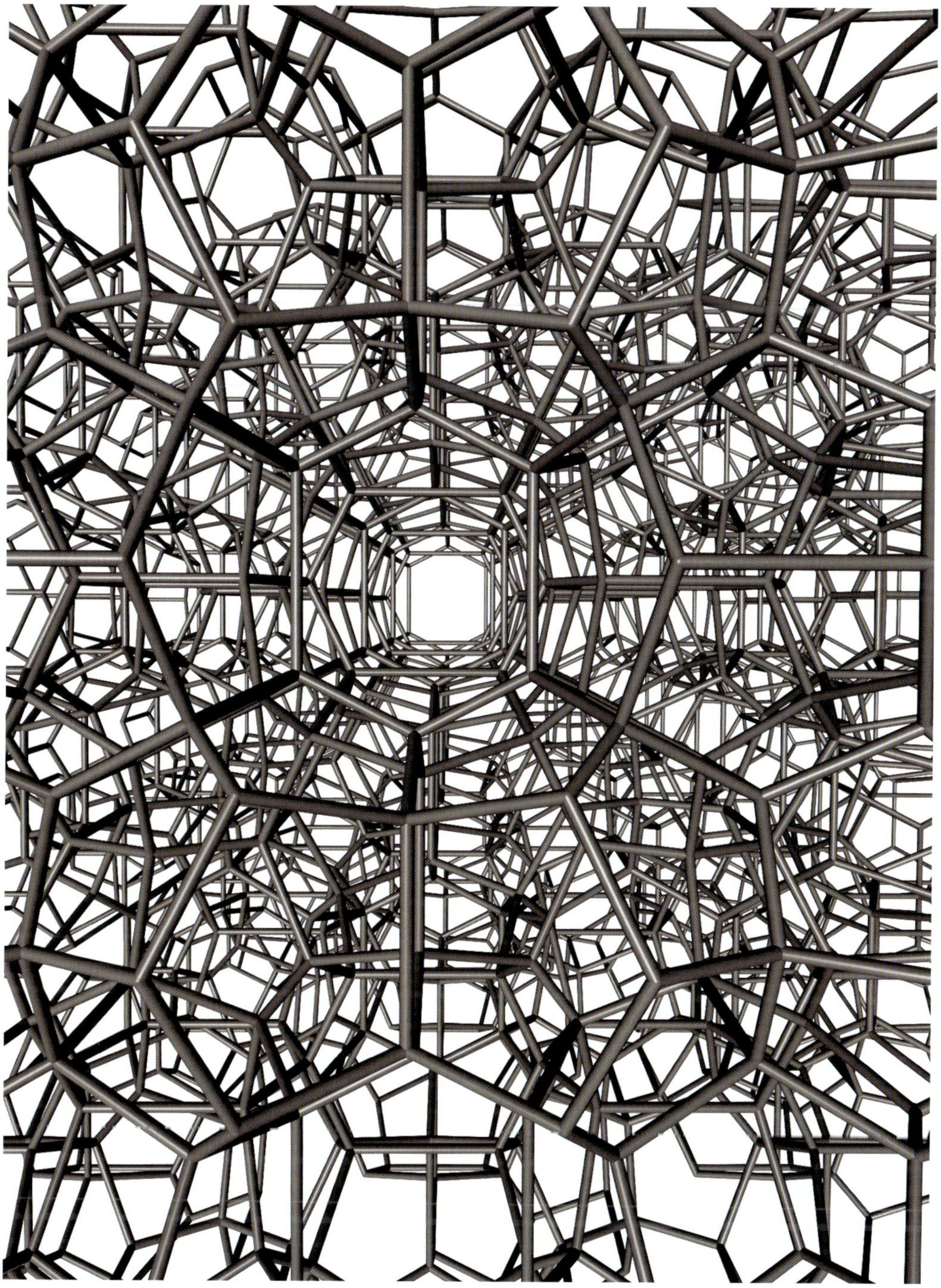

#S: 80
SV: 1130.97
sV: 14.14
bV: 2092.92
# of sides: 12, 14

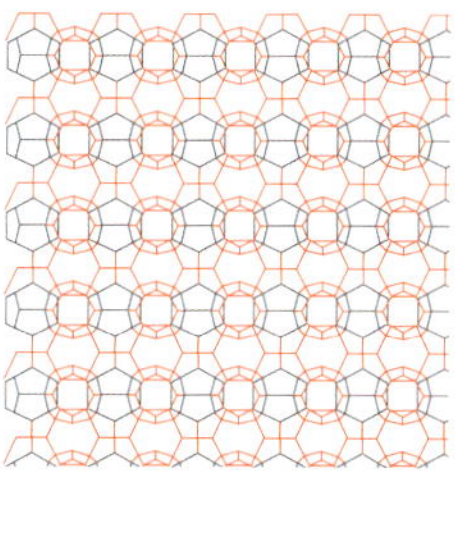

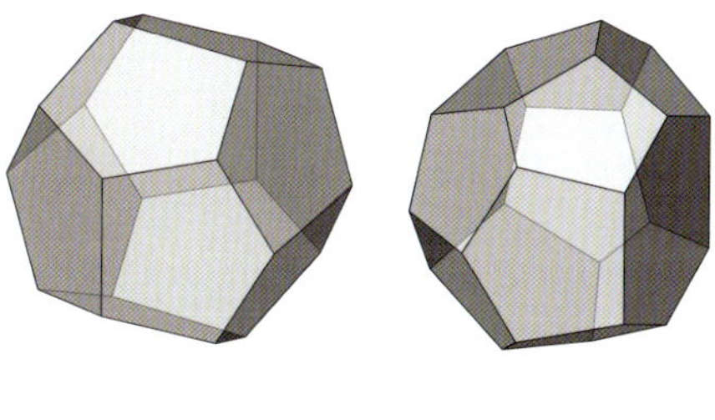

Special Packing Networks:
Weaire-Phelan Structure

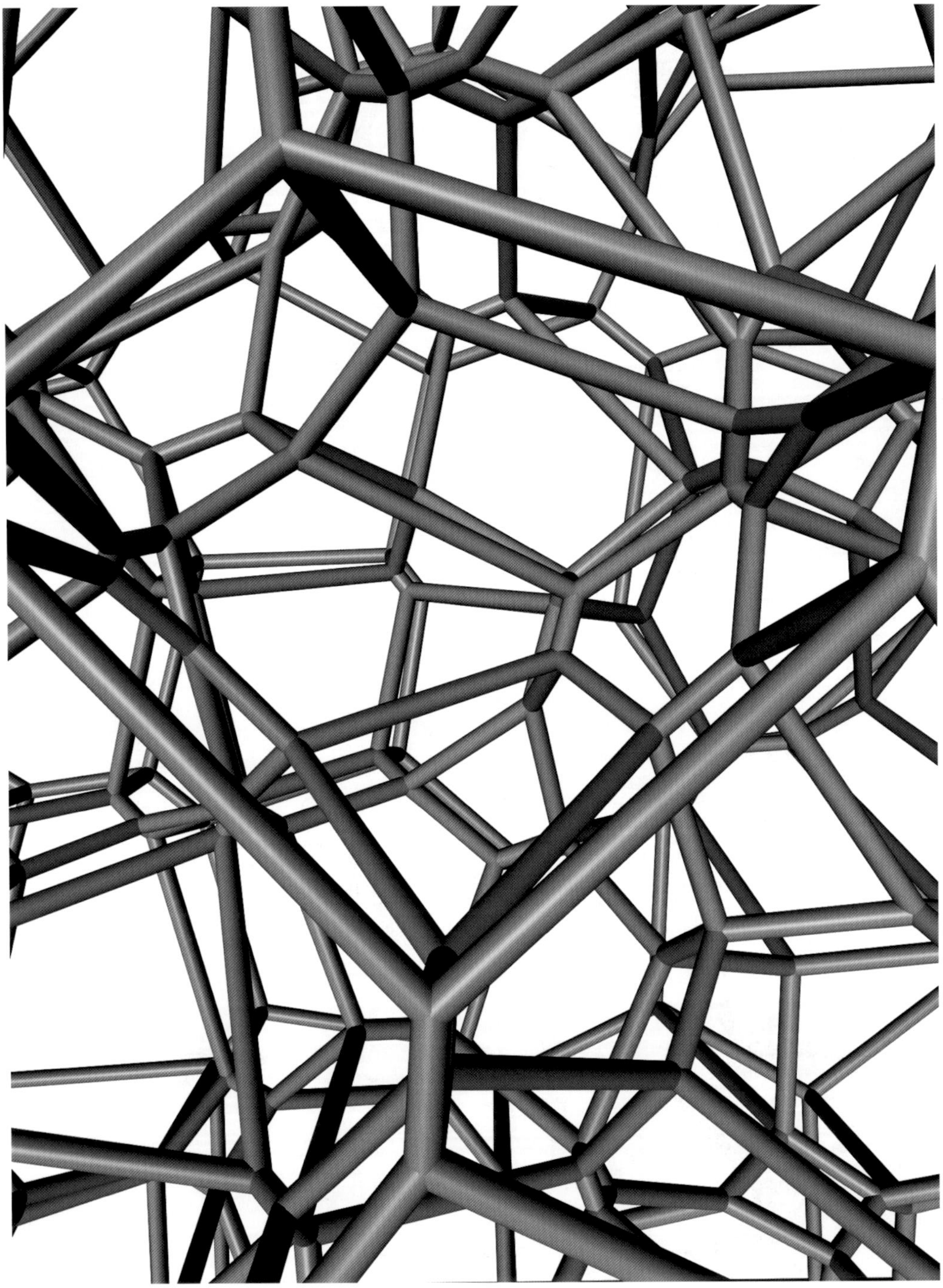

#S: 95
SV: 1343.03
sV: 14.14
bV: 3027.11
# of sides: 13

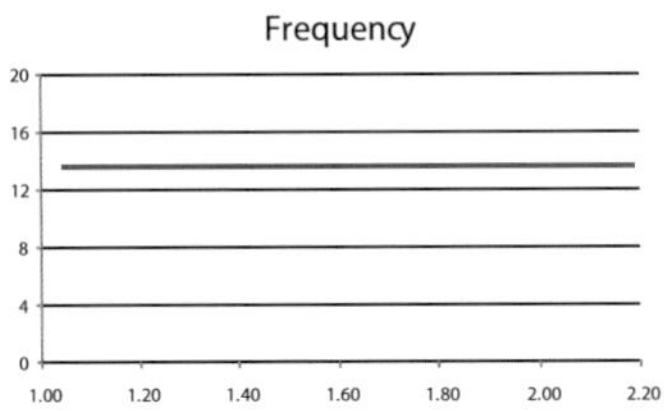

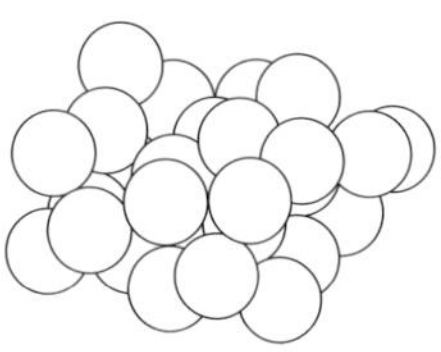

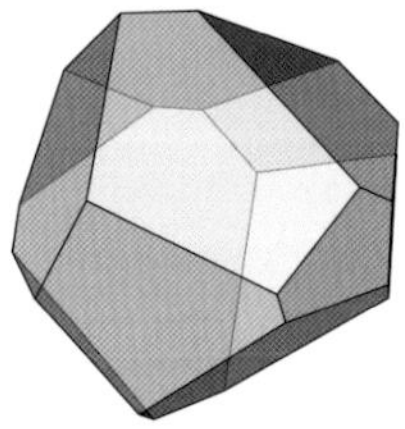

Irregular Packing Networks:
Mean Radius 1.5, Deviation 0.000

#S: 95
SV: 1494.28
sV: 15.73
bV: 3451.88
# of sides: 13

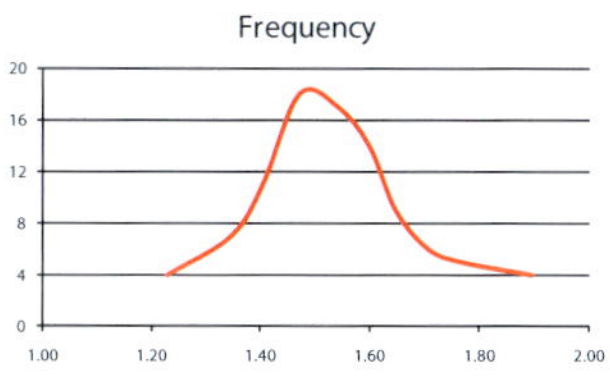

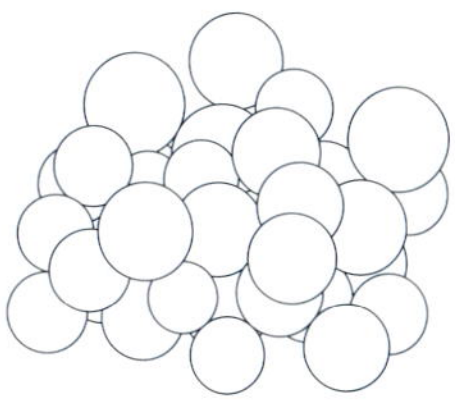

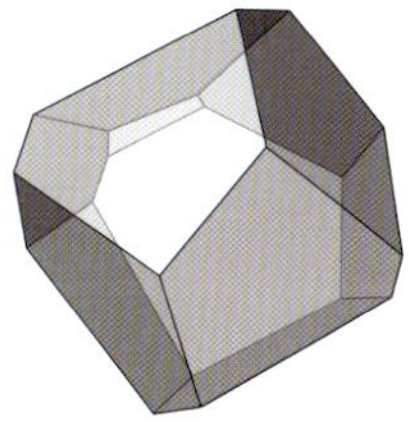

Irregular Packing Networks:
Mean Radius 1.5, Deviation 0.100

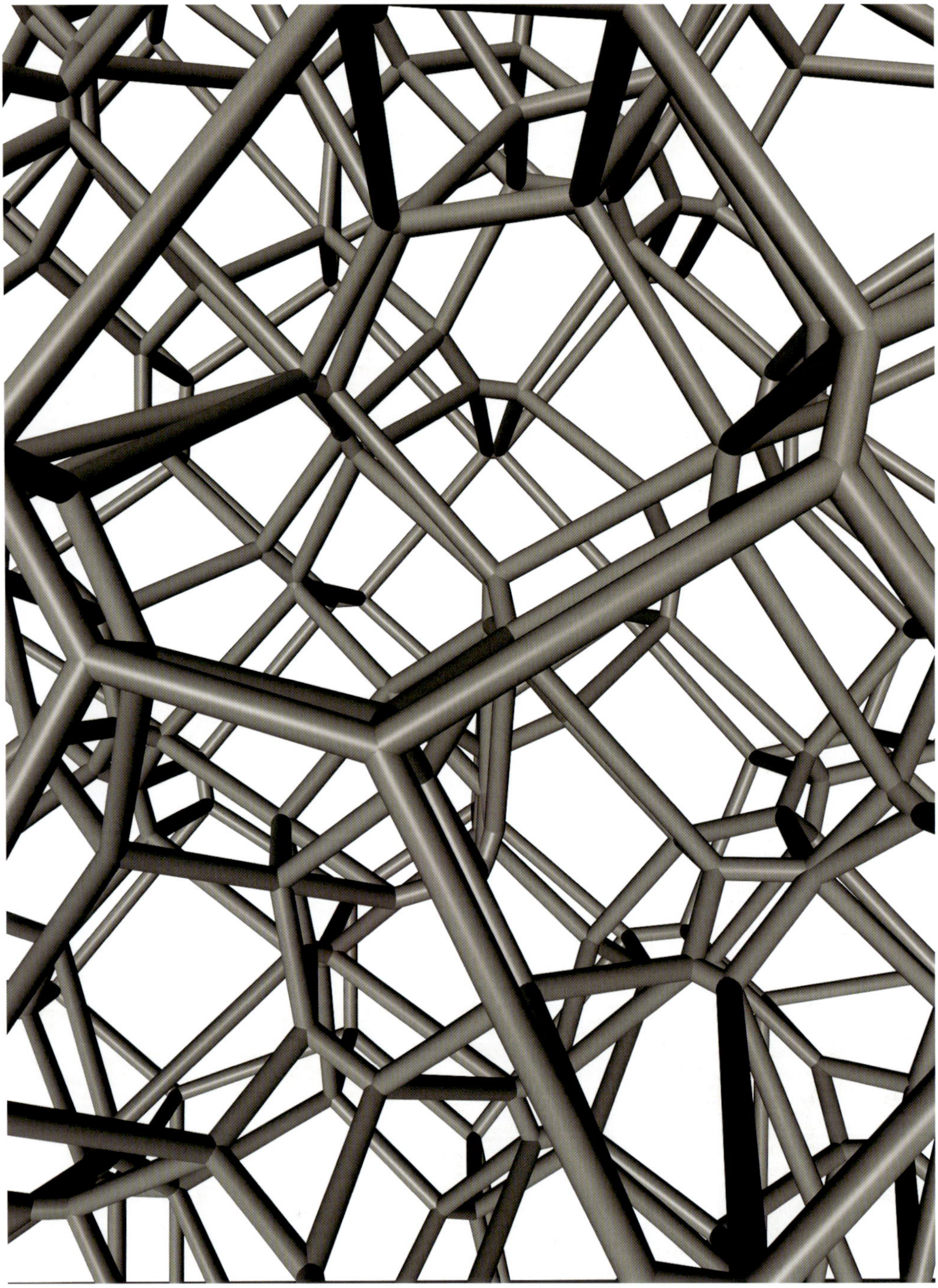

#S: 95
SV: 1456.55
sV: 15.332
bV: 3425.92
# of sides: 13

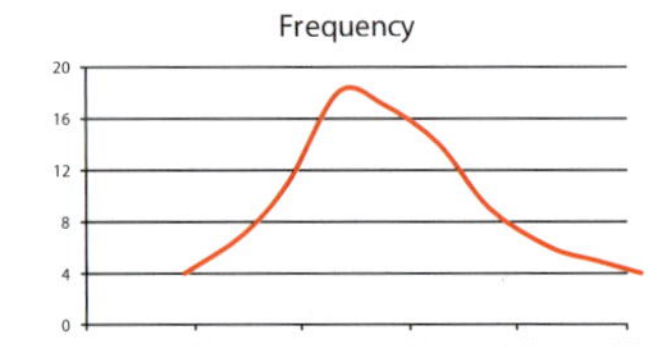

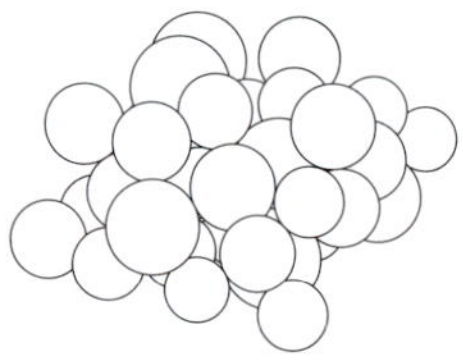

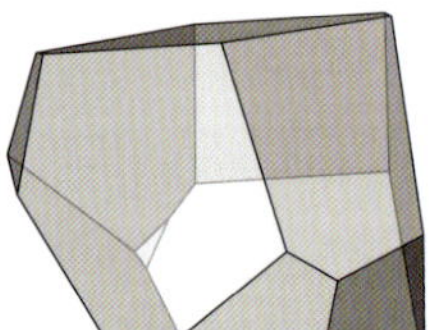

Irregular Packing Networks:
Mean Radius 1.5, Deviation 0.125

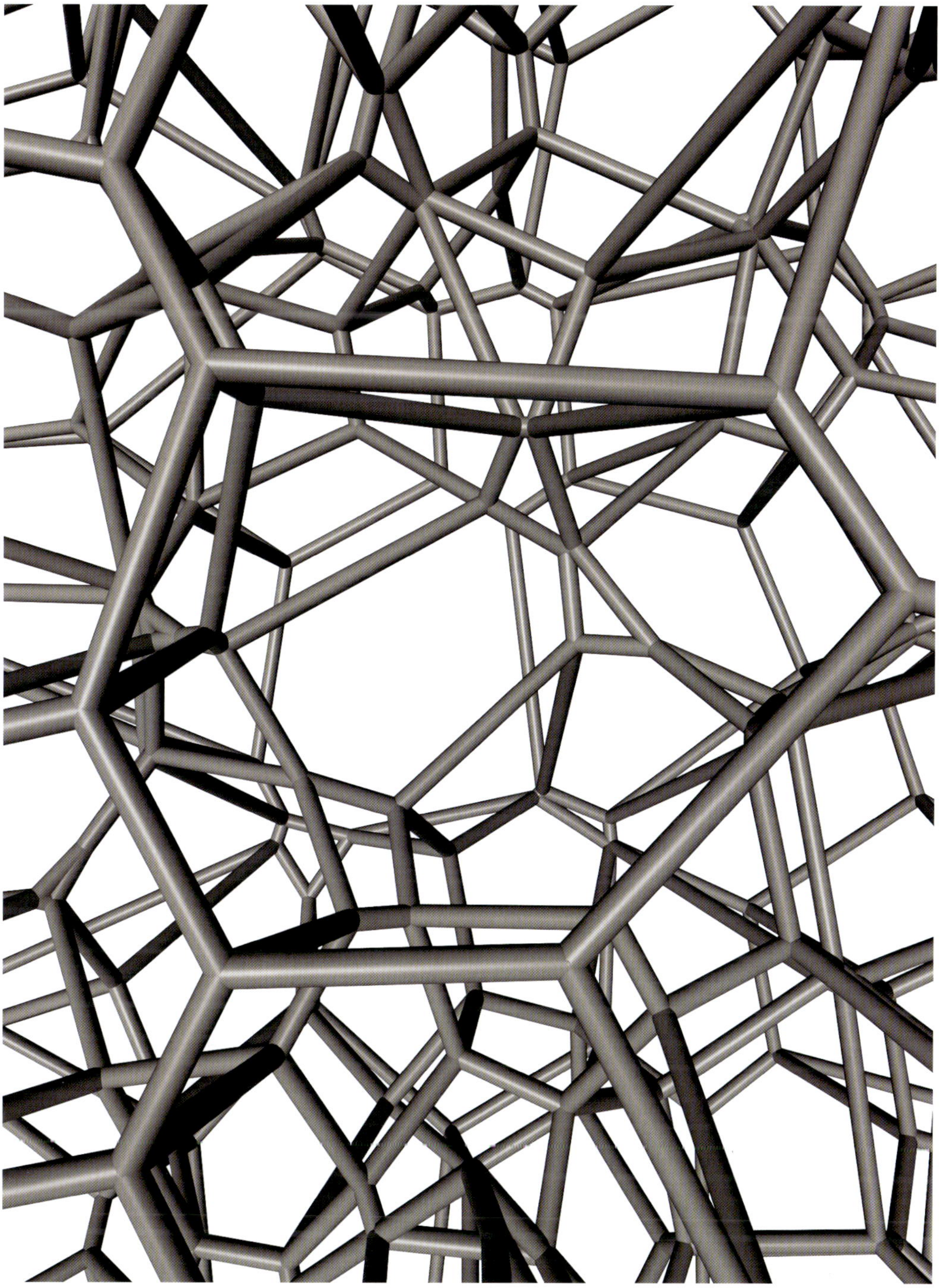

#S: 95
SV: 1431.30
sV: 15.066
bV: 3491.74
# of sides: 14

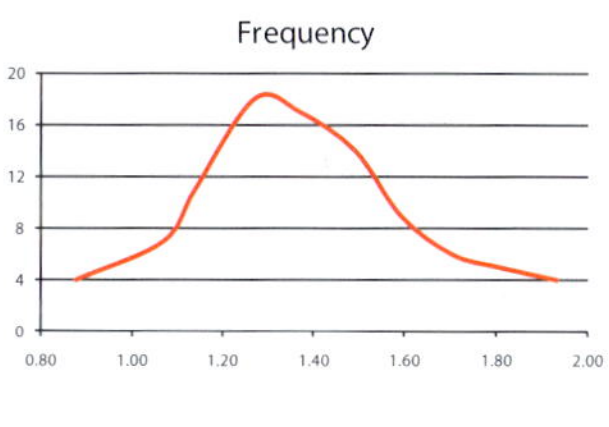

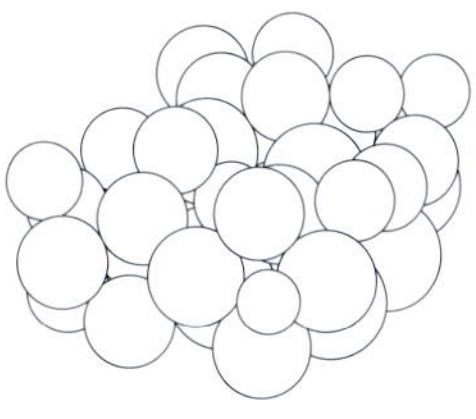

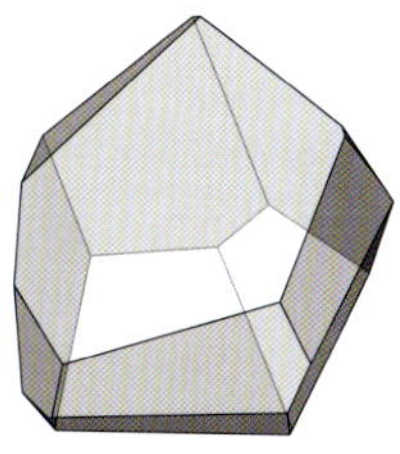

Irregular Packing Networks:
Mean Radius 1.5, Deviation 0.150

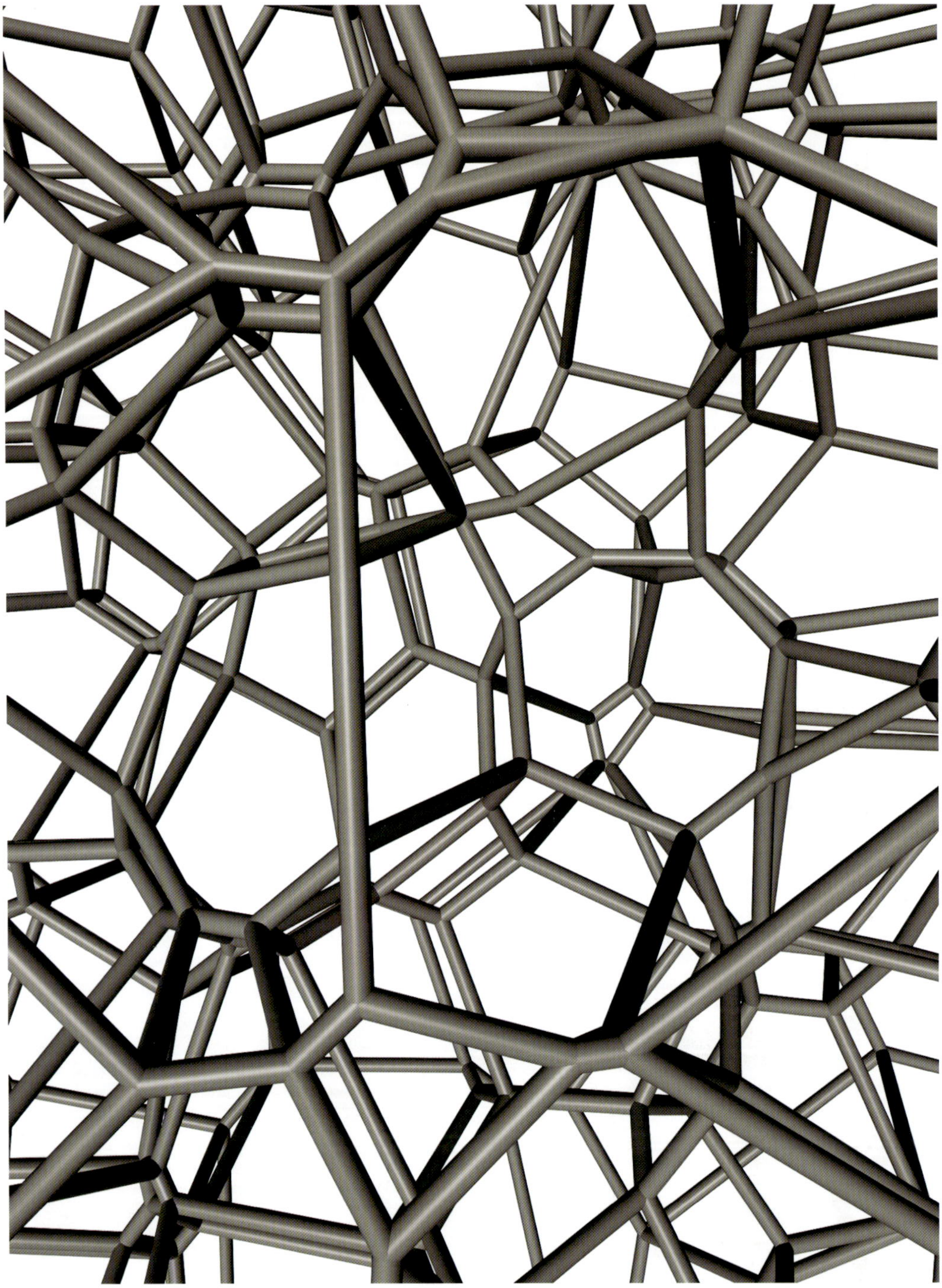

#S: 95
SV: 1591.24
sV: 16.781
bV: 3693.31
# of sides: 16

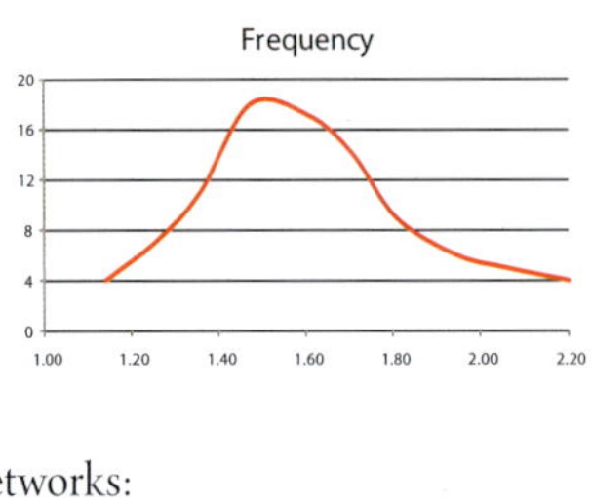

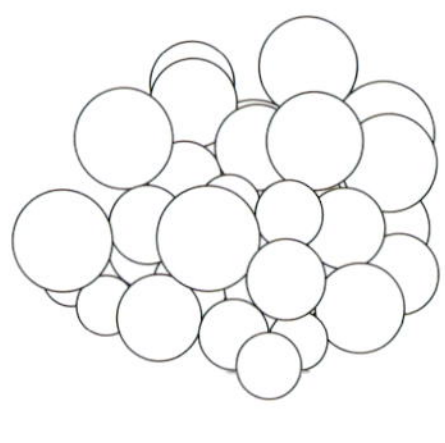

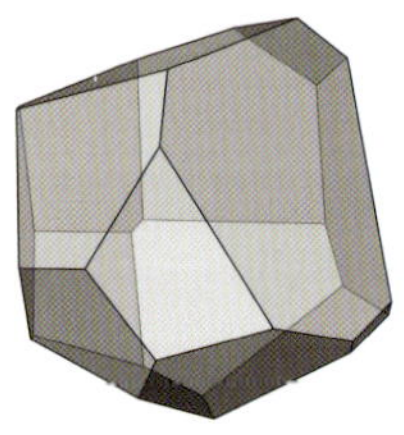

Irregular Packing Networks:
Mean Radius 1.5, Deviation 0.175

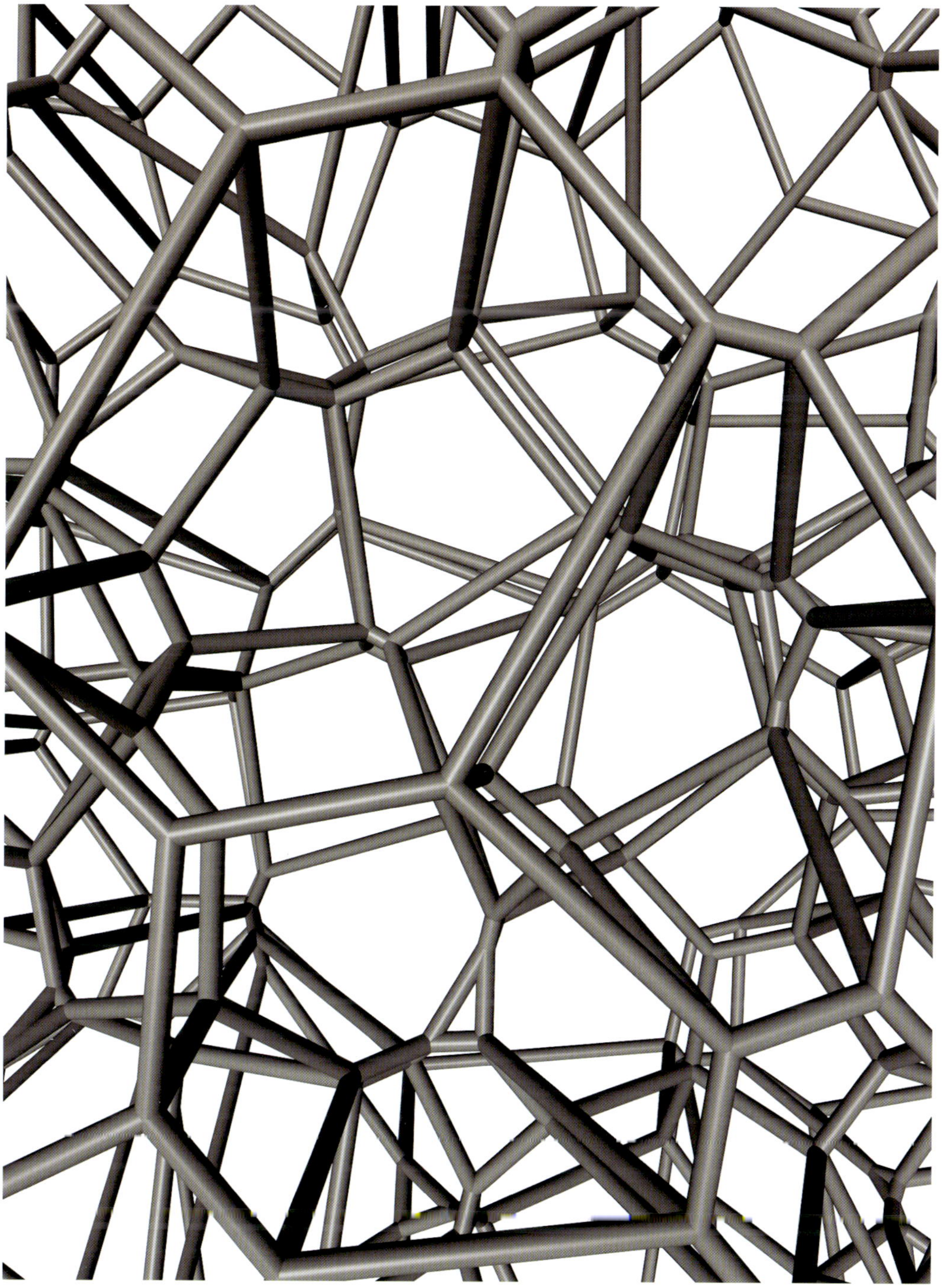

#S: 95
SV: 1494.95
sV: 15.731
bV: 3495.75
# of sides: 16

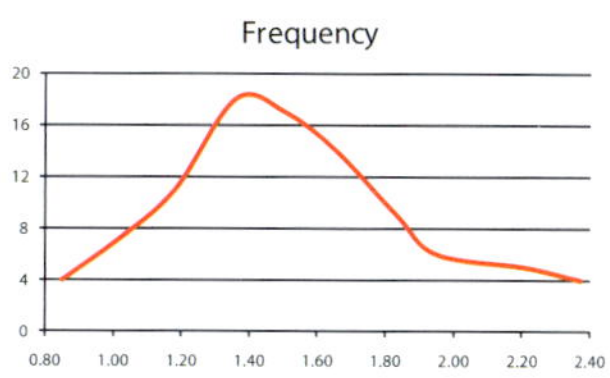

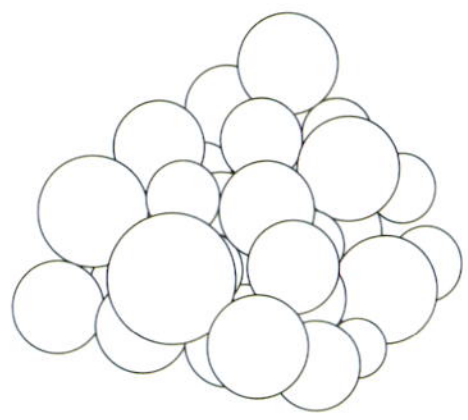

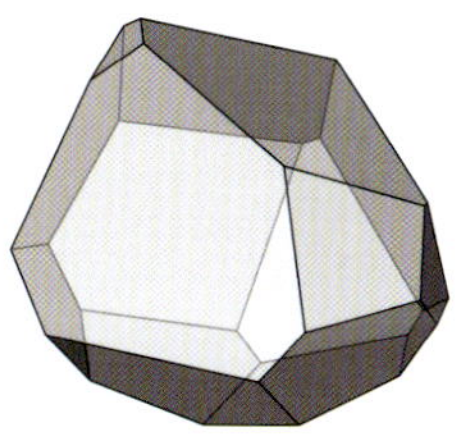

Irregular Packing Networks:
Mean Radius 1.5, Deviation 0.200

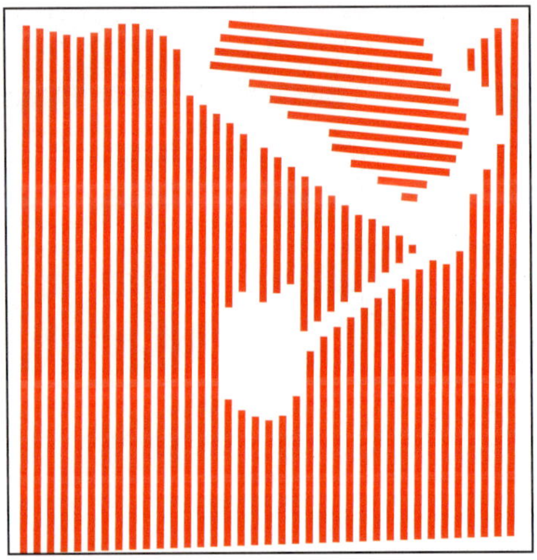

Length: 3005
Lines: 71
Solid: 0.77

Directions: 2
Regions: 2

Coherence Index = 2 : 4 = 0.50

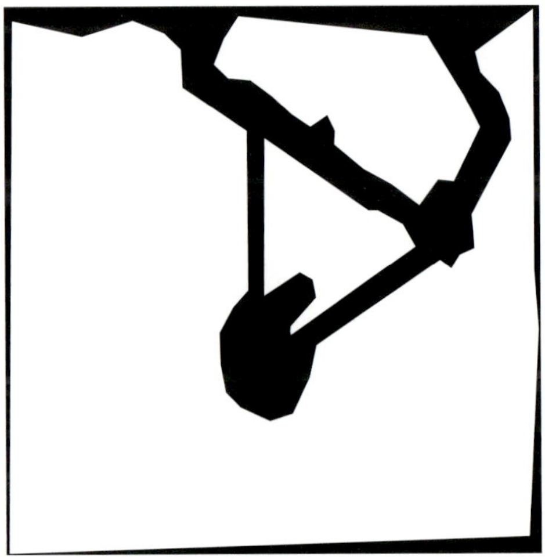

Islands: 4
Length: 781
Area: 7846

Tightness Index = 2 : 4 = 0.50

Length: 2488
Lines: 73
Solid: 0.64

Directions: 1
Regions: 1

Coherence Index = 1 : 4 = 0.25

Islands: 4
Length: 651
Area: 6422

Tightness Index = 1 : 4 = 0.25

Length: 2410
Lines: 80
Solid: 0.62

Directions: 4
Regions: 4

Coherence Index = 4 : 5 = 0.80

Islands: 5
Length: 768
Area: 6193

Tightness Index = 4 : 5 = 0.80

Length: 2670
Lines: 99
Solid: 0.68

Directions: 2
Regions: 3

Coherence Index = 3 : 6 = 0.50

Islands: 6
Length: 887
Area: 6642

Tightness Index = 2 : 6 = 0.33

Length: 2596
Lines: 75
Solid: 0.67

Directions: 3
Regions: 3

Coherence Index = 3 : 6 = 0.50

Islands: 6
Length: 697
Area: 6574

Tightness Index = 3 : 6 = 0.50

Length: 2393
Lines: 111
Solid: 0.61

Directions: 3
Regions: 4

Coherence Index = 4 : 10 = 0.20

Islands: 10
Length: 913
Area: 5967

Tightness Index = 3 : 10 = 0.30

Length: 2413
Lines: 96
Solid: 0.62

Directions: 4
Regions: 4

Coherence Index = 4 : 13 = 0.31

Islands: 13
Length: 903
Area: 6050

Tightness Index = 4 : 13 = 0.31

Length: 2266
Lines: 112
Solid: 0.58
Directions: 4
Regions: 5

Coherence Index = 5 : 11 = 0.45

Islands: 11
Length: 1018
Area: 5622

Tightness Index = 4 : 11 = 0.36

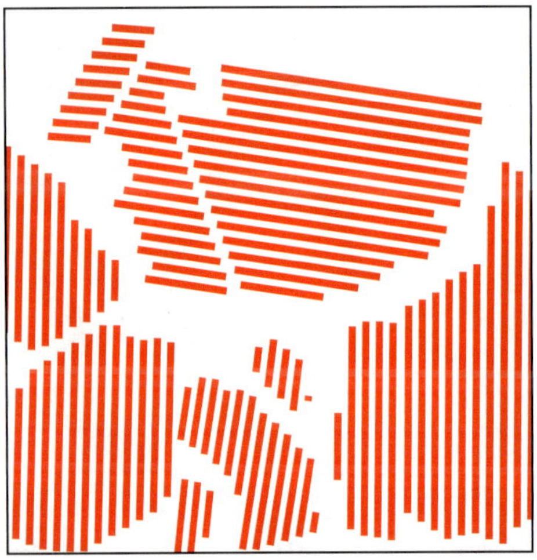

Length: 2591
Lines: 99
Solid: 0.66

Directions: 3
Regions: 4

Coherence Index = 4 : 10 = 0.40

Islands: 10
Length: 1044
Area: 6202

Tightness Index = 3 : 10 = 0.30

Length: 2159
Lines: 127
Solid: 0.55

Directions: 3
Regions: 7

Coherence Index = 7 : 13 = 0.54

Islands: 13
Length: 1075
Area: 5352

Tightness Index = 3 : 13 = 0.23

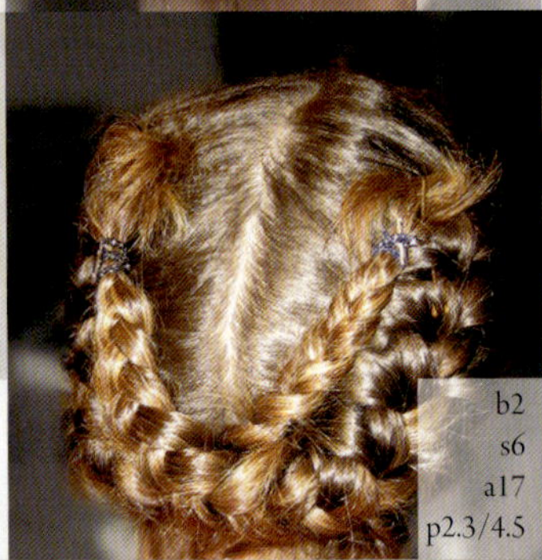

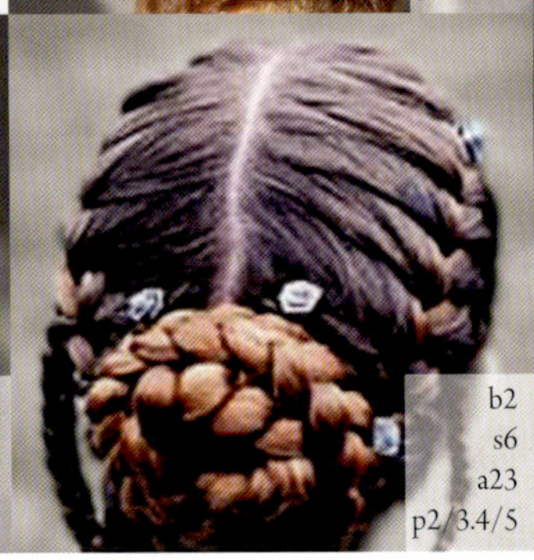

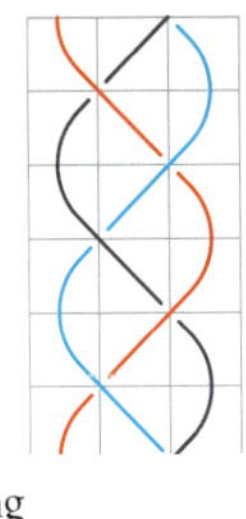

b1
s3

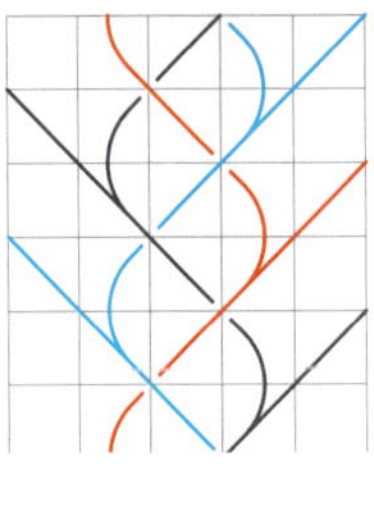

b1
s3
a5

b1
s3
a5
p1

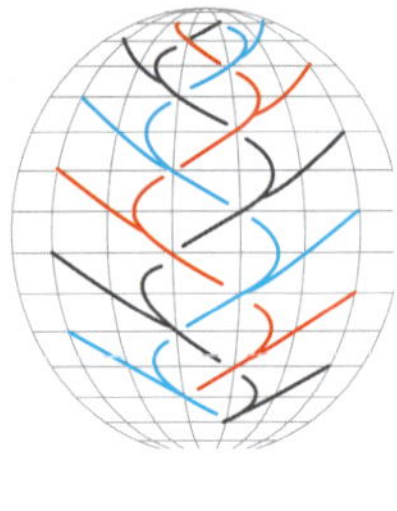

French Braiding

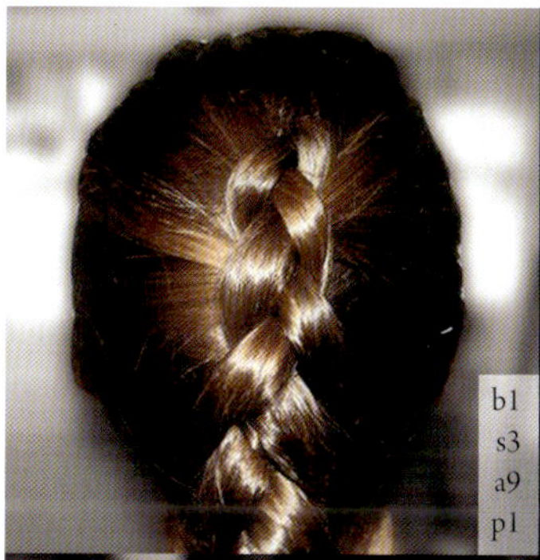

b1 s3 a9 p1

b2 s6 a39 p1.2.5

b2 s6 a35 p1.3.4

b1 s9 a15 p1

b1 s3 a21 p4.3.2

b1 s3 a39 p3.4.5.2

b1 s3 a89 p1.4.5.2.3

b2 s6 a67 p3.2.5.4/1-5

b1 s3 a15 p2.3/5.4

b s6 a31 p2.3/5.4

b1 s3 a p1-5

b2 s6 a29 p1-5

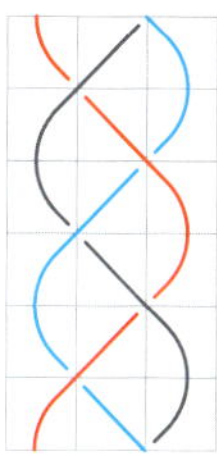

b1 s3

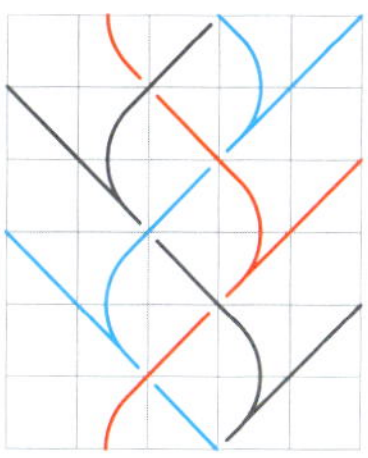

b1 s3 a5

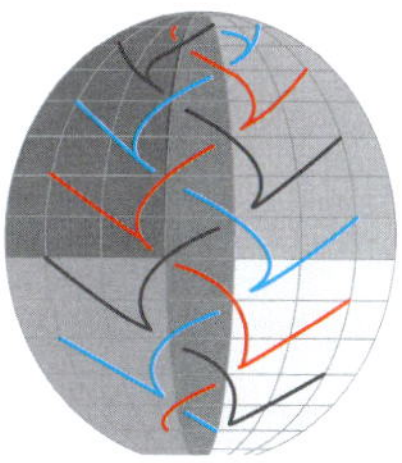

b1 s3 a5 p1

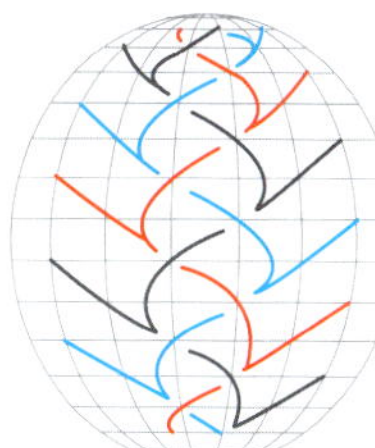

Dutch Braiding

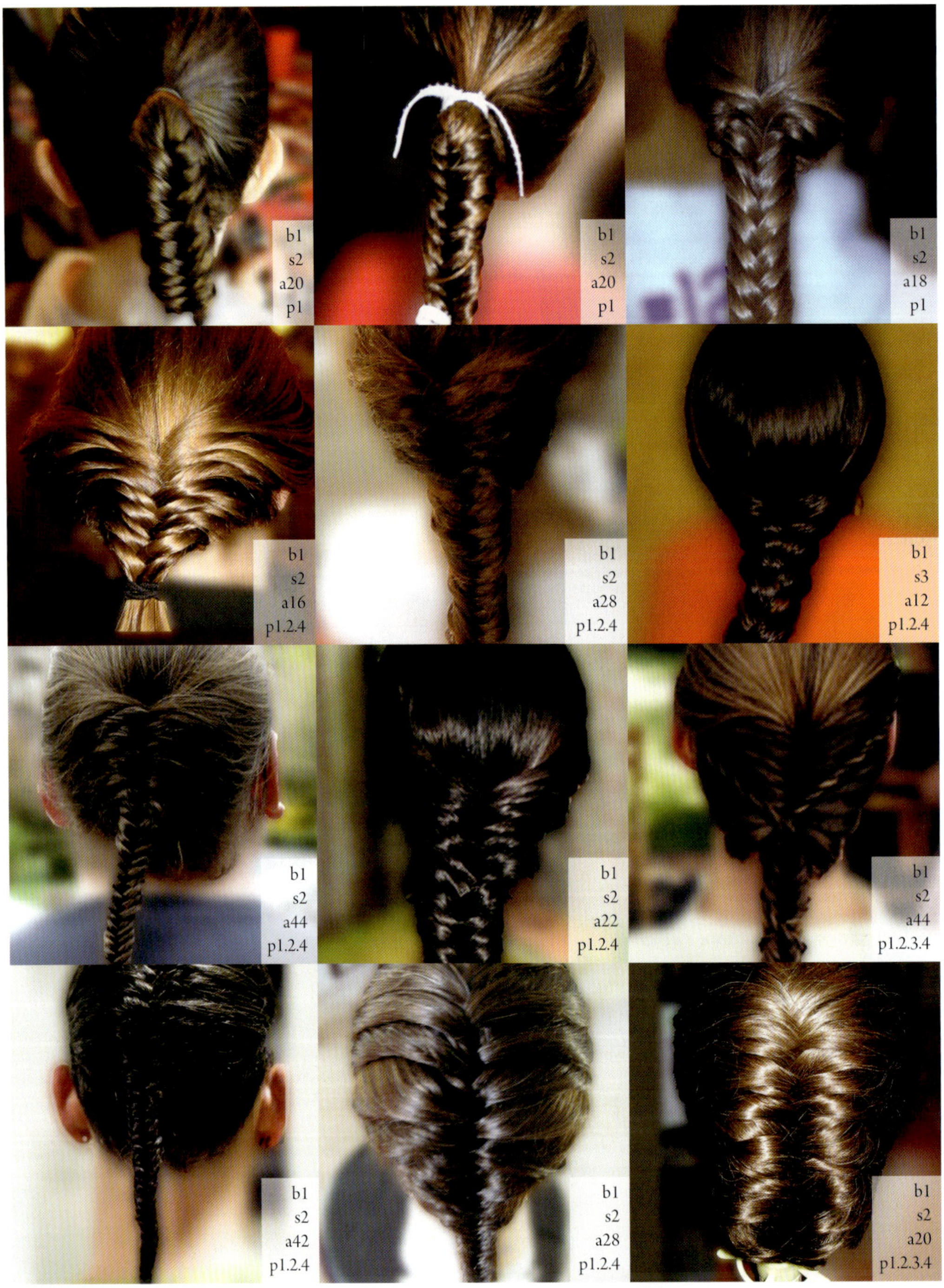

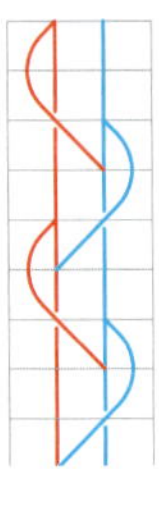

b1
s2

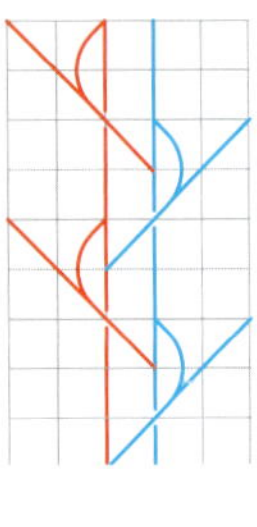

b1
s2
a4

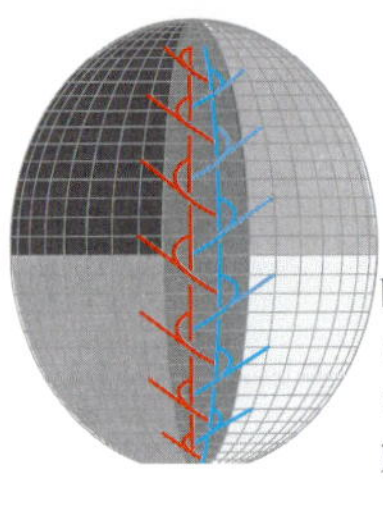

b1
s2
a4
p1

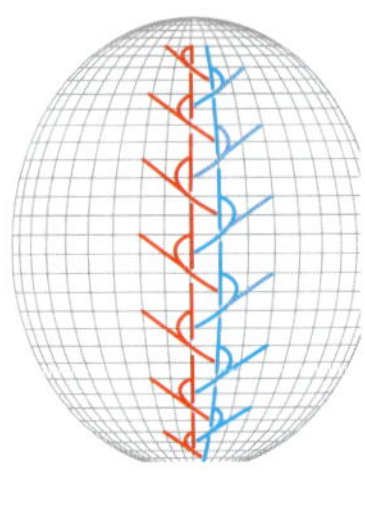

Herringbone Braiding

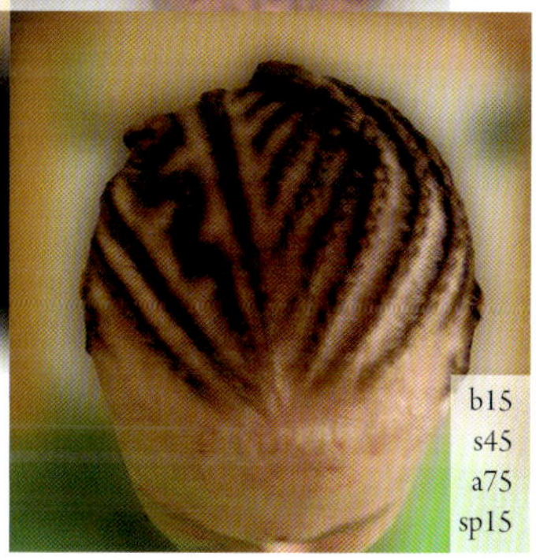

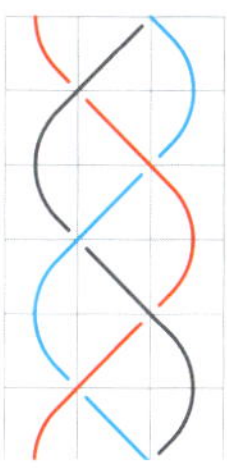

b1
s3

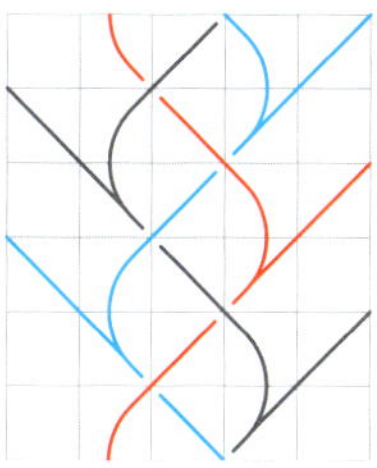

b1
s3
a5

b18
s54
a90
sp17

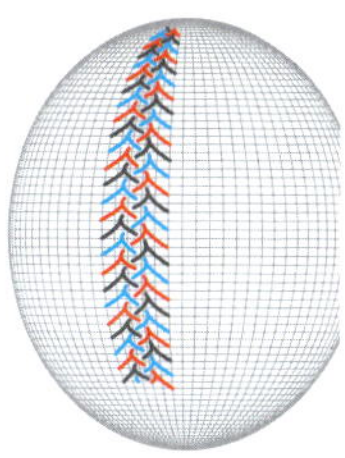

Cornrow Braiding

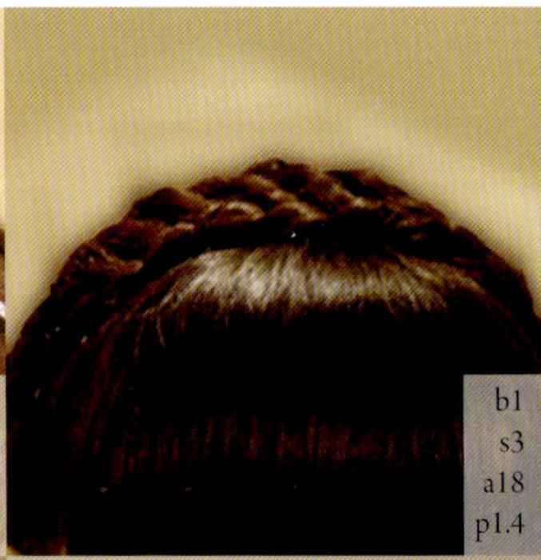

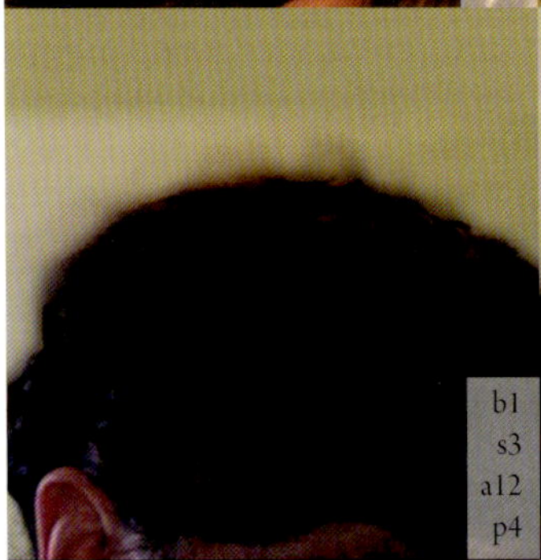

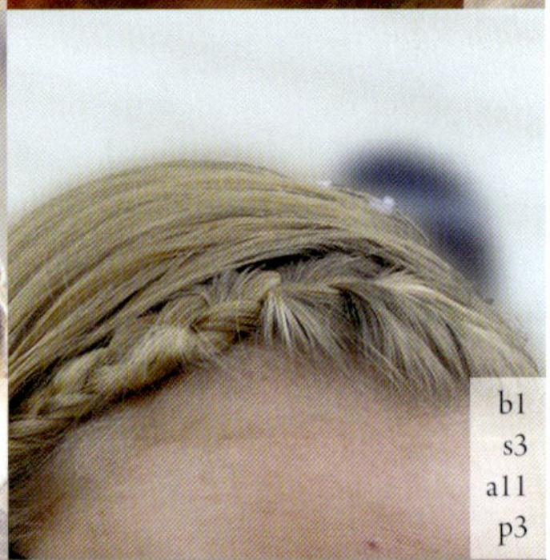

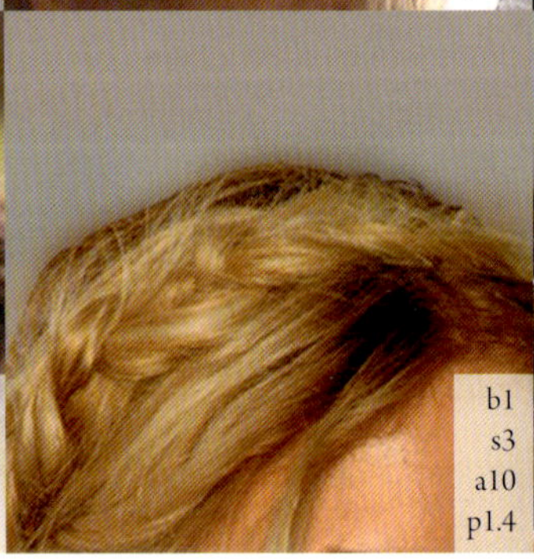

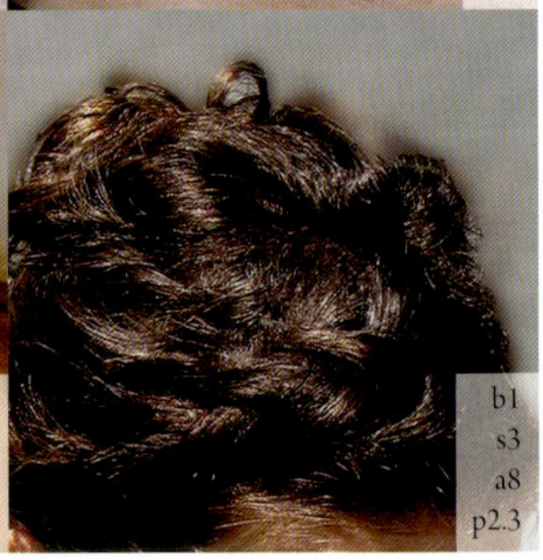

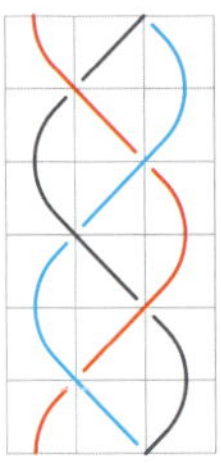

b1
s3

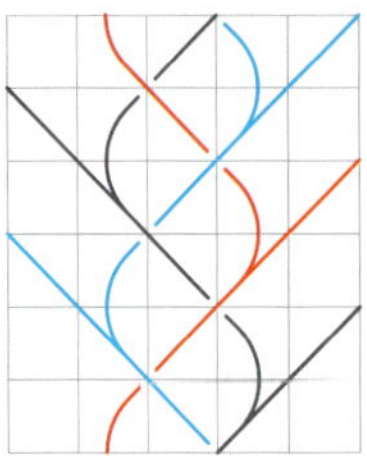

b1
s3
a5

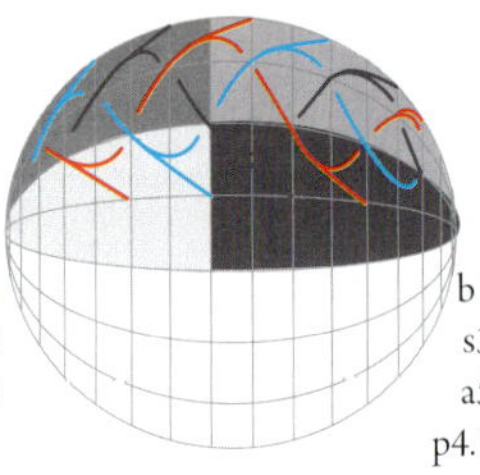

b1
s3
a5
p4.1

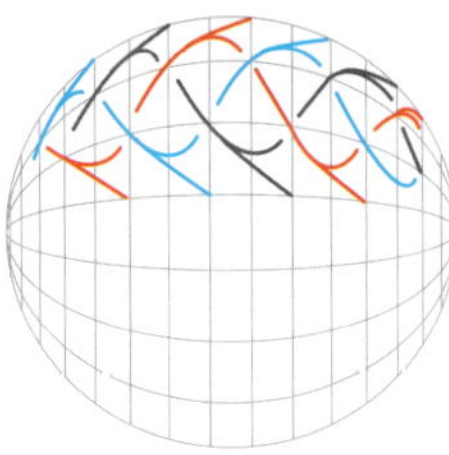

German Braiding

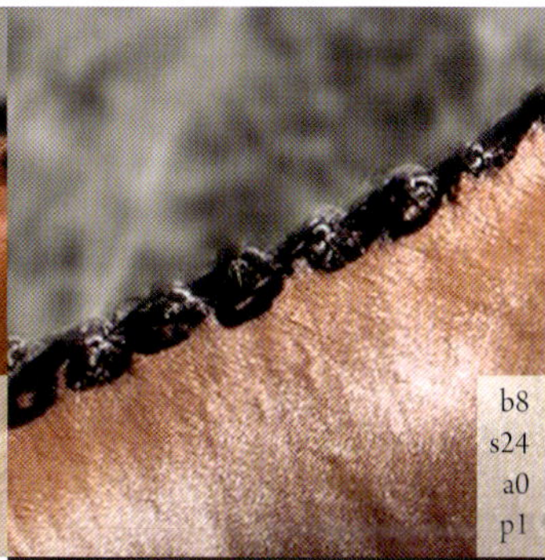

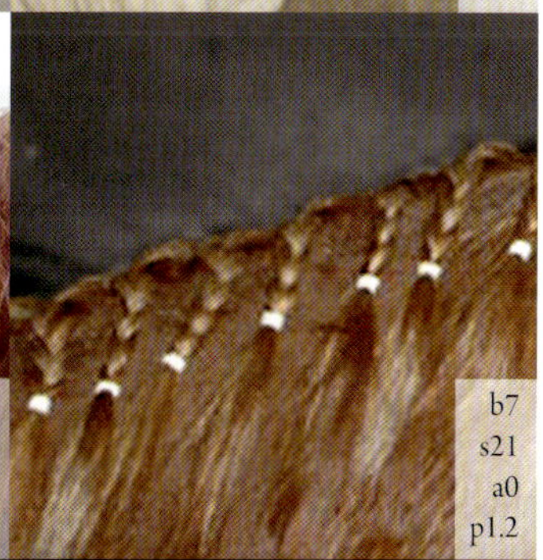

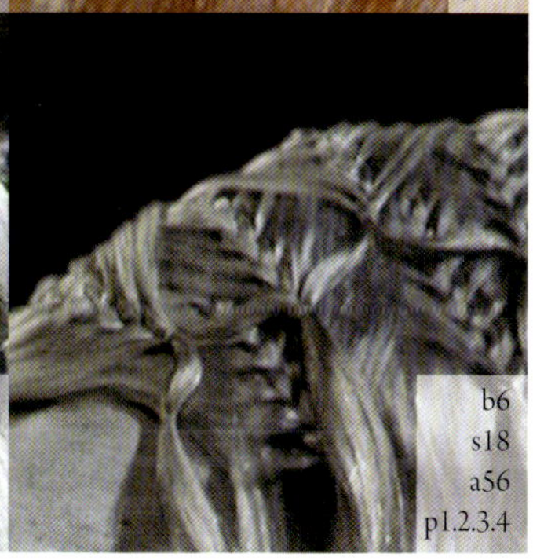

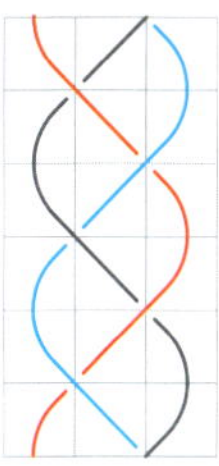

b1
s3

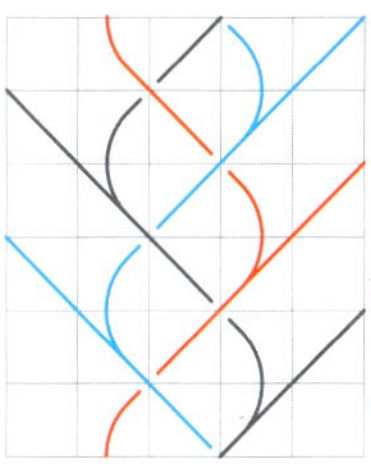

b1
s3
a5

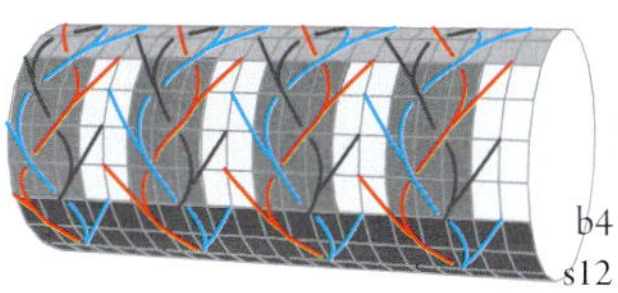

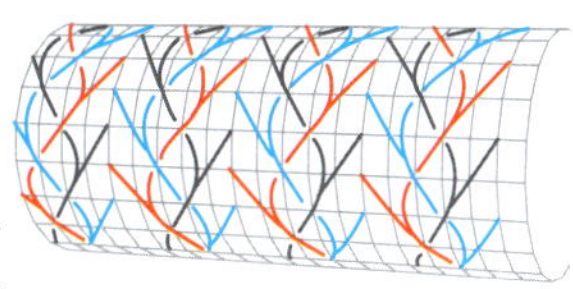

b4
s12
a28
p1.2.3.4

Mane Braiding

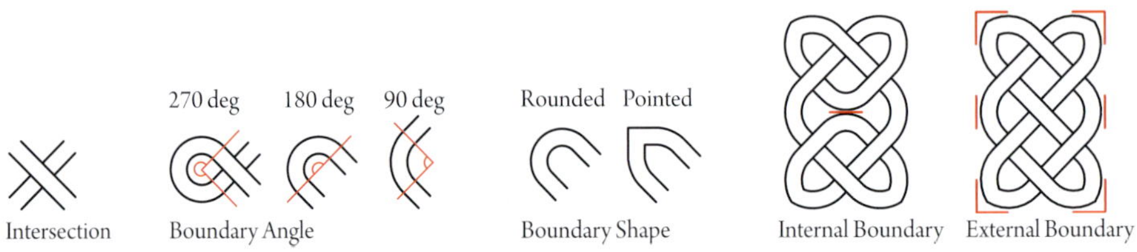

Celtic Knotwork Crosses
Continuous Knot, No Additional Panels

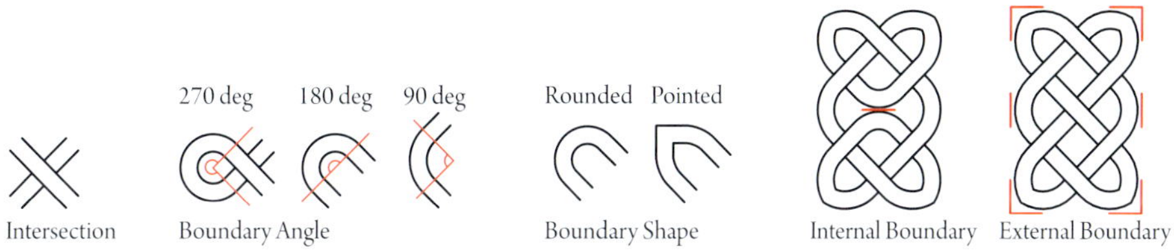

Celtic Knotwork Crosses
Discrete Knots, No Additional Panels

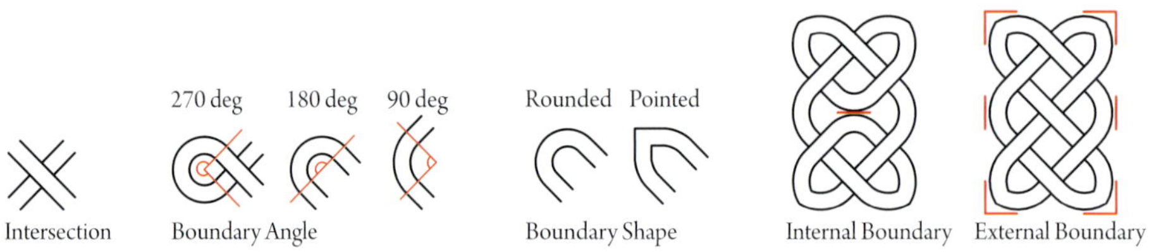

Celtic Knotwork Crosses
Continuous Knot, Additional Panels

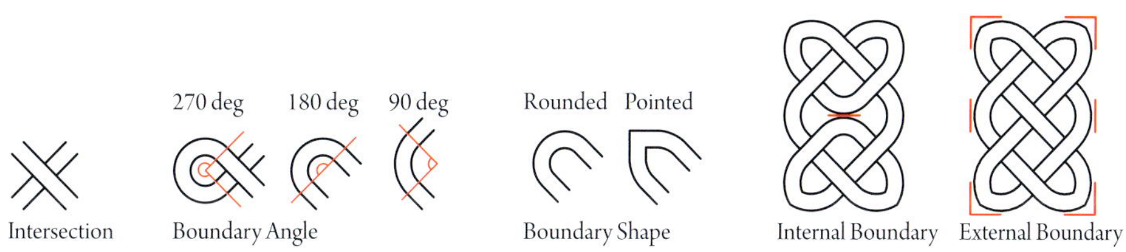

Celtic Knotwork Crosses
Continuous Knot, Additional Panels

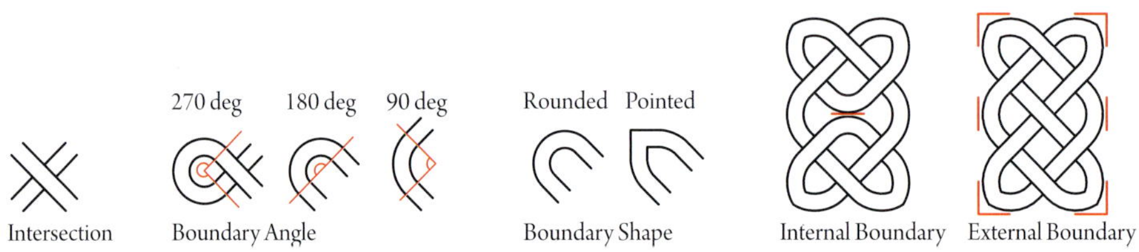

Celtic Knotwork Crosses
Discrete Knot, Additional Panels

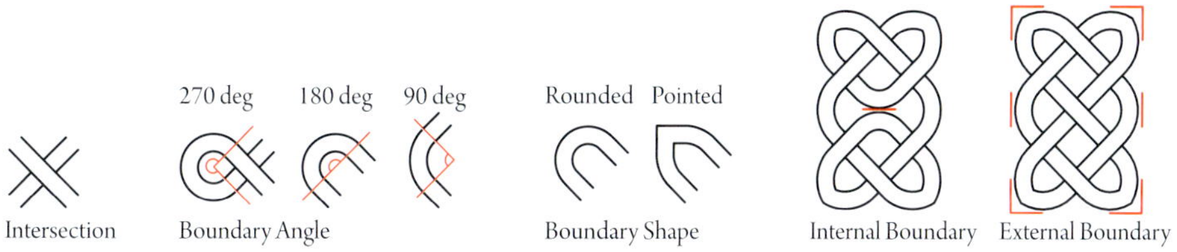

Celtic Knotwork Crosses
Discrete Knot, Additional Panels

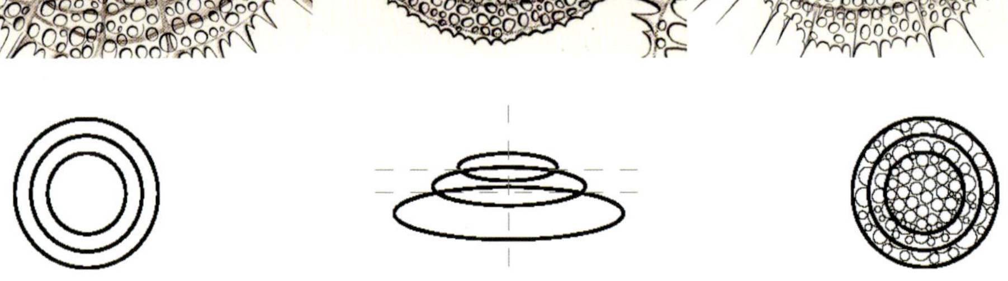

Circle Packing: Flat Surface
Open

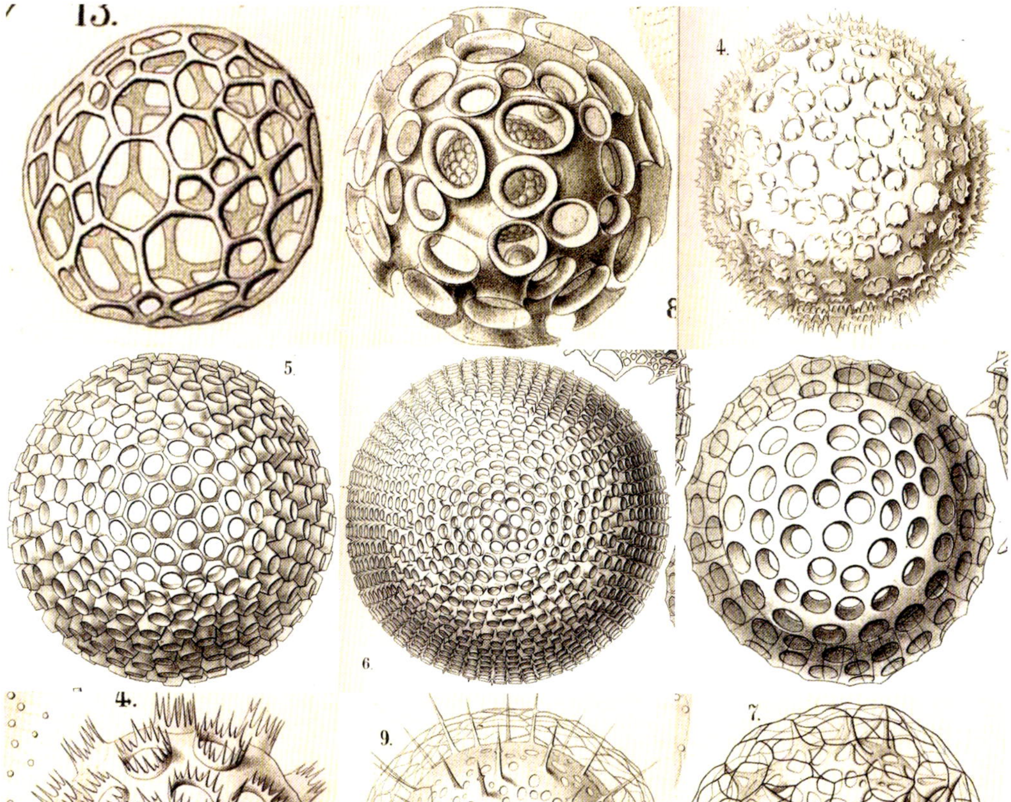

Circle Packing: Sphere
Closed

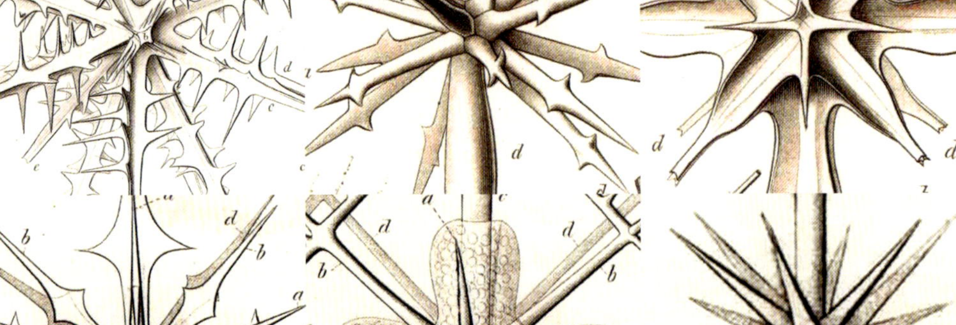

Spicule Star
Open

Spicule Star + Sphere
Closed

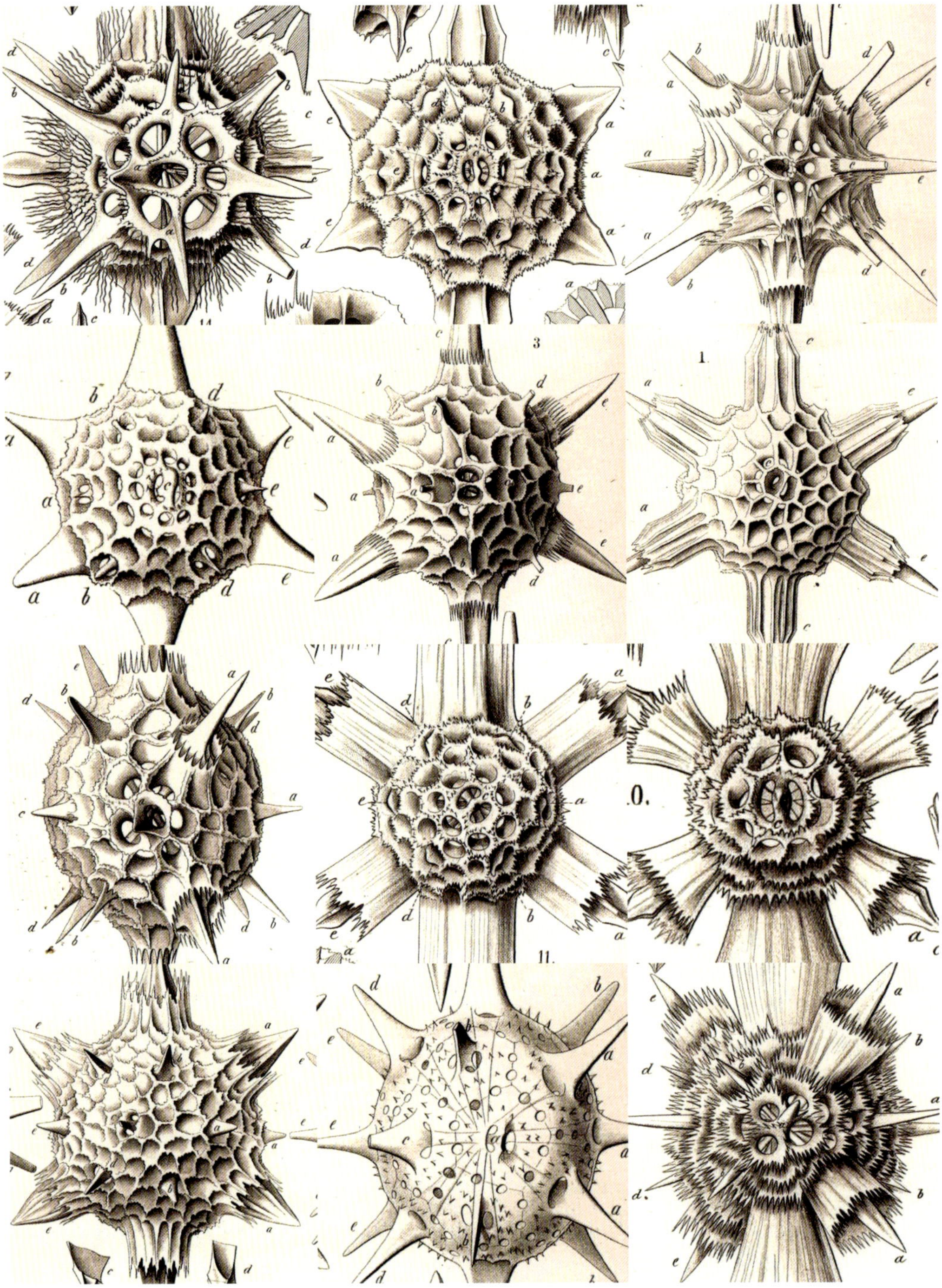

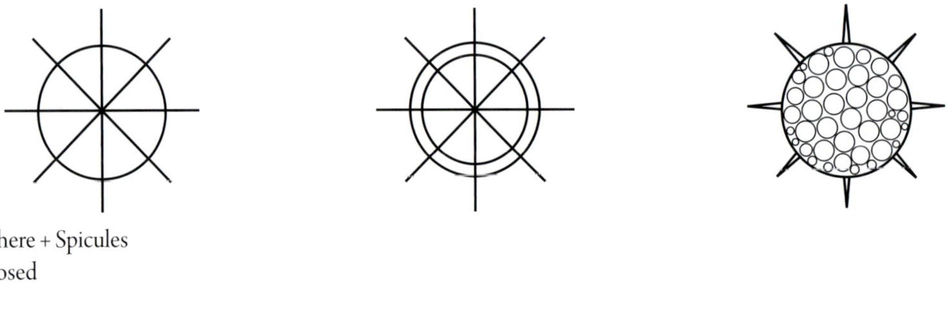

Sphere + Spicules
Closed

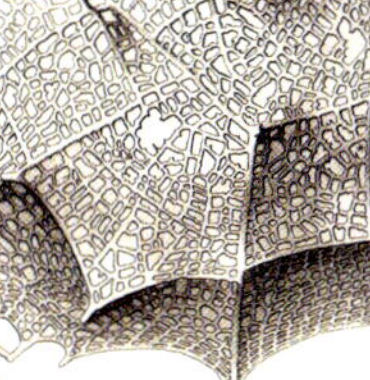

Convex Polyhedrons
Closed

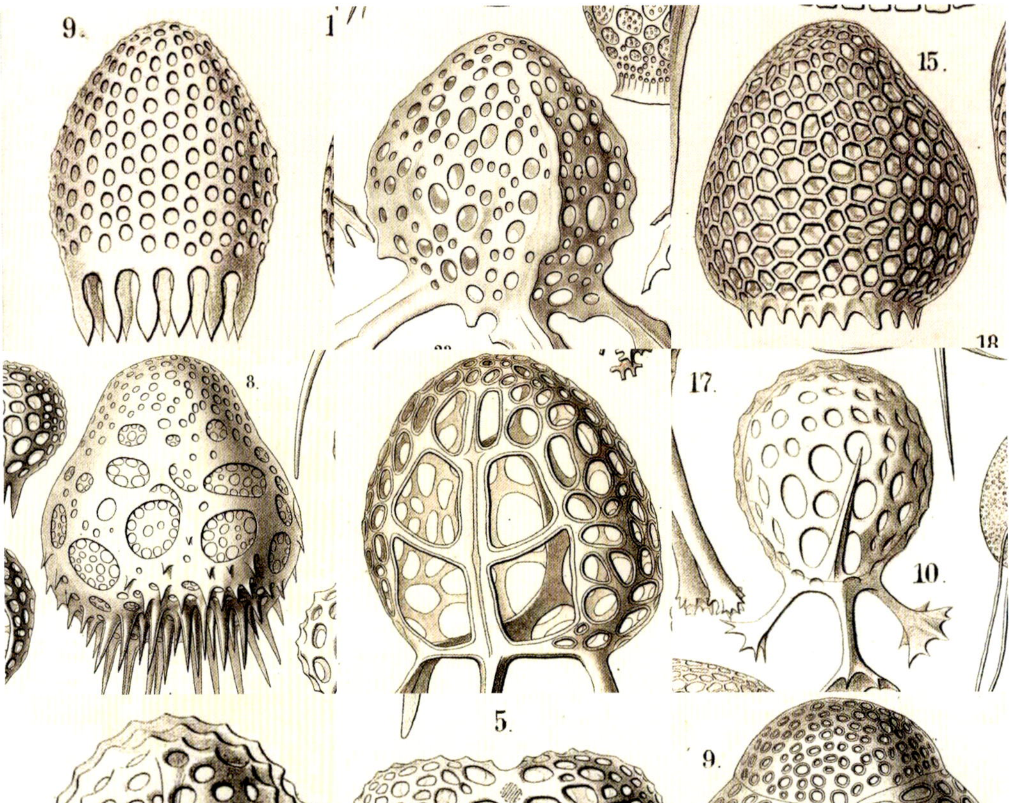

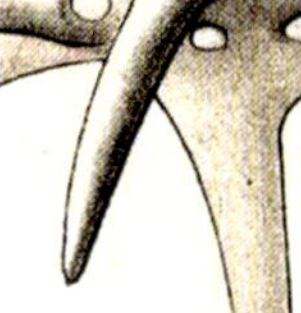

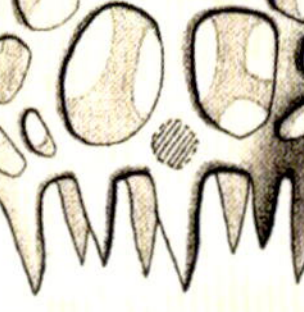

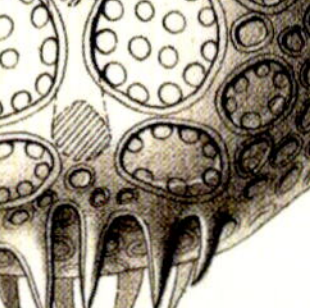

Sphere + Legs
Open

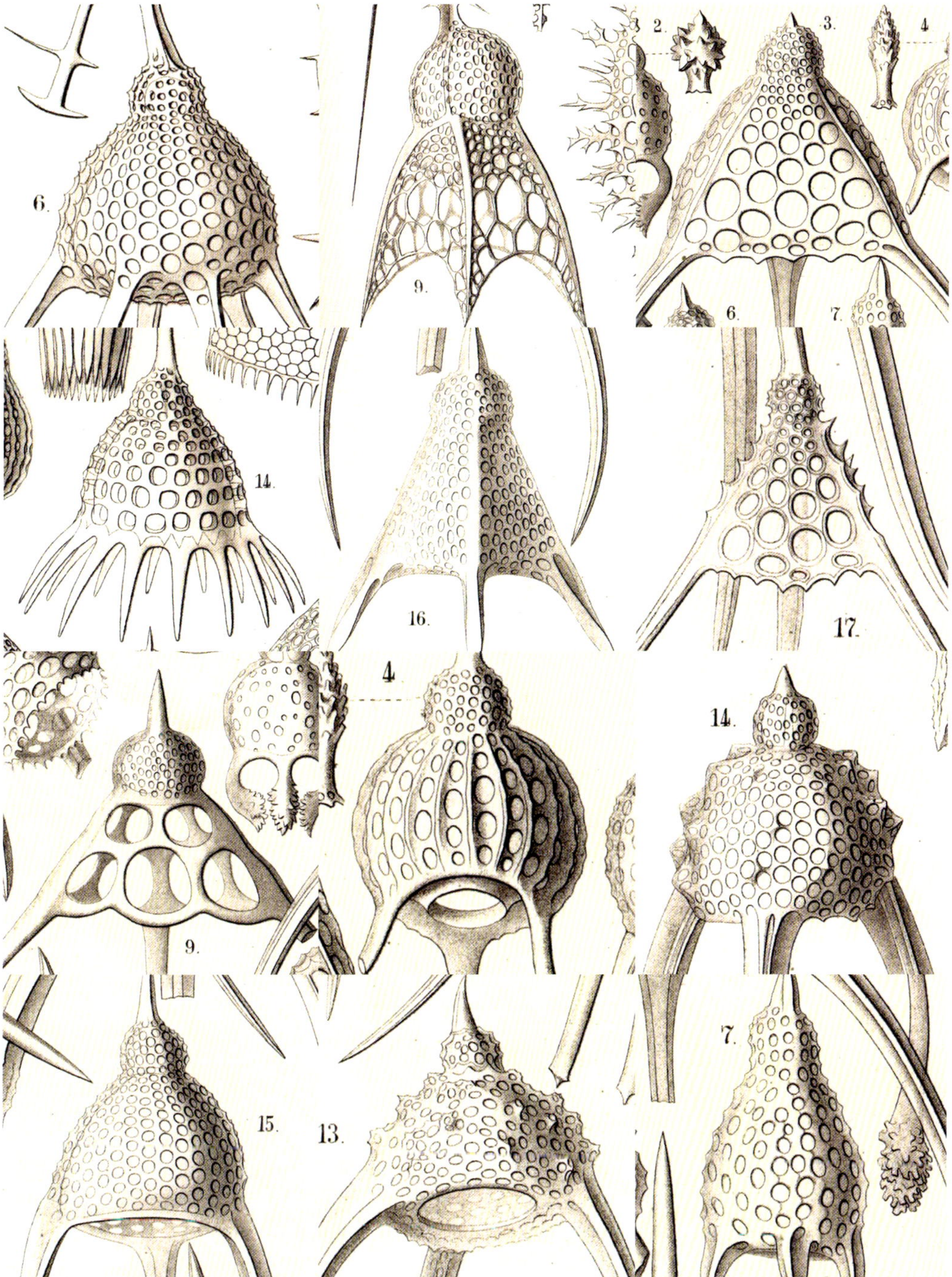

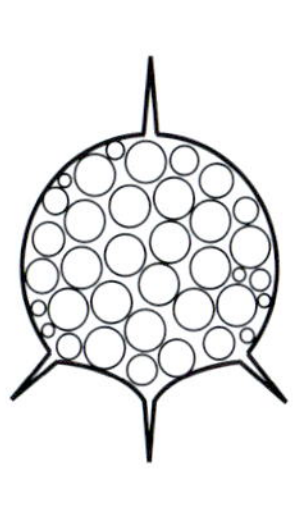

Sphere + Legs + Spicule
Open

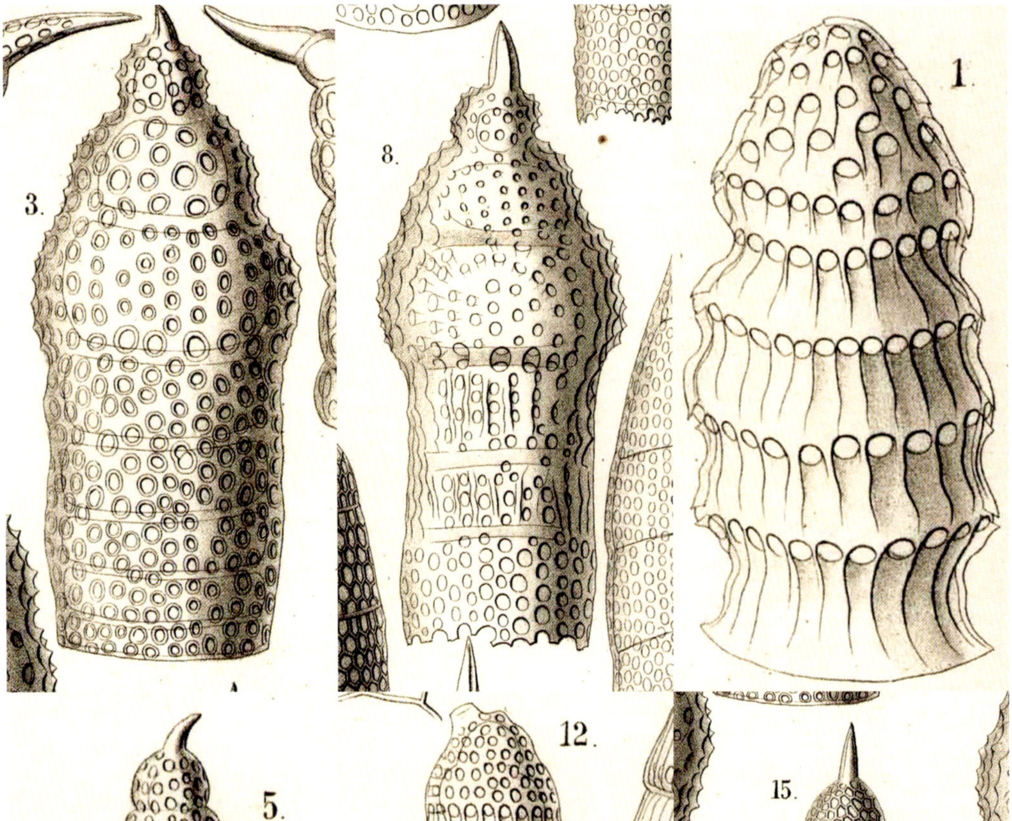

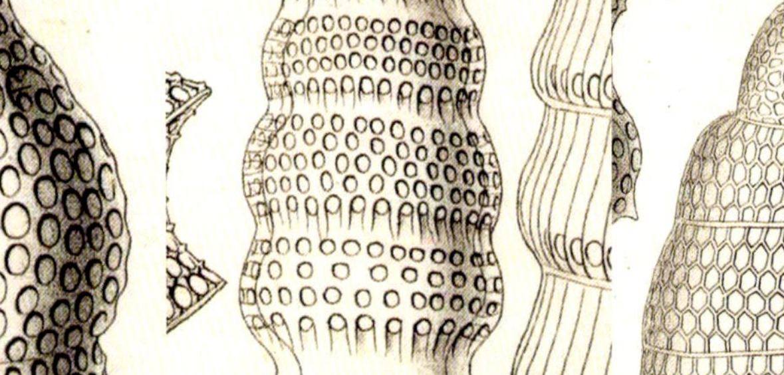

Multiple Spheres
Open

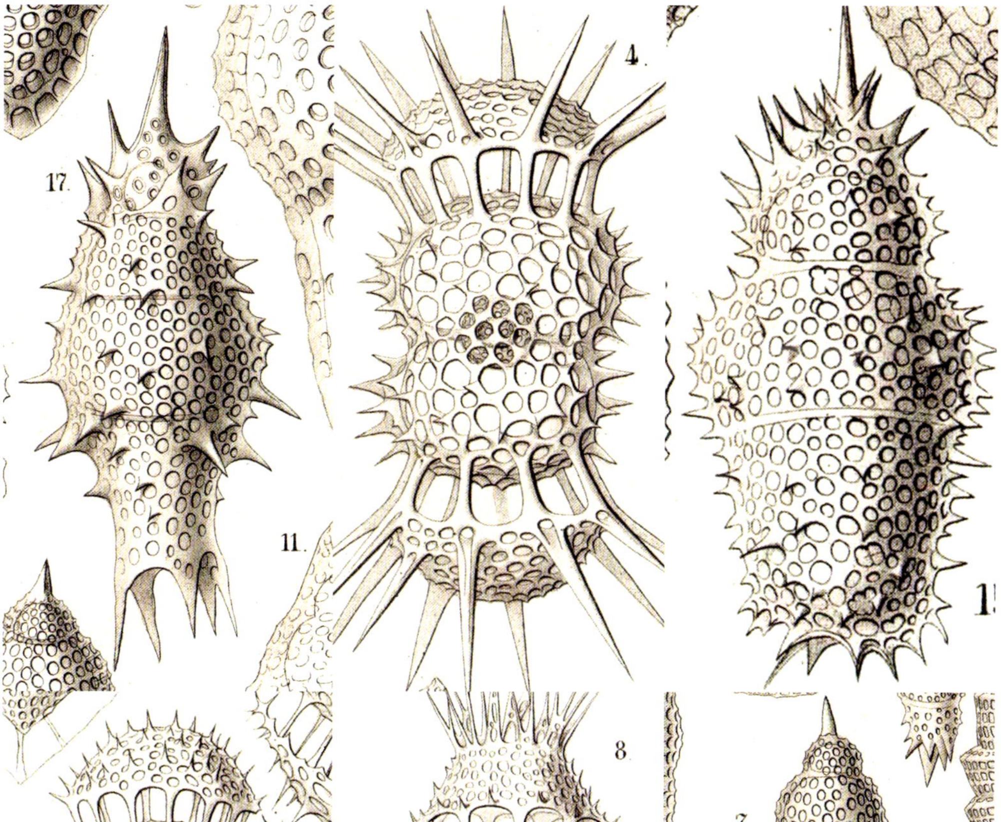

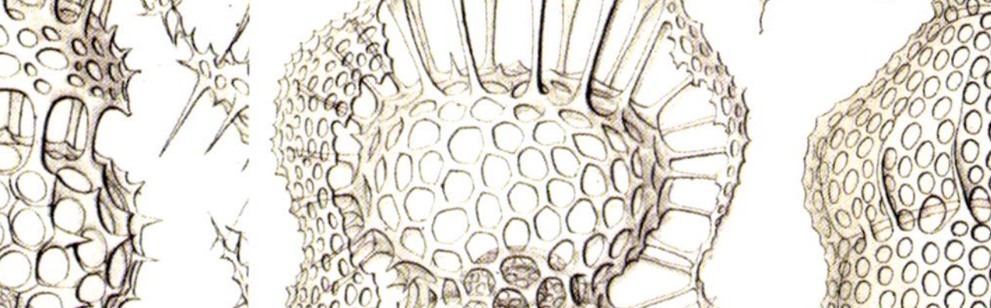

Multiple Spheres + Legs + Spicules
Open

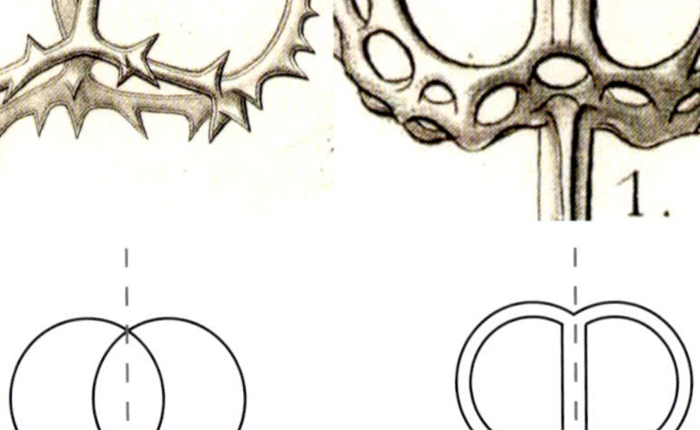

Skeletal Structure: Group of Two
Open

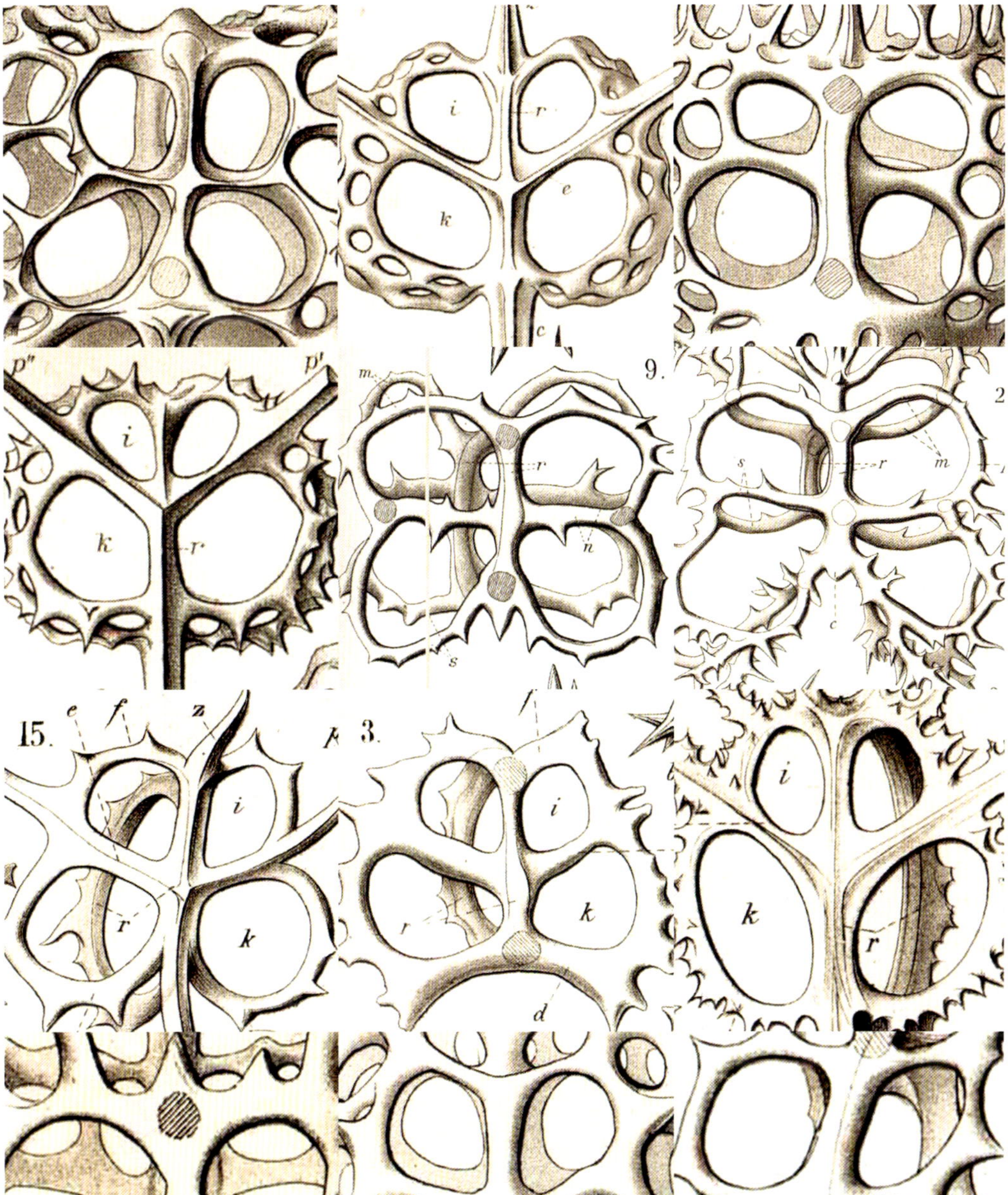

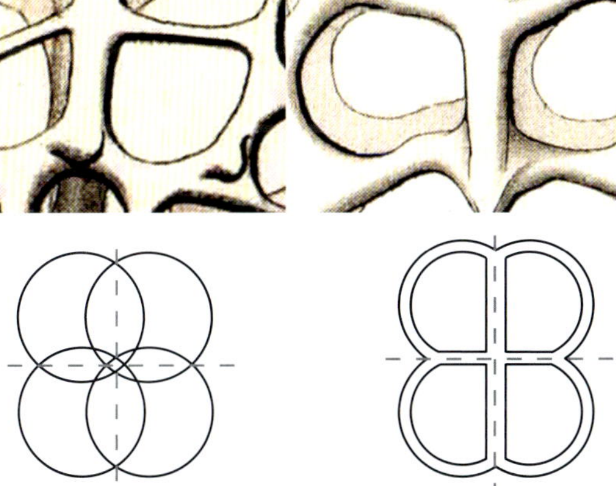

Skeletal Structure: Group of Four
Open

Textile Towers and Textile Façades

Lars Spuybroek

For *Textile Tectonics*, we deliberately strove to expand on the textile techniques developed in the first volume: macrame, crochet, braiding and knitting. Here, we have looked for systems that work via the activities of flexible elements ("agents") that enter into relationships with each other to form stable structures. Briefly, all these systems work by means of a relationship between figures and configurations, in which the former – looked at digitally – always have a certain amount of variation at their disposal and the latter emerge from rules of connection between the figures. The world of figures consists of movement, while that of configuration consists of rigidity and stability.

Of all the former textile techniques, we have kept only braiding, supplemented by other techniques, such as Frei Otto's wool-thread method, in which slack fibers are dipped in water, stick together, and form complex structures. Another method springs from studies of Ernst Haeckel's radiolaria, in which double-curved bodies are tesselated in a complex system of three-legged nodes, where irregular arrangements of pentagons, hexagons and other polygons lead to a closed, faceted surface. Mathematical examination of foam has not yet brought a full understanding of its complex geometry; mostly, they come with completely symmetrical and regular systems, but our students found solutions that make possible more variation of polygonal cells, and even systems that incorporate ruptures and shifts. Finally, of course, there is the Gothic, which – once we only look at the figure-configurations with our digital insect's eye – we suddenly realize is the mother of all architecture, and no longer the one of the Greek post-and-beam (which Morris disparagingly called "lintel architecture") but one of continuing variation and pattern.

We deliberately applied these five techniques (braiding, wool-thread wetting, Gothic interlacing, radiolarian tesselation and foam formation) to two completely different problems: those of the tower and the facade, or respectively of tectonics and ornamentation. The first group of students was given only the technique; they had to develop a tower typology from this and then find a program and location for the tower. We gave the students in the second group the same techniques, but we also later gave them an old modernist office building in downtown Chicago to dress. On the following pages, the reader will see how exactly the same techniques, placed in different hands and applied to different problems, can lead to completely different designs. Clearly, R&Design comprises a kind of reverse design technique: instead of giving students a type of building and location and then hoping they will make architecture out of it, we begin with the architecture and then take that to the location. Naturally, this architecture must be flexible, and moreover it must be organizational and not formal, so that it can adapt to the different site forms and programs. R&Design offers a methodology that certainly makes the lives of teachers of architecture much more pleasant: start the process with beauty and structure, and end it with site and program.

Radiolaria Tower

Jonathan Aprati, Valerie Bolen, Jin Cong Hong & Kim Wadelton

Radiolaria are a type of microorganism commonly found in nature, and first studied in depth by Ernst Haeckel. Classified as zooplankton under the phylum radiolaria, they are sometimes further divided into three classes: polycystinea, ancantharea and sticholonchea. Radiolaria range in size from 30 microns to 2 mm in diameter, and can be found in waters of many temperatures and depths. Their distinct silica skeletal system forms many complex structural geometries based in the theory of packed water droplets. Competition for silica between zooplankton is strong and the water droplet structures are an efficient system of minimal material and maximum porosity. This also aids in their buoyancy. Some Radiolaria may have a raised vertical rib running down their length, spicules, or interior layered structure made up of a series of shells and bars and beams. We have investigated the architectural advantages of the Radiolaria systems to minimize material use and maximize openings for light and views. In the Radiolaria Tower it is also advantageous to reduce the building's weight as the number of floors increases.

The Radiolarian patterns of structure and openings may be approximated by circles packed on regular and irregular surfaces. This creates a natural structural system which supports weight, but has the largest number of possible openings. Therefore we may create a building which is supported entirely by is exterior skin, providing ample interior flexibility of space. Interestingly, the most complex surfaces require smaller, more numerous and diverse circles where they not only change scale but may become irregular in shape. This naturally creates additional structural support in the areas which need it most, while fitting closely to the curvature of the form, allowing for a fluid and natural structural solution to even the most complex building forms.

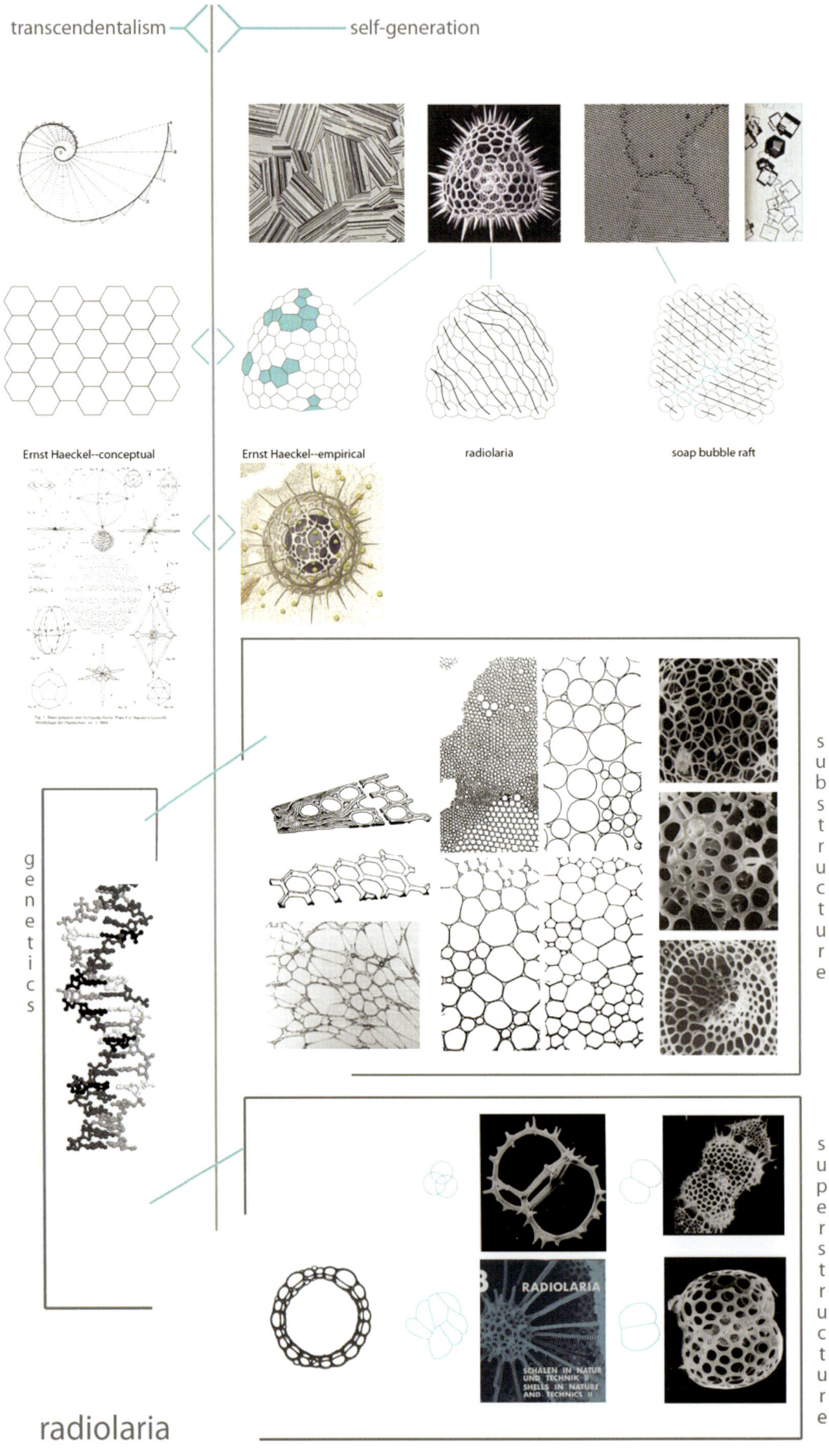
transcendentalism
self-generation
Ernst Haeckel--conceptual
Ernst Haeckel--empirical
radiolaria
soap bubble raft
genetics
substructure
superstructure
RADIOLARIA
SCHALEN IN NATUR UND TECHNIK II
SHELLS IN NATURE AND TECHNICS II

radiolaria

Organic examples

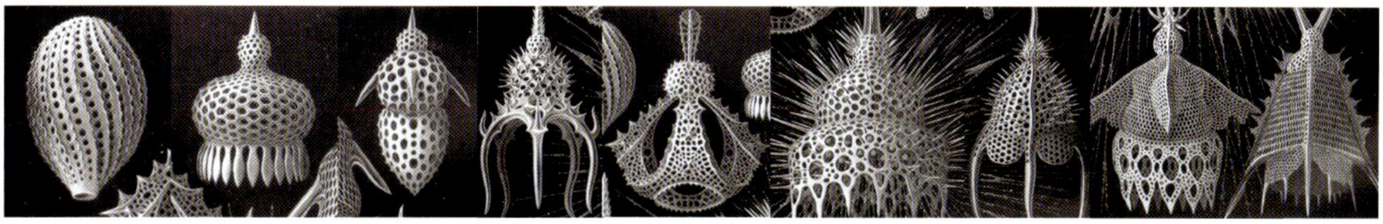

Empirical research

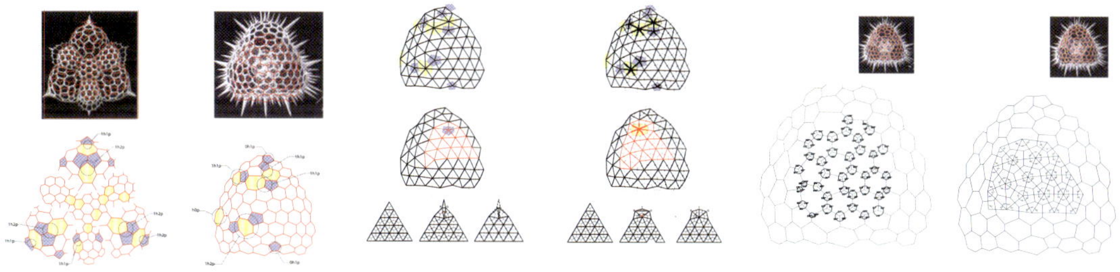

Transformation study

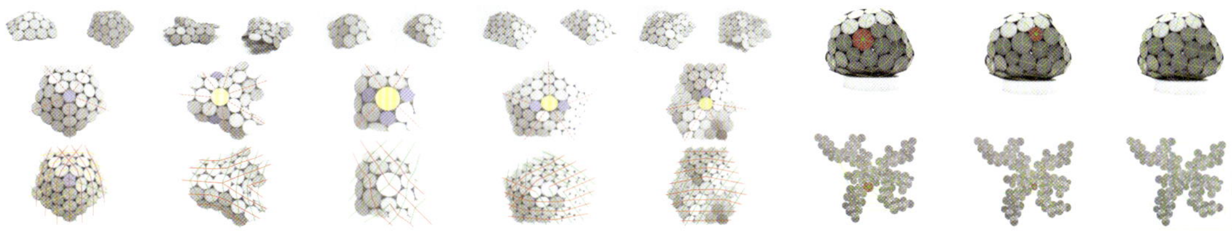

Tesselation process

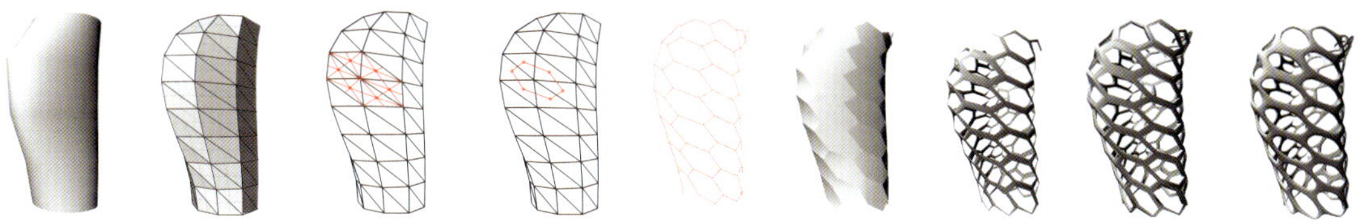

Formal menu part I

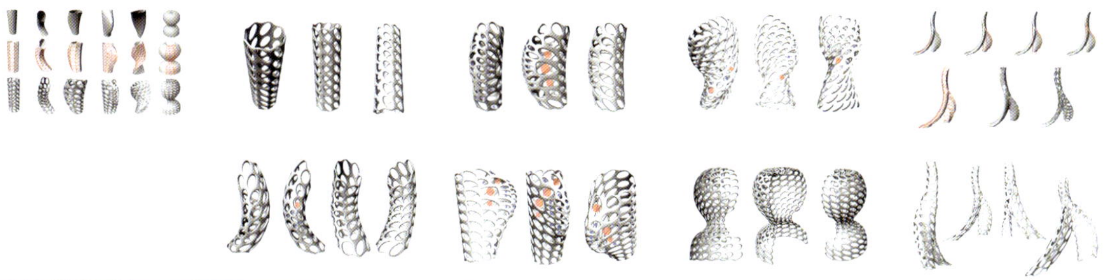

Formal menu part II

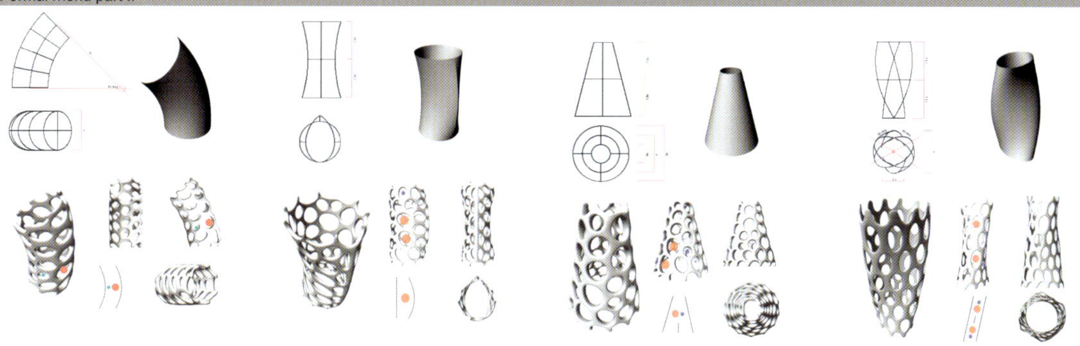

Uniform Cylinder

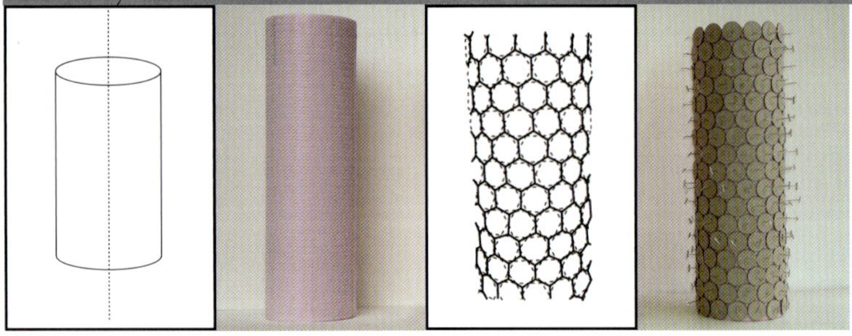

In a uniform cylinder circles of equal size pack the surface evenly. This is the same as even packing of hexagons of equal side length. This is the simplest, ideal case.

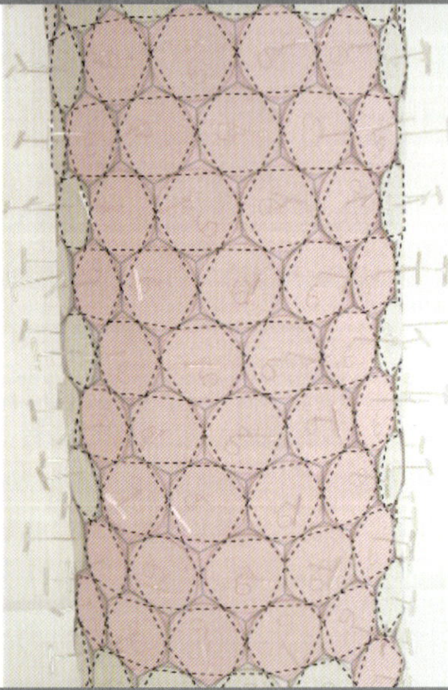

Curved Cylinder

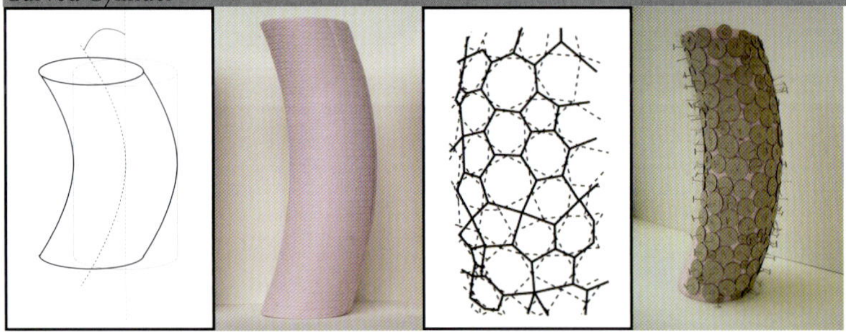

In a curved cylinder areas of expansion and contraction appear. Smaller and larger circles must be added to the mix in order to fill the surface smoothly. This is the same as adding heptagons and pentagons to the hexagonal grid surface. All hexagons pentagons and heptagons have equal side length, but the reduction or expansion in the number of sides allows for curvature to occur.

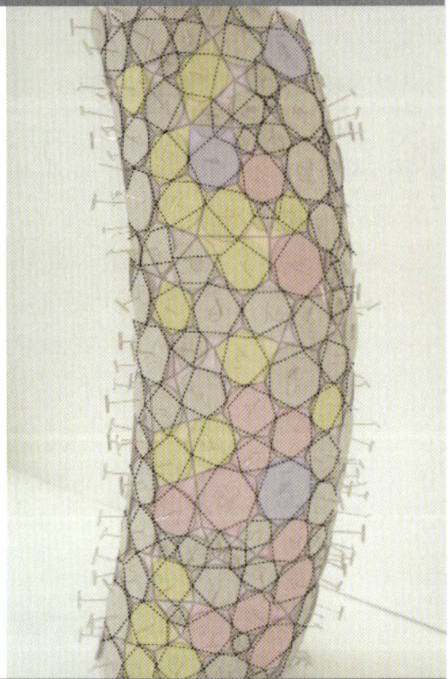

Double Curved Cylinder

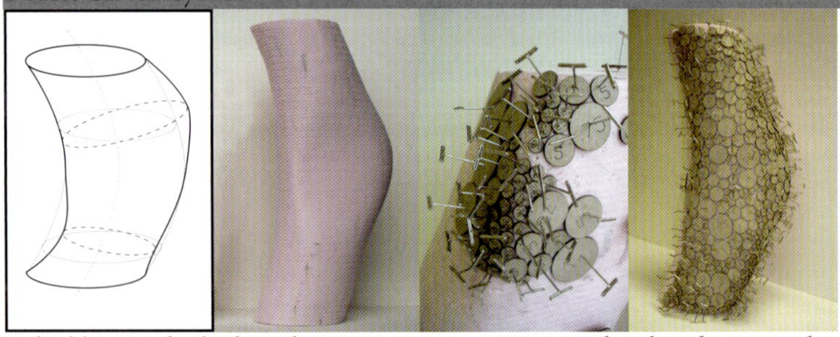

A double curved cylinder is the more extreme case. Here, rather than distortion along a single axis, the standard cylinder is distorted along two axes. To continue to pack the surface smoothly a large variety of sizes of circle must be employed. Again this is equal to packing a number of hexagons, pentagons, and heptagons but, in the most extreme areas of surface distortion triangles begin to appear.

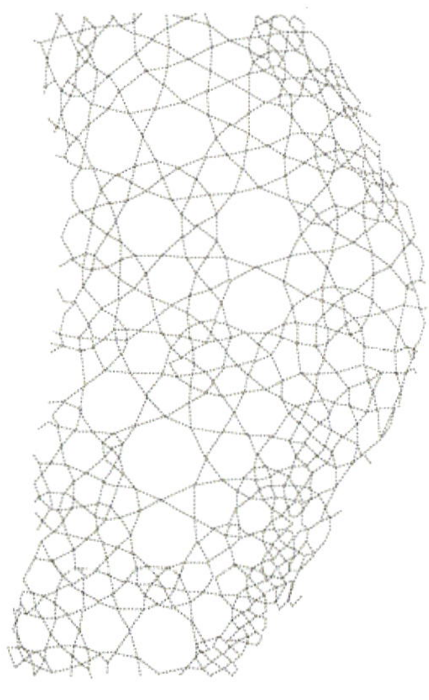

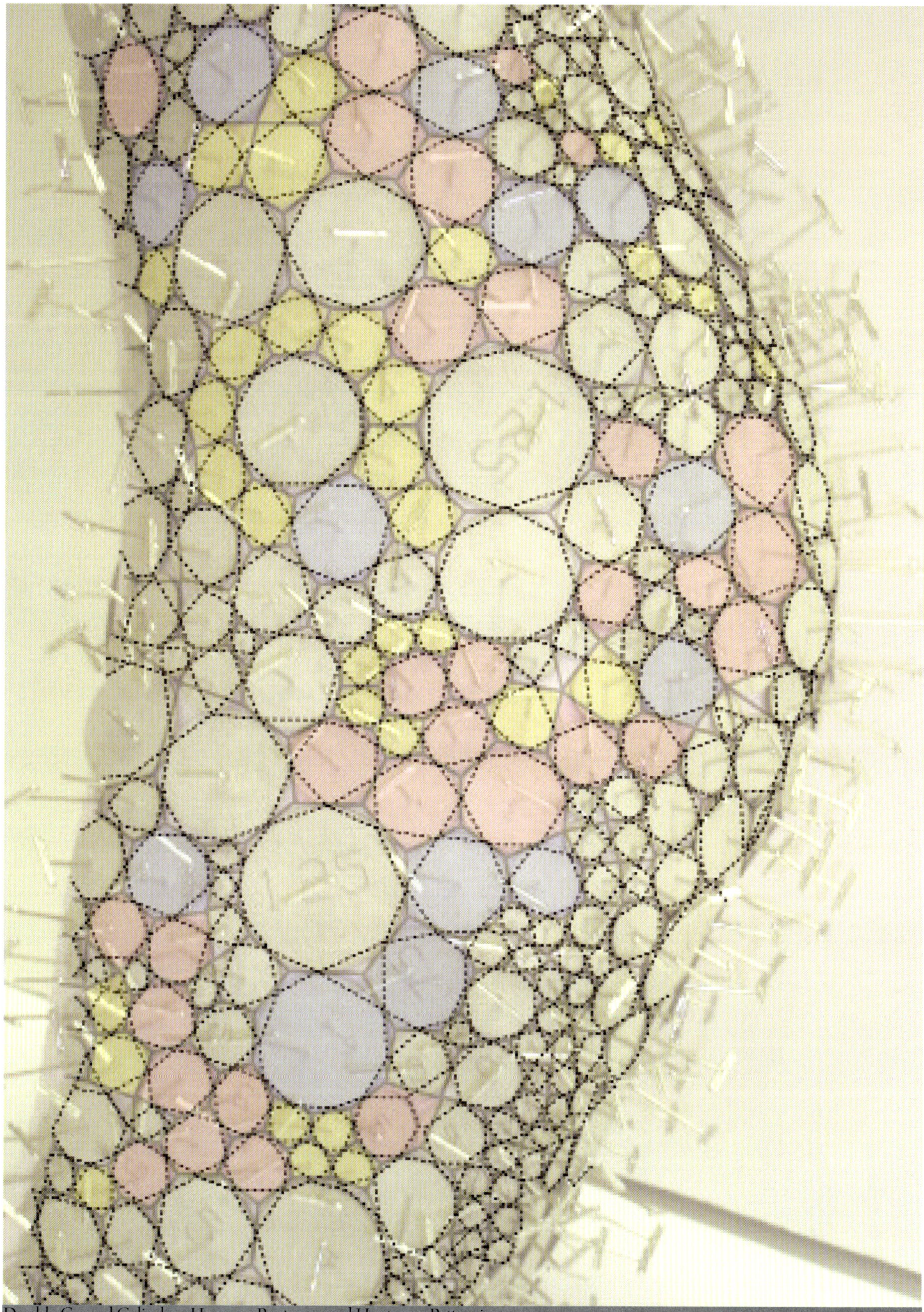

Double Curved Cylinder - Hexagon Pentagon and Heptagon Patterning

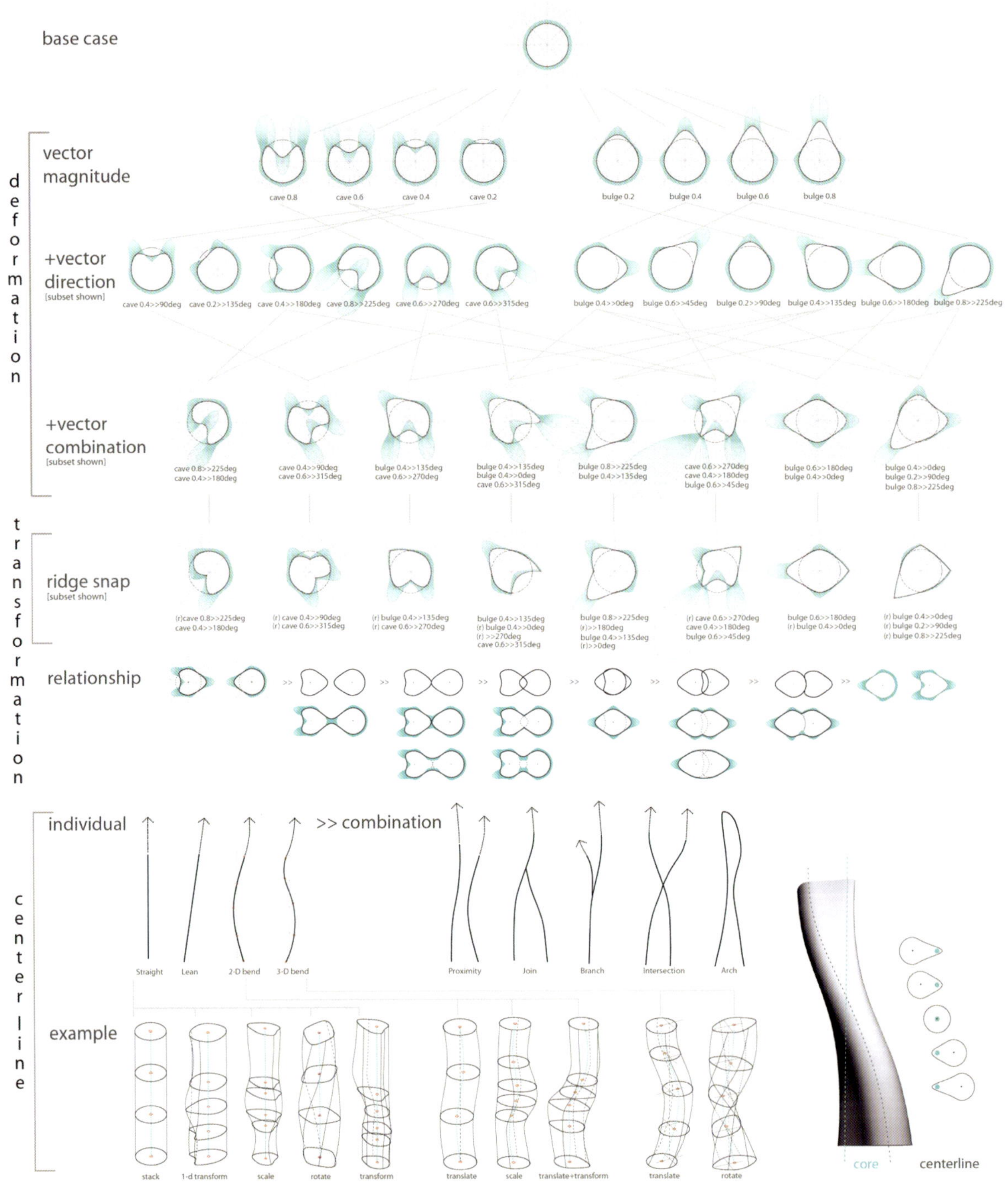

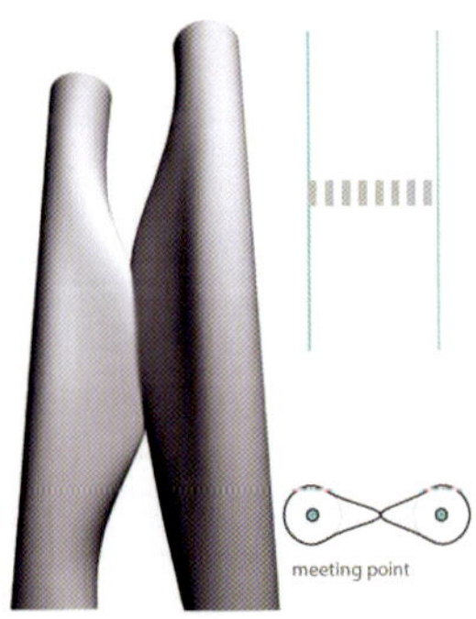

bulge merge (straight towers)

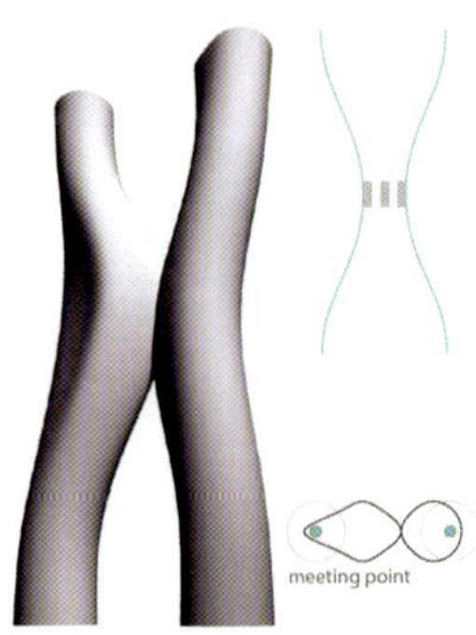

bulge merge (engaged towers)

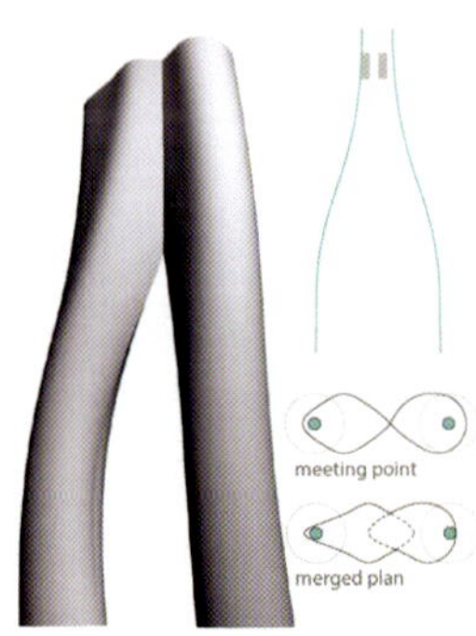

single ridge merge

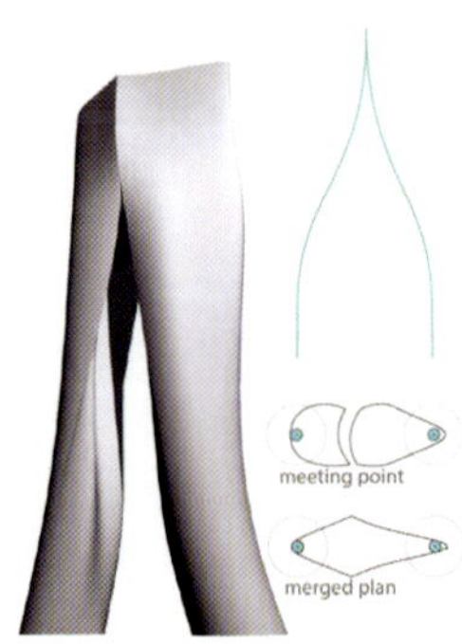

double ridge merge

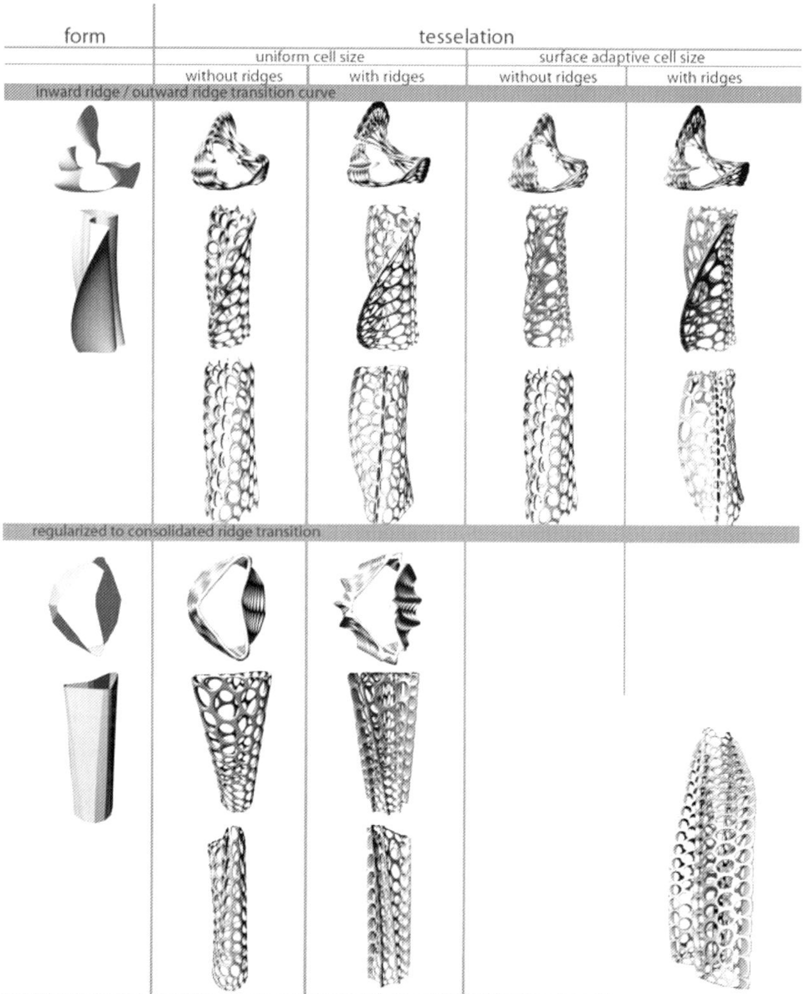
form
tesselation
uniform cell size
surface adaptive cell size
without ridges
with ridges
without ridges
with ridges
inward ridge / outward ridge transition curve
regularized to consolidated ridge transition

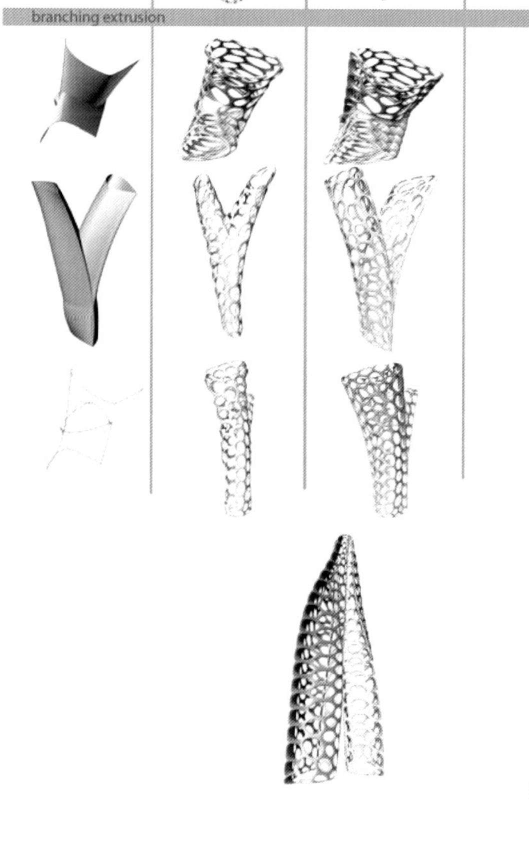
branching extrusion

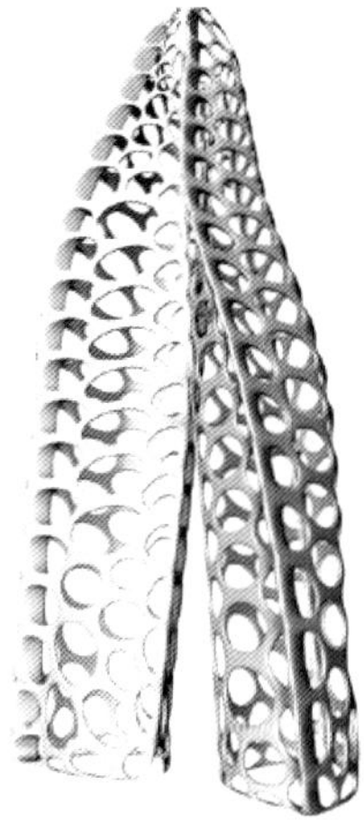

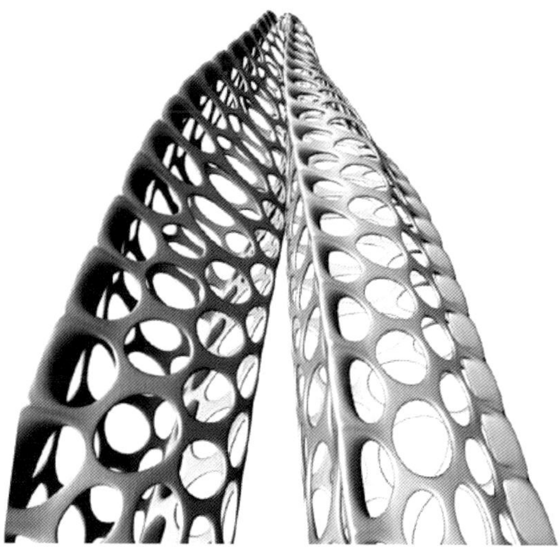

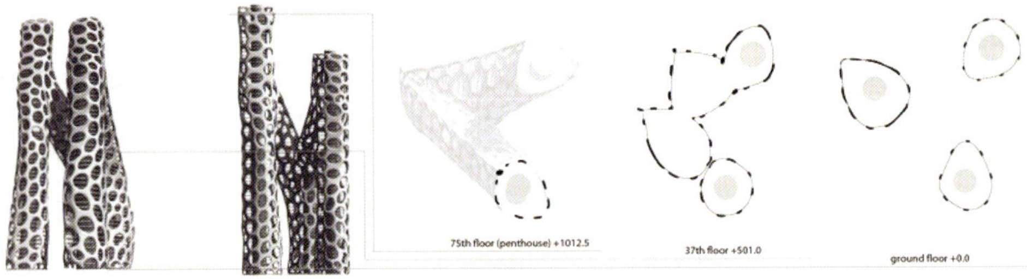
75th floor (penthouse) +1012.5
37th floor +501.0
ground floor +0.0

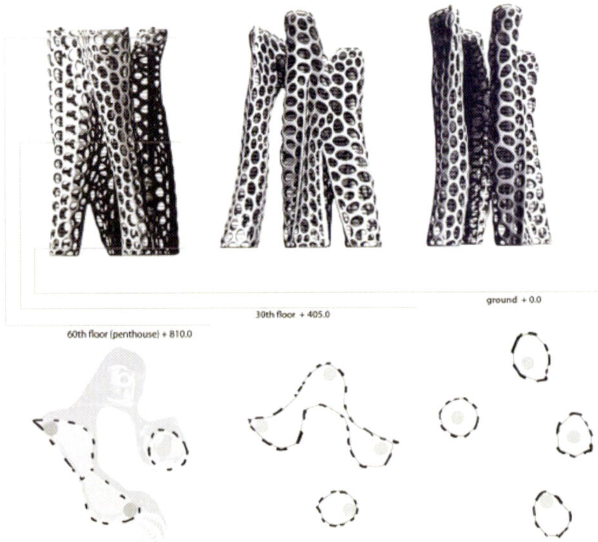
ground + 0.0
30th floor + 405.0
60th floor (penthouse) + 810.0

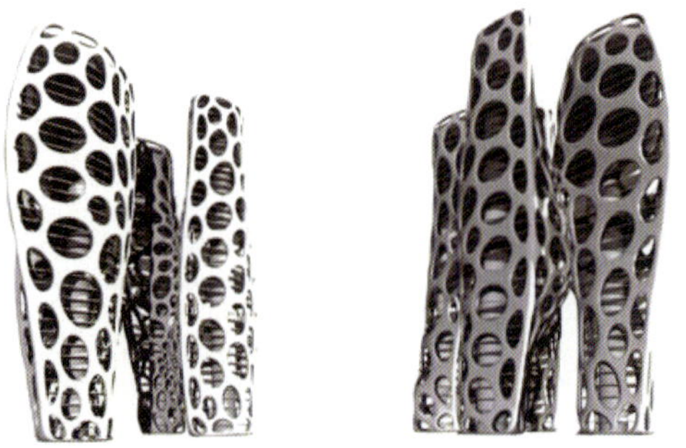

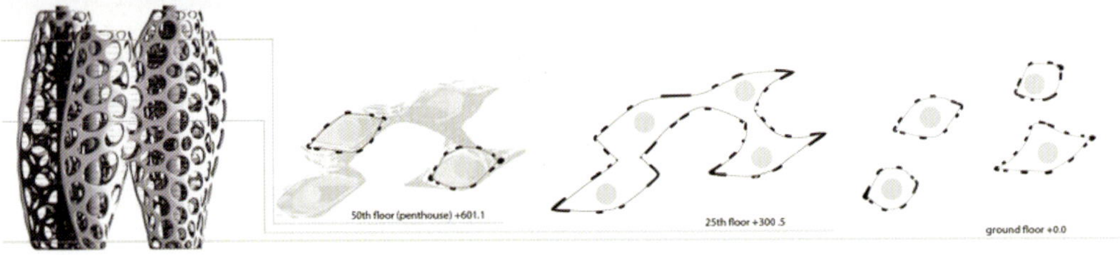
50th floor (penthouse) +601.1
25th floor +300 .5
ground floor +0.0

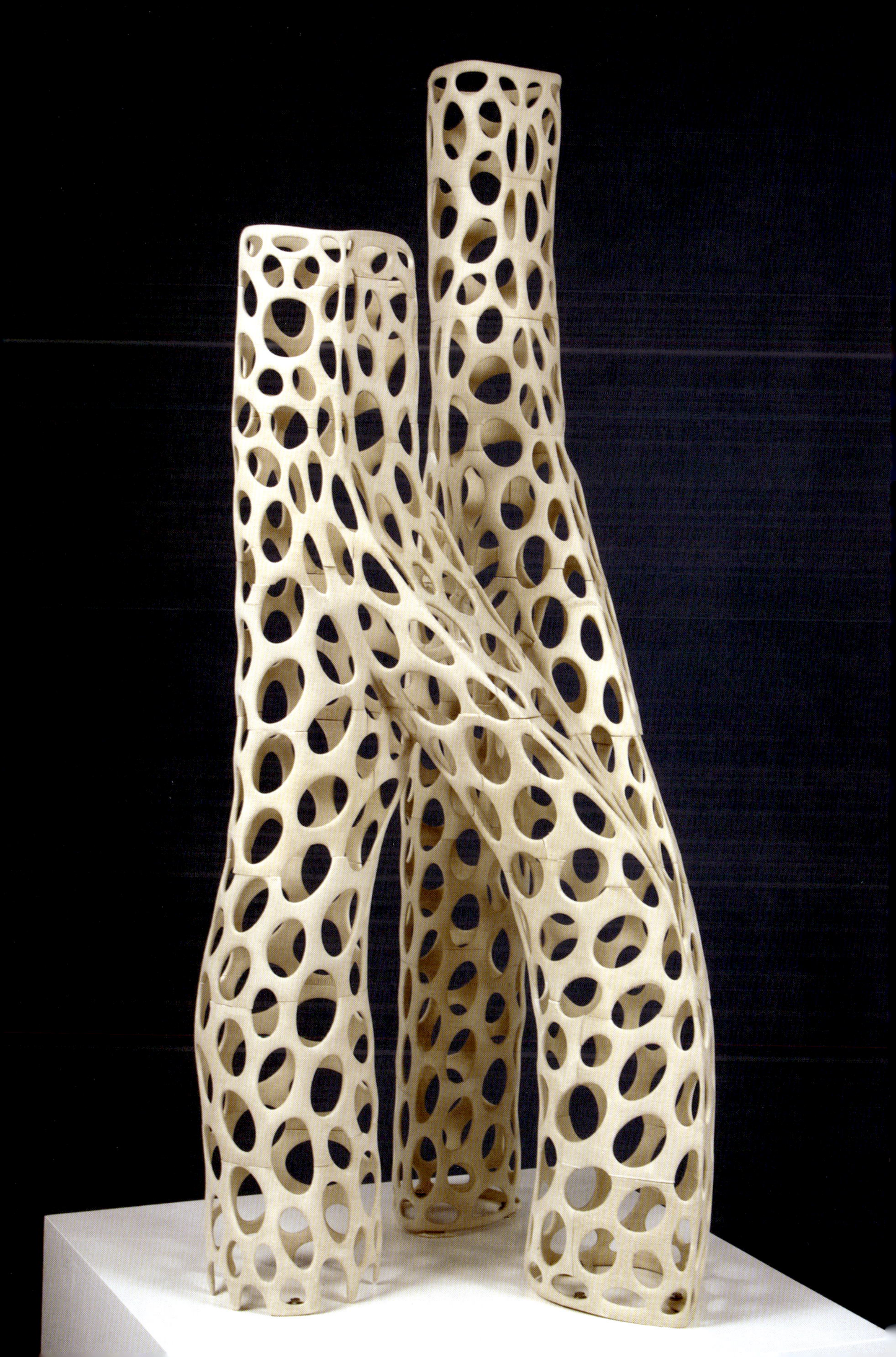

Z - Corp Testing

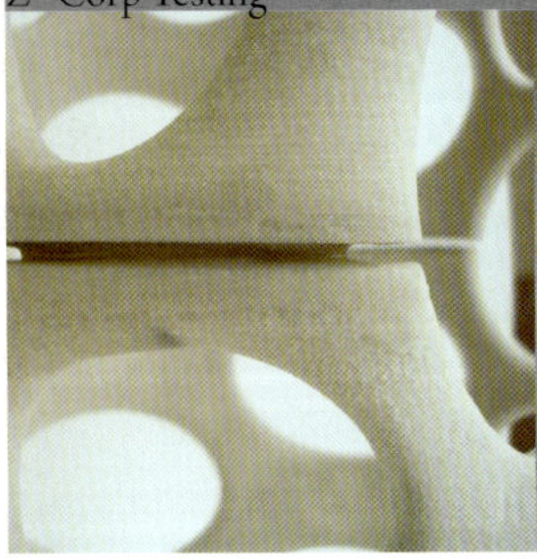
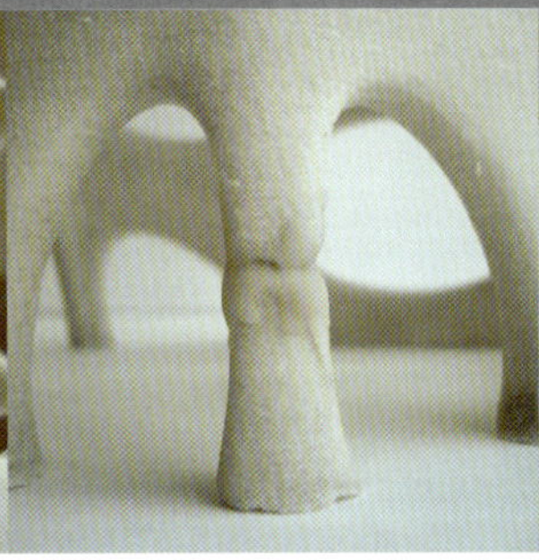
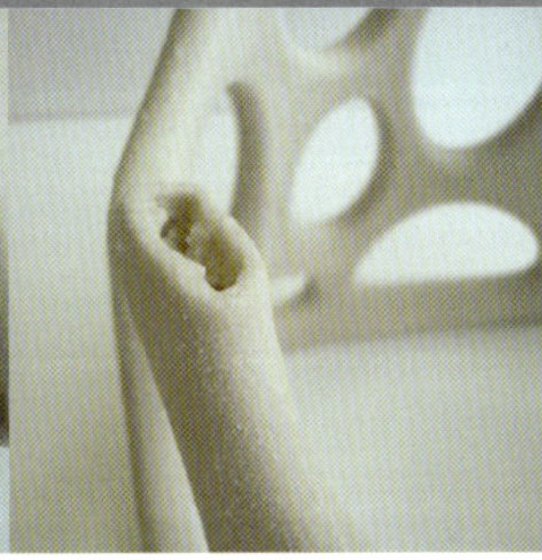

Digital Modeling

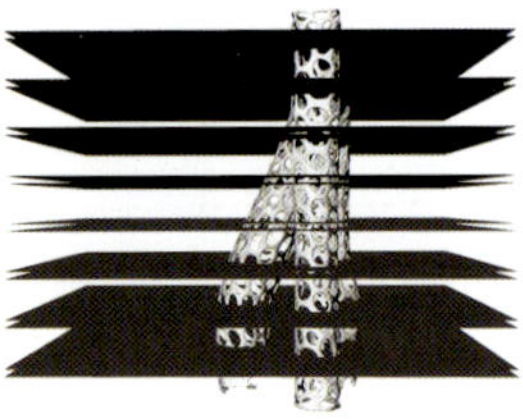
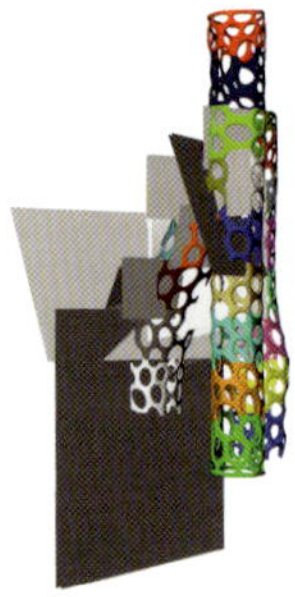

Model Assembly

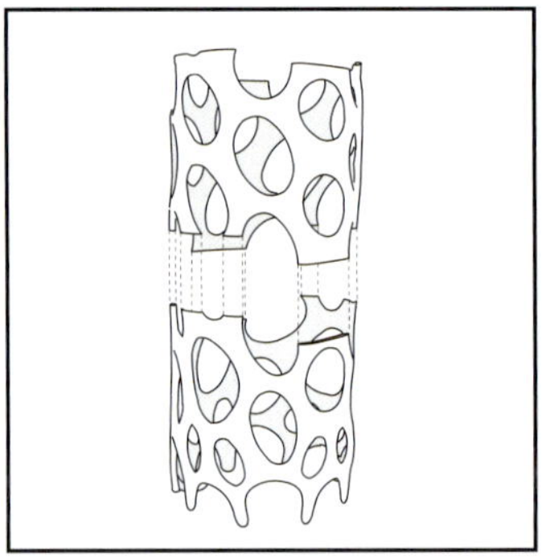
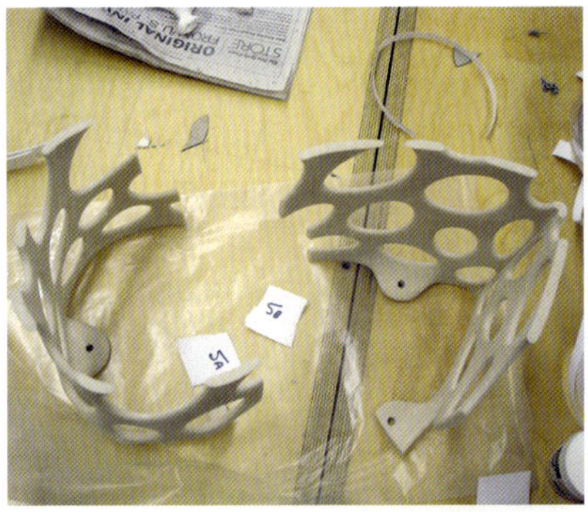

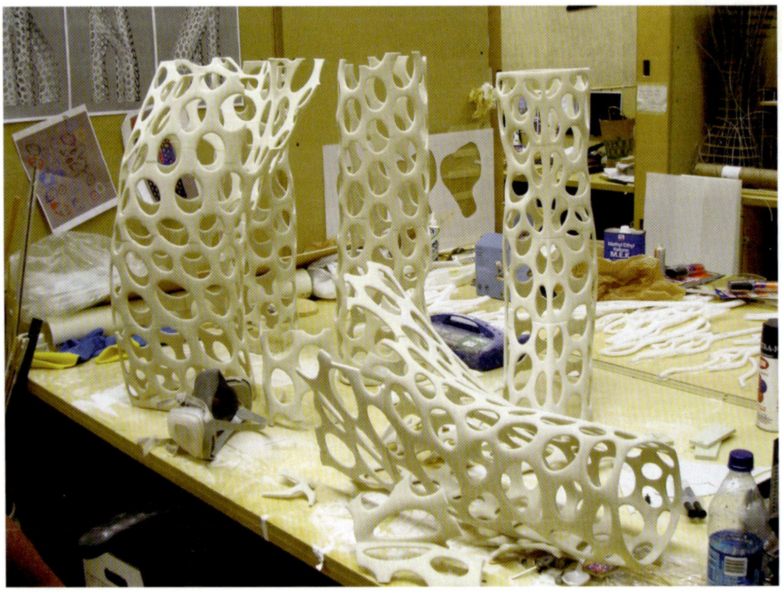
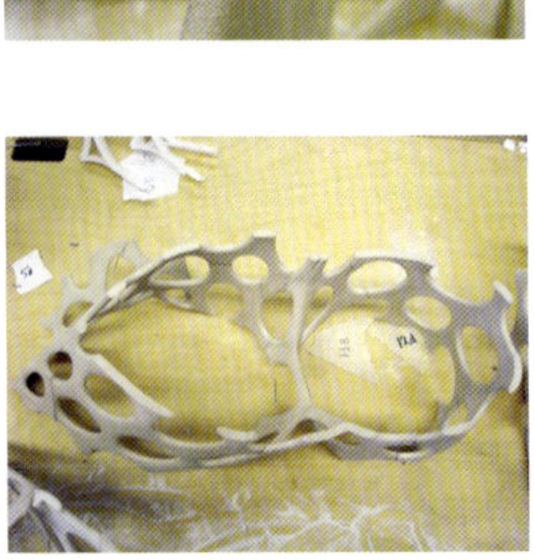

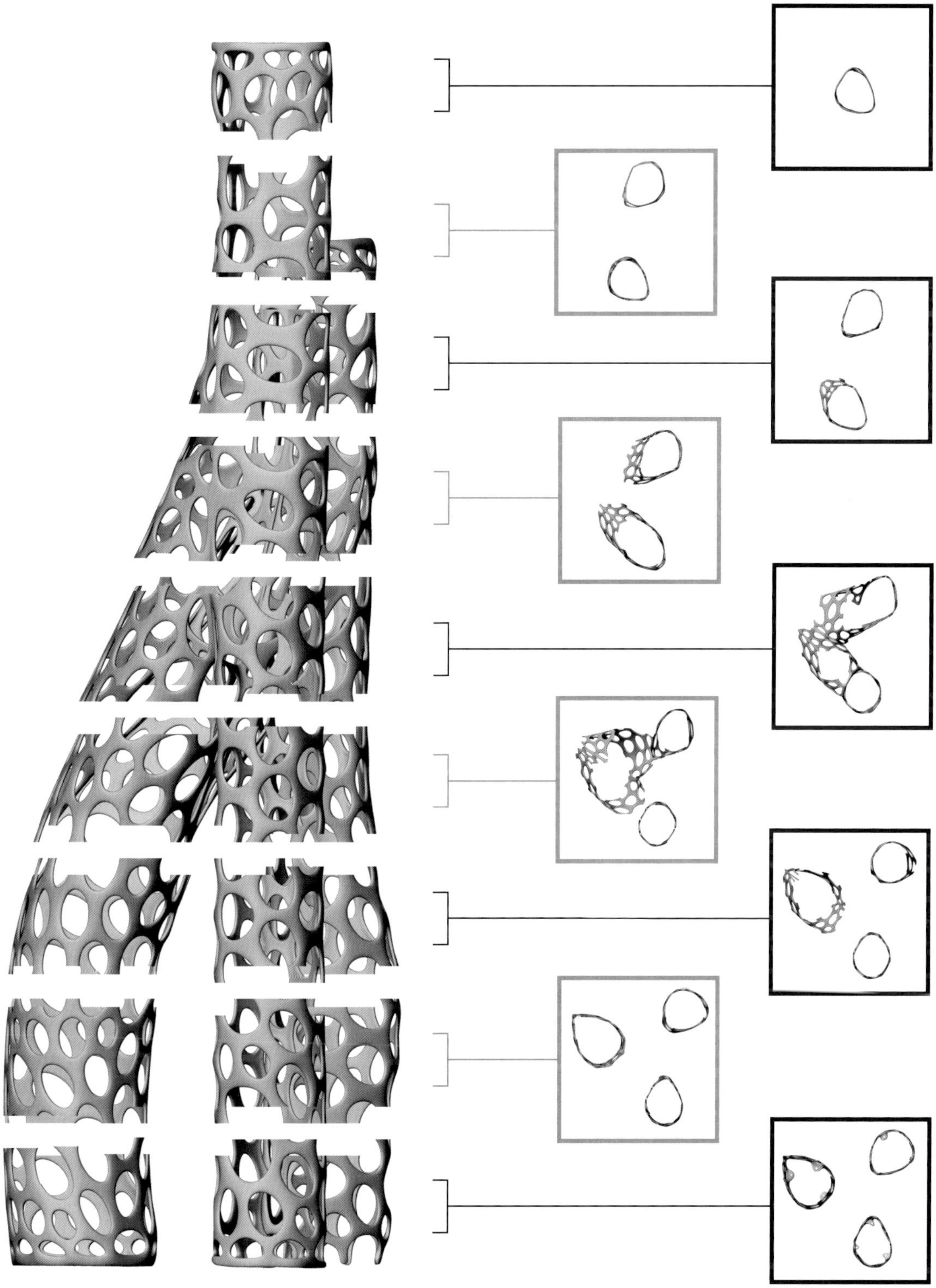

AREVA

Wool Thread Tower

Matt Erwin & Adam Sauer

This project focuses on analog computing techniques forming unique yet highly efficient optimized path systems that can be interpreted into efficient structural systems. Here, using Frei Otto's technique of wool thread models, we studied 'optimized path systems,' similar to Gaudi's catenary curves. These models where made by pulling taught thread through a 25 x 25 grid drilled into top and bottom plates. Next the thread was slacked by 8% and dipped into water. Through cohesion and gravity the threads rearranged into an efficient path system that was used to establish the methodology of our network. This network informed our tower structural system that was further developed through digital and physical models, creating a unique and highly efficient structural system. The rules informed by these 'wet grids' were digitally reconstructed into an integrated structural system, in which building skins, floor slabs and the programmatic needs of a high-rise tower are intertwined. The integration of program and circulation components into the tower structure were based on a similar logic of connectivity and optimization that was driven by the organization of the dynamic strucutral column "grid." For example, the circulation cores do not effect the internal structural system but rather are placed in the void spaces that exist in the structure having no structural bearing. This allows the internal circulation cores to be independent of the structure, unlike most towers built today that rely on circulation cores to offset compressive forces. Through our research we found that three base configurations formed the entire network, the X-node, Tangent, and Y are the parent configurations that form endless possibilities while still maintaining the singular topology. Using these three parent shapes and the calculated interaction capabilities, the system was further explored through the development of digital models and built physical models both illustrated in the following pages. By three dimensionally recreating the wool thread system using the connectivity calculations, and 2D networking configurations, we where able to create a 3D-matrix of 21 possible structural tower systems. Each of these structural systems can be fully developed into tower configurations using the same procedure described, creating near endless tower configurations based on our research.

Wool Thread Models

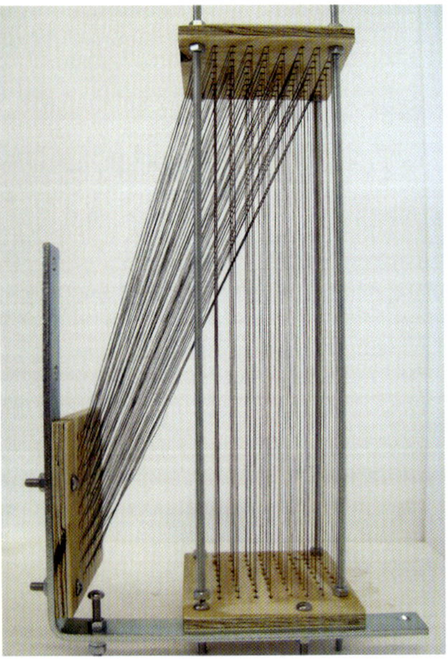

1. taught model

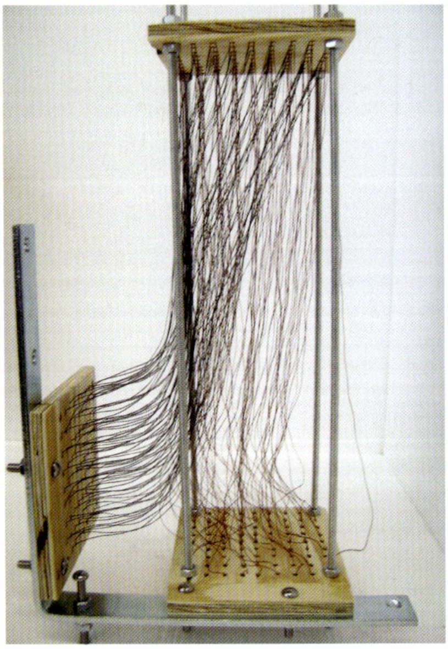

2. 8% slacked model

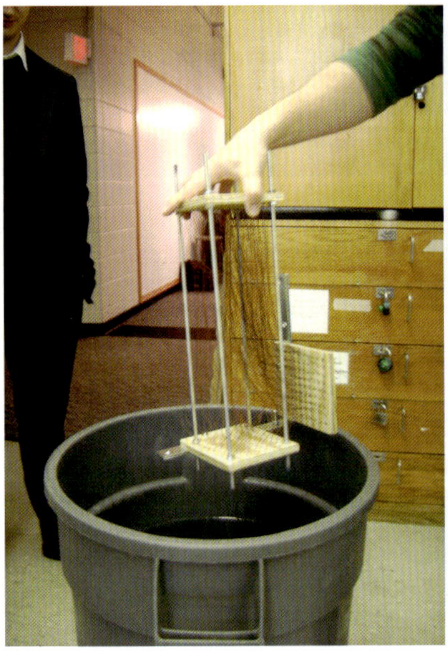

3. model dipped in water

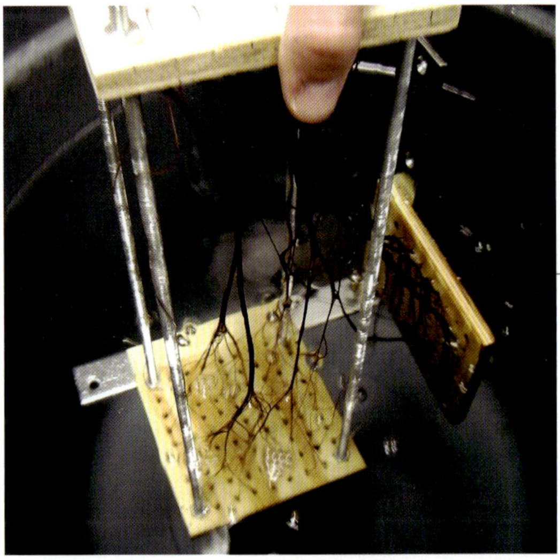

Physical Model

a physical representation of the 3D tower system, made from 3/8" silicon tubing and aluminum wire

2D Matrix Configurations

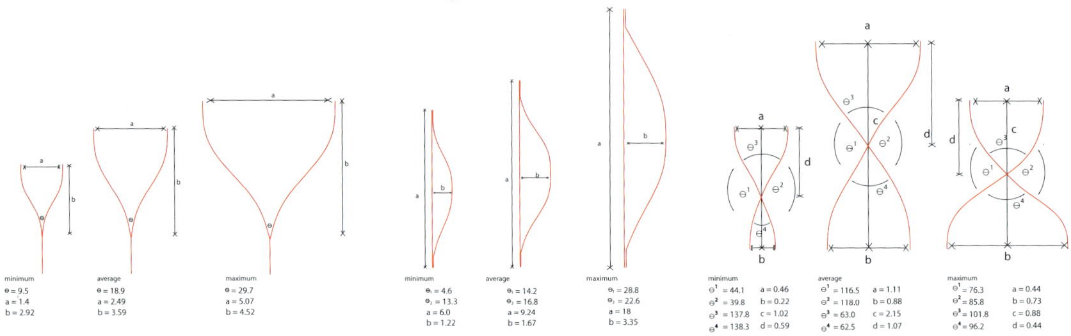

X-node Study

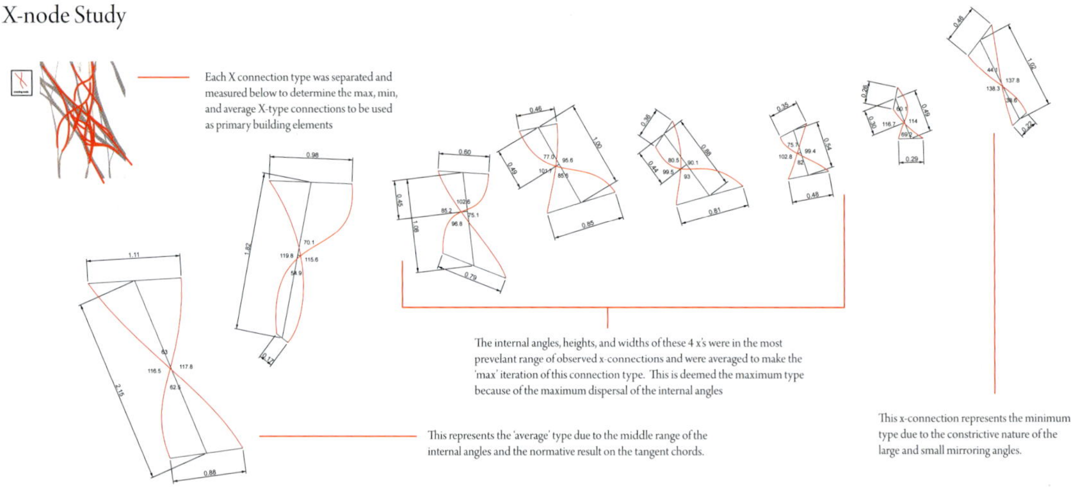

Each X connection type was separated and measured below to determine the max, min, and average X-type connections to be used as primary building elements

The internal angles, heights, and widths of these 4 x's were in the most prevelant range of observed x-connections and were averaged to make the 'max' iteration of this connection type. This is deemed the maximum type because of the maximum dispersal of the internal angles

This represents the 'average' type due to the middle range of the internal angles and the normative result on the tangent chords.

This x-connection represents the minimum type due to the constrictive nature of the large and small mirroring angles.

Component Configuration Matrix

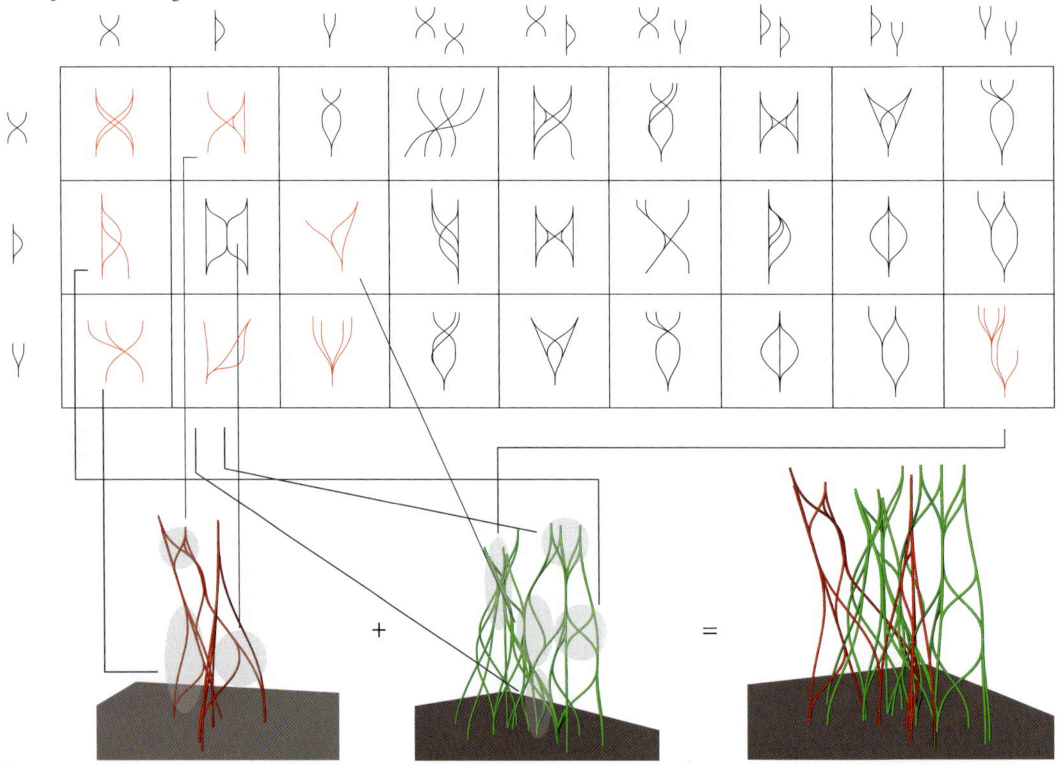

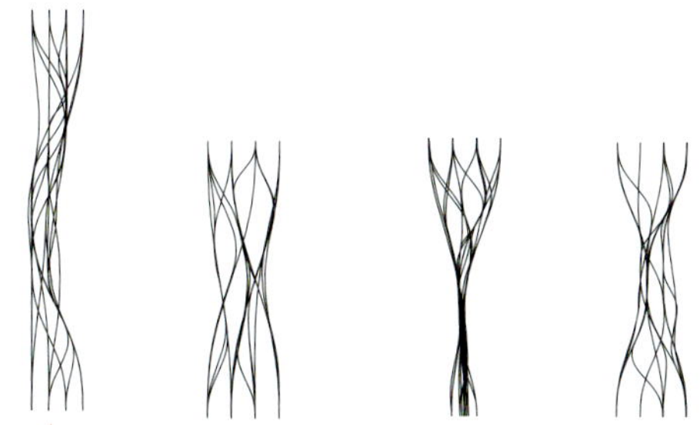

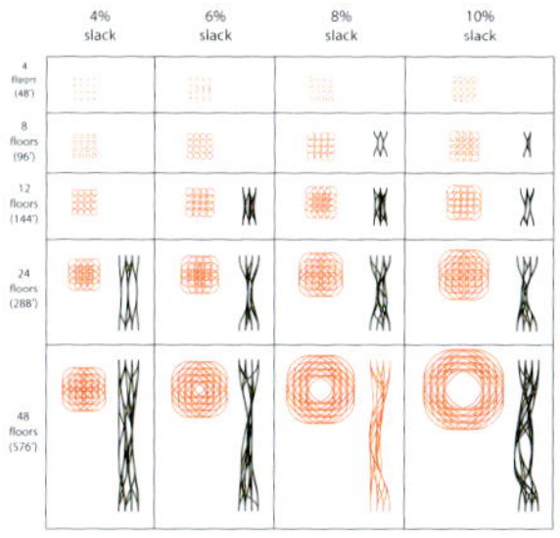

Thread Length vs. Percent Slack Matrix

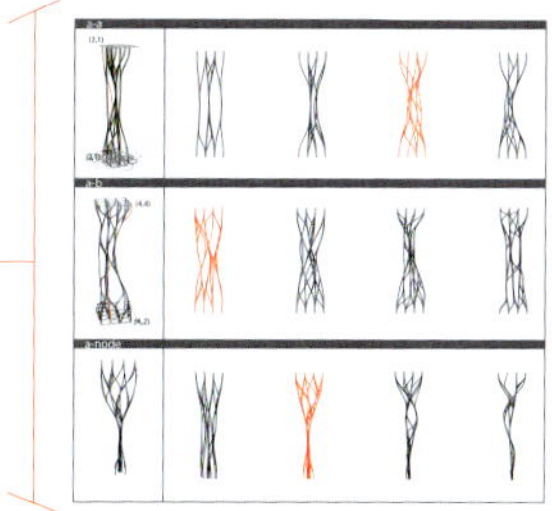

Length vs. Slack Matrix Modified by Connection Type

576'Tower - 8% Slack - A to A Connections

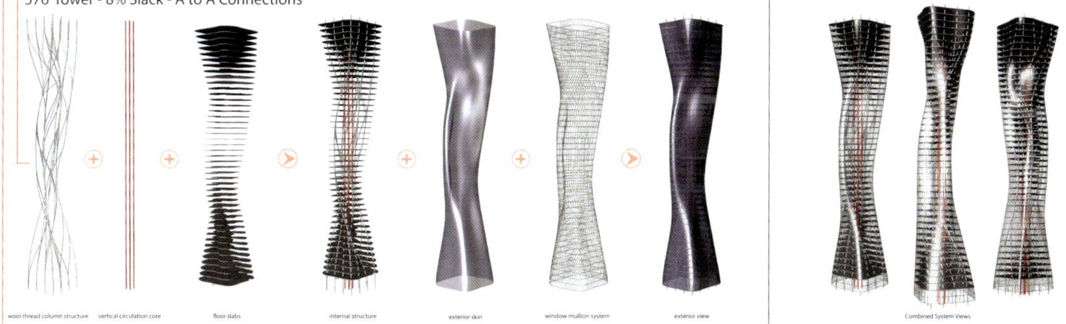

288'Tower - 4% Slack - A to B Connections

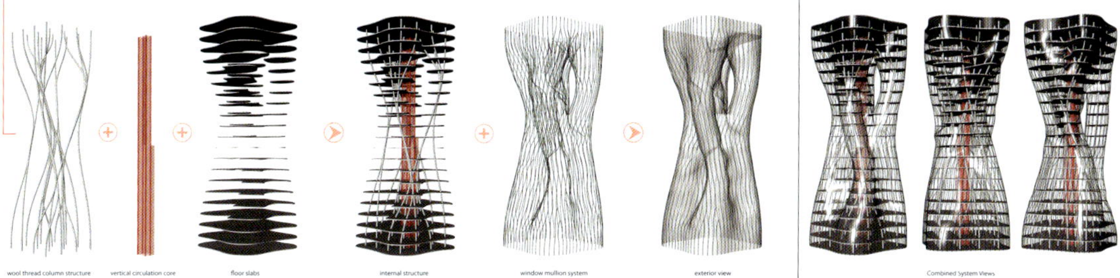

288'Tower - 8% Slack - A to A Connections

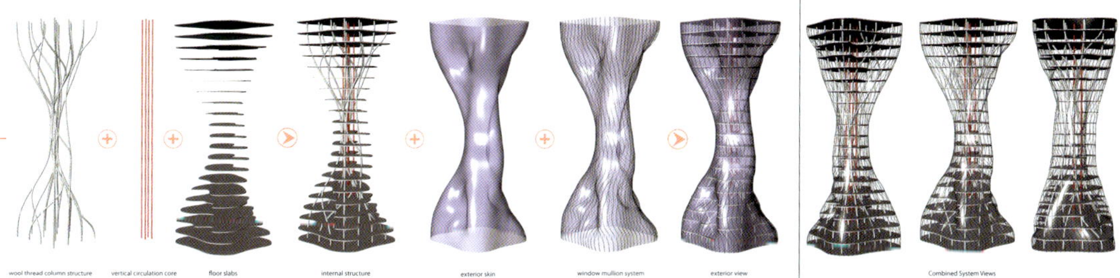

288'Tower - 6% Slack - A to Node Connections

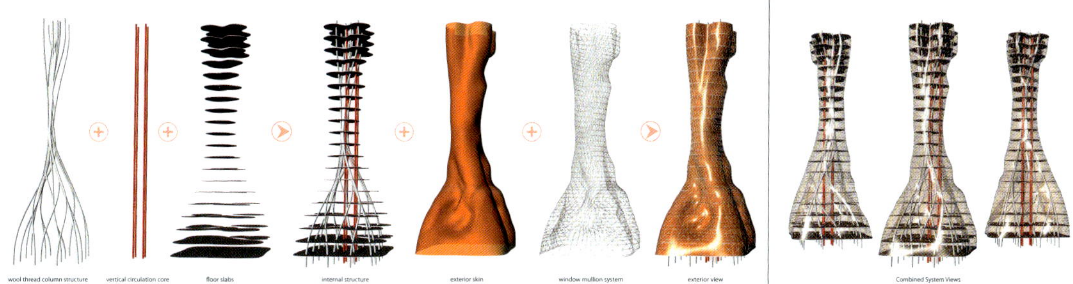

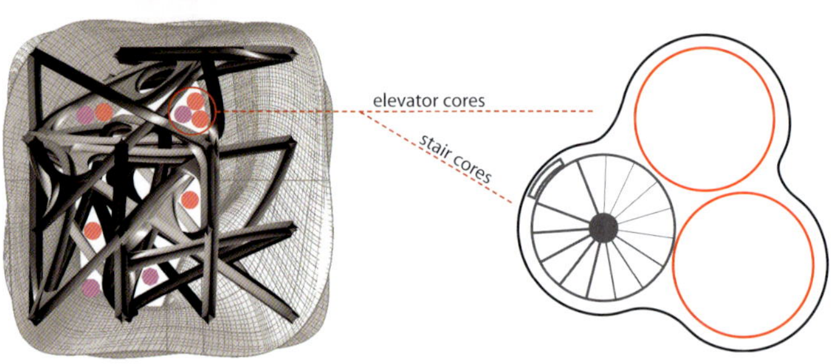

elevator cores
stair cores

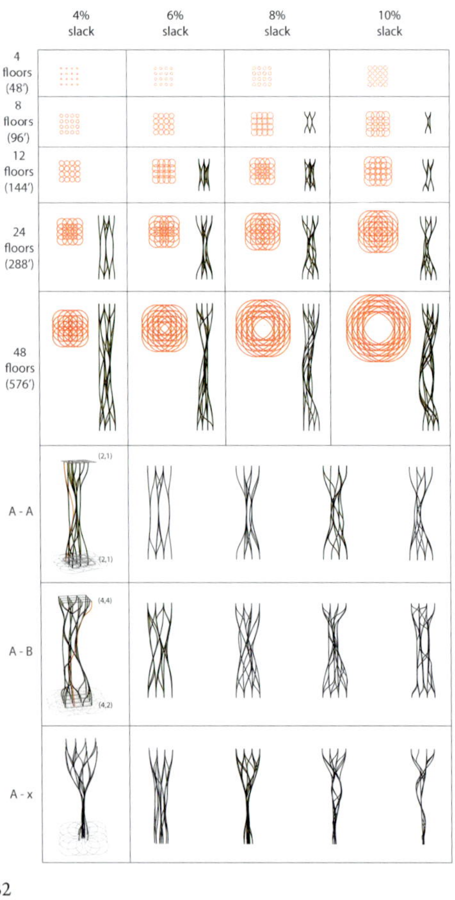

4% slack
6% slack
8% slack
10% slack
4 floors (48')
8 floors (96')
12 floors (144')
24 floors (288')
48 floors (576')
A - A
A - B
A - x

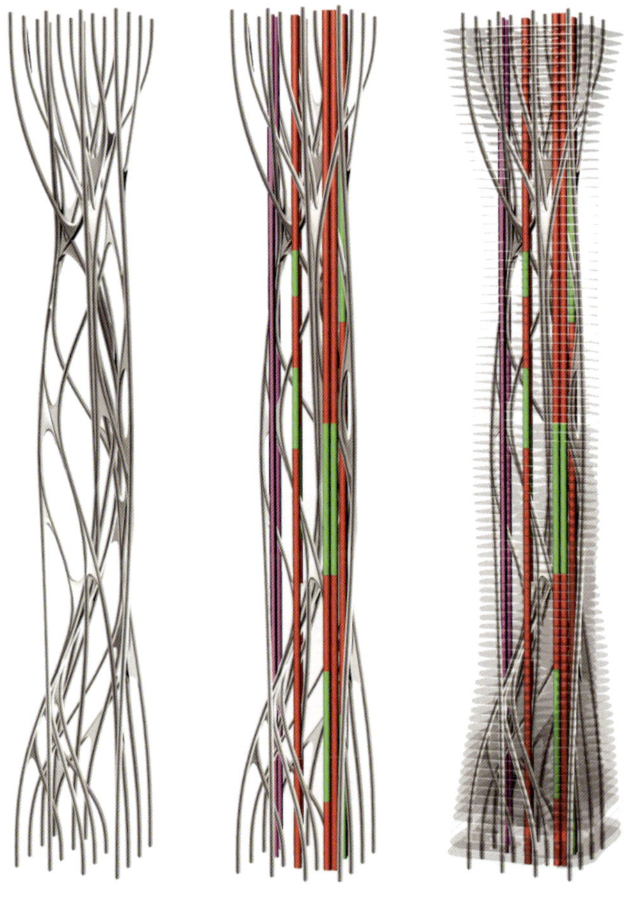

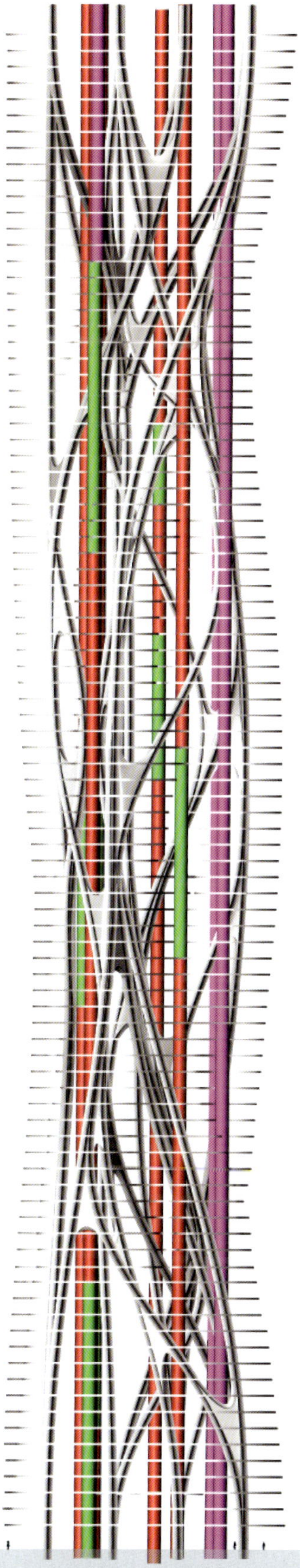

Right Elevation

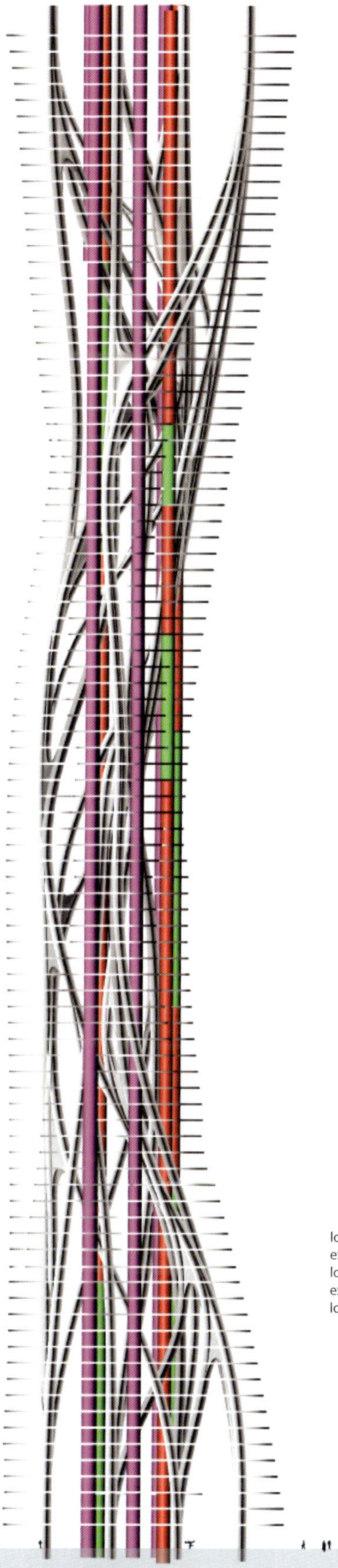

Front Elevation

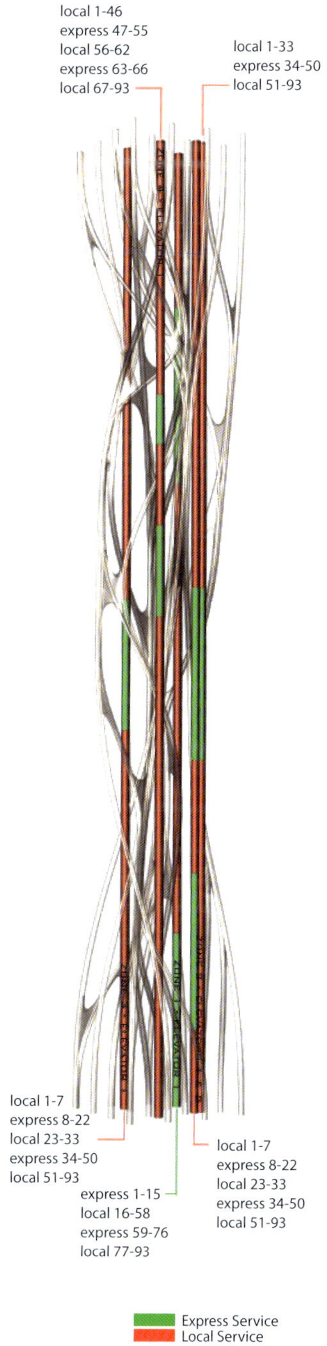

fabrication

the process of slicing the digital model for FDM printing, organizing print trays, and fastening techniques are shown in the diagram below

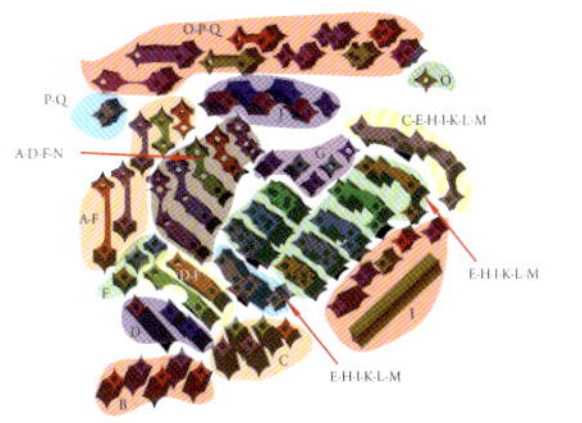

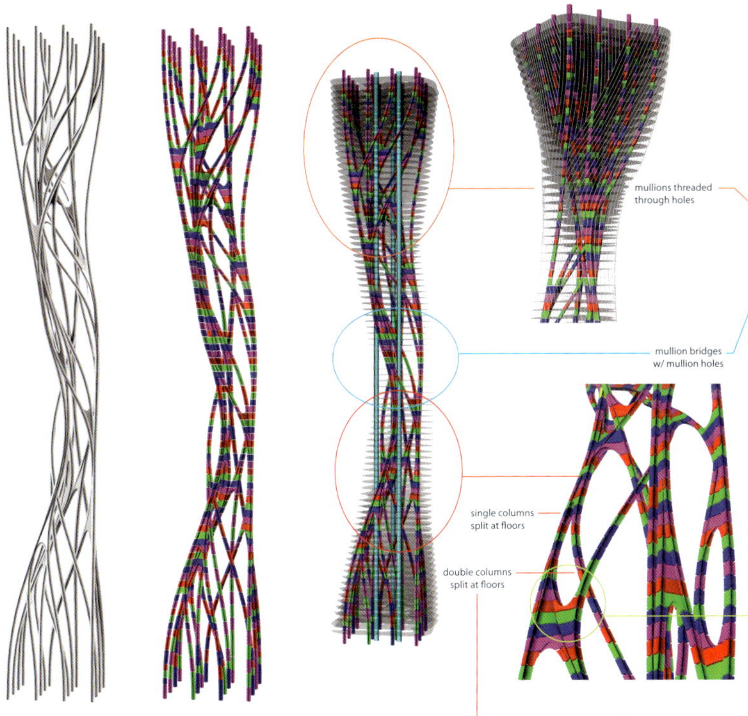

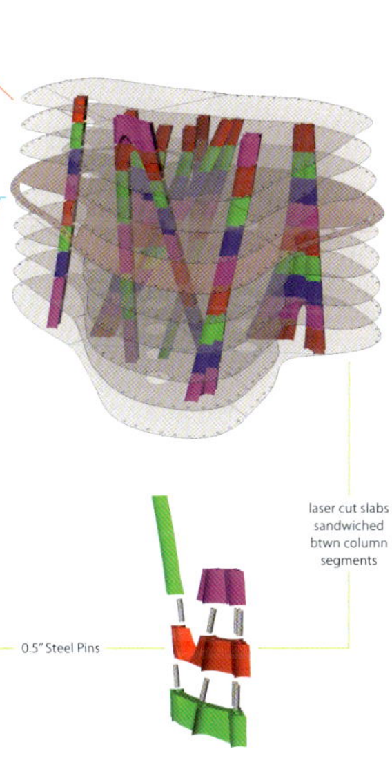

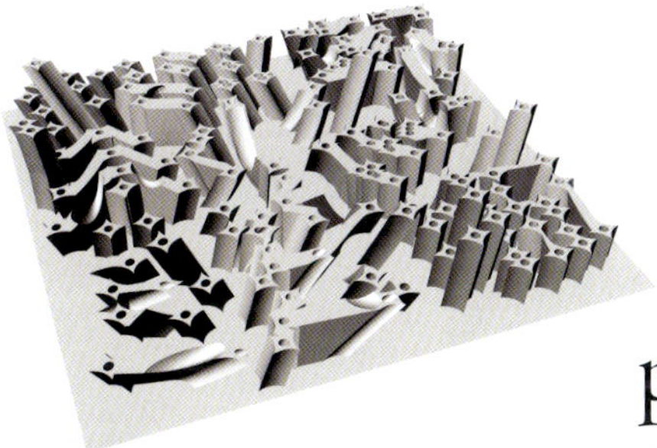

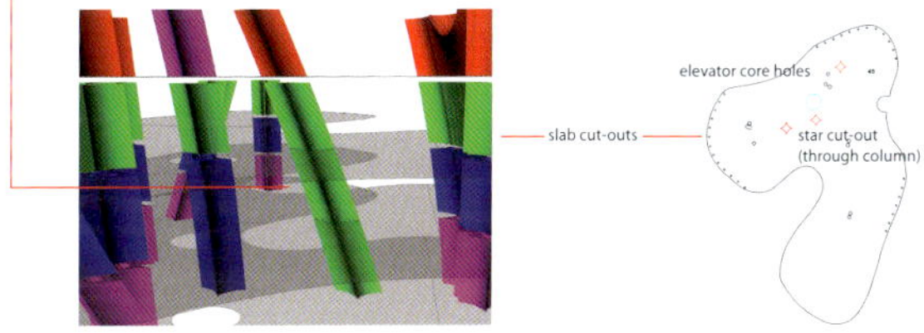

printing

the FDM print trays where labeled and numbered for assembly . The acrylic floor slabs were laser cut and prepped for assembly.

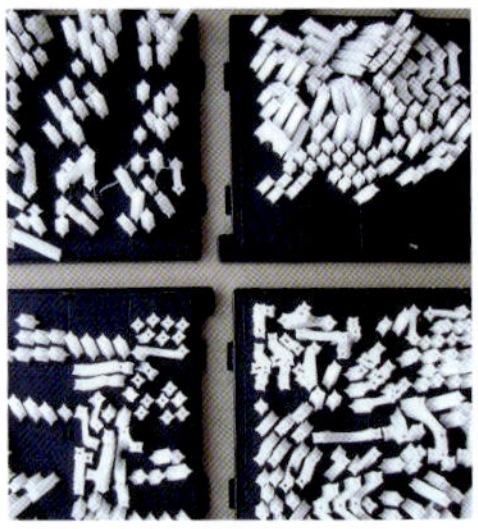
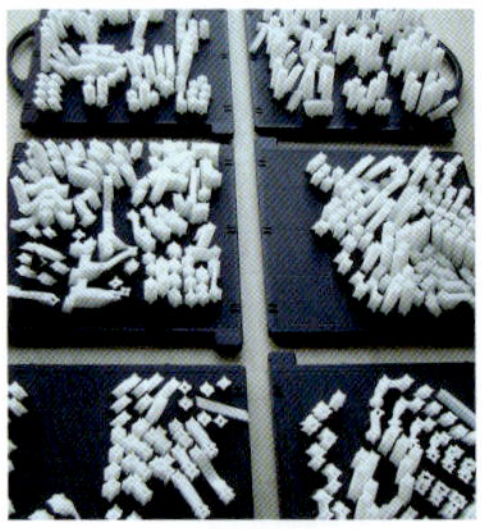
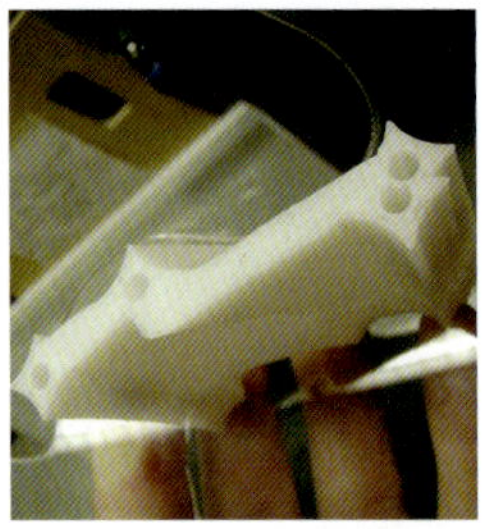

F
F
F
C
C
C
A/B
A/B
A/B
A/B

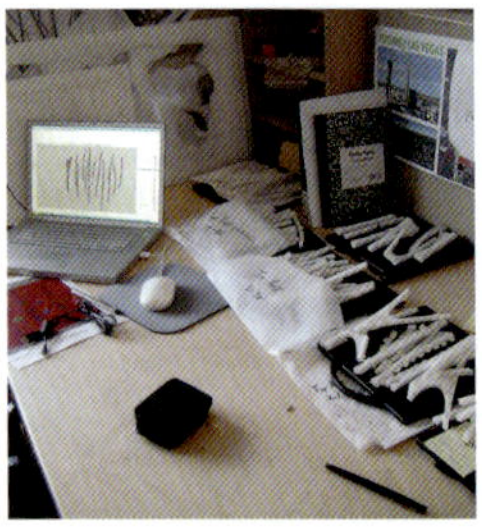

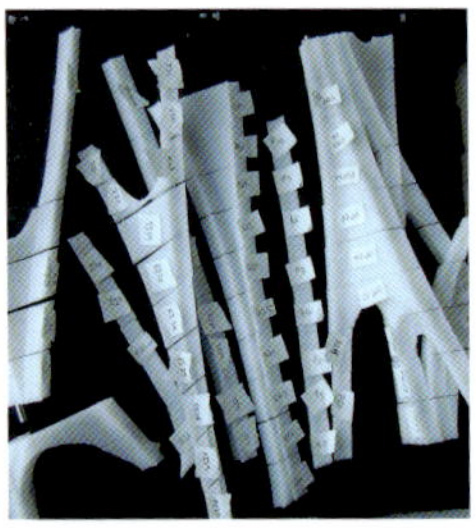
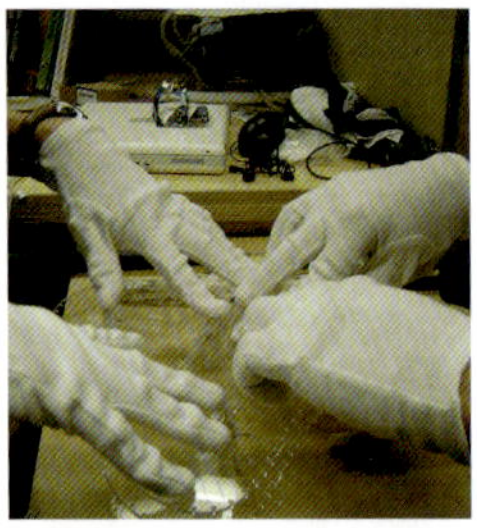

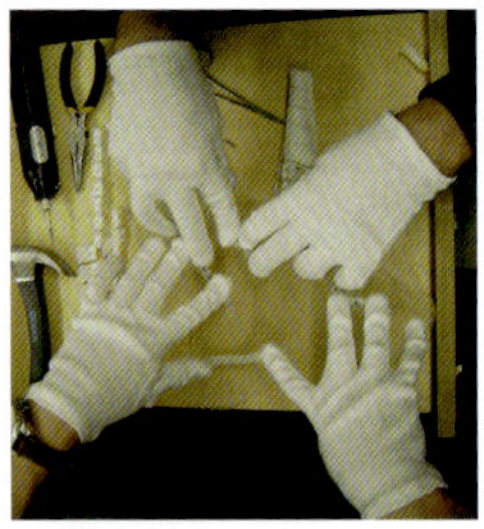
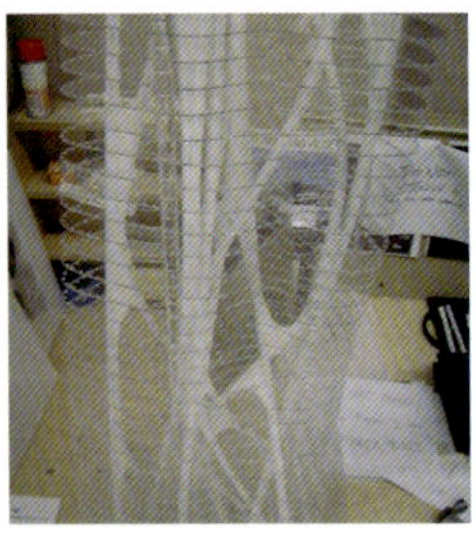
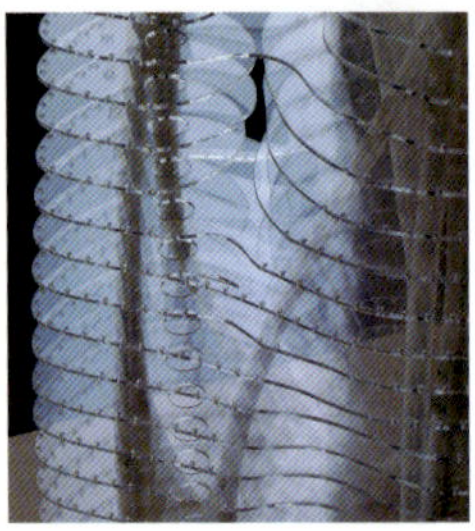
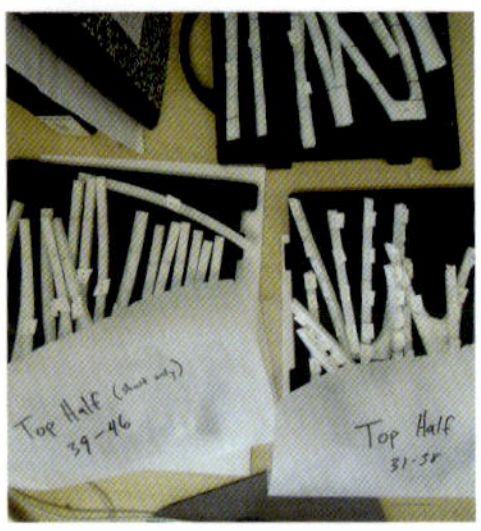
Top Half
Top Half

FUTURE LAS VEGAS
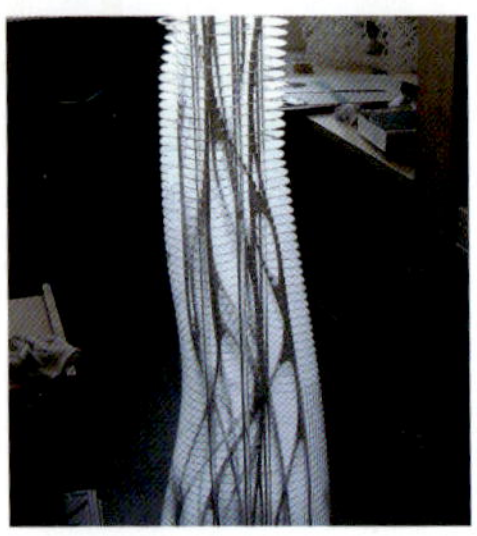

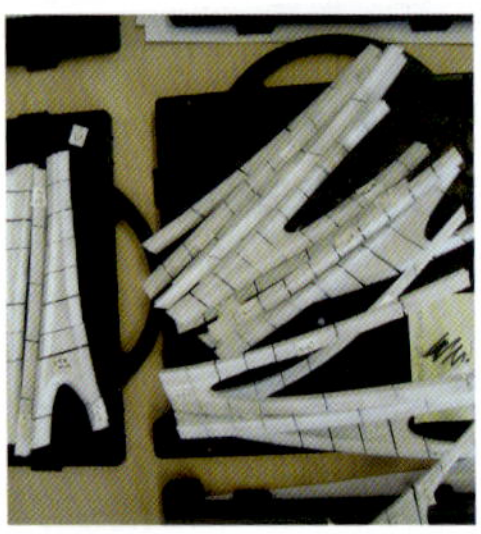

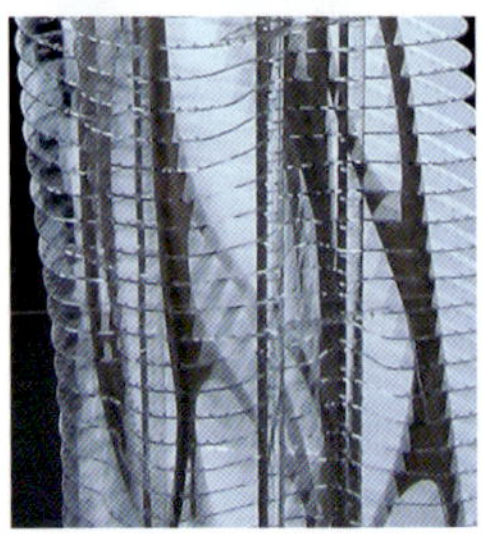

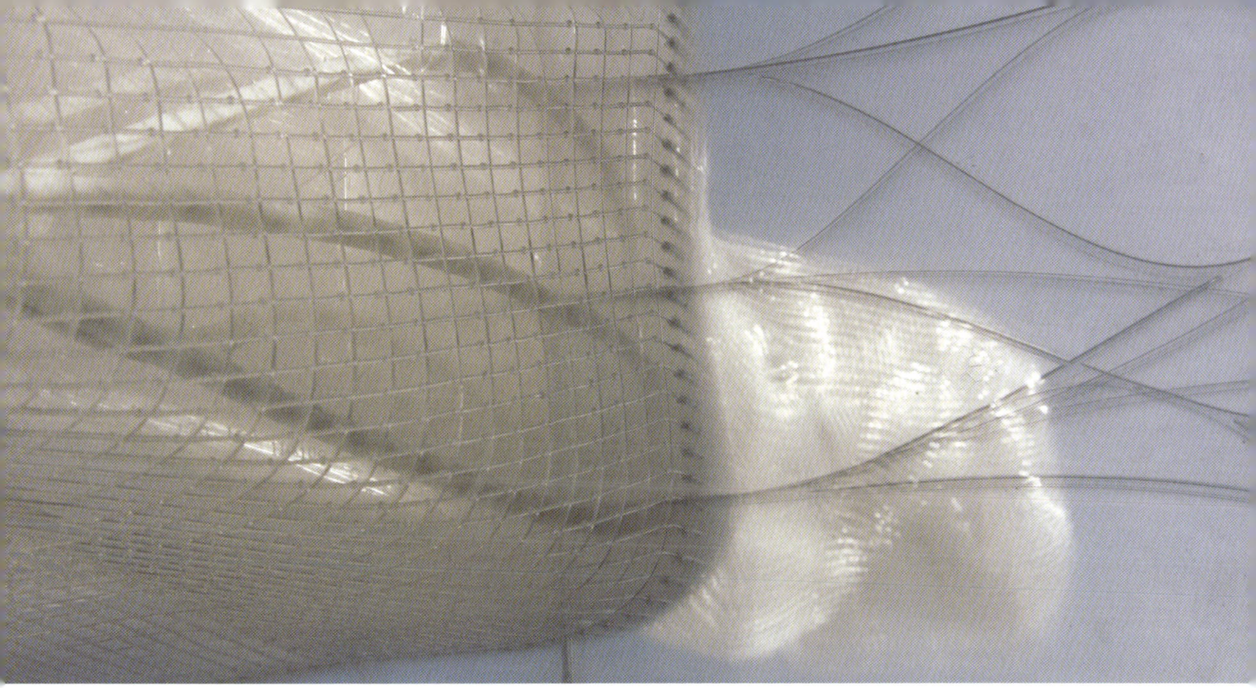

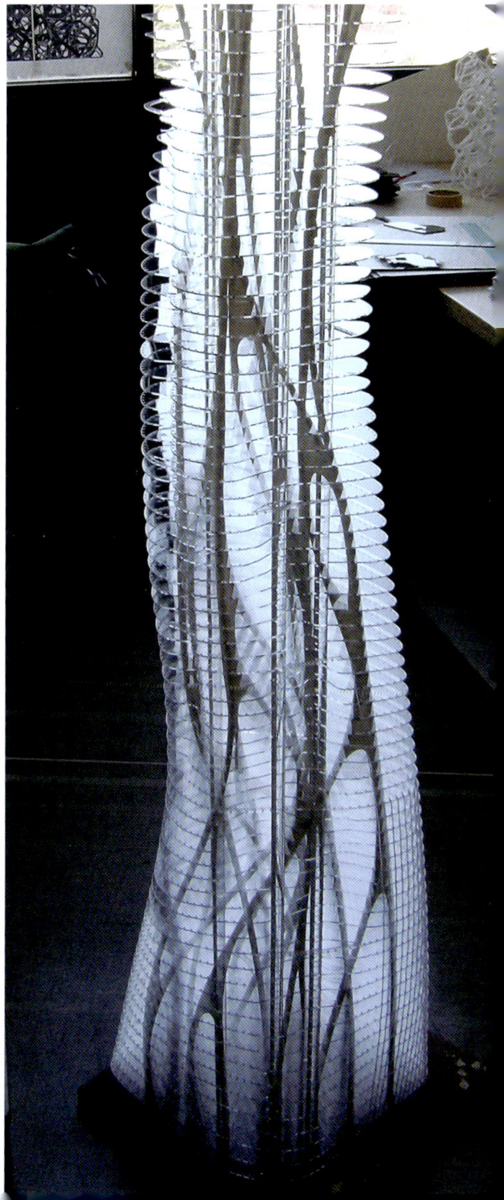

Hong Kong site analysis

The chosen site is located in the Wan Chai District of Hong Kong. Today Wan Chai is described as the heart of the city, representing the epitome of the Hong Kong lifestyle. Within the district is a well-established arts centre, the large exhibition and conference complexes, luxury apartments, five-star and other hotels, shopping malls, metropolitan office towers and a large government building cluster. Due to the diversity of building types we felt the Oracle Corporation would reinforce this internationally important district of Hong Kong. We have chosen a large site allowing the building to impact only a portion of the site developing the rest of the site as a public green space which are few and far between in this dense district of Hong Kong.

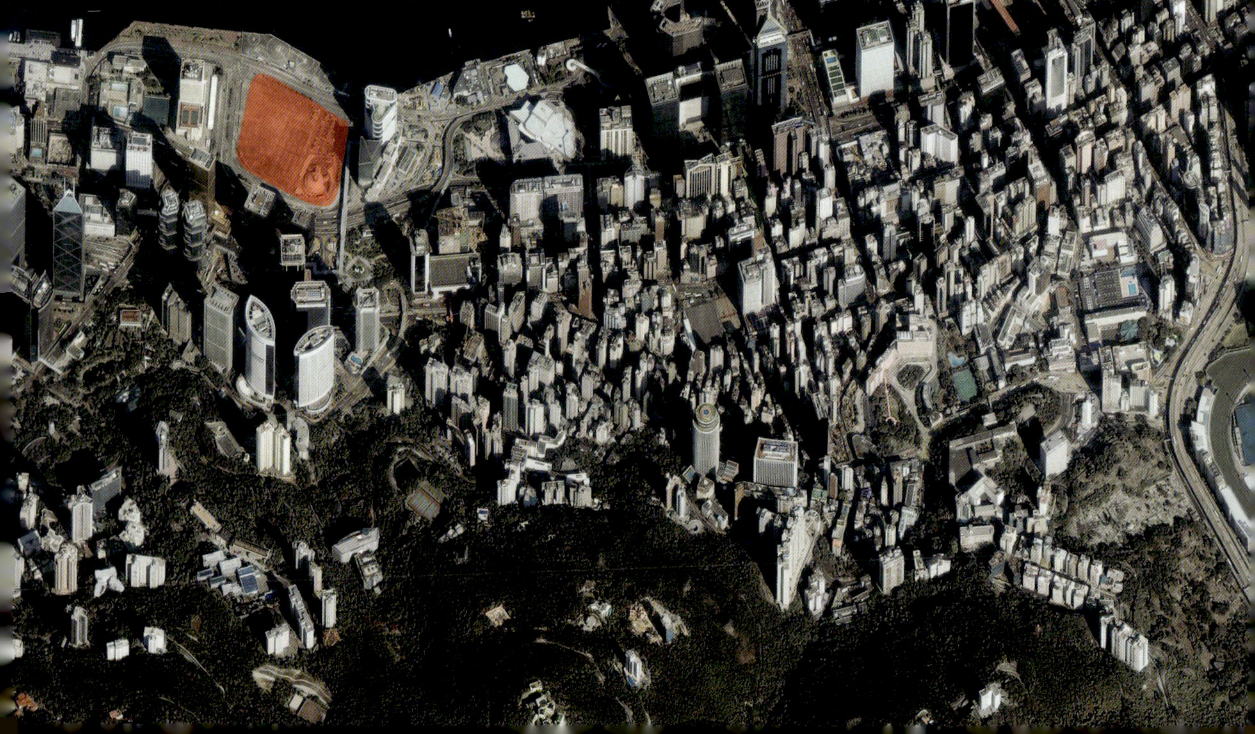

Program Analysis

Oracle is a company leaping from its grid platforms into flexible, adaptable networks seeking to provide dynamic, yet reliable systems to its broad customer base. The reach of Oracle extends exponentially past the single-market industry, combining a staggering array of industry-leading companies and applications under one name. The adaptable cluster framework supported by the company is also a concept from which it grows - adjusting and expanding through strong connections and tangential vectors which form the fabric of operation. With such a range of unique and diverse groups and ideas under one name, the need for diverse space and application environments are readily evident.

In the Oracle Tower, we have captured and embedded many of these concepts into the structure of the building itself. Exerting the natural influence of flexible networks onto a system of Grid Control has yielded a space of diverse connectivity and unique application potential. Dynamic in the integration of open-based framework and cross-application transaction, the structure grid is a physical product of inhabitable connectivity, as well as a 'maximum unique architecture' providing a wide menu of custom spaces suited for a mega-facited operation.

We have essentially gotten the most out of our Grid.

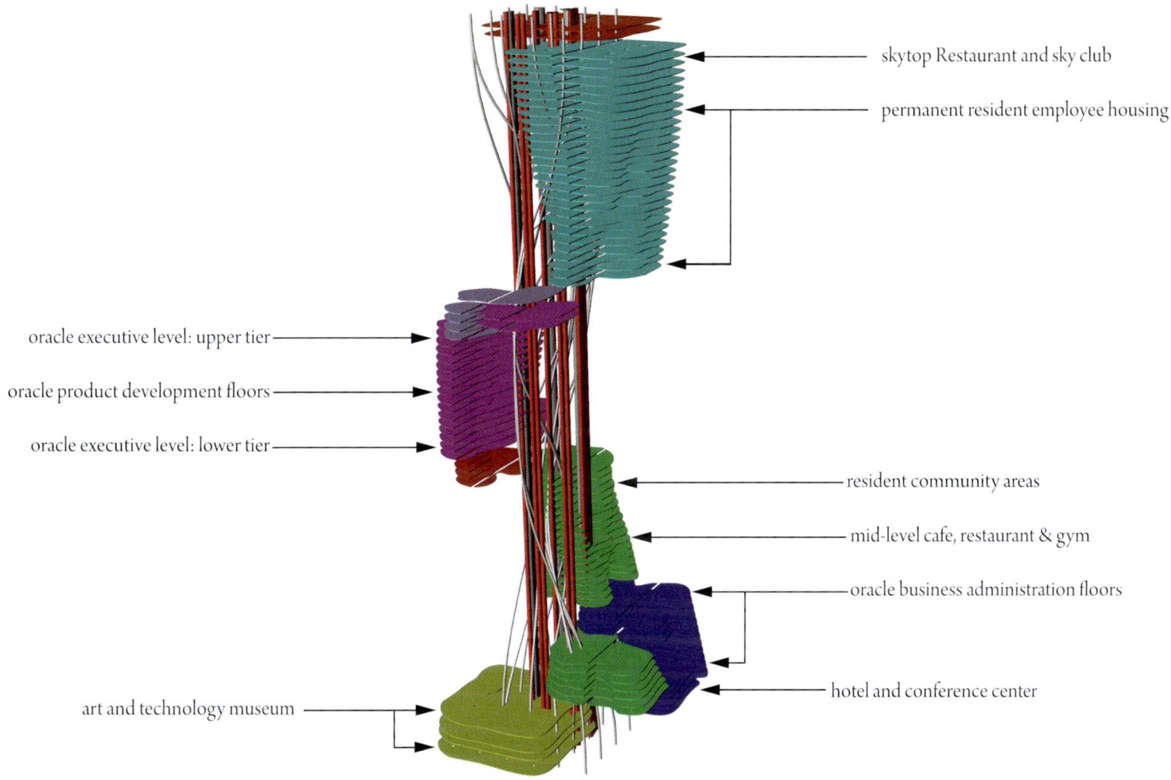

SHARP

EPSON

Braiding Tower

Cameron Bishop & Mara Neumann

The Braiding Tower is based on an understanding of both the aesthetic and technical possibilities afforded by the textile technique of braiding. Braiding can be simply defined as "interweaving three or more strands, strips, or lengths in a diagonally overlapping pattern". Because braiding already exists as a technique used to create useful and culturally expressive constructs (baskets, ropes, plaiting, hair braiding, etc) it is easy to imagine its potential to accommodate both structural and aesthetic needs. The Braiding Tower represents just such a confluence of structure and ornament, performance and aesthetics, technology and culture.

The simplicity of how braiding is defined might defy the complexity and abundance of its possible applications but it is precisely this vagueness of definition that allows for variation within the system. The diagonal, over-under relationship of strands is essentially the only rule and so the relative nature of the relationship of strands; either in size, shape, orientation, or proximity; allows for a variety of features and conditions within the system. Two of the main operations performed within this system rely on proximity of strands (or strand density) as well as the twisting of strands (or strand orientation). In theory the strongest and most compact braided envelope (if made of flat strands) would be of maximum density and of uniform orientation. However, this system would not lend itself as a building envelope. The system must undergo deformations and transformations to accommodate the programmatic requirements of a skyscraper such as lighting, connectivity, and variations in size and use.

There is an overriding tensile logic based on a series of implied ribs that follow a catenary curve from the top of the tower to the ground. The building's surface drapes from one catenary rib to the next. A core of vertical columns acts in compression and carries the load of the tensile ribs to the ground. A series of strands braids diagonally across the surface creating a tensile membrane that both supports the floor slabs and creates the building envelope. The twisting of the strands opens the system forming window-like apertures while the density of the strands is increased at the ribs to accommodate the increased load. At times the system undergoes a dramatic transformation when strands are broken and reorganize to form a new system that branches out like an appendage briding between towers.

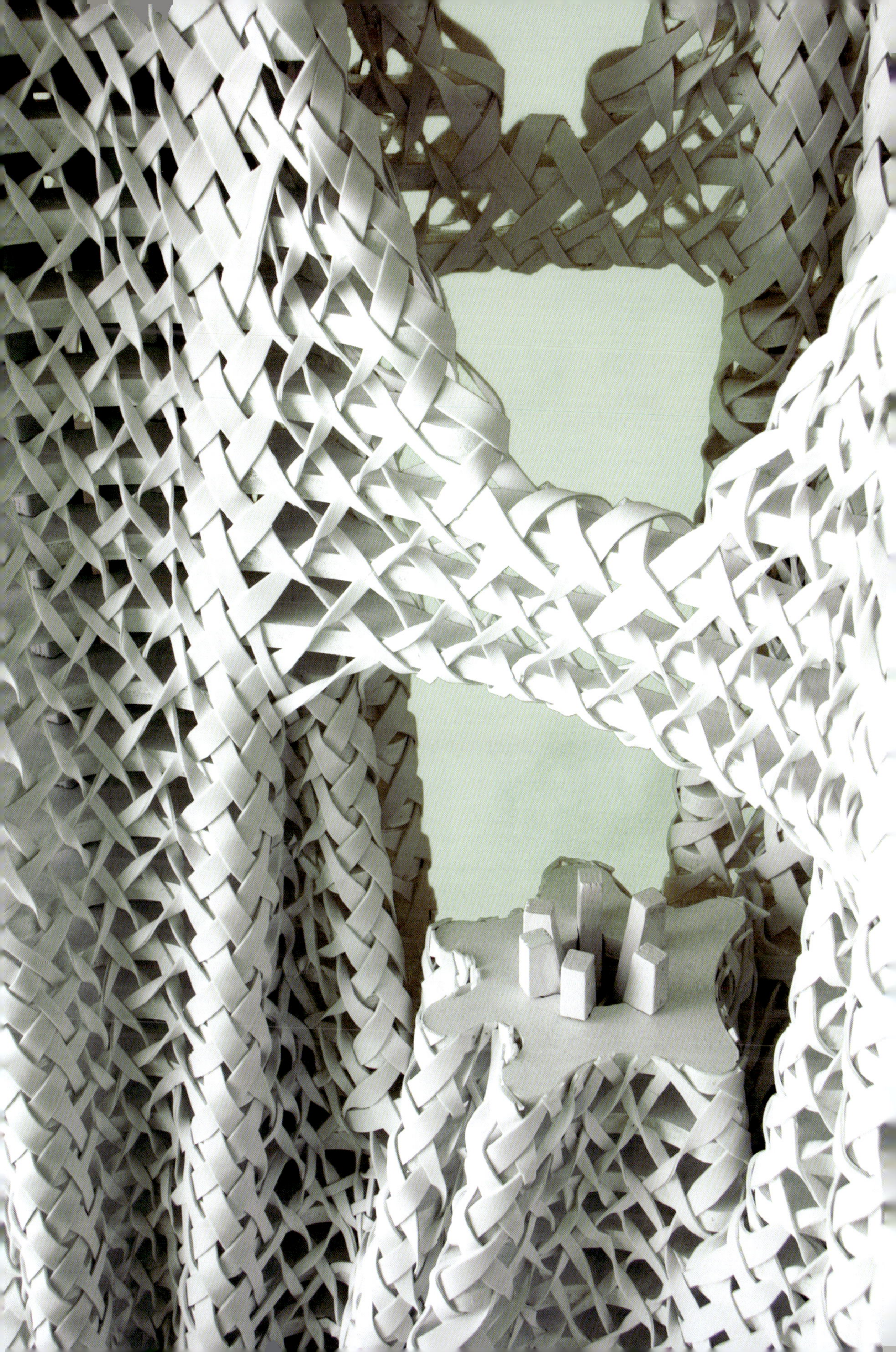

ORDINAL

CARDINAL

quantity. counting numbers or rationa
numbers
for example: 1, 2, 3, . . .

idealize — represent — realize

1D — 2D — 3D

concept — diagram — object

BRAIDING

\brā-diŋ

a. to interweave three or more strands, strips, or lengths in a diagonally overlapping pattern in which each strand crosses every other strand given a regular continuous pattern.
b. to create (something) by such interweaving: braid a rug.
c. to style (the hair) by such interweaving.
d. to mingle (discrete elements, for example) as if by such interweaving: braided the ideas into a complex thesis.

NOT BRAIDING

knot
a. an interlacing, twining, looping, etc., of a single cord, rope or the like.
b. a piece of ribbon or similar material tied or folded upon itself.
c. (topologically) embedding of a circle in 3D euclidian space.

twist
z to combine, as two or more strands or threads, by winding together.
b. to wind or coil (something) about something else.

weave
a. to interlace as to form a fabric or material out of warp (vertical) threads and weft (horizontal) threads that do not necessarily interact with all other threads in the material.

configuration

(at least 3 strands)
flat

strand

round
(at least 4 strands)

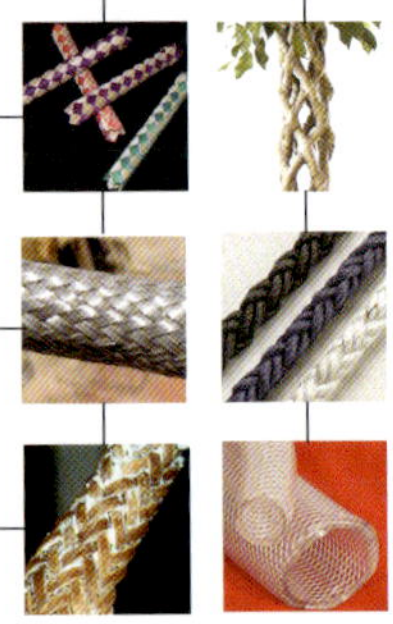

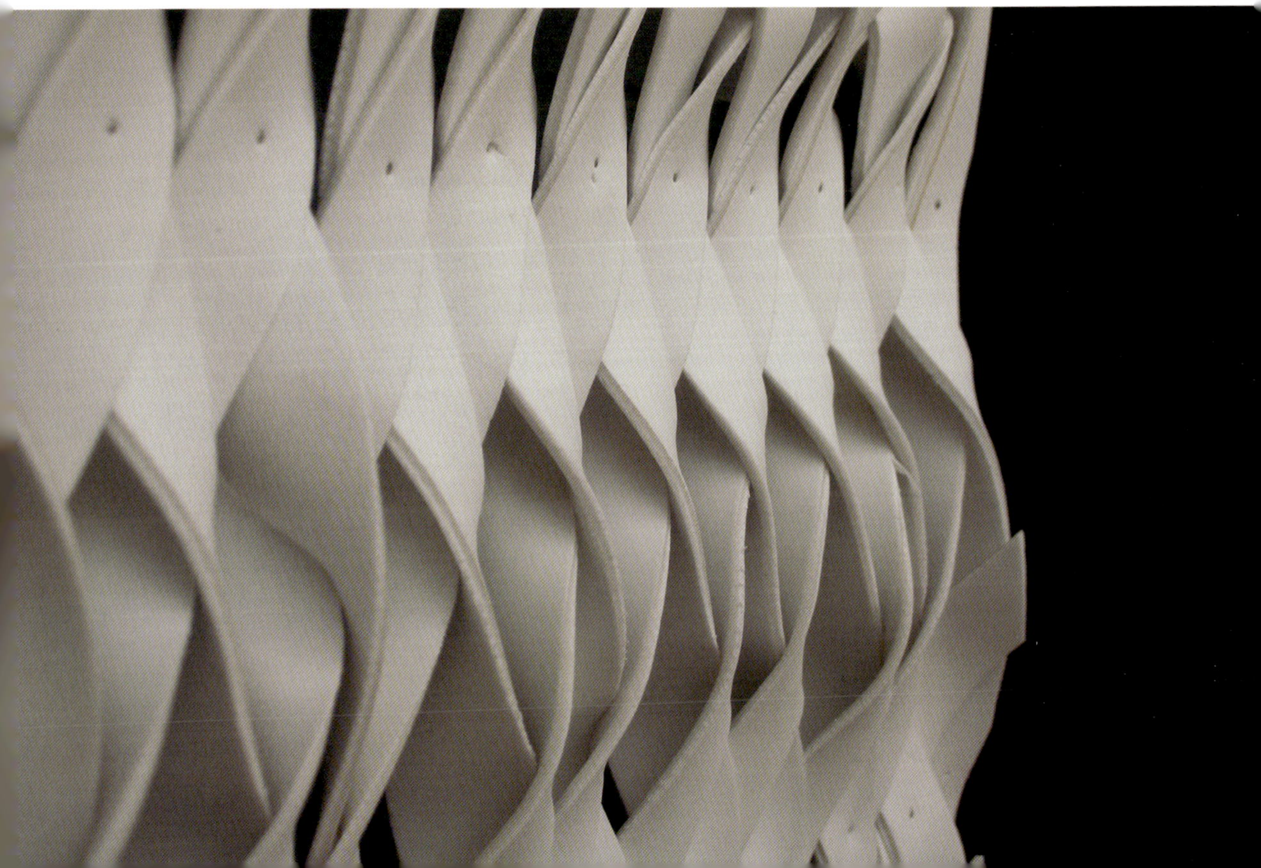

3d flat braids

EX: 4 - 1a.2a.3b.4b...

(4) - (1) (a) . (2) (a) . (3) (b) . (4) (b) . (..)

KEY: (strand#) - (position) (rotation) . (position) (rotation) . (position) (rotation) . (position) (rotation) . (repeat)

position read: left to right ; top to bottom

a: rotation away from braid center

b: rotation toward braid center

therefore a braid described as : 4 - 1a.2a.3b.4b... looks like this:

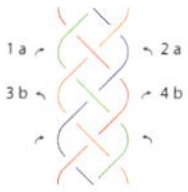

3 - 1_.2_.3_.4_...

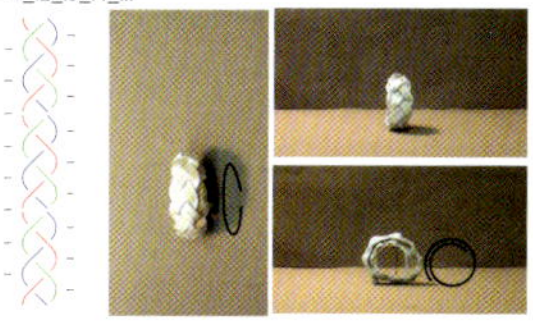

4 - 1_.2_.3_.4_...

3 - 1a.2b.3a.4b...

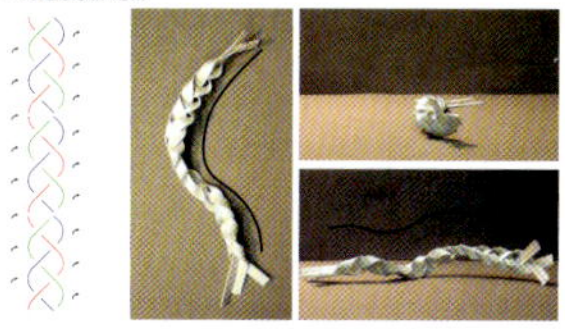

4 - 1a.2b.3a.4b...

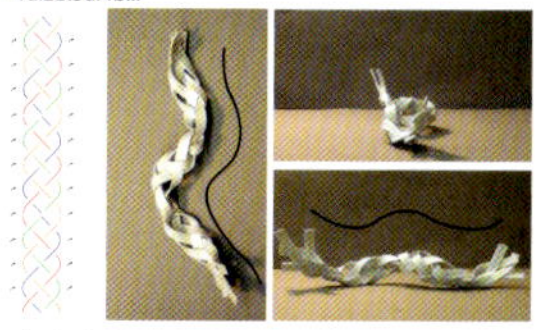

3 - 1a.2a.3a.4a...

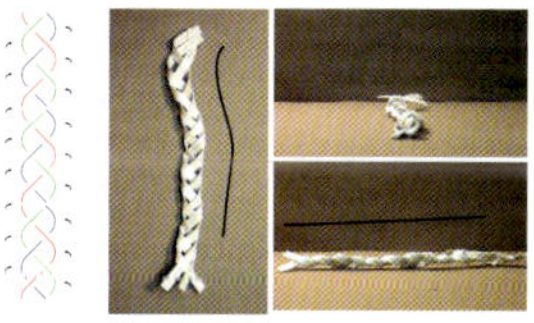

4 - 1a.2a.3a.4a...

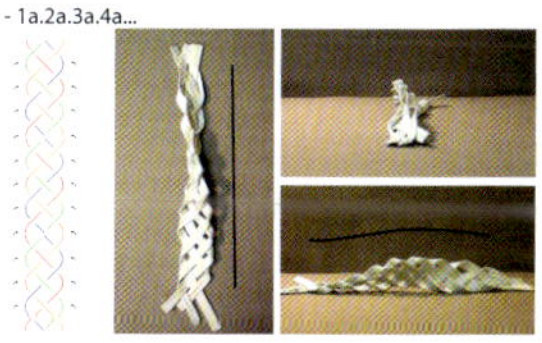

3 - 1b.2b.3b.4b...

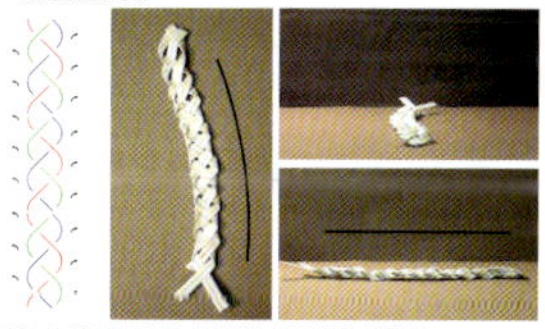

4 - 1b.2b.3b.4b...

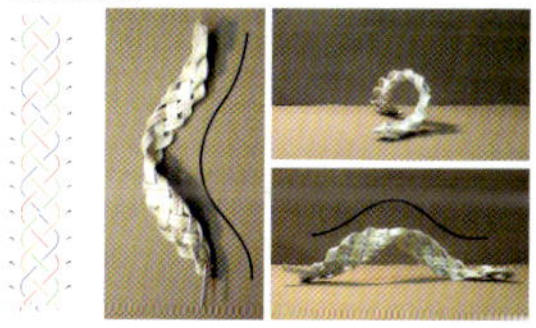

3 - 1a.2a.3b.4b...

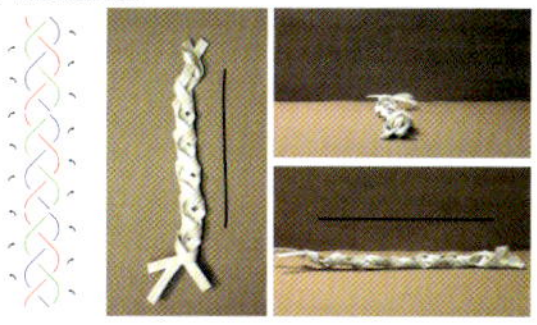

4 - 1a.2a.3b.4b...

3 - 1a.2b.3b.4a...

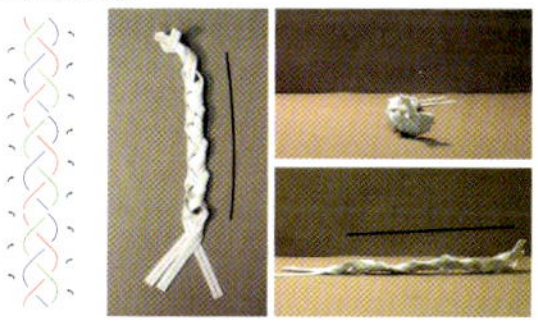

4 - 1a.2b.3b.4a...

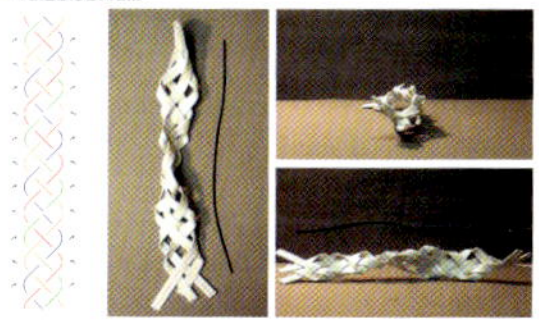

7 & 8 STRAND ANALOG BRAIDS

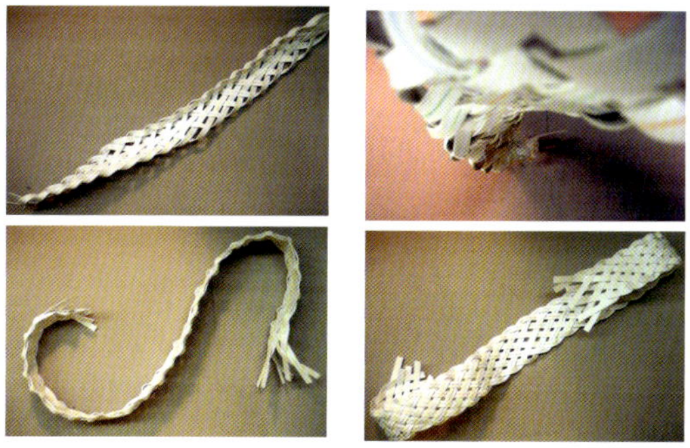

3d round braids

local variations

regular

switch

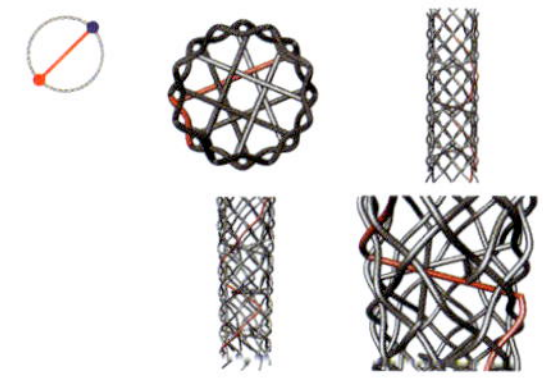

stray

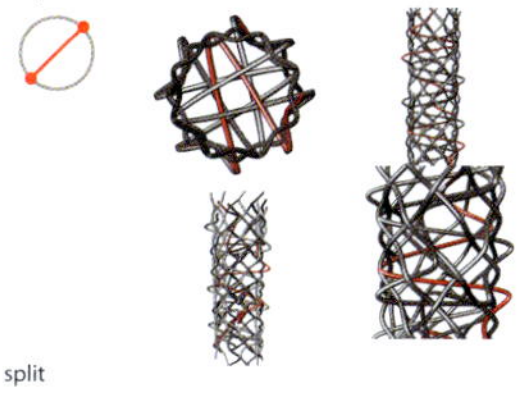

split

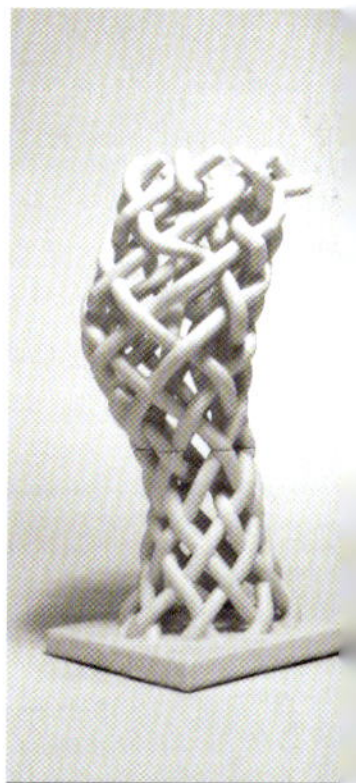

system variations

furcation

branching

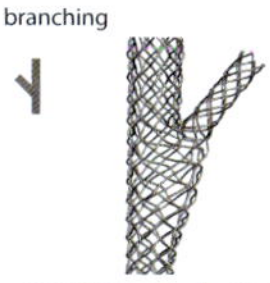

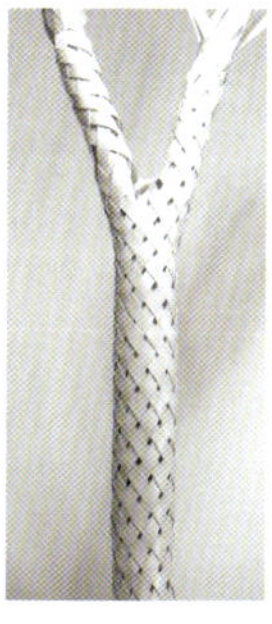

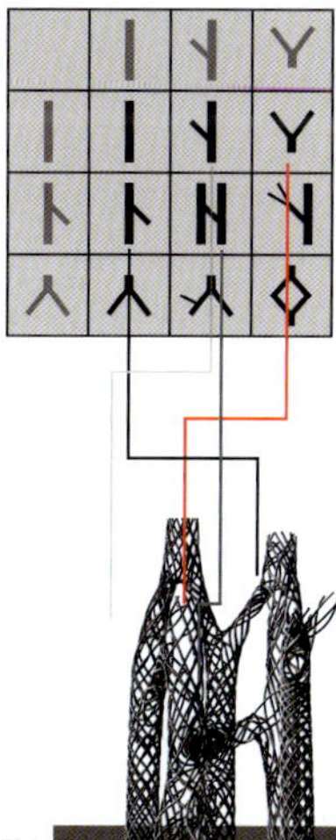

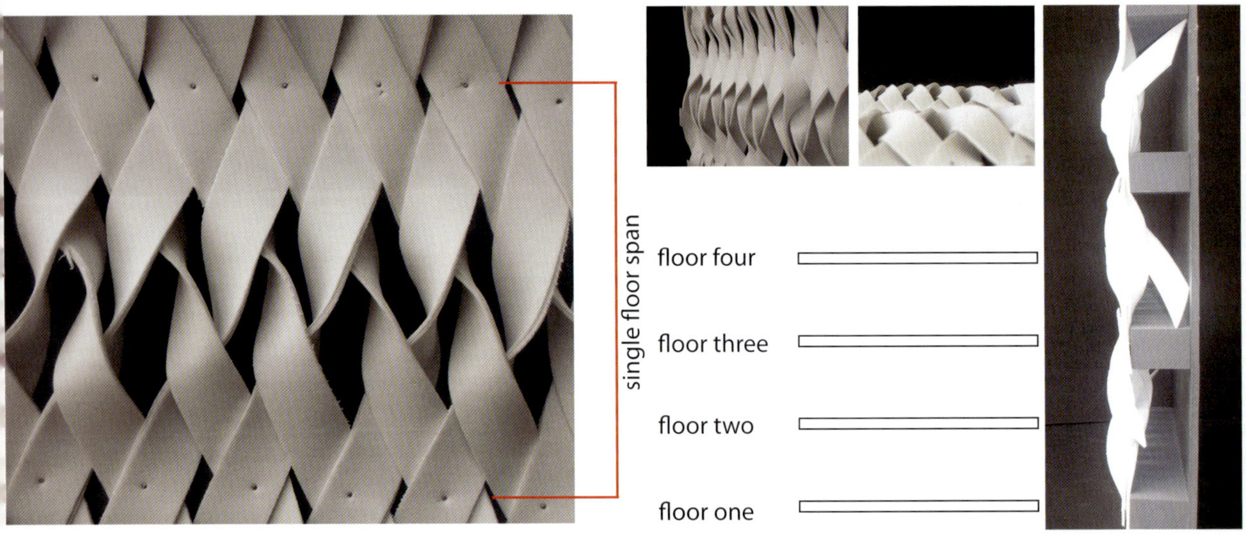
single floor span
floor four
floor three
floor two
floor one

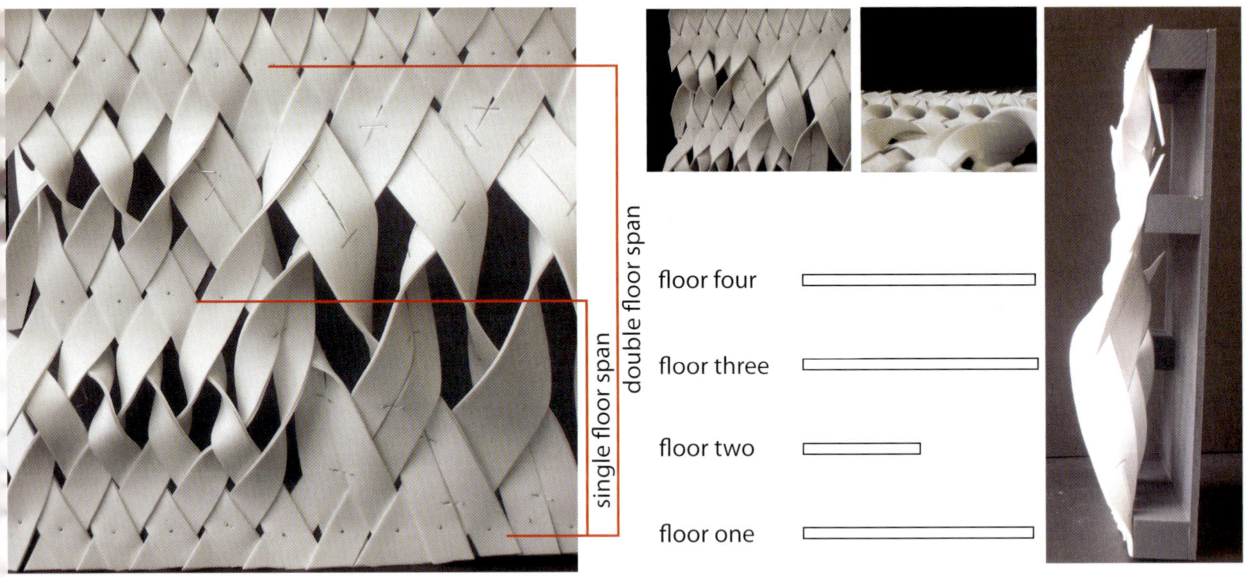
single floor span
double floor span
floor four
floor three
floor two
floor one

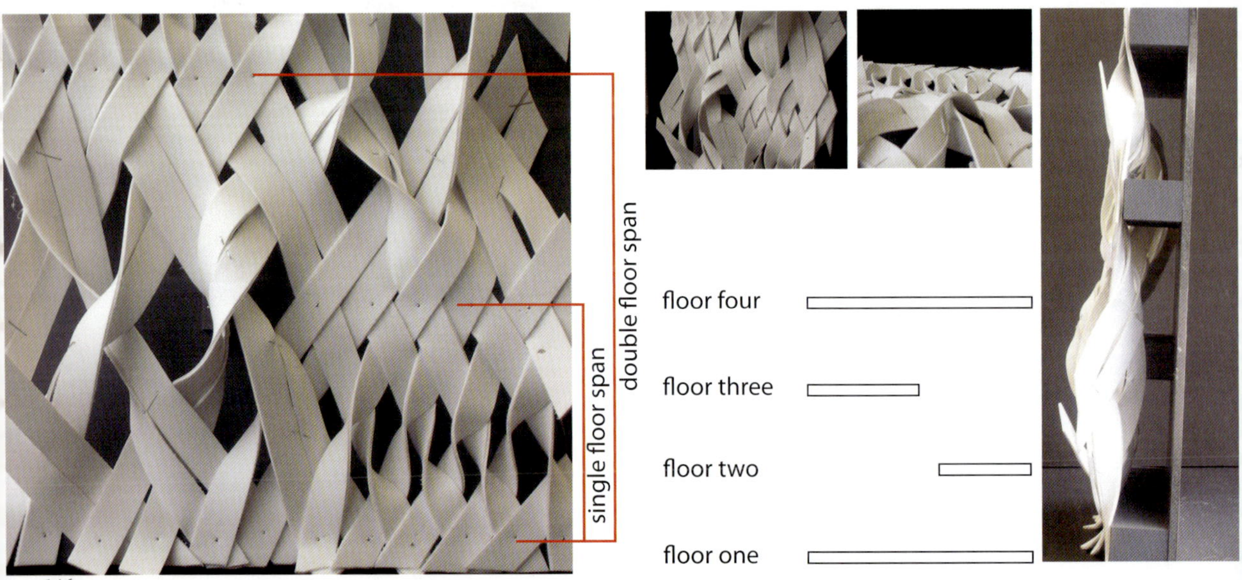
single floor span
double floor span
floor four
floor three
floor two
floor one

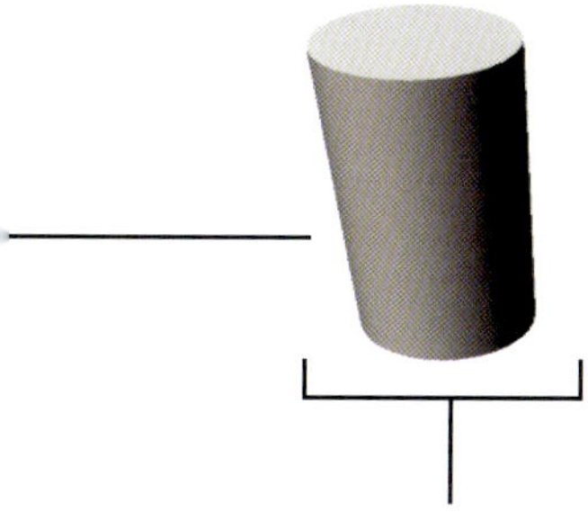

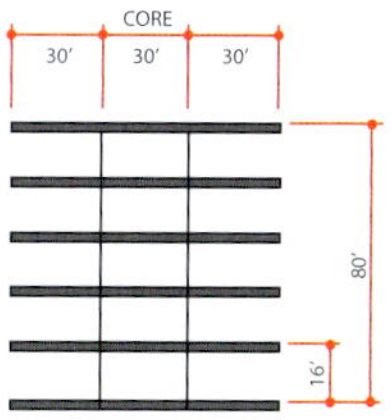

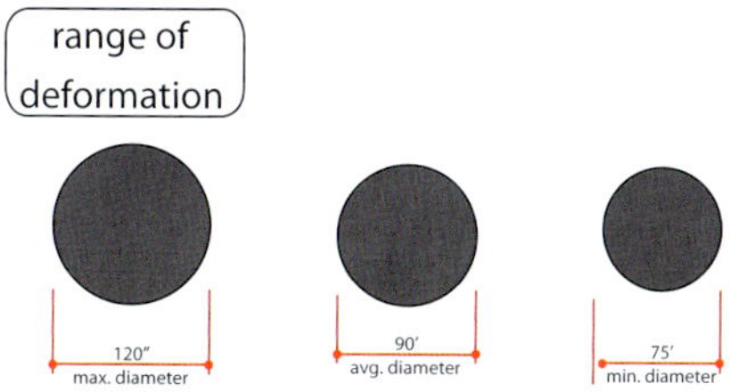

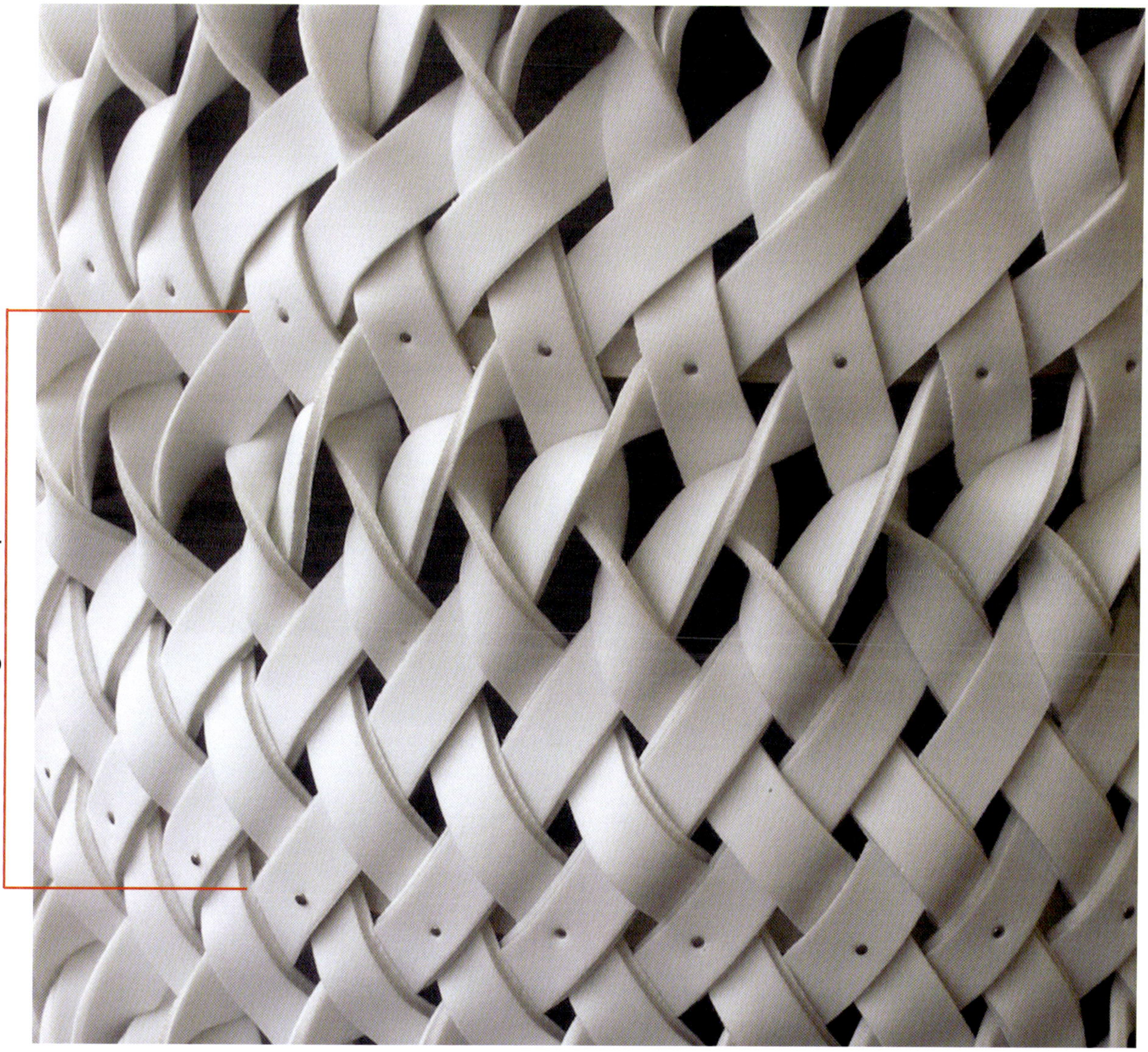

single floor span

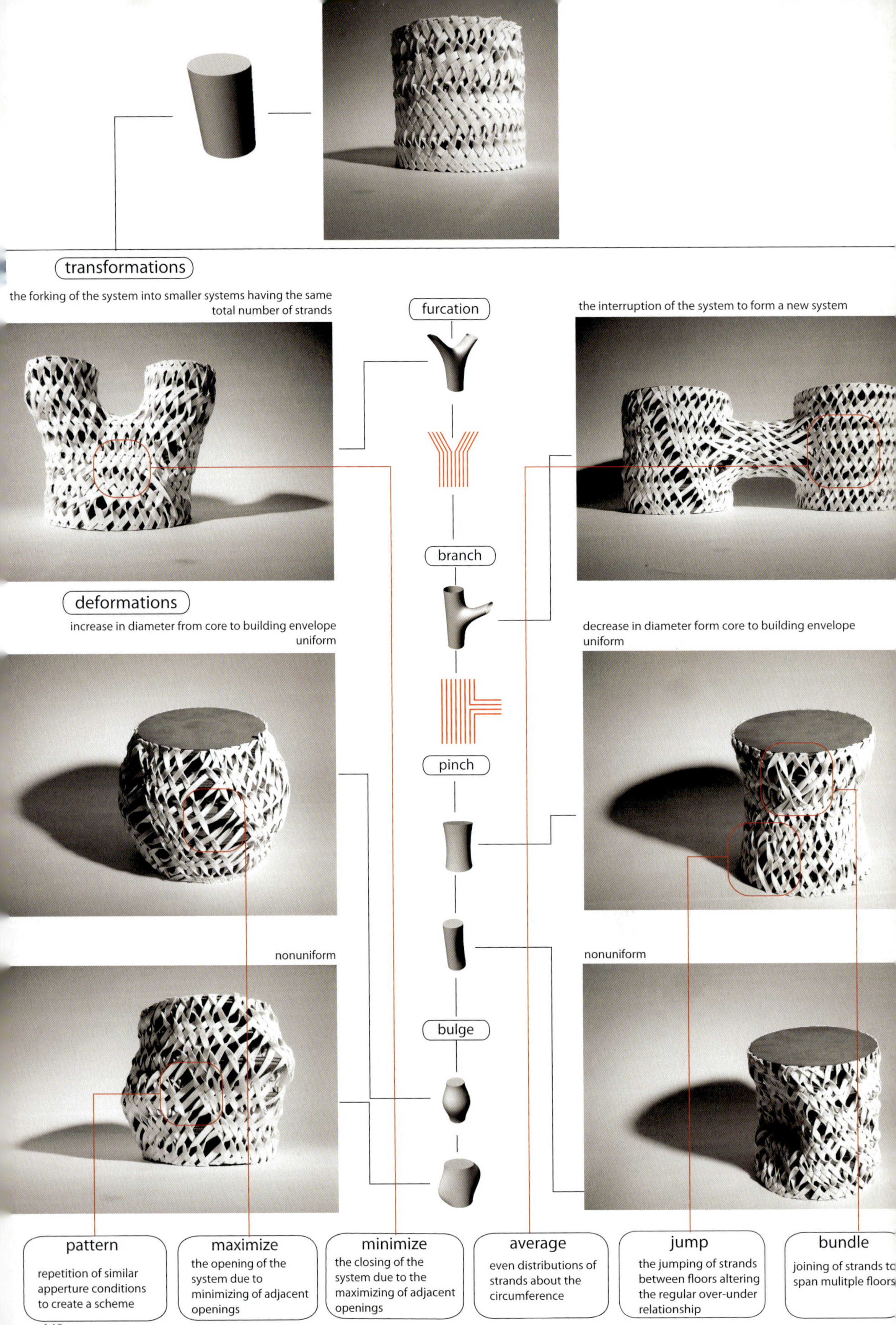
transformations
the forking of the system into smaller systems having the same total number of strands
furcation
the interruption of the system to form a new system
branch
deformations
increase in diameter from core to building envelope
uniform
pinch
decrease in diameter form core to building envelope
uniform
nonuniform
bulge
nonuniform
pattern
repetition of similar apperture conditions to create a scheme
maximize
the opening of the system due to minimizing of adjacent openings
minimize
the closing of the system due to the maximizing of adjacent openings
average
even distributions of strands about the circumference
jump
the jumping of strands between floors altering the regular over-under relationship
bundle
joining of strands to span mulitple floors

gaudi inverted

catenary variations

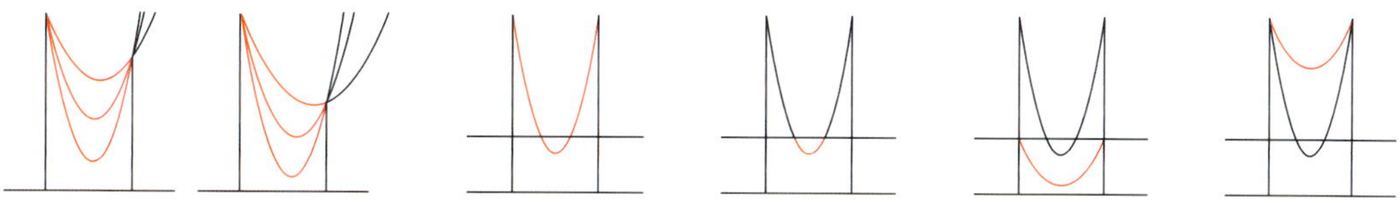

possible connections

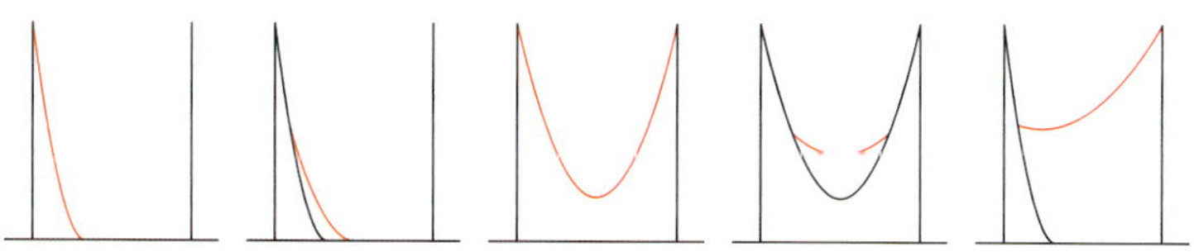

suspension bridge study

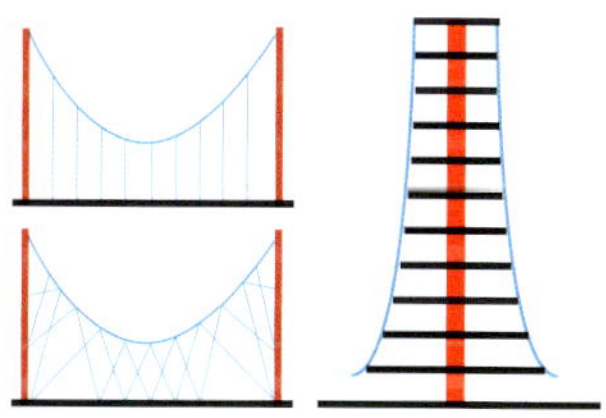

catenary + surface

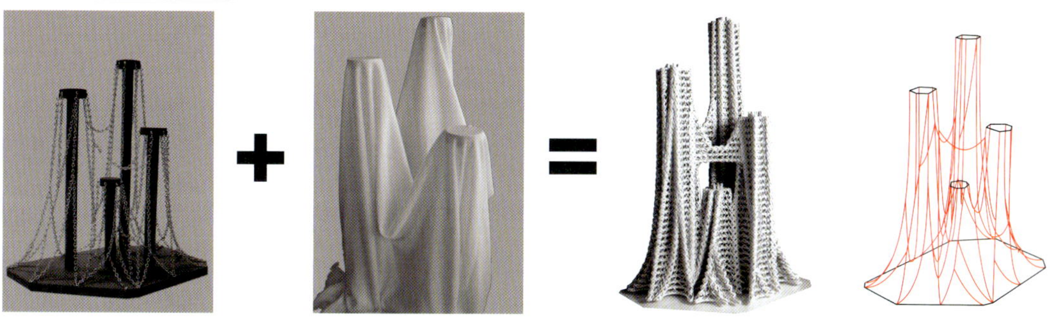

dubai

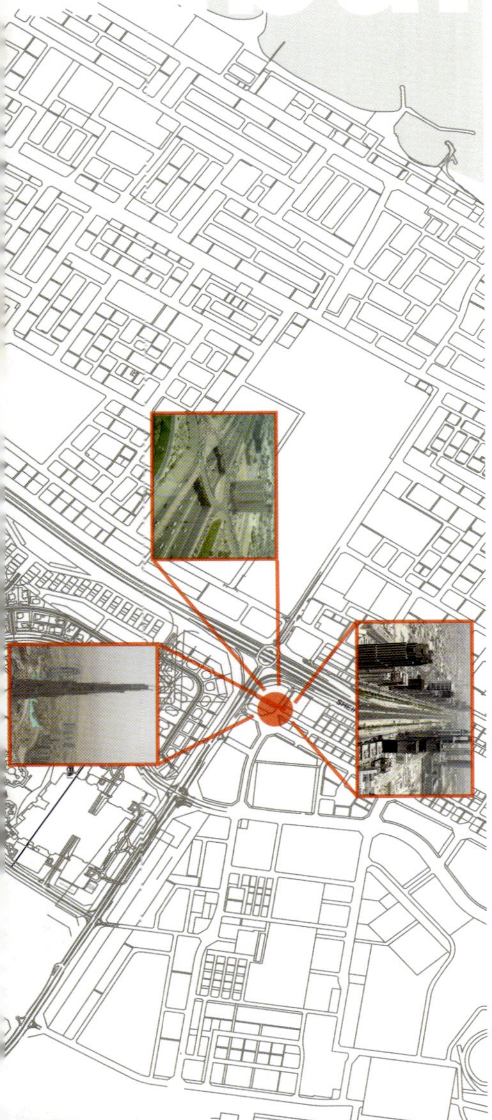

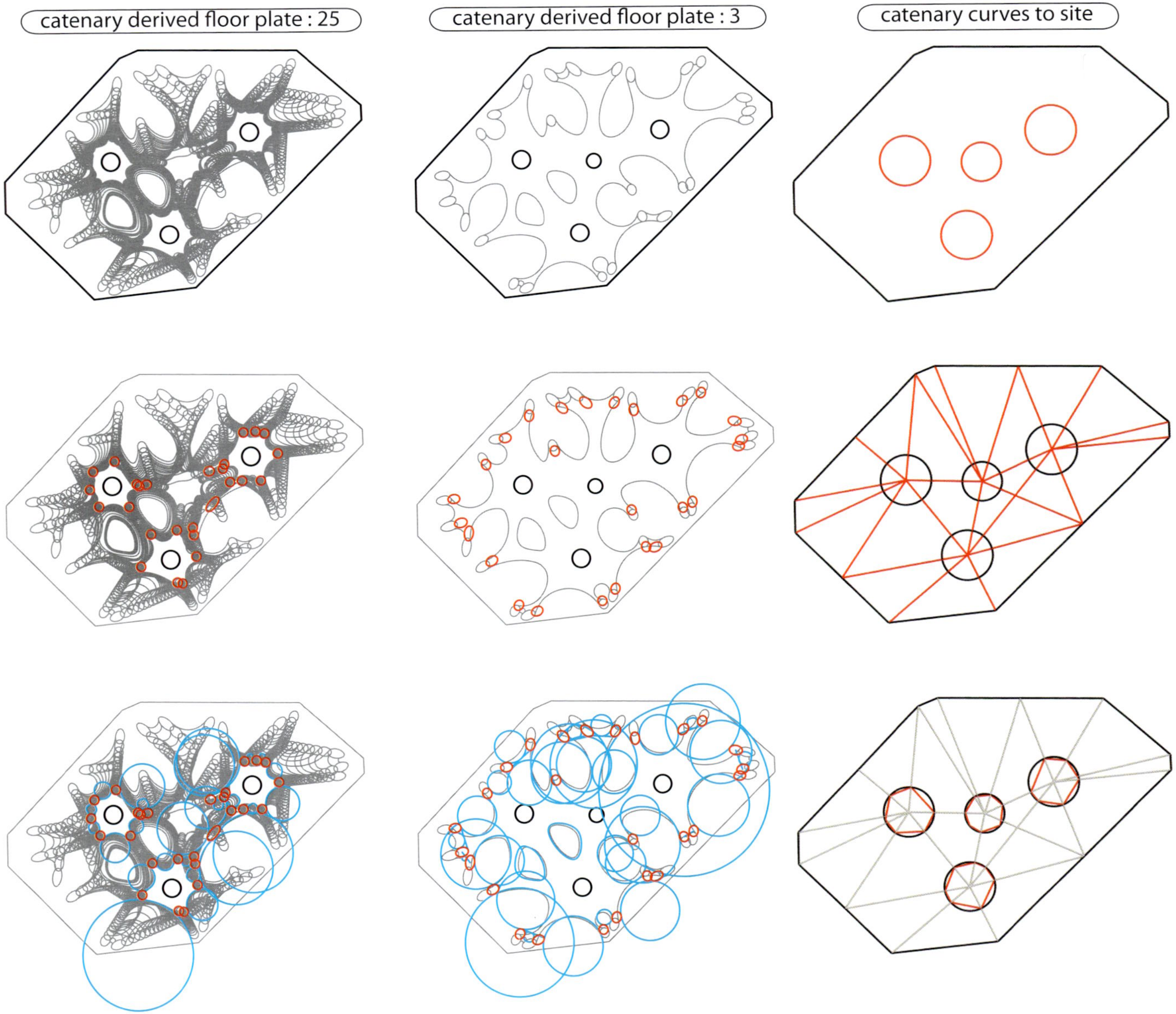
catenary derived floor plate : 25
catenary derived floor plate : 3
catenary curves to site

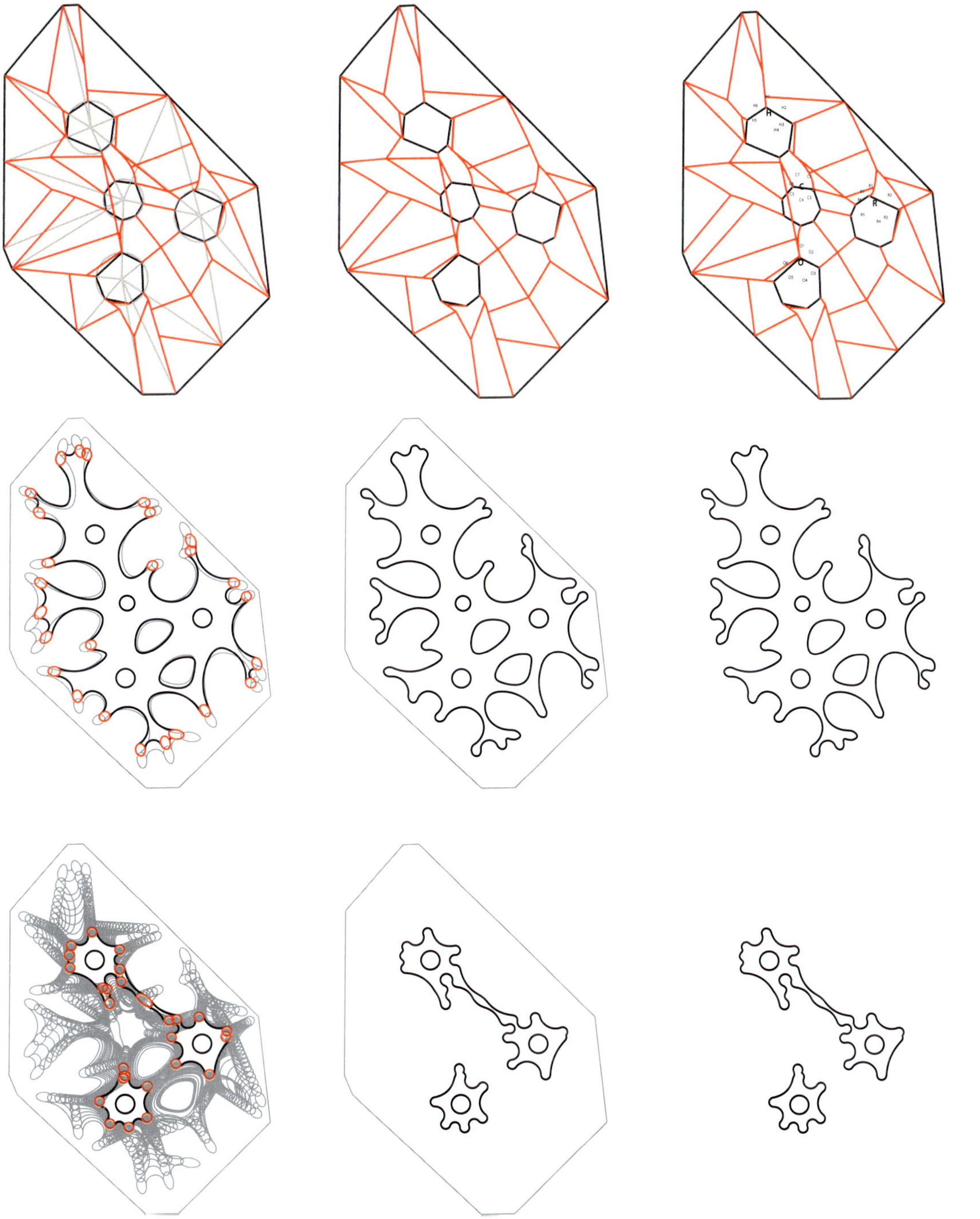

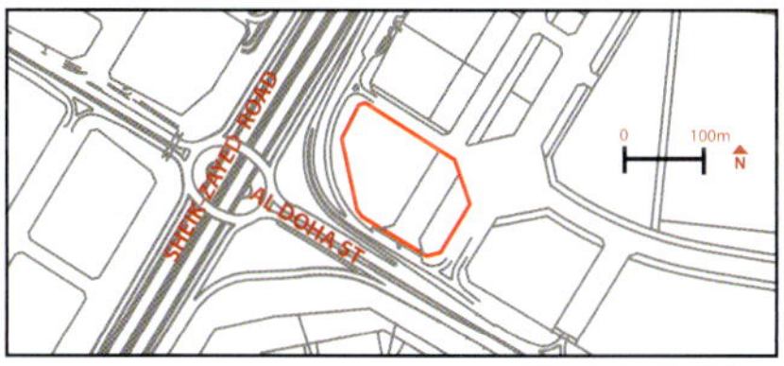

SHEIK ZAYED ROAD
AL DOHA ST
0
100m
N

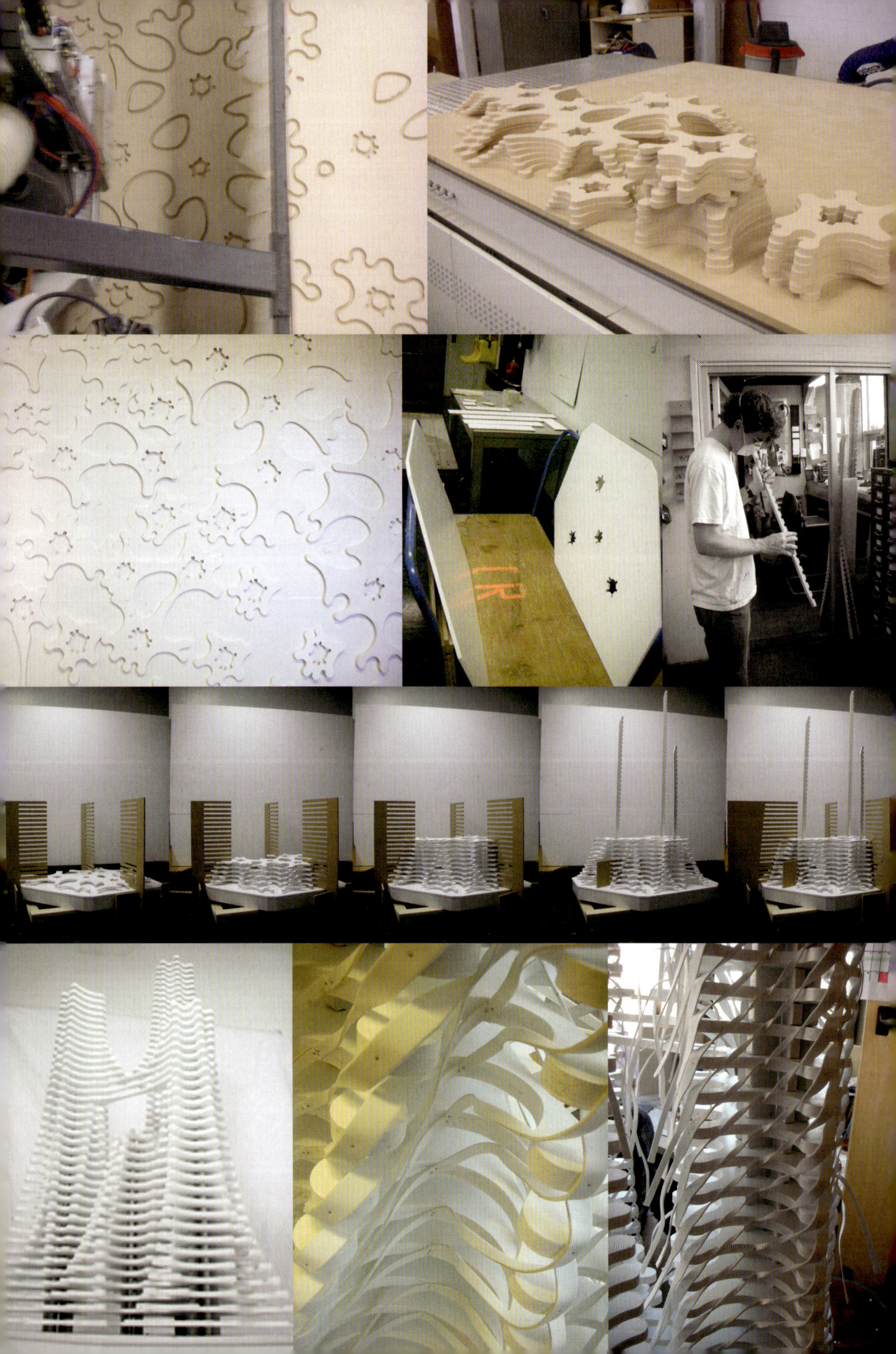

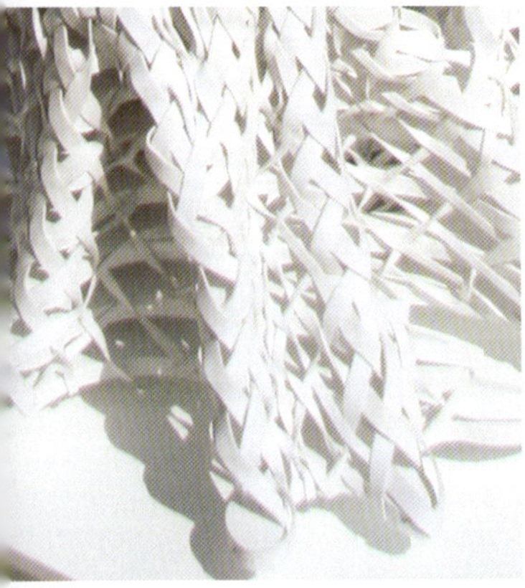

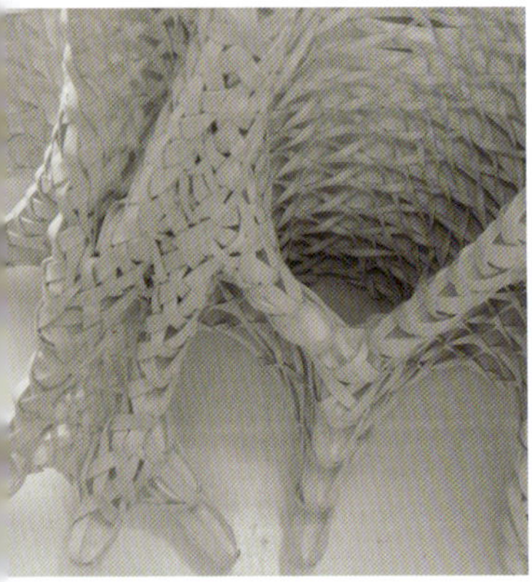

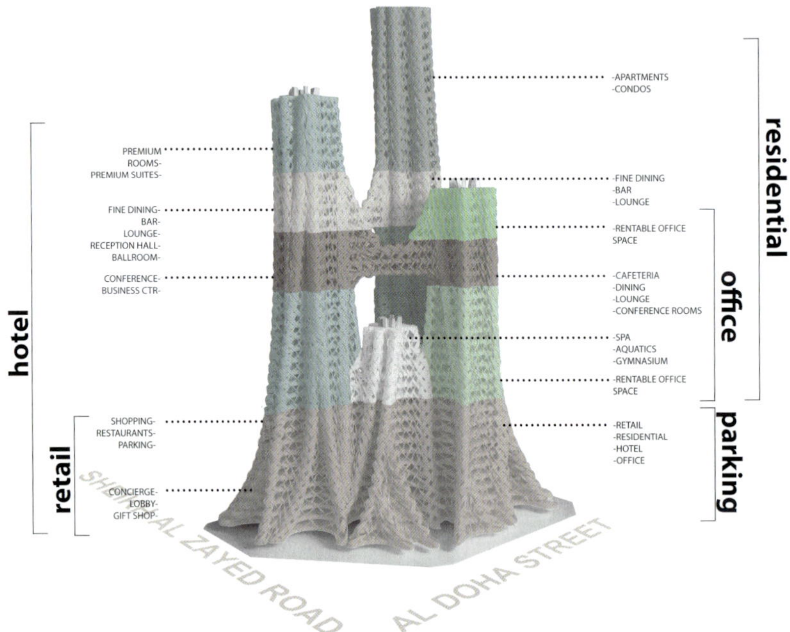

tensile construction

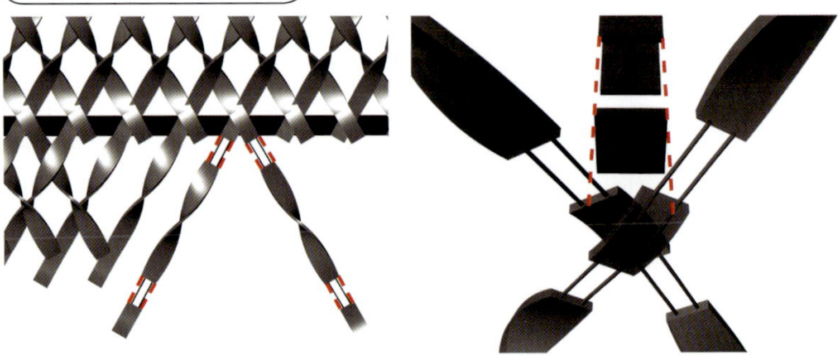

Gothic Tower

Sookie Kim & Rae Smith

"The gothic architect approached stone with a desire for purely spiritual expression, that is to say, with structural intentions conceived artistically and independently from stone, and for which stone was only the external and submission means for realization." *Form in Gothic,* Wilhelm Worringer

The Gothic Tower explores the various figures found in the lattice work of gothic ornament as a diagram for a skyscraper's structure. According to Worringer, an abstract system of construction is the result of stone playing a merely tectonic, yet not intentionally artistic, role. By divorcing the figures from the material they are wed to by the gothic cathedrals, the figures are allowed to become a diagram that can contribute to the aesthetic and sensorial qualities of a space. Gothic figures are particularly becoming of the skyscraper's program through their inherent verticality. The project is based on the classic idea of the Gothic: the interlacing, the networking of curved lines into complex configurations. These configurations are then self-stabilizing as they are specifically linked through researched methods of gothic figure pairing.

Through a rigorous process of simplifying gothic ornament into three figures; a J-curve, S-curve, and C-curve; we have created a tool for varying and re-interpreting gothic forms into structural components. This process identifies potential figures, places the figures into pairs and the pairs into fields as a basis for developing of new techniques of geometrical articulation in the tower's massing. The idea is that the variability of a figure is directly connected to an emergent effect of configuration. Because of the system of continuity, the structure does not need distinguished structural elements, rather, the forces gradually transfer through the bundled columns in a way resembling the structural logic of gothic cathedrals.

FIGURE GEOMETRY

PIN CONTROL TANGENT CONTROL

spear

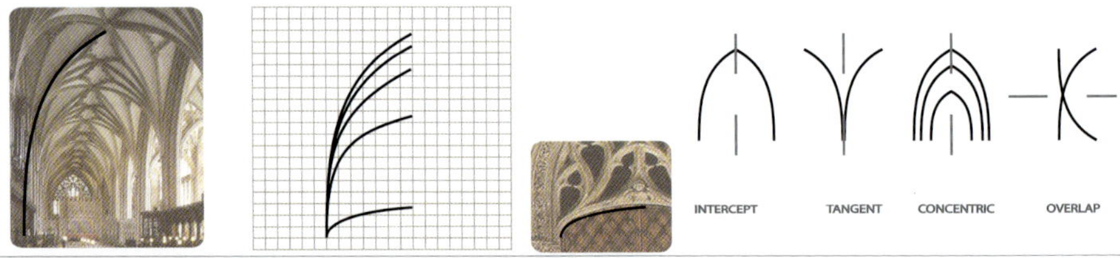

INTERCEPT TANGENT CONCENTRIC OVERLAP

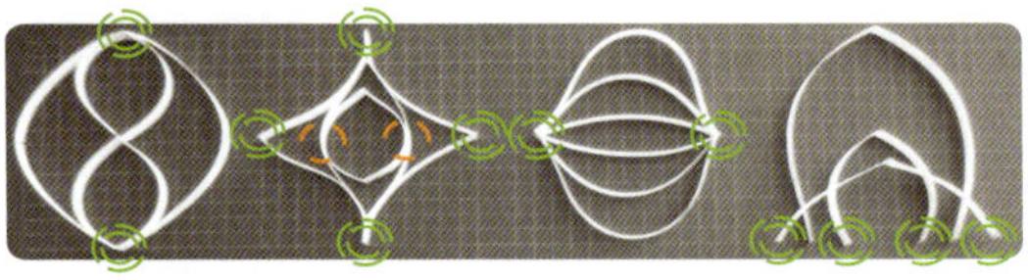

INTERCEPT TANGENT CONCENTRIC OVERLAP

PAPER / PIN MODELS

CONTROL STUDY

c-curve

INTERCEPT TANGENT CONCENTRIC OVERLAP

CONTROL STUDY

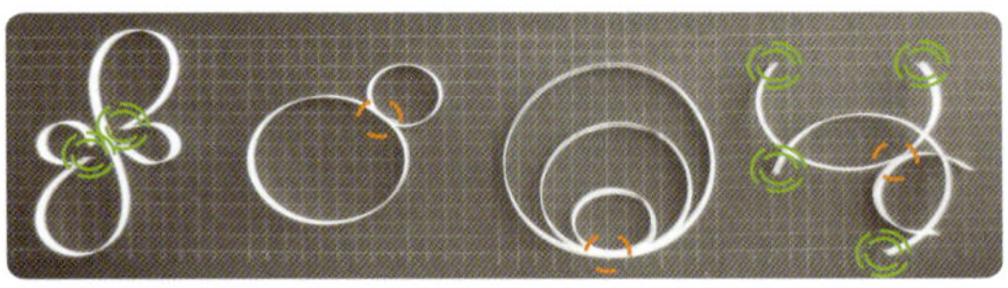

INTERCEPT TANGENT CONCENTRIC OVERLAP

PAPER / PIN MODELS

j-curve

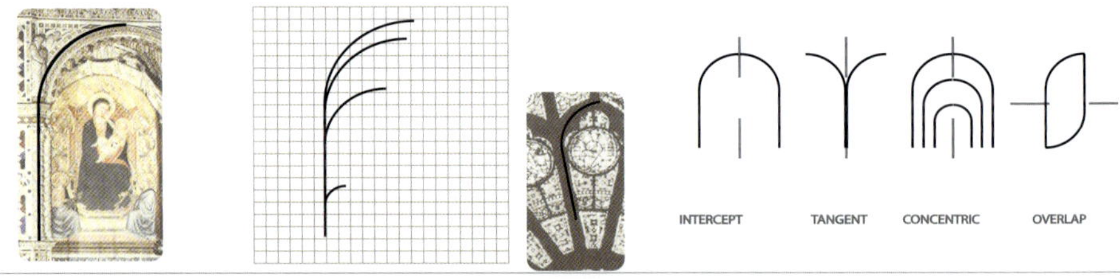

INTERCEPT TANGENT CONCENTRIC OVERLAP

INTERCEPT TANGENT CONCENTRIC OVERLAP

PAPER / PIN MODELS

CONTROL STUDY

s-curve

INTERCEPT TANGENT CONCENTRIC OVERLAP

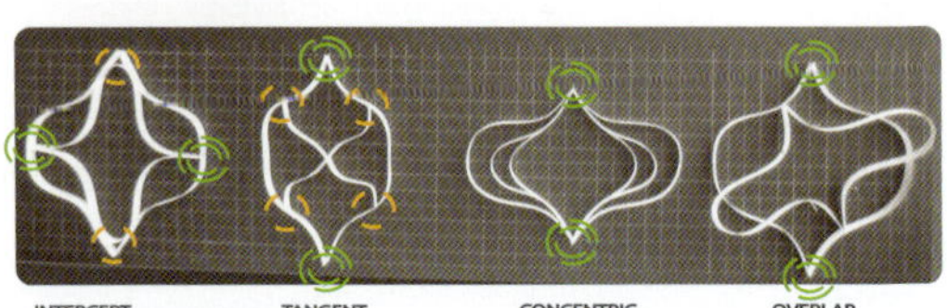

INTERCEPT TANGENT CONCENTRIC OVERLAP

PAPER / PIN MODELS

CONTROL STUDY

CONFIGURATIONS

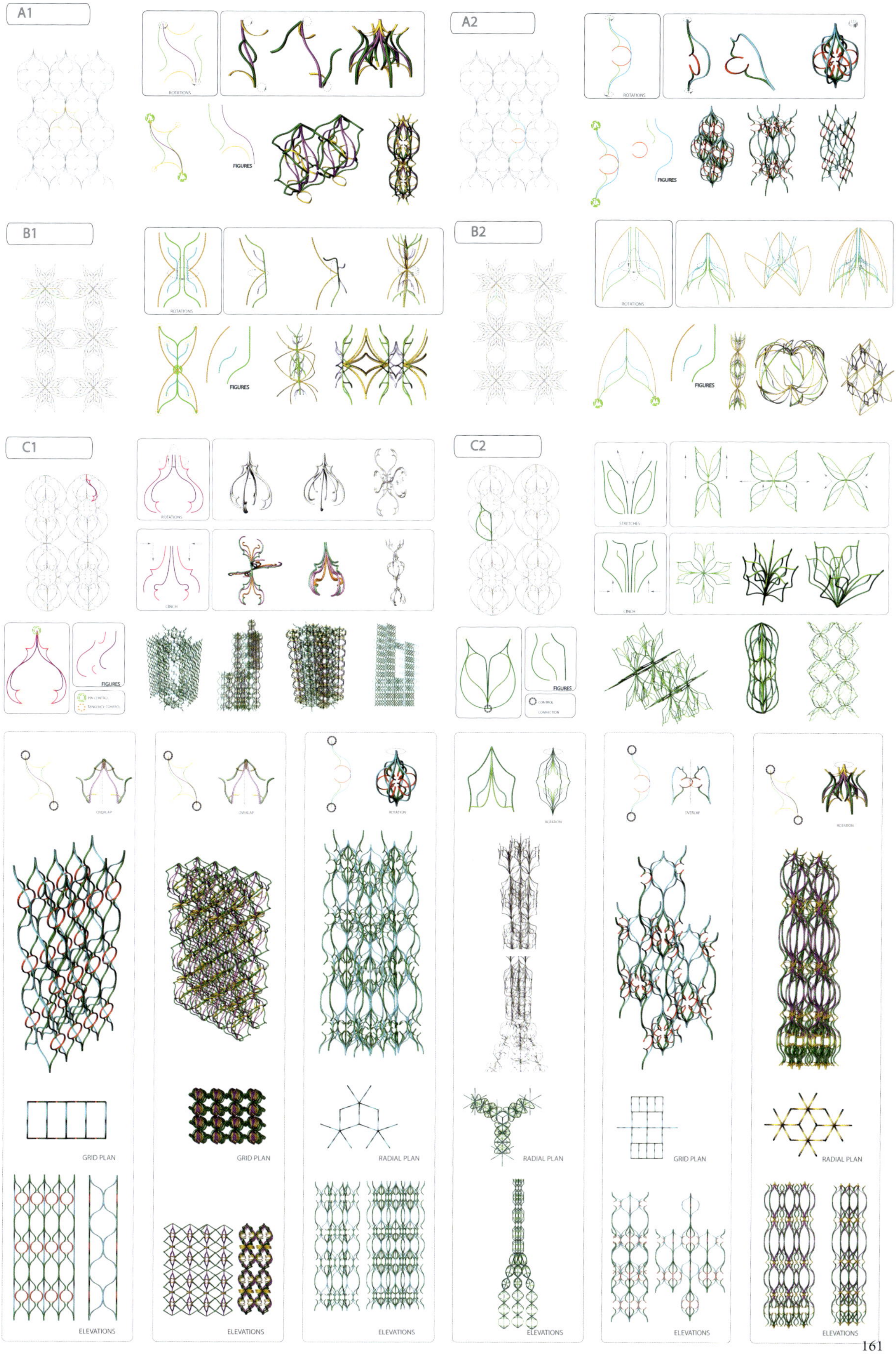

DIGITAL MODEL

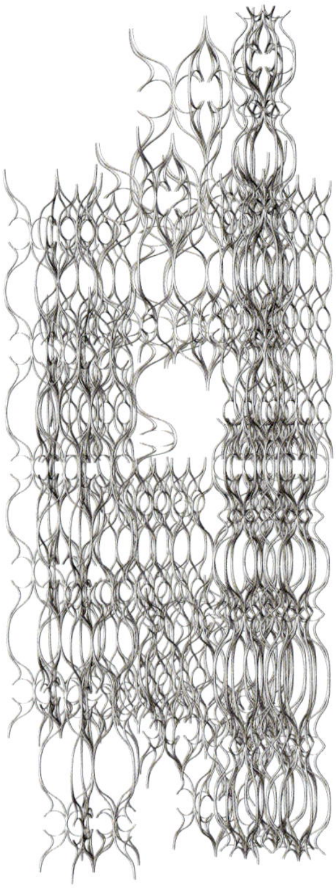

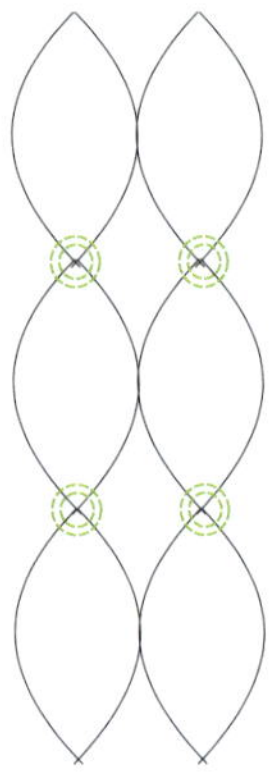

END POINT STACK

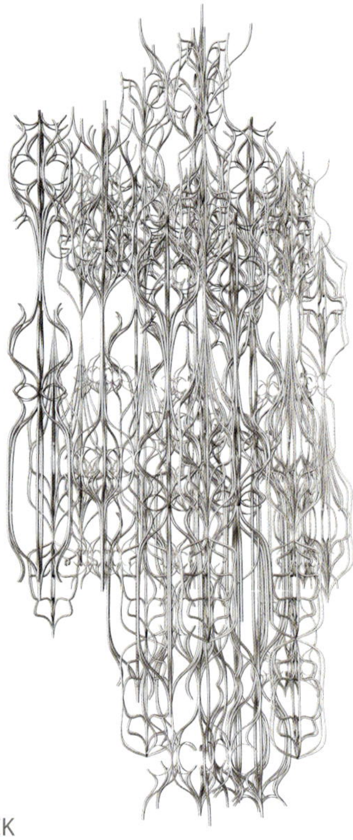

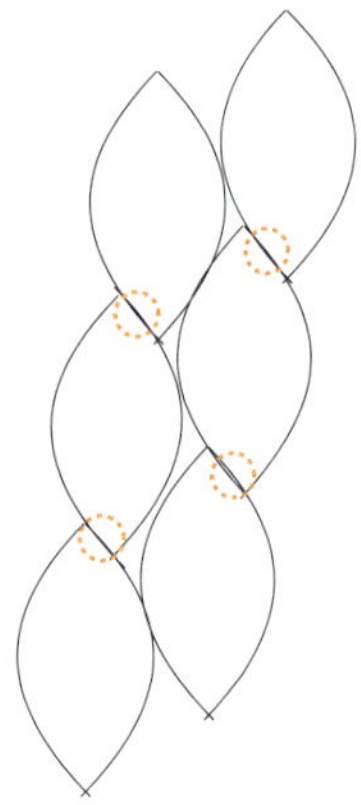

TANGENCY STACK

ANALOGUE MODEL

TECHNIQUES

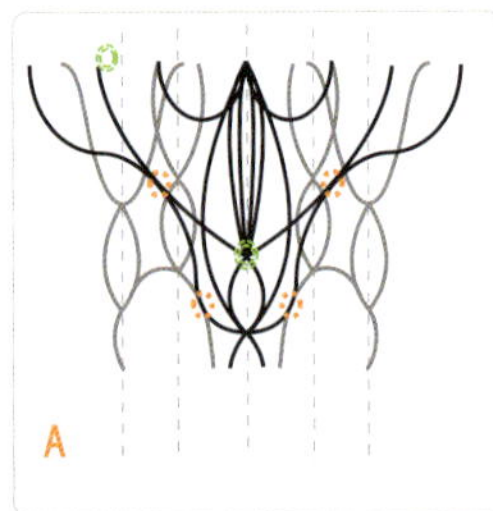

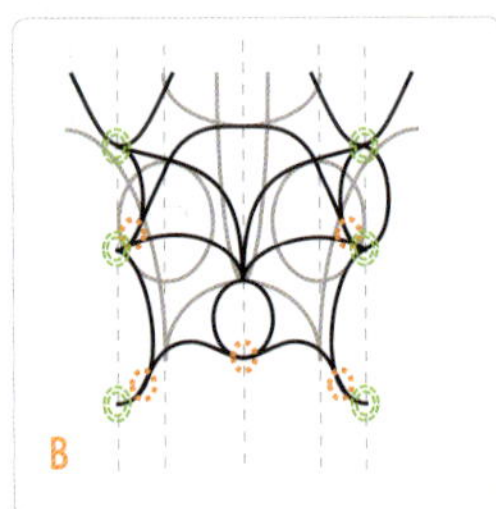

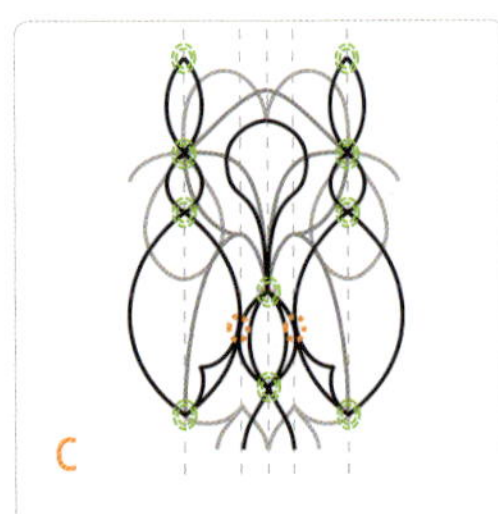

FLOOR SYSTEMS ANALYSIS

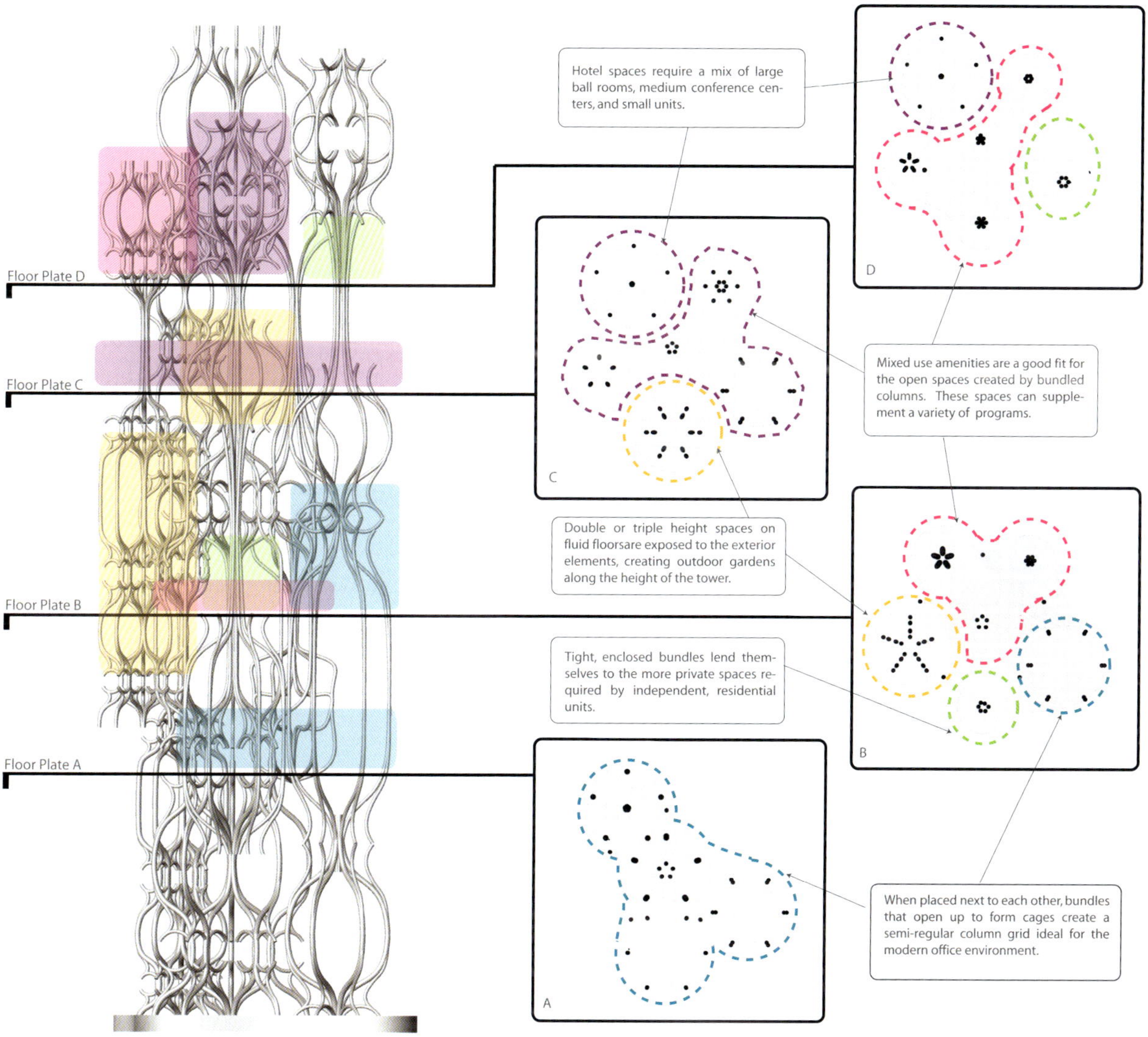

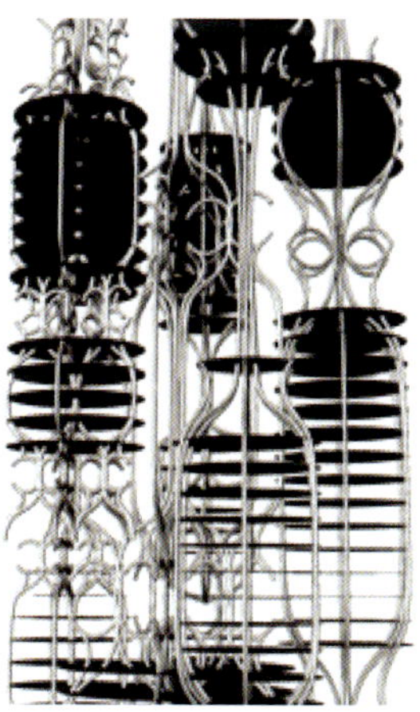

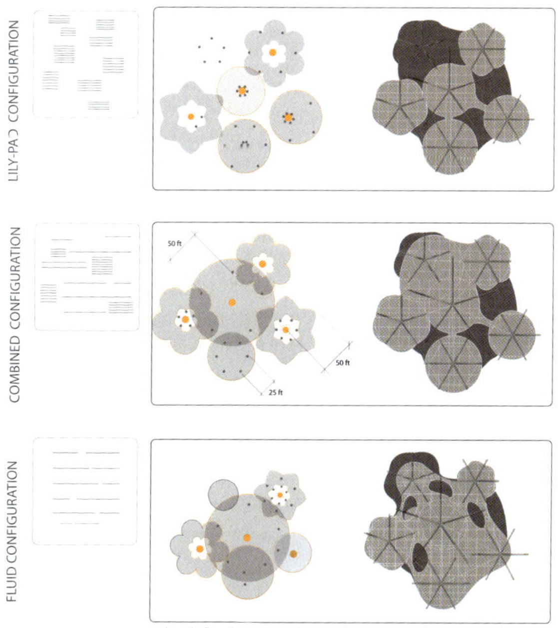

Analyzes the floor plates as derived from control points that were created by section plane through all the configuration bundles.

PROGRAM ANALYSIS

- - - - RESIDENTIAL
individual units
multi-family

- - - - OFFICES
build out

- - - - HOTEL
rooms
restaurant

- - - - OPEN
viewing deck

- - - - MULIT-USE AMENITIES
meeting rooms
fitness centers
auditorium

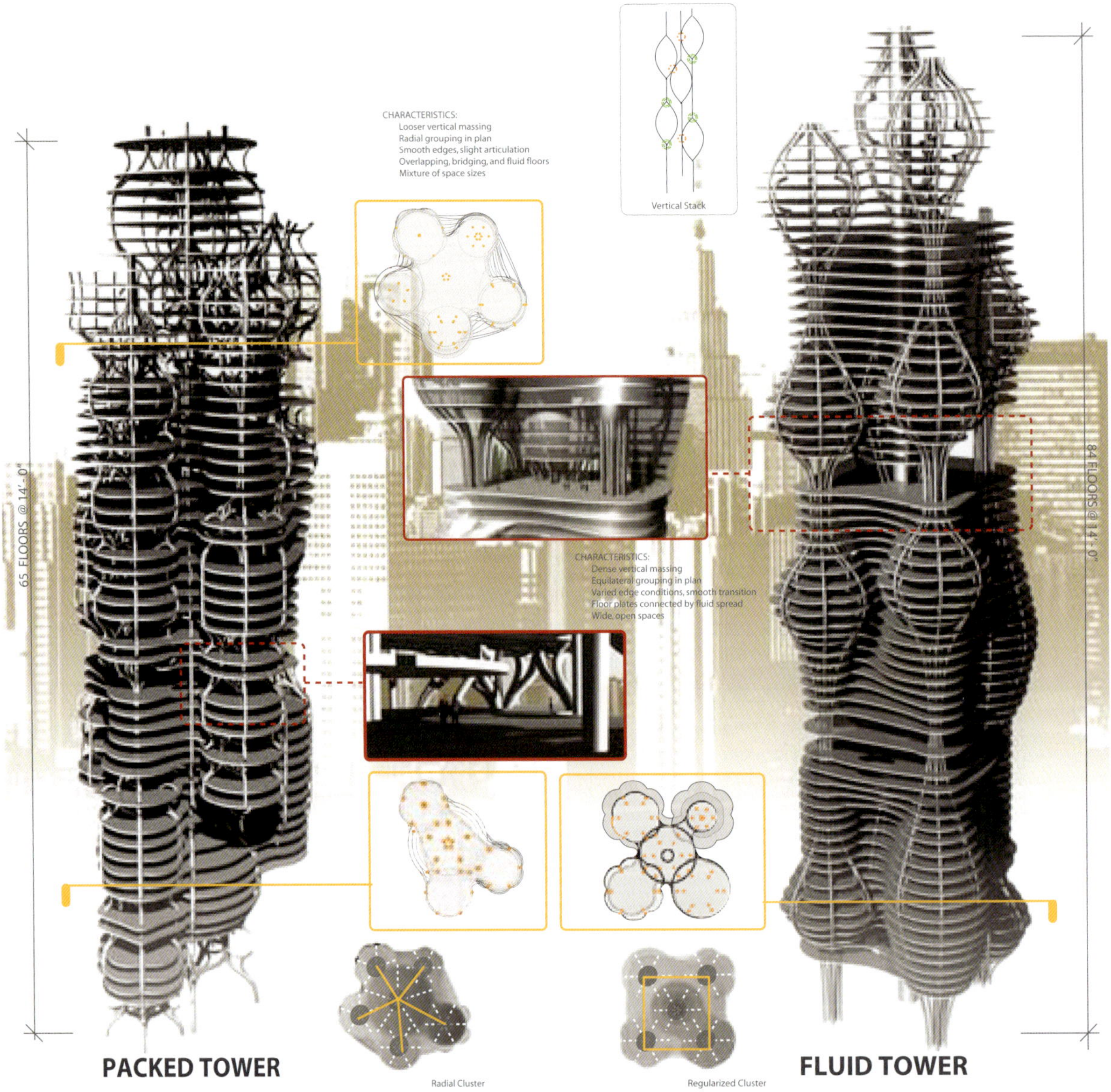
CHARACTERISTICS:
Looser vertical massing
Radial grouping in plan
Smooth edges, slight articulation
Overlapping, bridging, and fluid floors
Mixture of space sizes
Vertical Stack
65 FLOORS @ 14'-0"
84 FLOORS @ 14'-0"
CHARACTERISTICS:
Dense vertical massing
Equilateral grouping in plan
Varied edge conditions, smooth transition
Floor plates connected by fluid spread
Wide, open spaces
PACKED TOWER
Radial Cluster
Regularized Cluster
FLUID TOWER

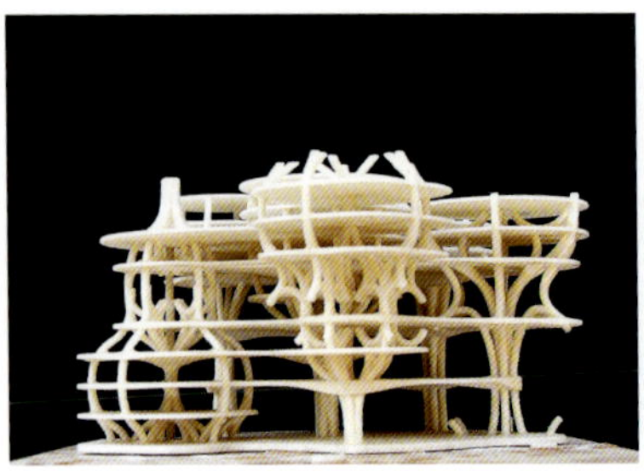

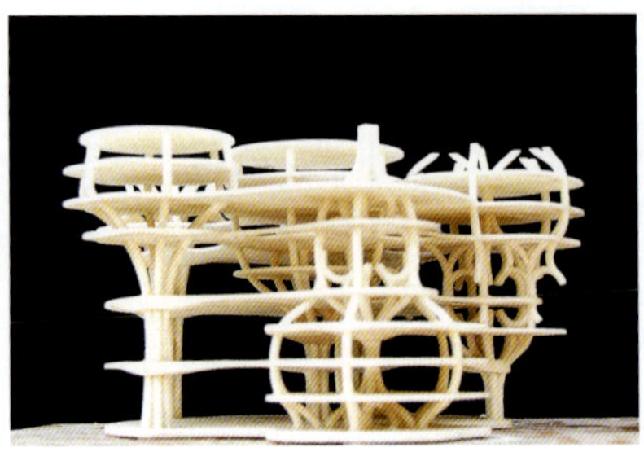

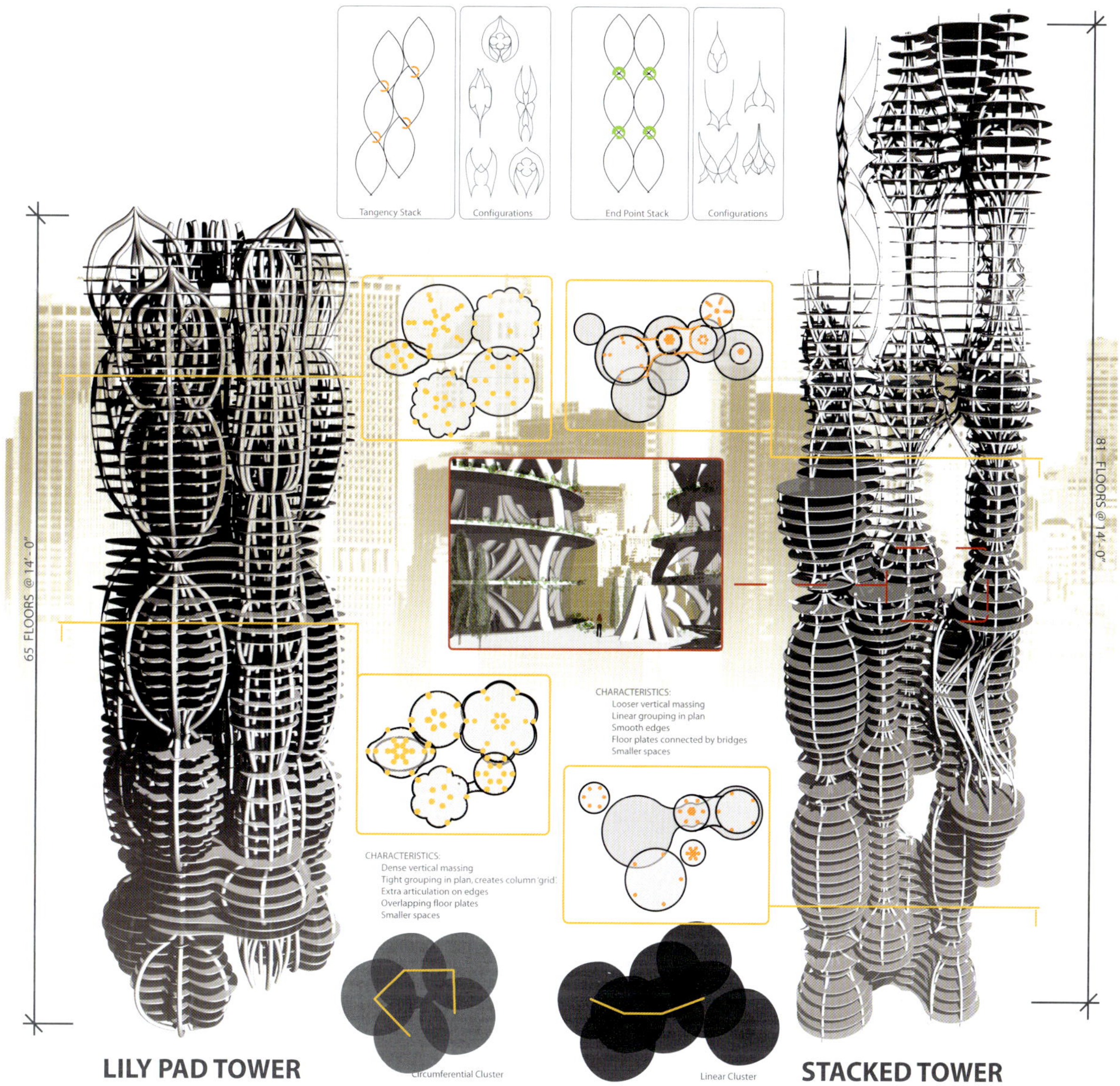

Tangency Stack
Configurations
End Point Stack
Configurations
65 FLOORS @ 14'-0"
81 FLOORS @ 14'-0"
CHARACTERISTICS:
Looser vertical massing
Linear grouping in plan
Smooth edges
Floor plates connected by bridges
Smaller spaces
CHARACTERISTICS:
Dense vertical massing
Tight grouping in plan, creates column 'grid'
Extra articulation on edges
Overlapping floor plates
Smaller spaces
Circumferential Cluster
Linear Cluster
LILY PAD TOWER
STACKED TOWER

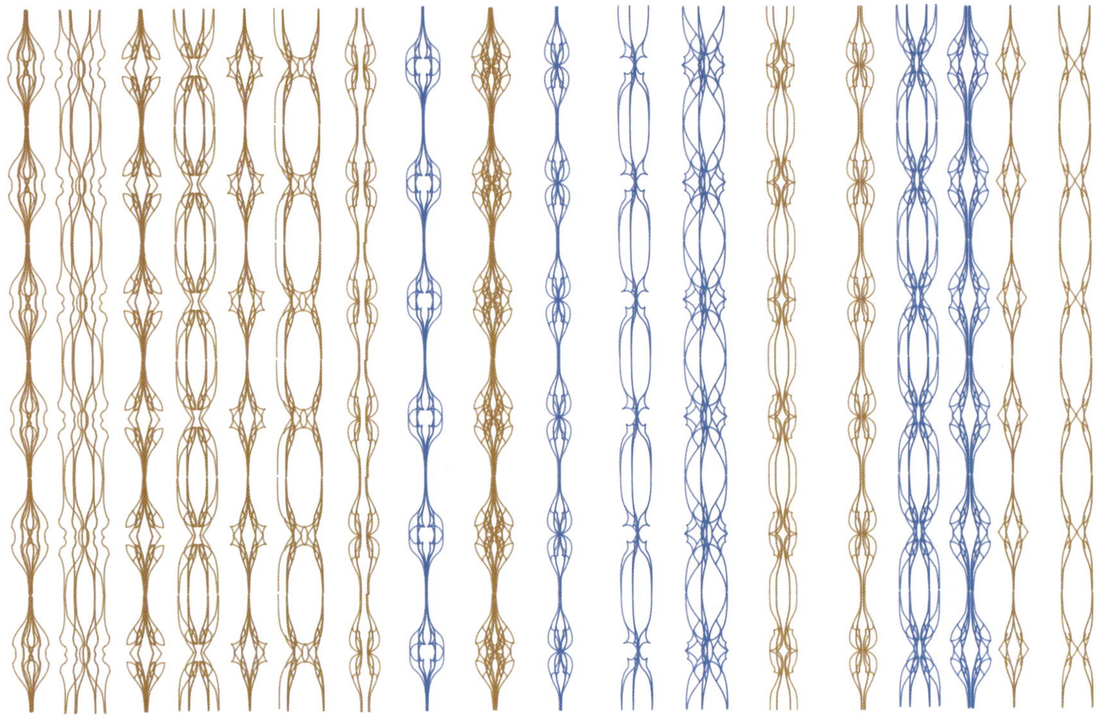

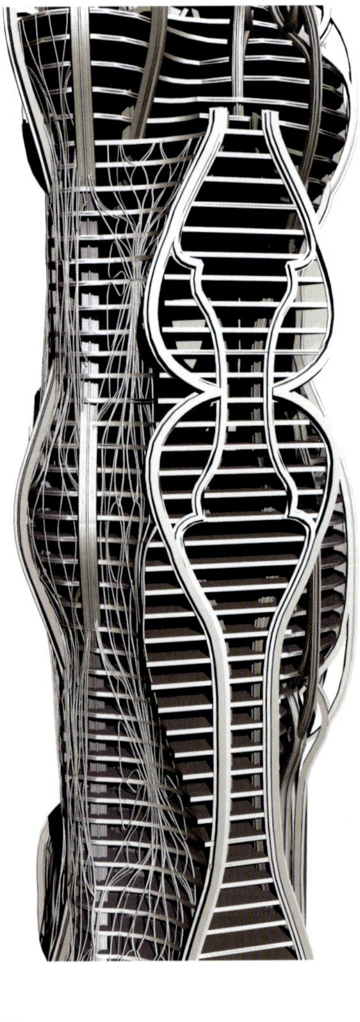

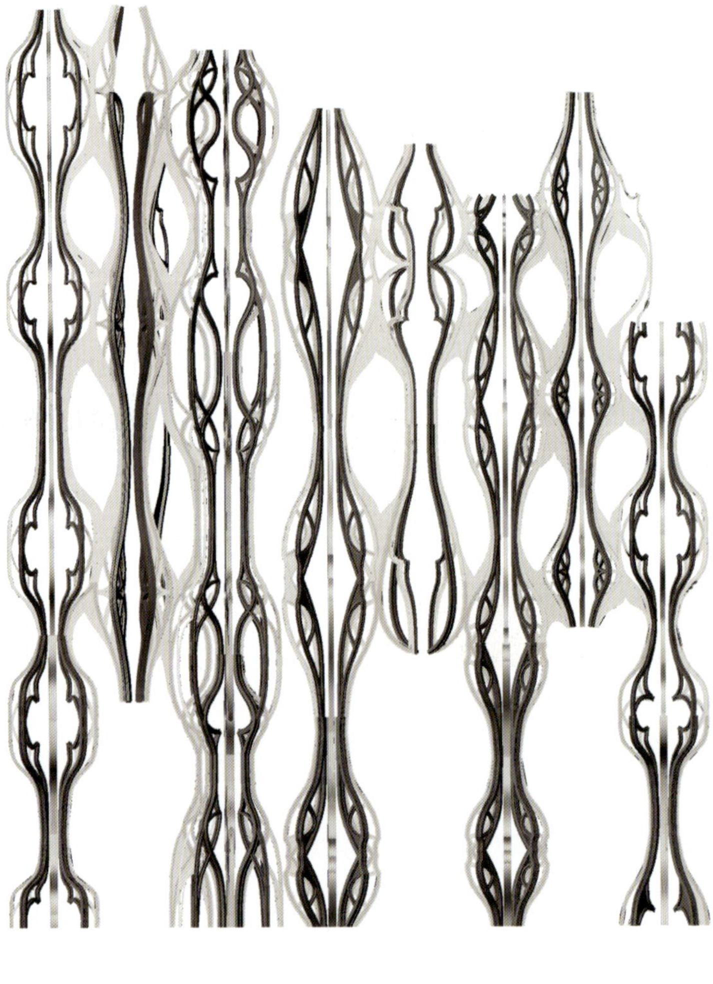

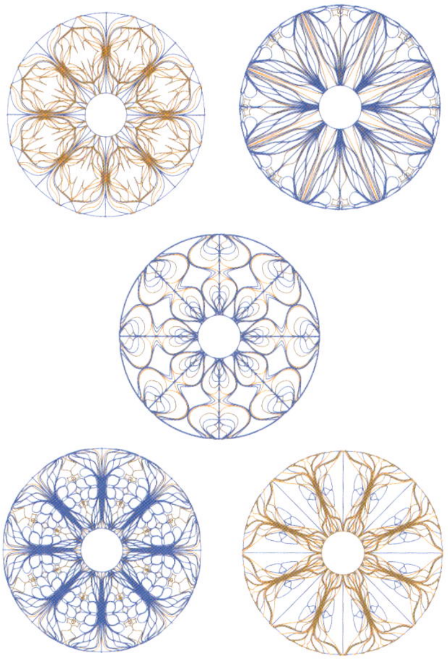

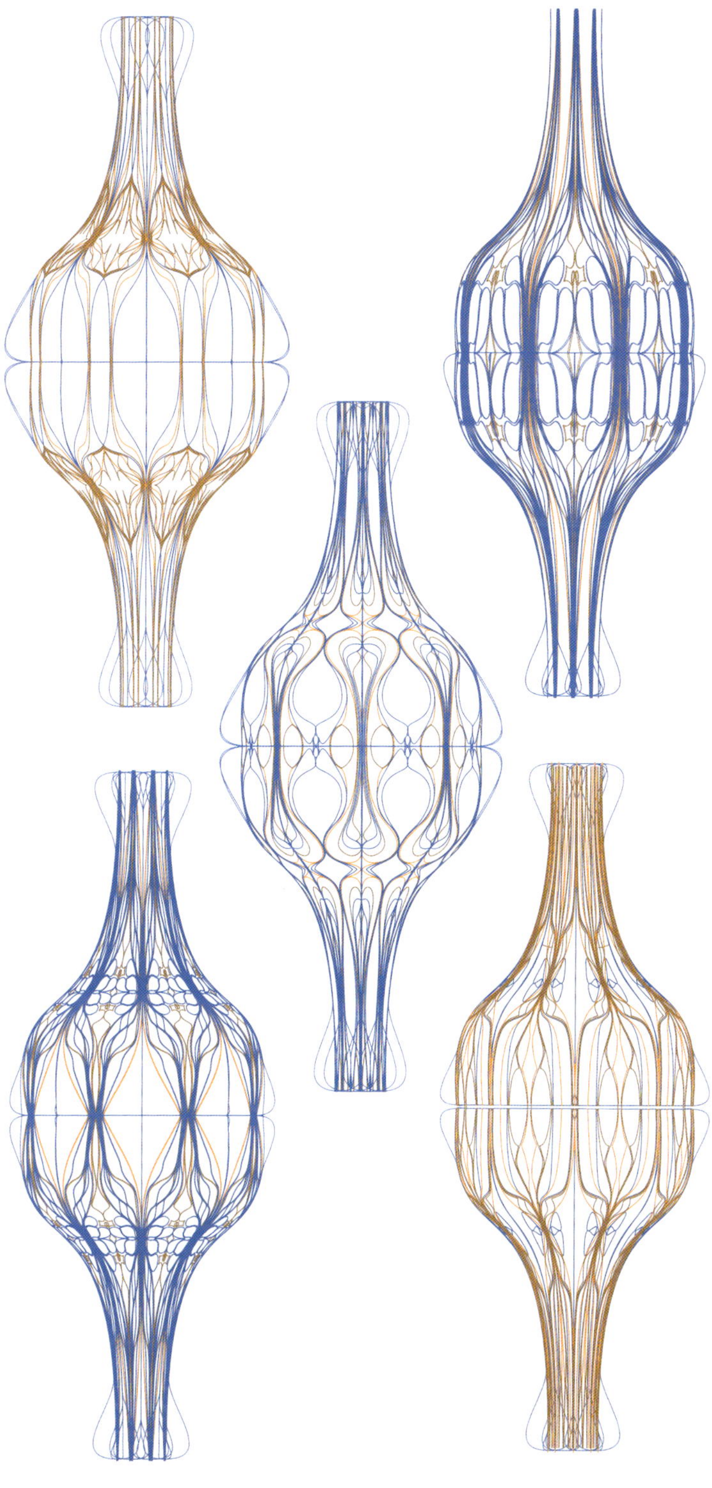

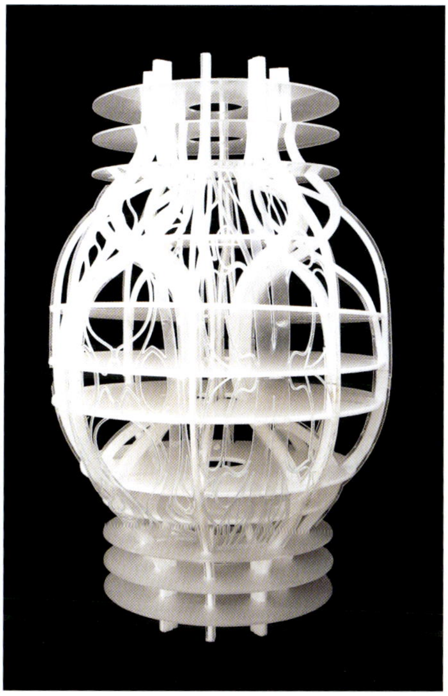

Figure Lattices

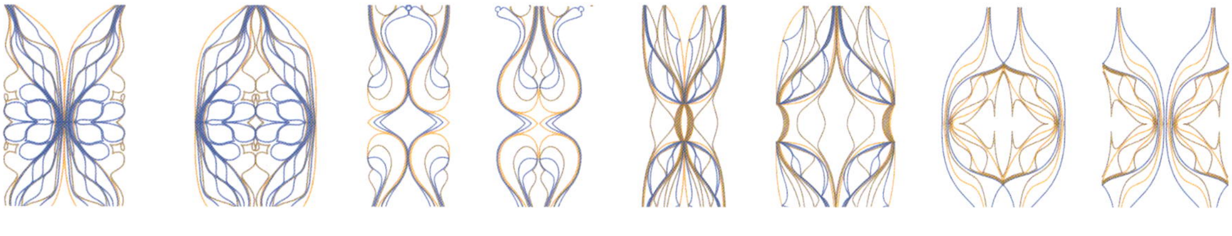

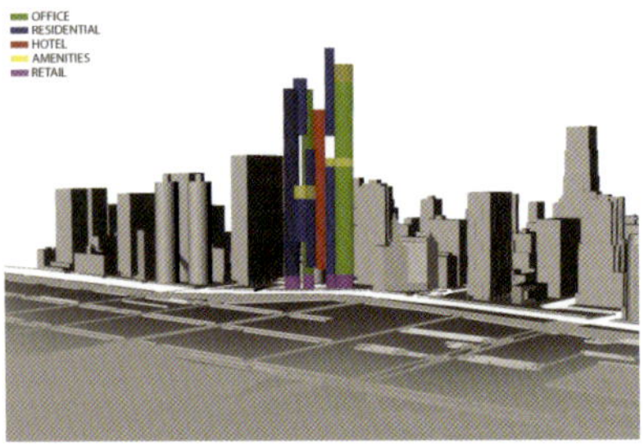
OFFICE
RESIDENTIAL
HOTEL
AMENITIES
RETAIL

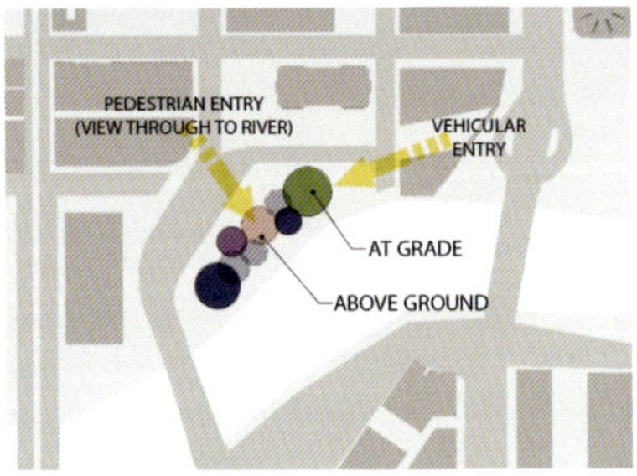
PEDESTRIAN ENTRY
(VIEW THROUGH TO RIVER)
VEHICULAR
ENTRY
AT GRADE
ABOVE GROUND

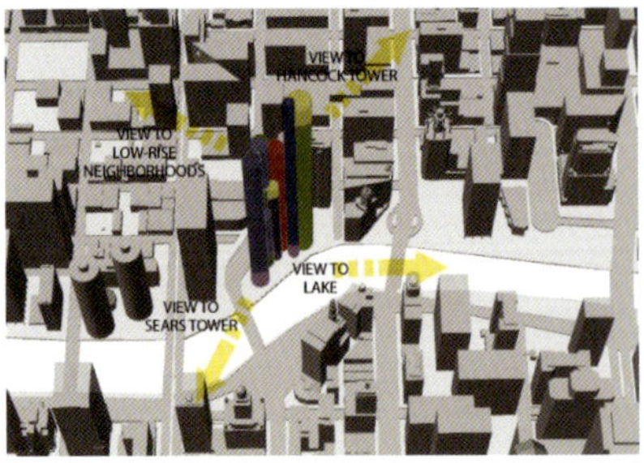
VIEW TO
HANCOCK TOWER
VIEW TO
LOW-RISE
NEIGHBORHOODS
VIEW TO
SEARS TOWER
VIEW TO
LAKE

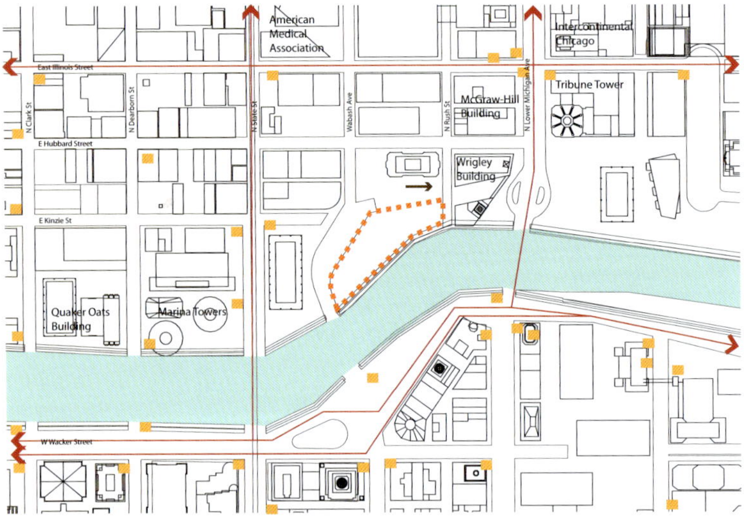
American
Medical
Association
Intercontinental
Chicago
East Illinois Street
Tribune Tower
McGraw-Hill
Building
N Clark St
N Dearborn St
N State St
Wabash Ave
N Rush St
N Lower Michigan Ave
E Hubbard Street
Wrigley
Building
E Kinzie St
Quaker Oats
Building
Marina Towers
W Wacker Street

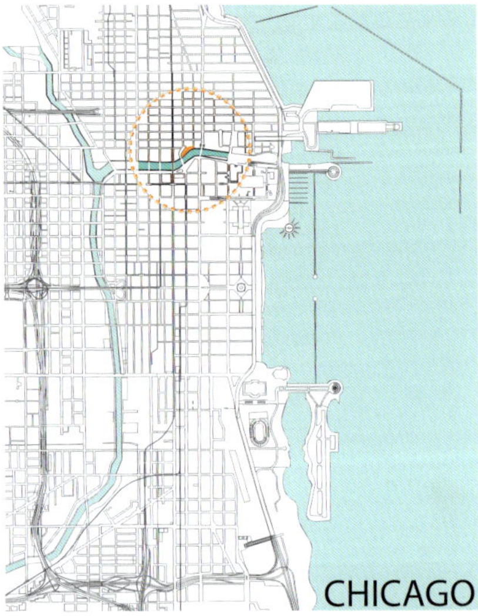
CHICAGO

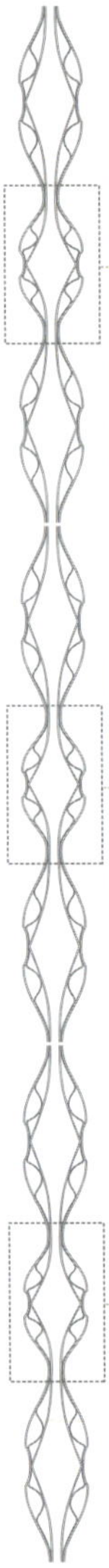

FLOOR CONSTRUCTION TYPE 1
"SLIP"

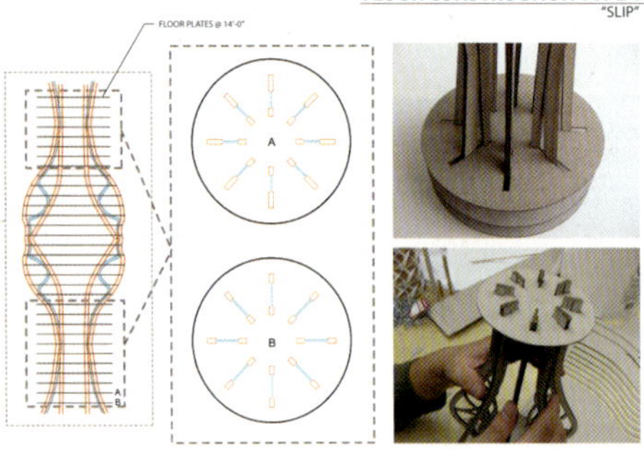

AREAS WHERE FLOOR EXTEND BEYOND THE STRUCTURE

FLOOR CONSTRUCTION TYPE 2
"SNAP"

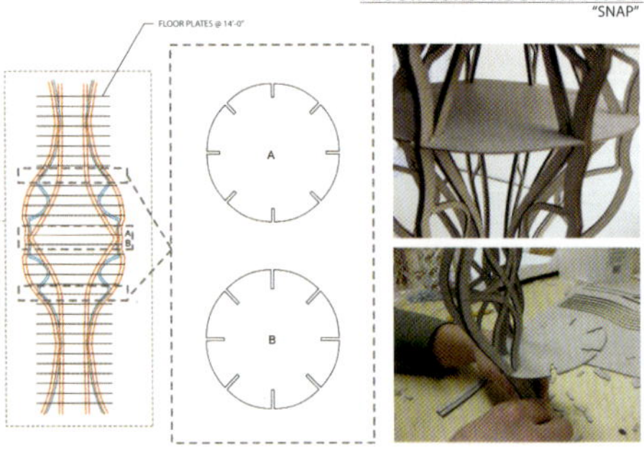

AREAS WHERE FLOOR ALIGNS WITH THE STRUCTURE

FLOOR CONSTRUCTION TYPE 3
"SKEWER"

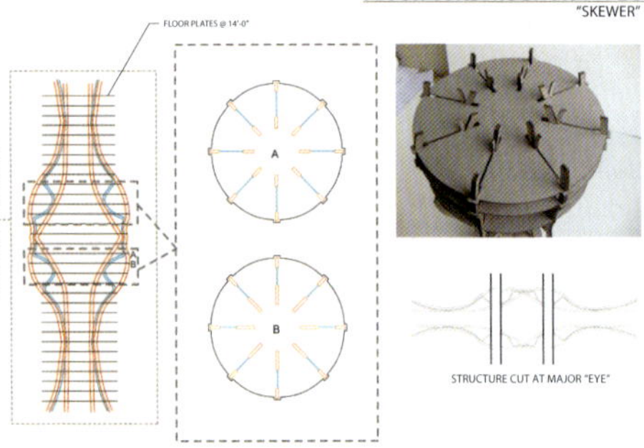

AREAS WHERE STRUCTURE MOVES INTO THE FLOOR PLATES

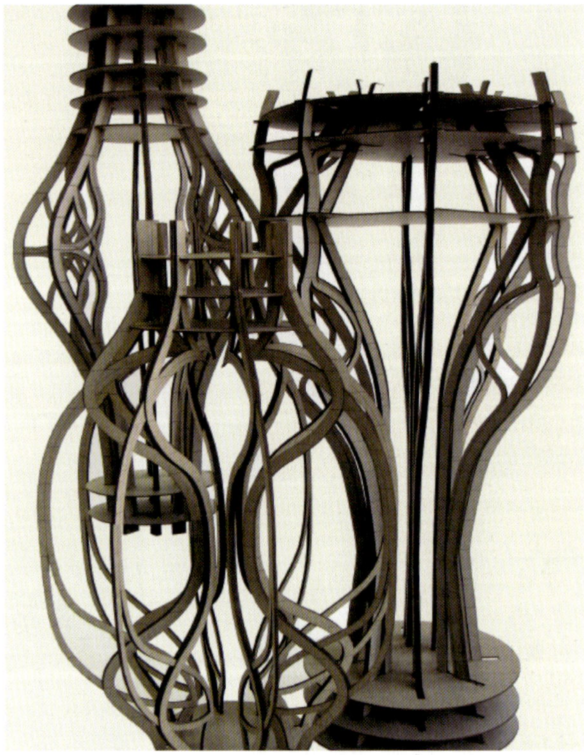

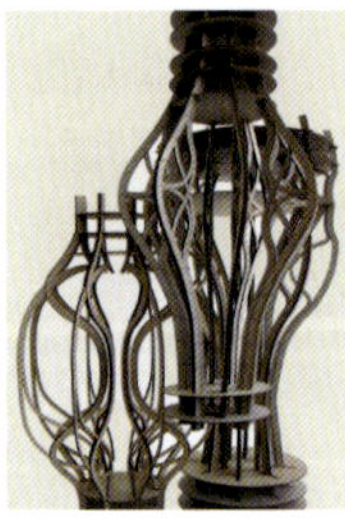

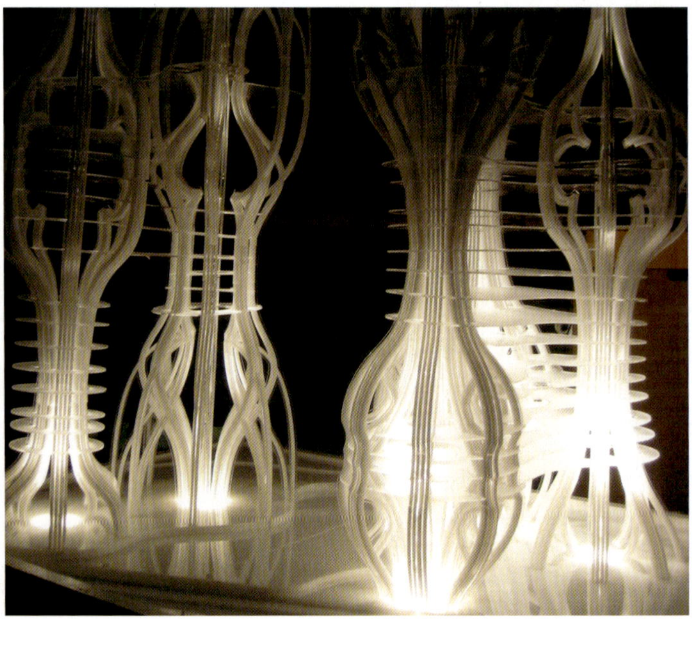

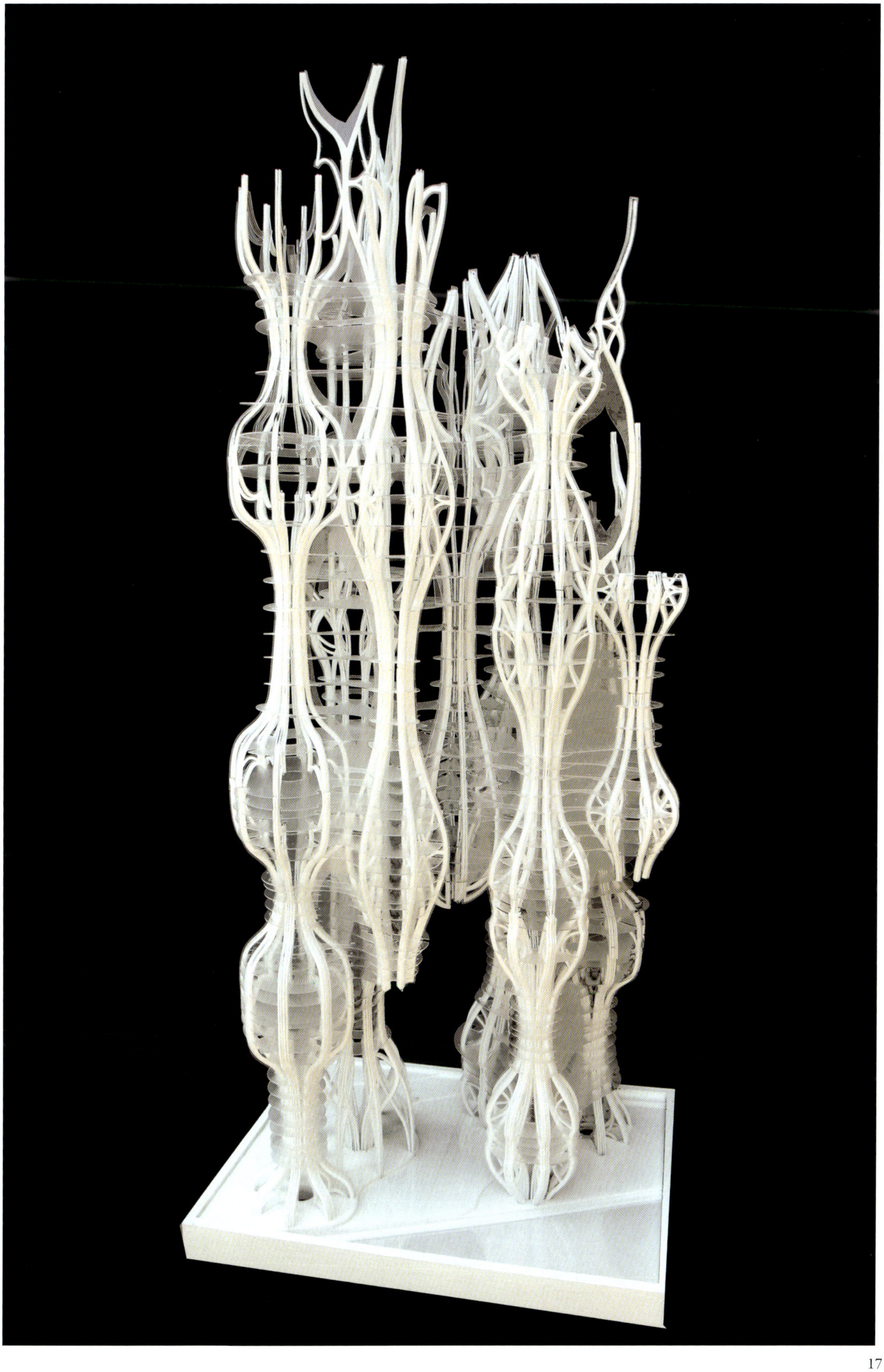

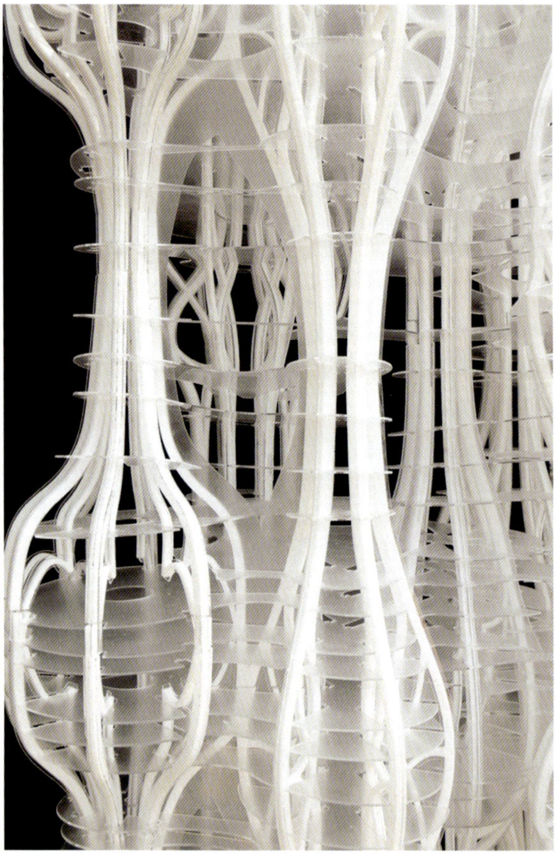

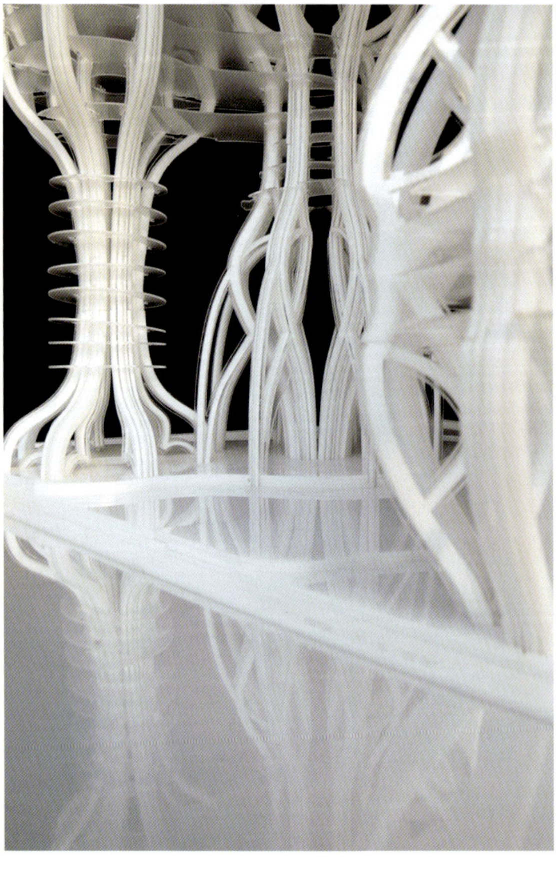

Foam Tower

Geoffrey Braiman & Dave Beil

The challenge of three dimensional packing is a classic mathematical problem dating back to the times of Plato and one developed by Archimedes, Newton, and countless other classical thinkers. Our research focuses on the specific 3D-packing problem of irregular polyhedral networks in natural foaming systems. Foaming networks are inherently efficient in terms of material usage while maintaining strength in all directions.

Networks in foaming systems are defined by the radical plane, which is described as the precise location and angle of the boundary plane between two spheres that results in a seamless system of polyhedra. This network informs all foaming systems. Assuming a system of non-uniform sphere radii and locations, the algorithm describes an irregular polyhedral network, where each sphere's resulting polyhedra's size and location is determined by the size and location of all other three dimensionally packed spheres in the network.

The implications of this research in architecture are complicated to conceptualize because the modern world exists in stacked space only. Some of the immediate benefits include the ability to cantilever and span great distances because of seemingly endless vectors of lateral bracing while utilizing the smallest amount of material possible. This spatial development also creates a multi-adjacency between polyhedra; the average number of sides for each polyhedra in a foaming network is between eleven and seventeen.

Our immediate reaction was to think about the tower in terms of discrete, clearly defined units of space. Housing programs work nicely with this kind of spatial division due to the history of property boundaries, but also because of the concept of neighborhood. Utilizing the multi adjacency in the system allows for a level of interaction never seen in typical housing towers. Spaces within the tower are sold in cubic feet instead of square feet: Each polyhedra is a single family residence. Circulation is managed by a system of elevators and escalators.

We fabricated the physical model using selective laser sintering (SLS) techniques. It is a composite of fused nylon, acrylic and epoxy.

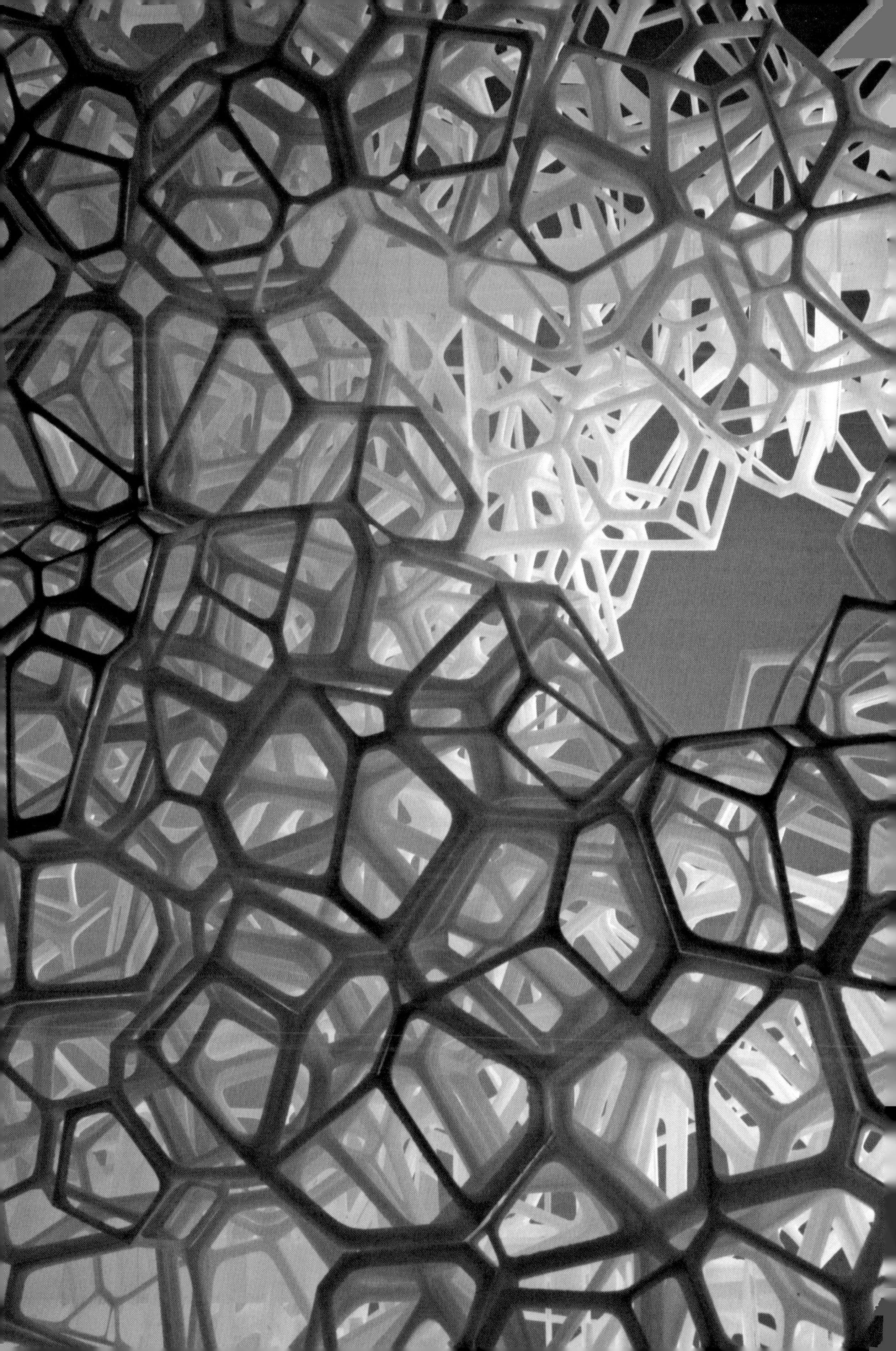

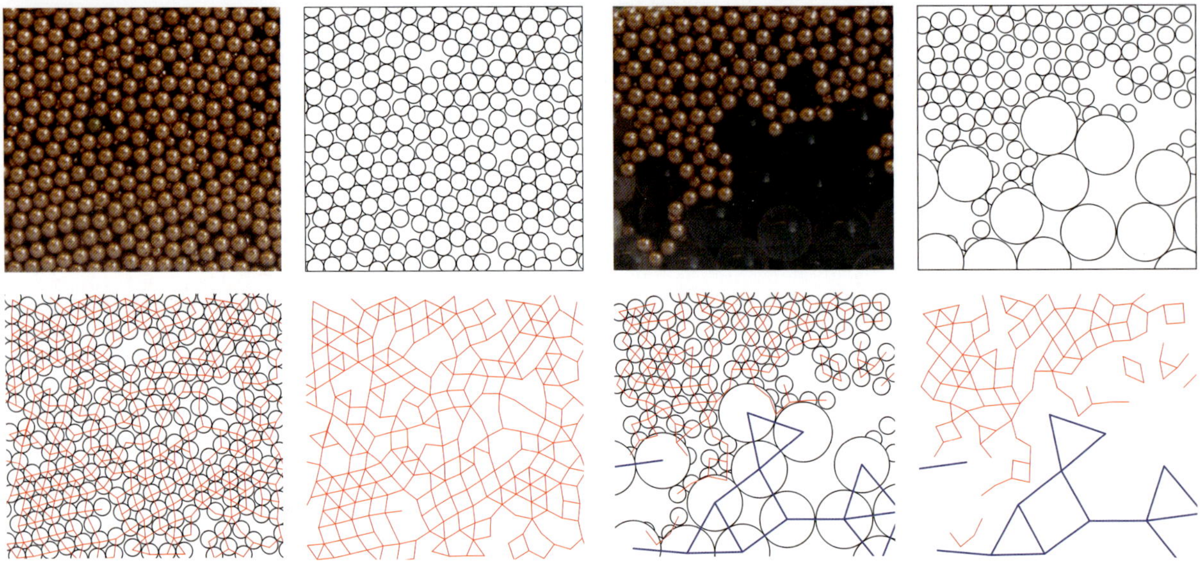

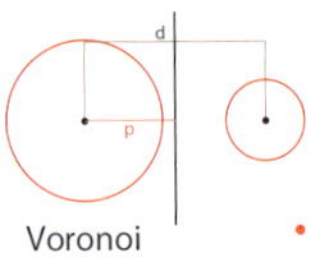

$p = \frac{d}{2}$

Voronoi

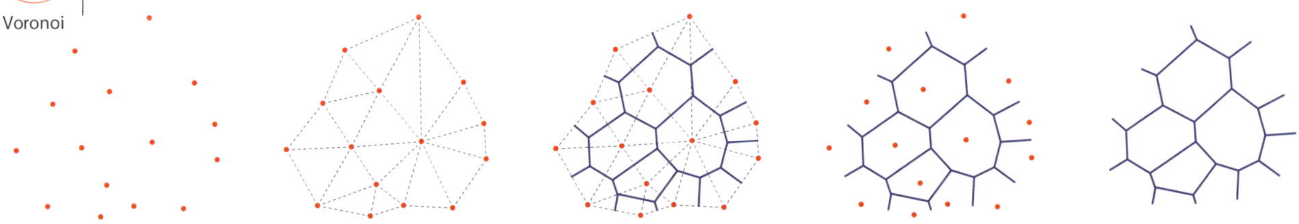

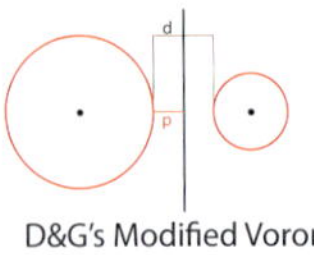

$p = \frac{d}{2}$

D&G's Modified Voronoi

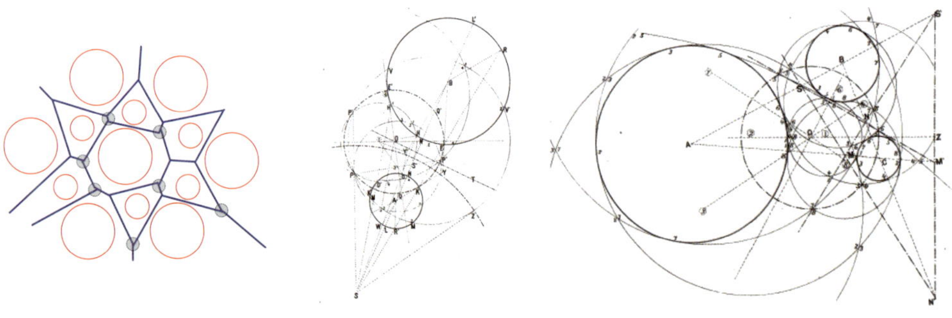

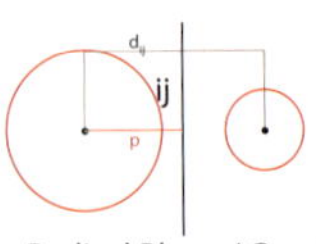

$p_{ij} = \frac{(d_{ij})^2 + (r_i)^2 - (r_j)^2}{2d_{ij}}$

Radical Plane / Constrained Voronoi

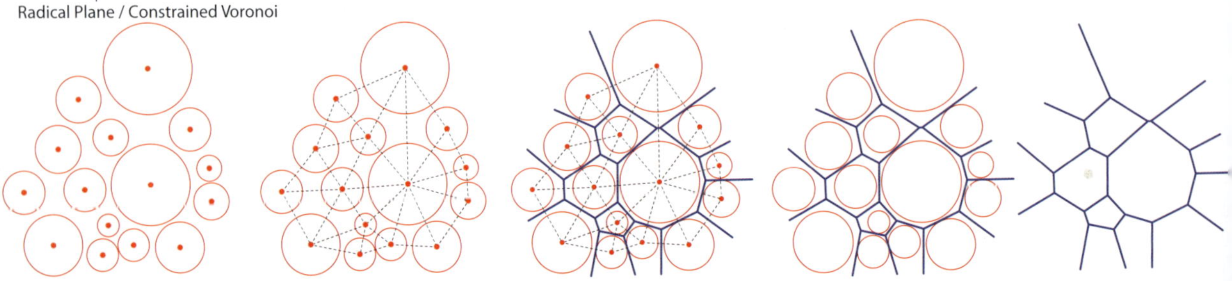

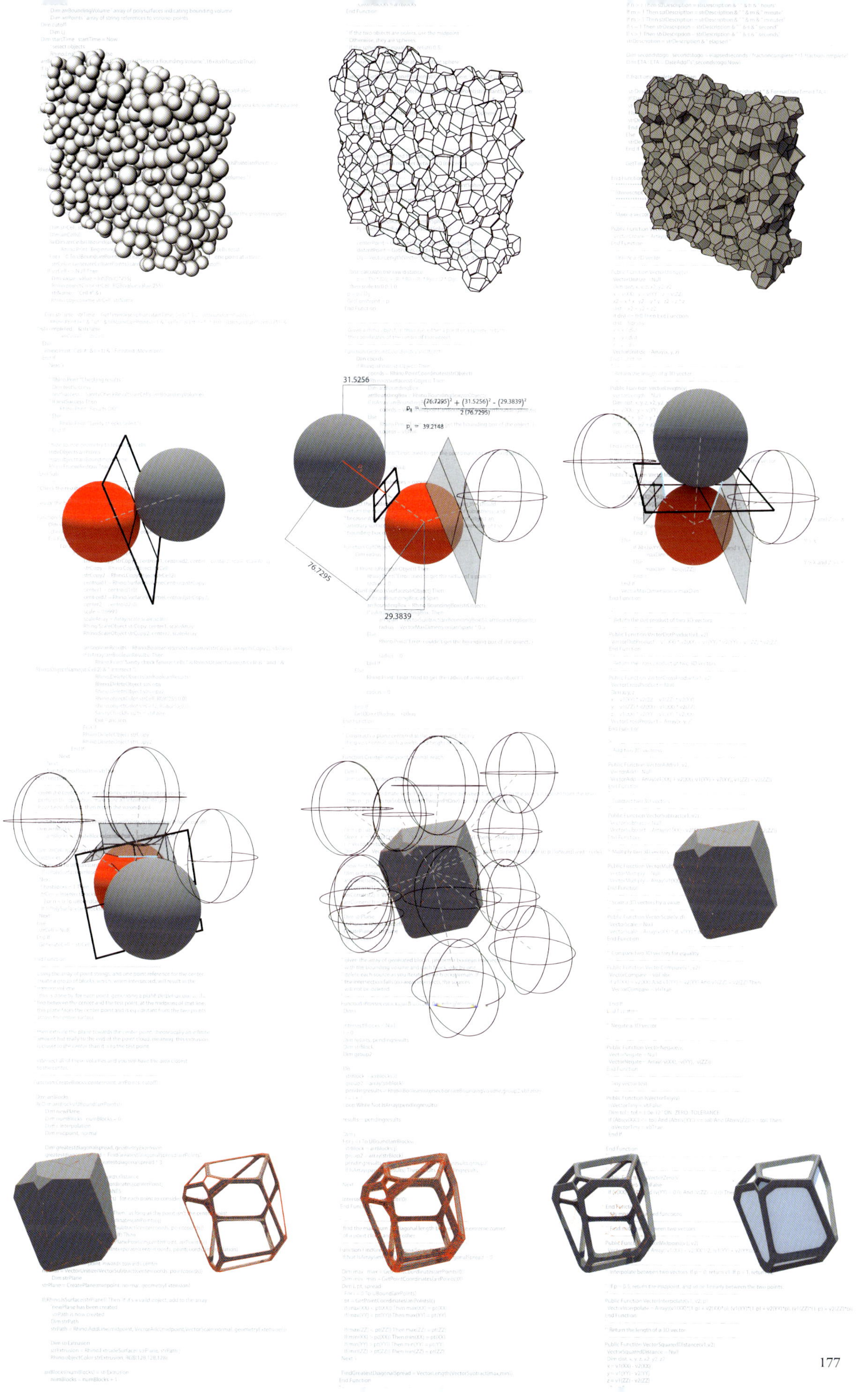
31.5256
$P_x = \frac{(76.7295)^2 + (31.5256)^2 - (29.3839)^2}{2\,(76.7295)}$
$P_x = 39.2148$
76.7295
29.3839

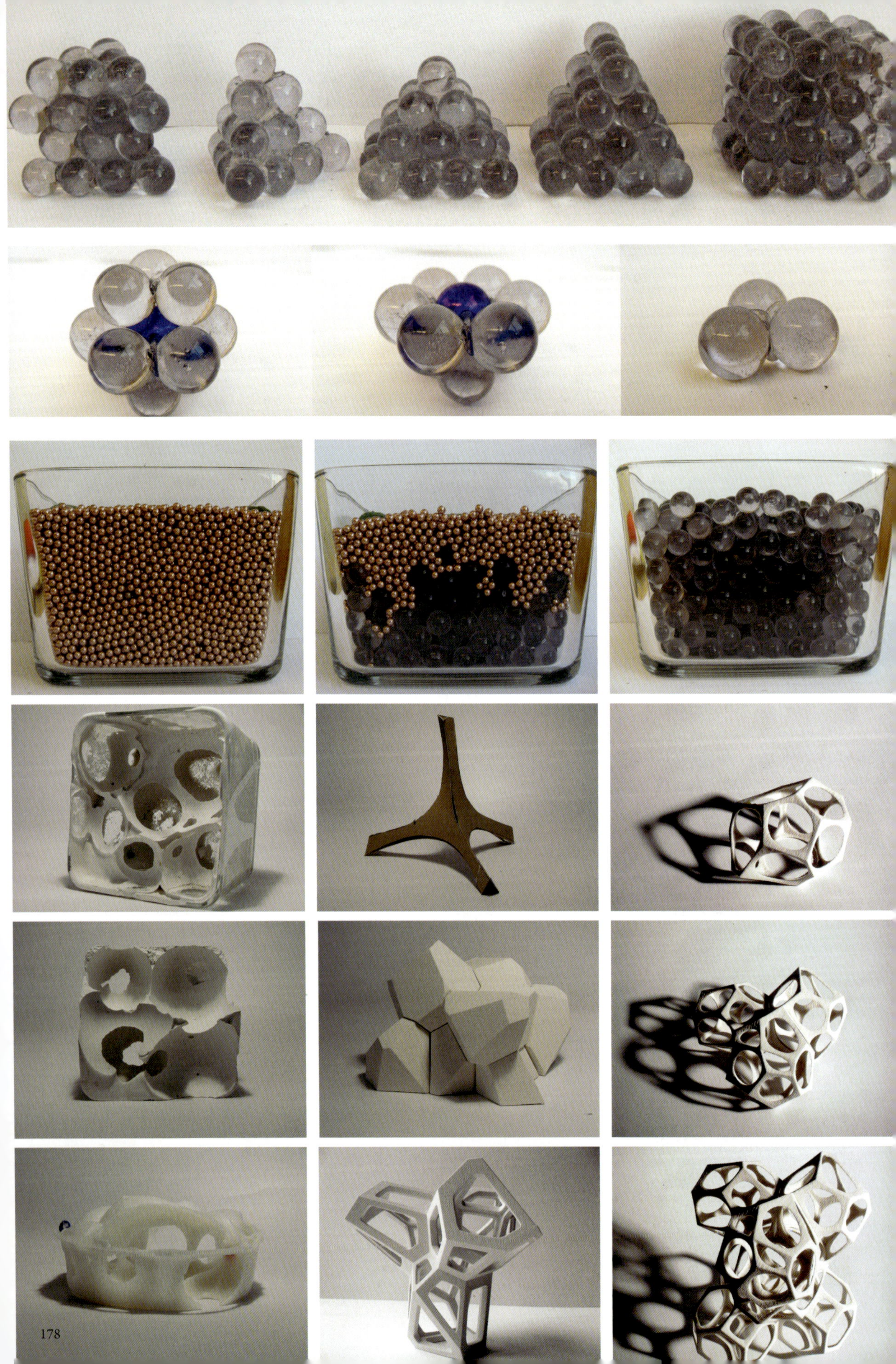

Dodecahedron
12 Sided
Only Pentagons

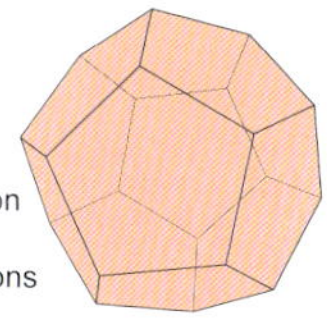

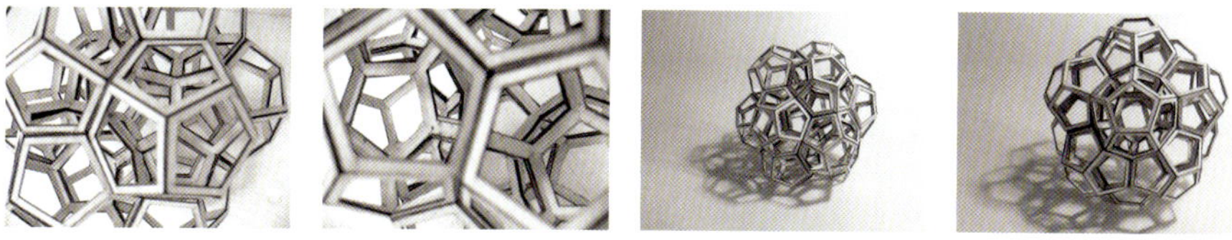

Truncated Octahedron
14 Sided
8 Hexagons
6 Squares

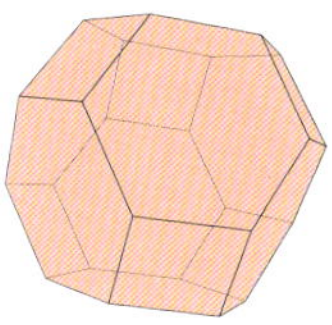

REGULAR TESSELATION

DEFORMED TESSELATION

REGULAR TO IRREGULAR TESSELATION

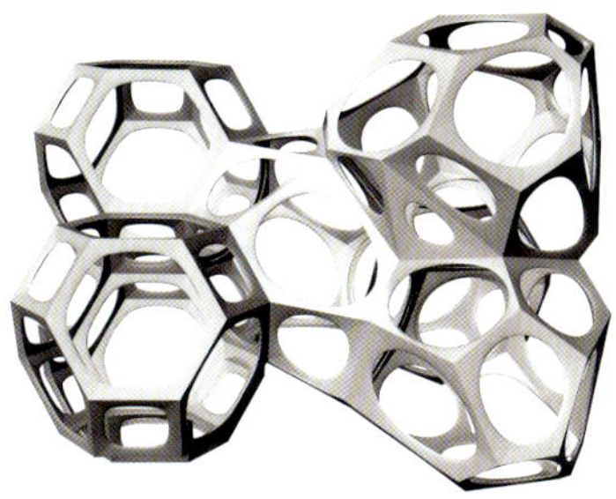

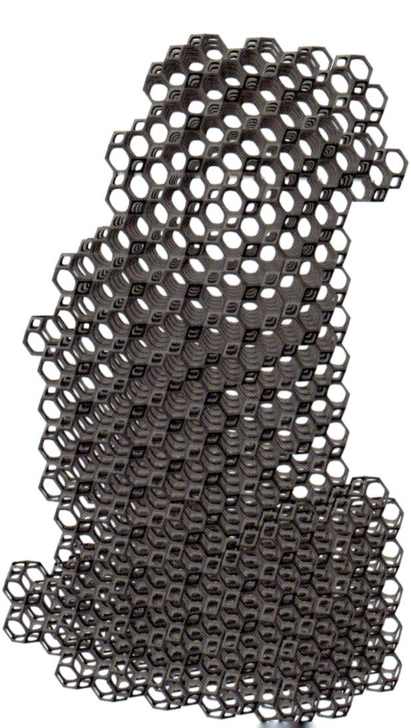

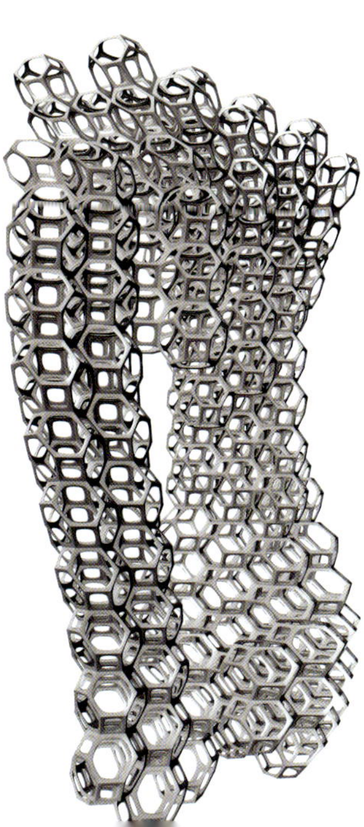

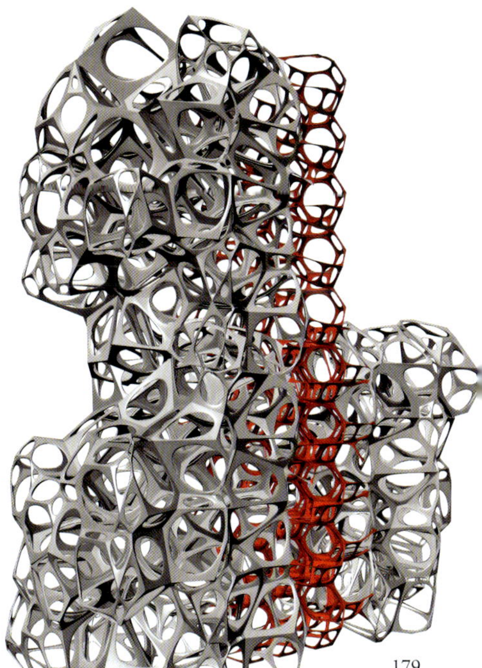

STRUCTURAL LOGIC

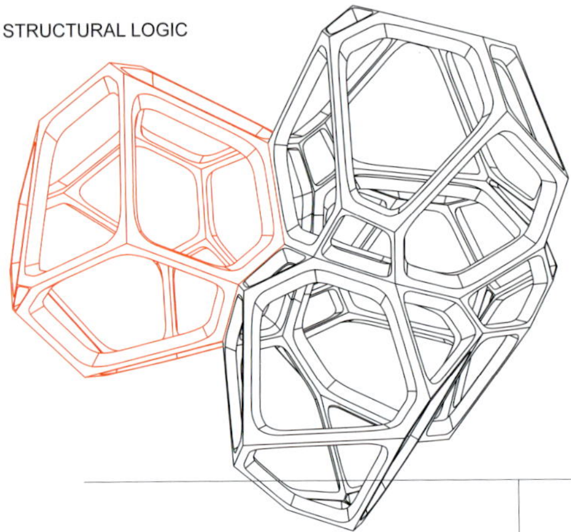

EXPLODED STRUCTURE

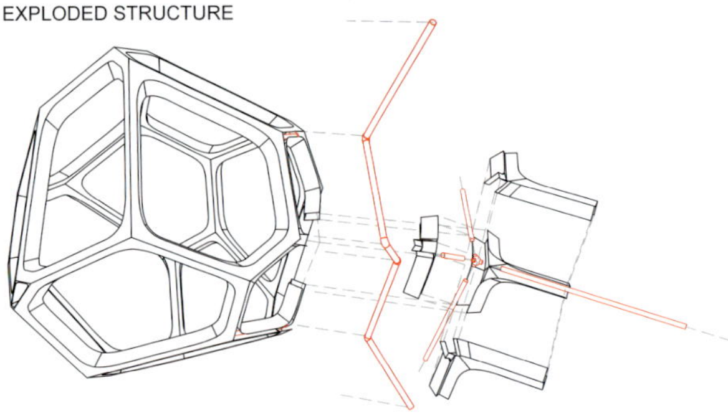

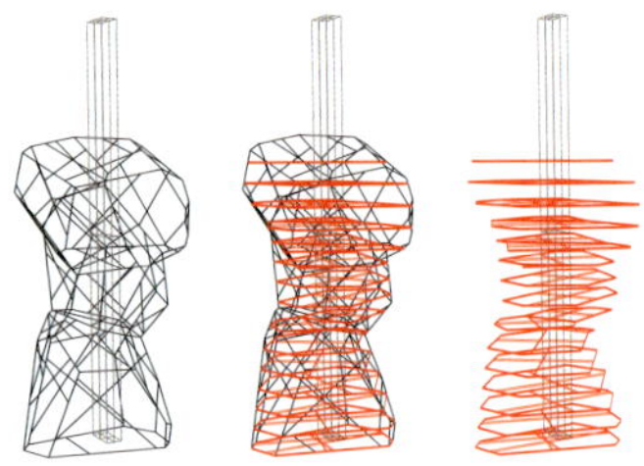
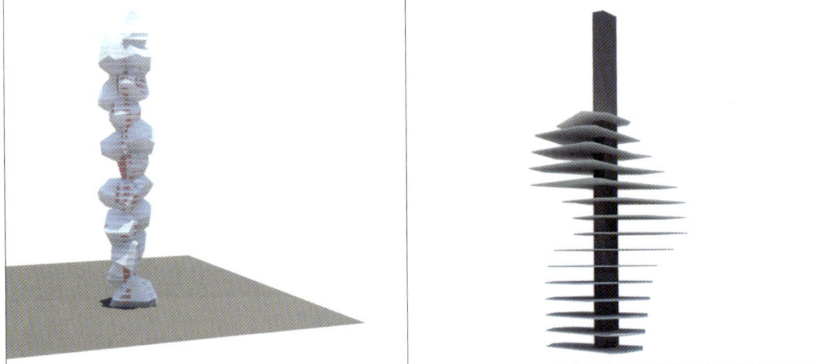

ELEVATOR DIAGRAMS

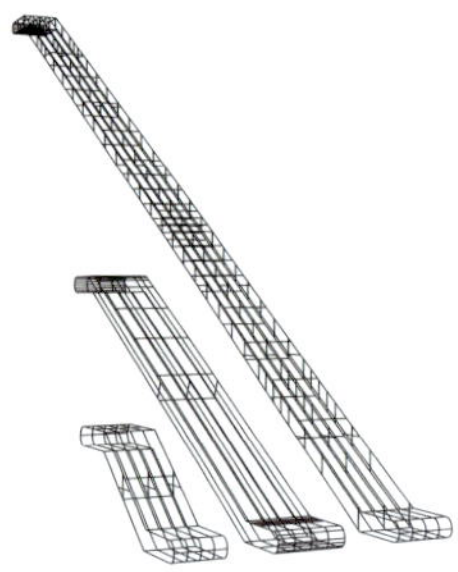
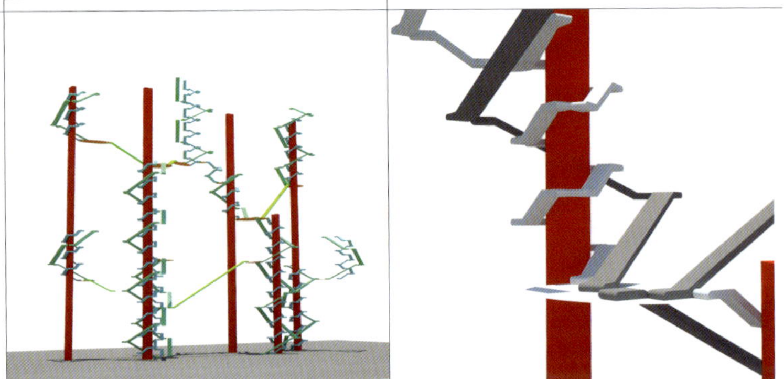

ESCALATOR DIAGRAMS

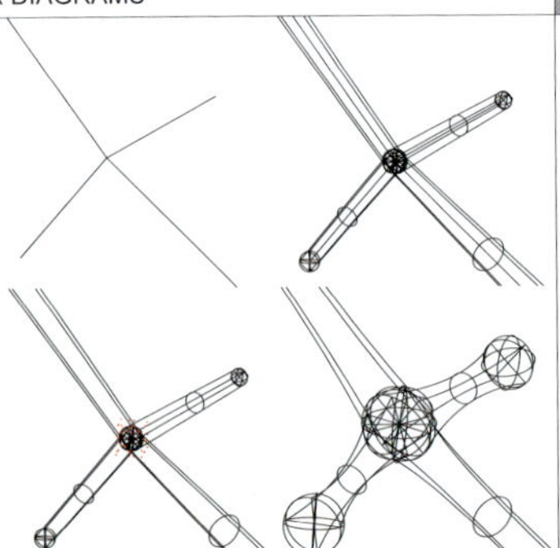
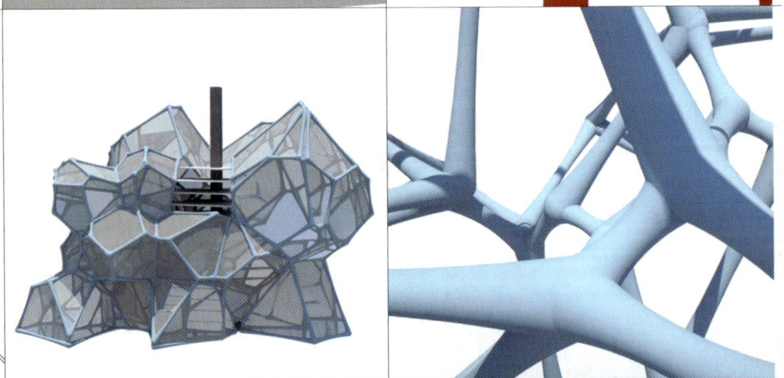

4-LEGGED NODE DIAGRAMS

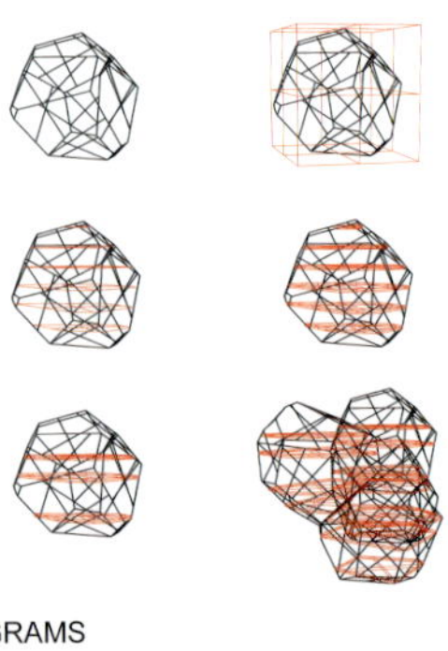
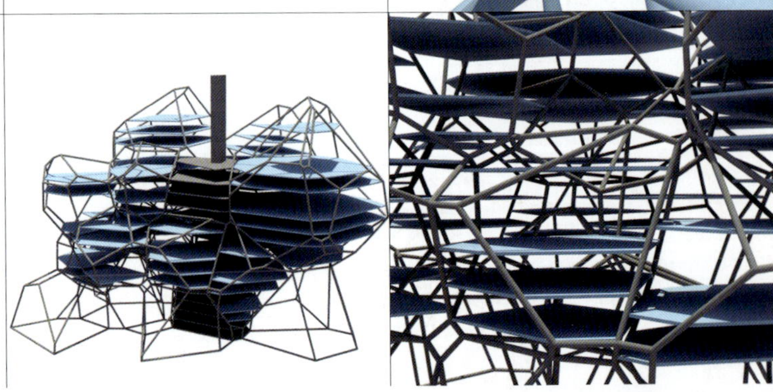

FLOOR SLAB DIAGRAMS

SITE PLAN

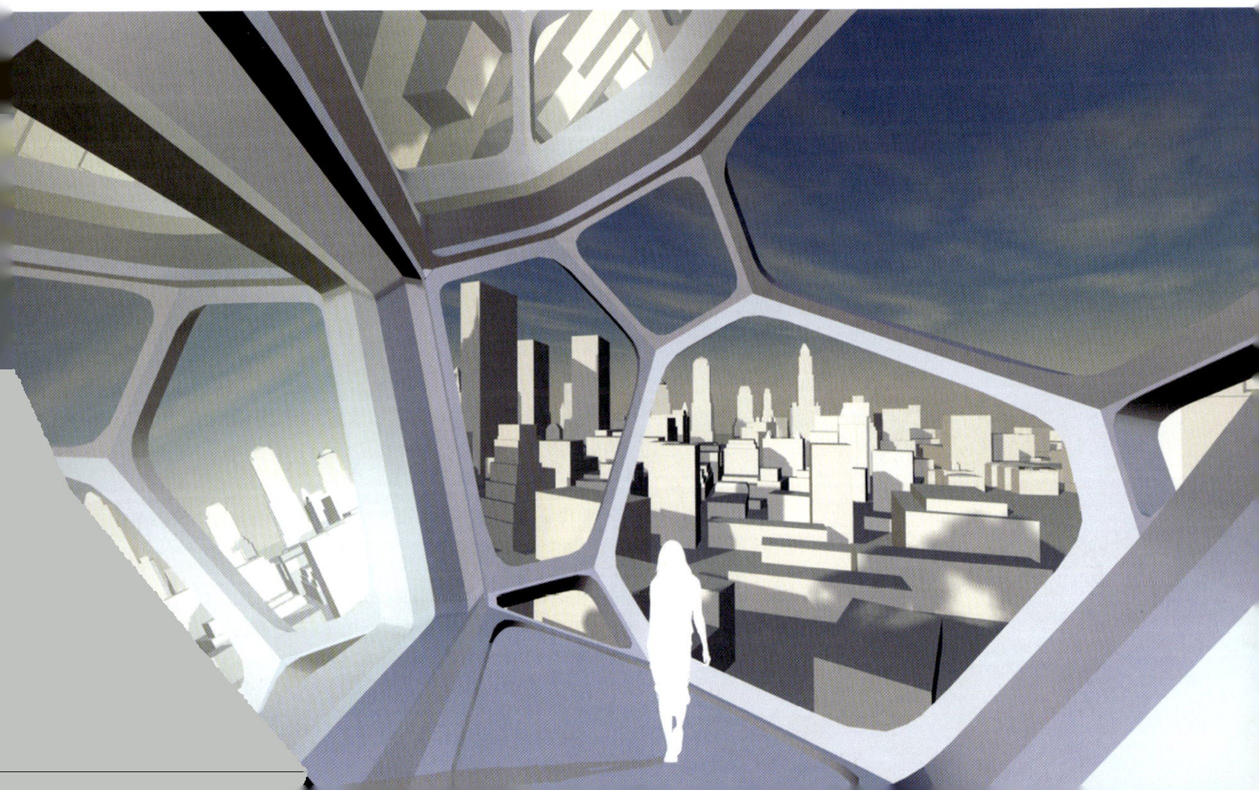

RURAL SUBURBAN URBAN FOAM

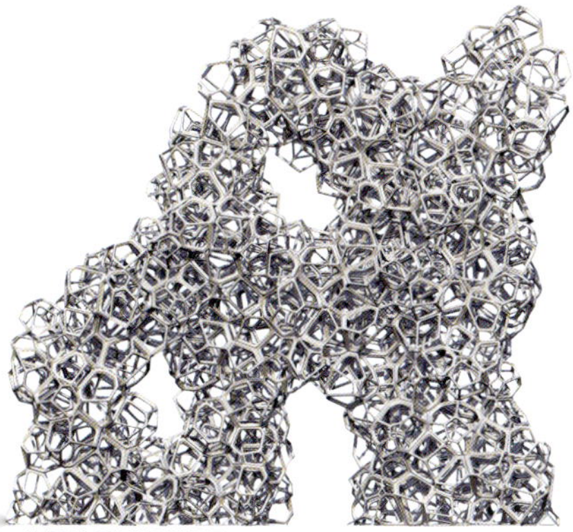

INFRASTRUCTURE 0 yr

PIONEERS 1yr

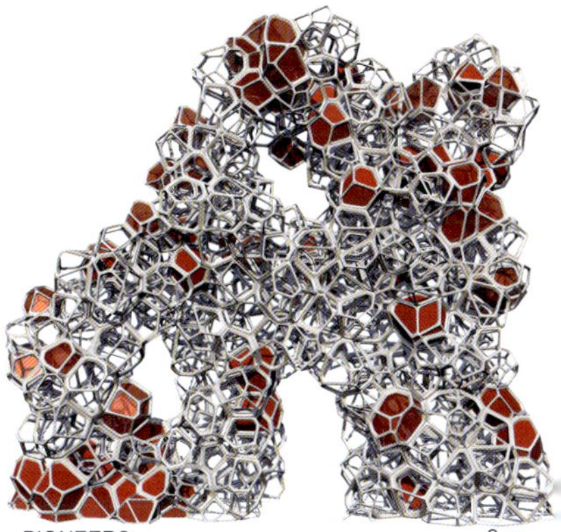

PIONEERS 2 yr

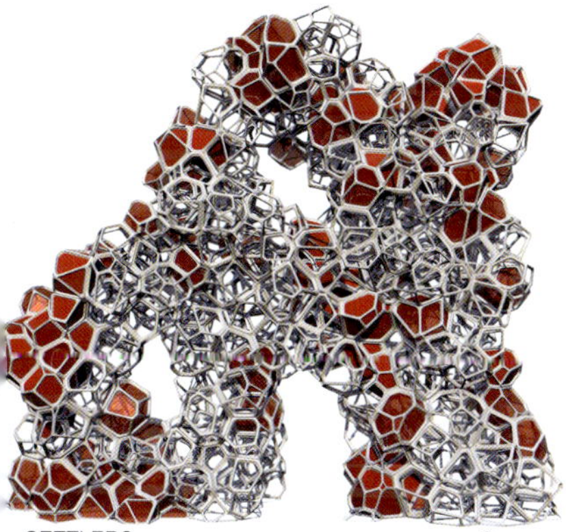

SETTLERS 3 yr

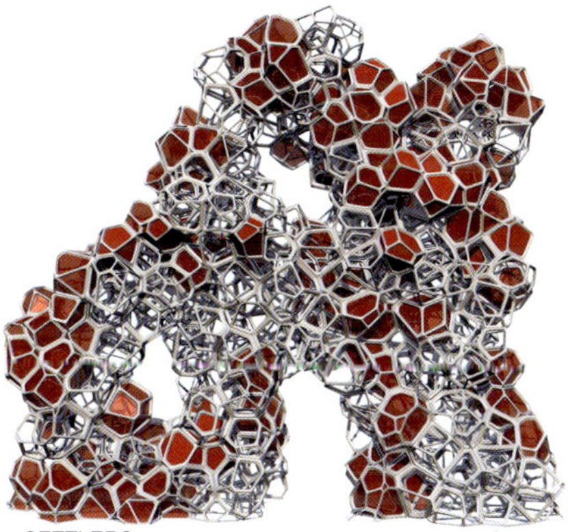

SETTLERS 4 yr

SETTLERS 5 yr

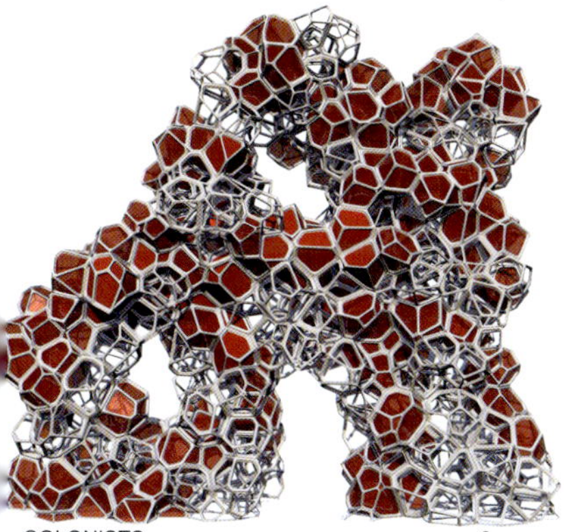

COLONISTS 6 yr

COLONISTS 7 yr

COLONISTS 8 yr

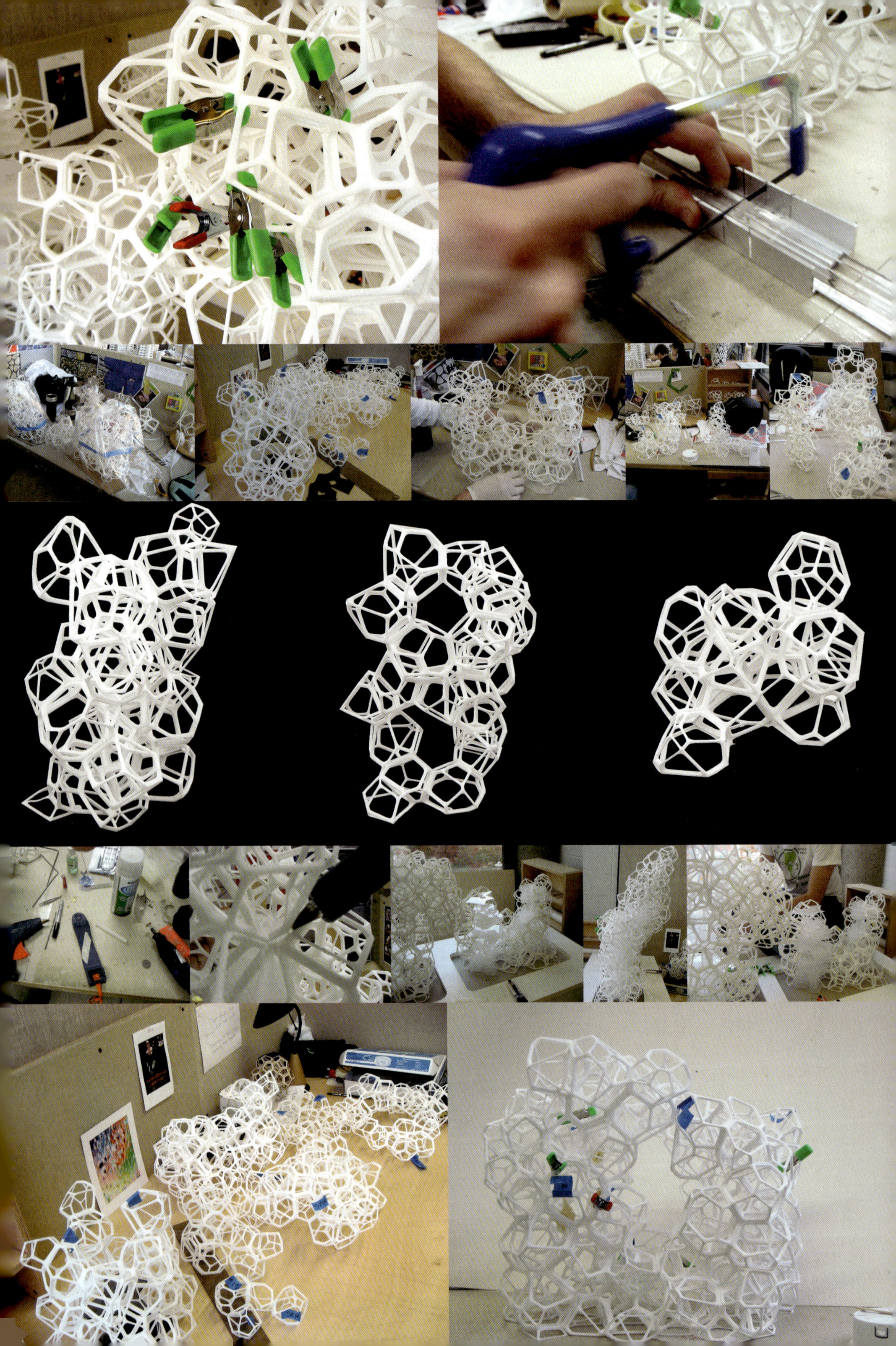

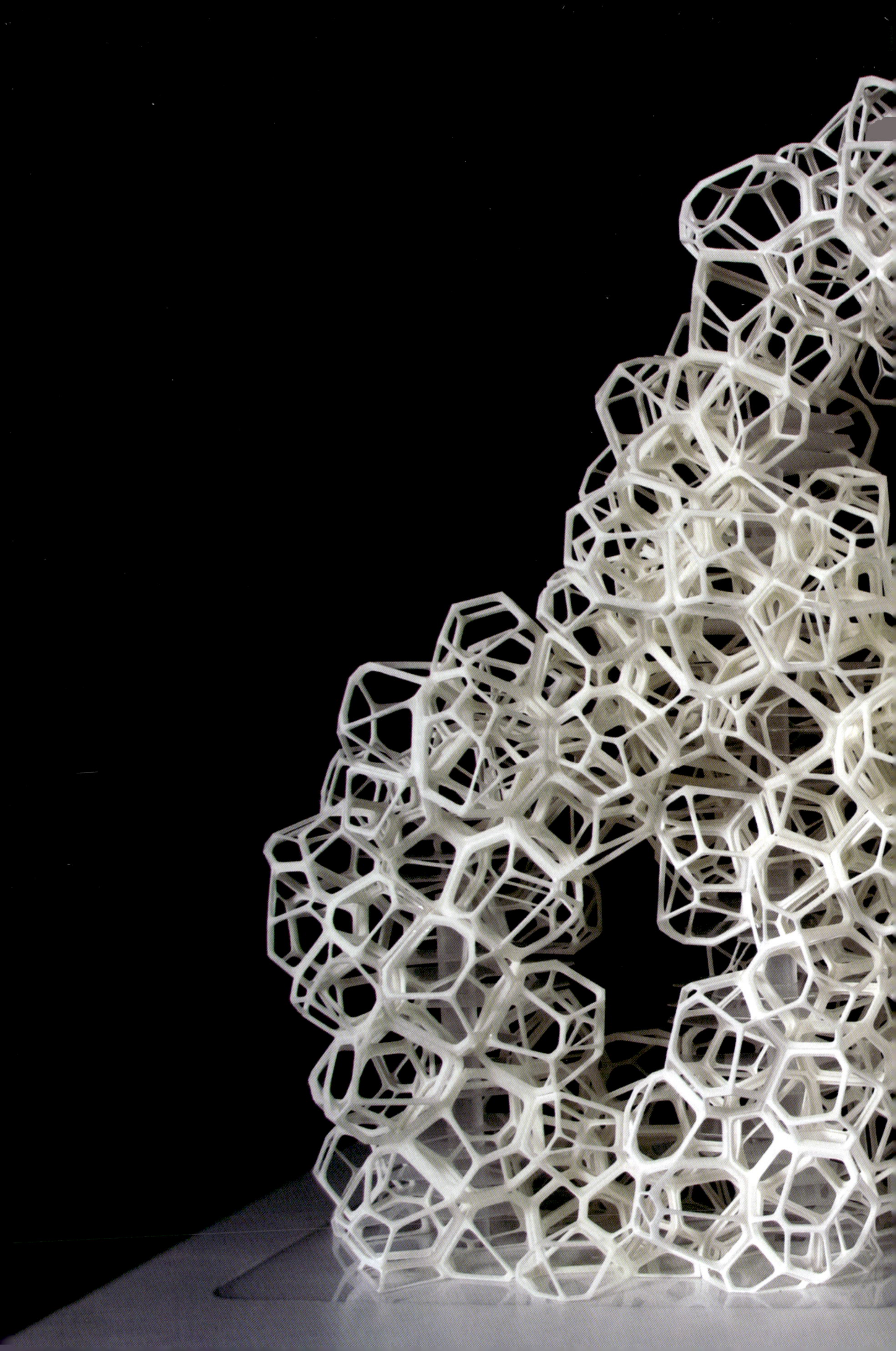

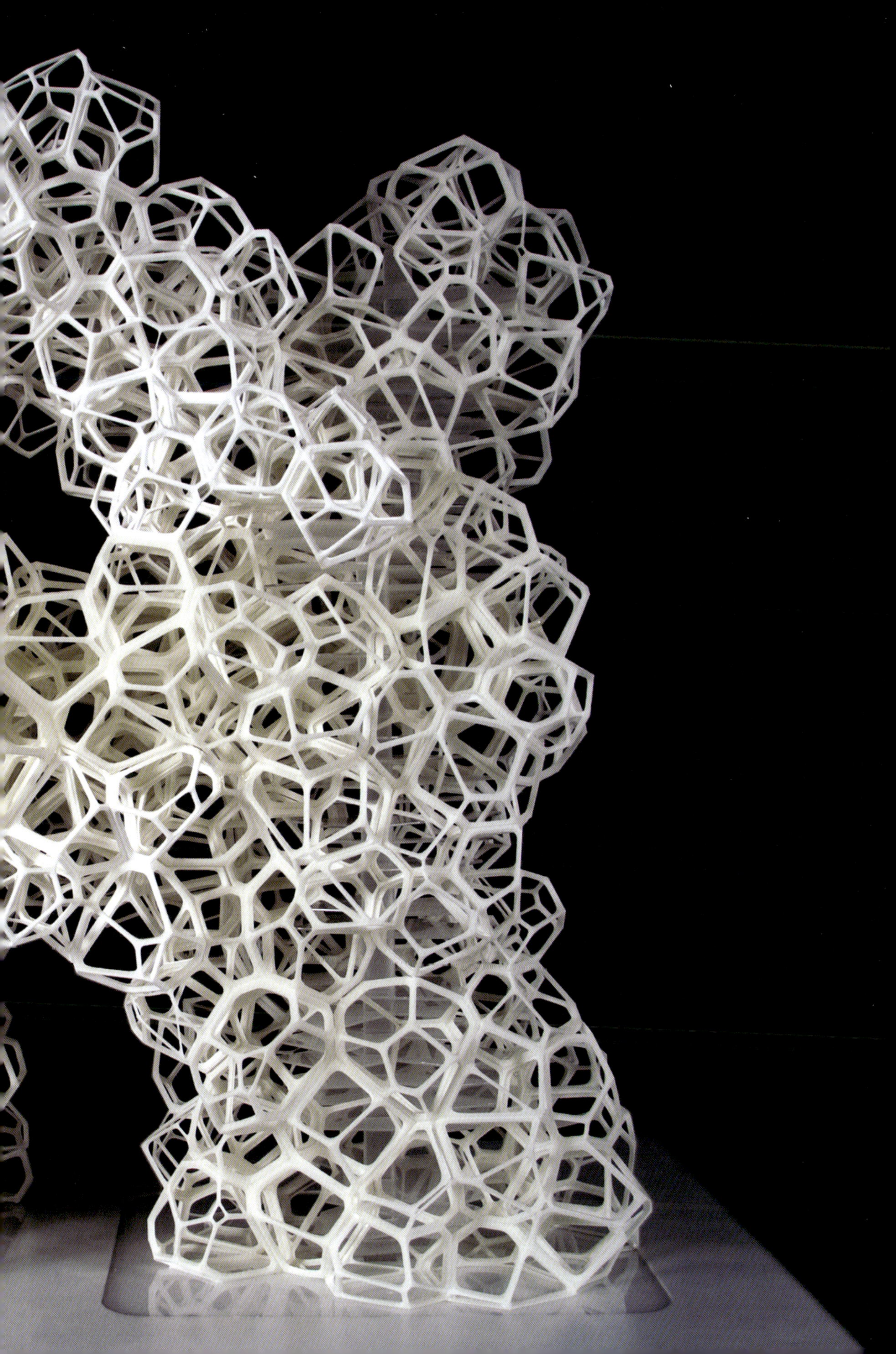

Crystallized Colors

Derek Tao-Han Liu

This project is designed based on the wool thread method. This is a technique used by Frei Otto in which slackened wool threads formed a self-organizing network of optimized path after they were dipped in water. When this technique is deployed, one must become responsive to the fact that free movement of materials is merely not enough to generate architectural complexity. Prior to any process of materiality, an analogue machine and its mechanism must be proposed, in which a framework is provided where the material may traverse freely, while constrained by typological parameters.

In contrast to the framework in Frei Otto's model, which is horizontal and circular, the analogue machine designed for this project is vertical and rectangular, so that the resulted frameworks are in a comparable dimension to a skyscraper's façade. Three primary figures are identified and derived from the numerous framework produced by the machine. The X-node, Y-node, and Tangent are the fundamental constituents of a tectonic network. In addition, each figure type essentially signifies a singular stratum of a completed network. Then the fabrication of this façade system follows such tectonic principles consequently. That is, X-nodes outline and establish the fundamental configuration (foundation network), Y-nodes re-enforce the correlated structure (varied depth and girth of the mullions), and Tangents completes the aesthetic delicacy of the network (varied shapes and sizes of the glass).

The color selection for the glass, as well as the title of this project, is directly inspired by the Bauhaus artist Paul Klee, and his painting 'Kristall-Stufung (Crystal Gradation).' In this painting Paul Klee used the chiaroscuro technique that was weighted in selected colors only, which suggested a crystallized transition of colors. The colored glass and the varied breadth of the mullions also advocate a direct relationship of the exterior façade system and the interior programmatic issues. Furthermore, with the grand entrance corridors, the final façade is hoped to bring forward an aesthetic quality that places itself in between the realms of Gothic and Art Nouveau.

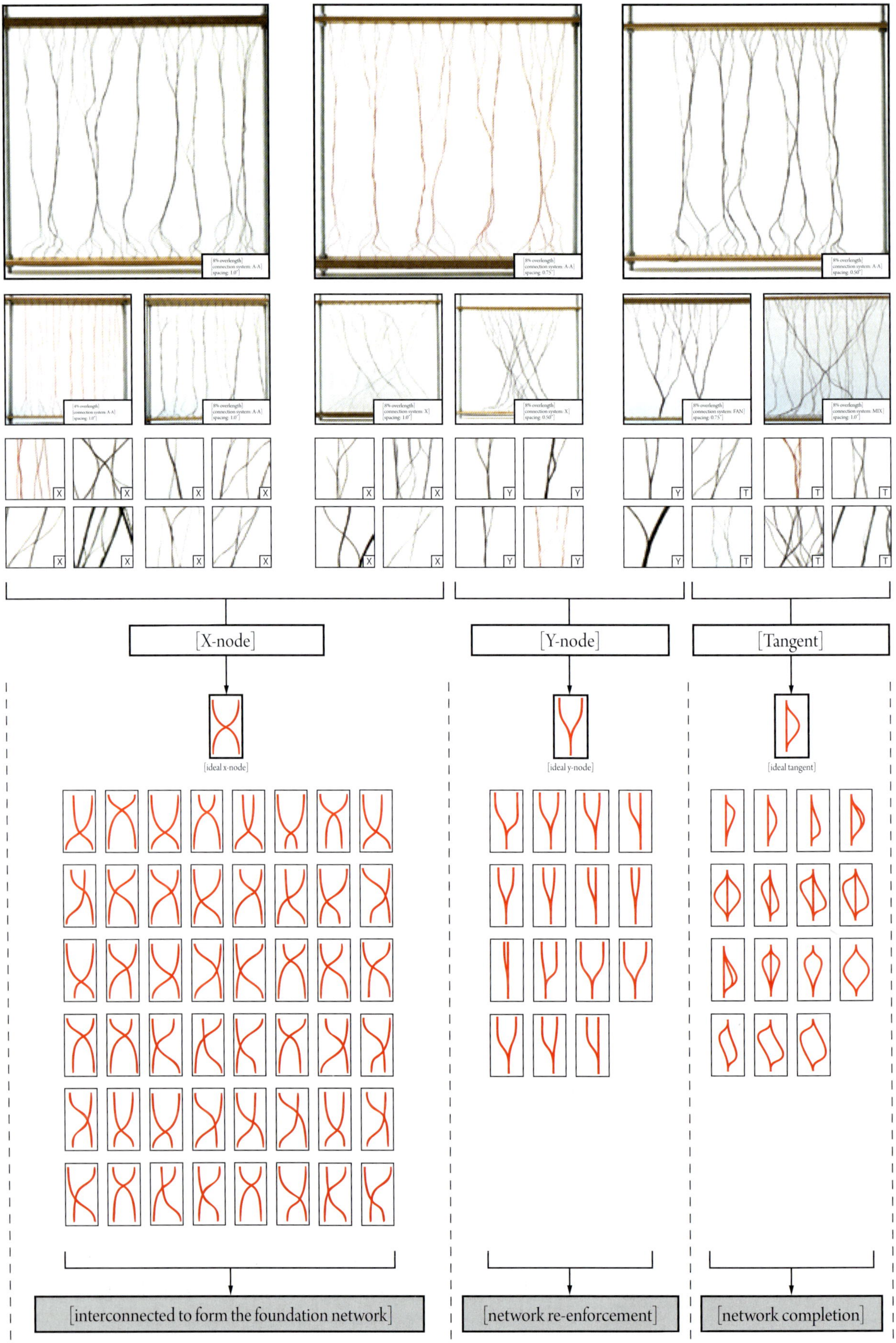

[X-node]
[Y-node]
[Tangent]
[ideal x-node]
[ideal y-node]
[ideal tangent]
[interconnected to form the foundation network]
[network re-enforcement]
[network completion]

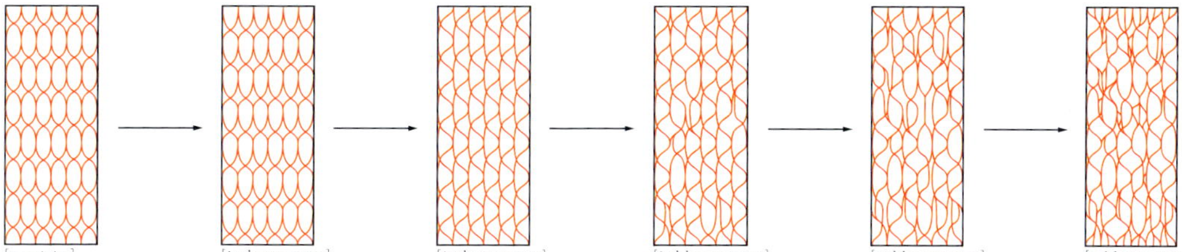

[no variation]
[only ideal X figures]

[1st degree variation]
[ideal X replaced with varied X]

[1st degree variation]
[ideal X replaced with varied X]

[2nd degree variation]
[irregular interconnection of varied X]

[2nd degree variation]
[network reenforcement with Y]

[3rd degree variation]
[configuration completion with T]

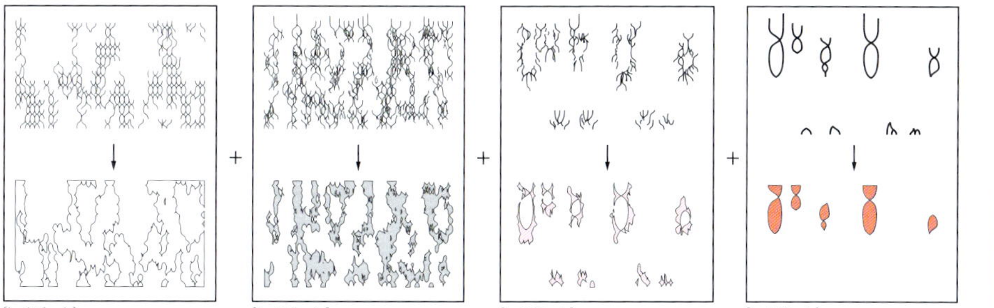

[level 1 façade]
> glass technique.5% transparency
> color technique.white (0,0,0,0)

[level 2 façade]
> glass technique.15% transparency
> color technique.gray (0,0,0,20)

[level 3 façade]
> glass technique.40% transparency
> color technique.pink (0,19,5,0)

[level 4 façade]
> glass technique.80% transparency
> color technique.red (0,61,46,4)

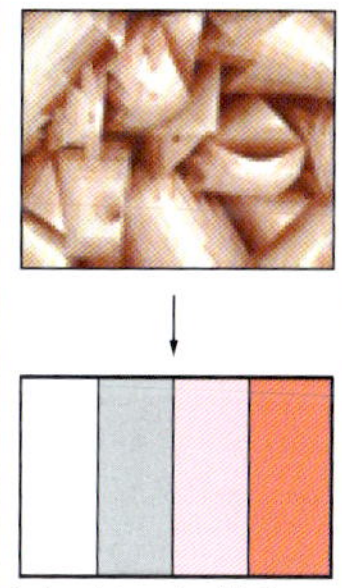

[color technique of paul klee]

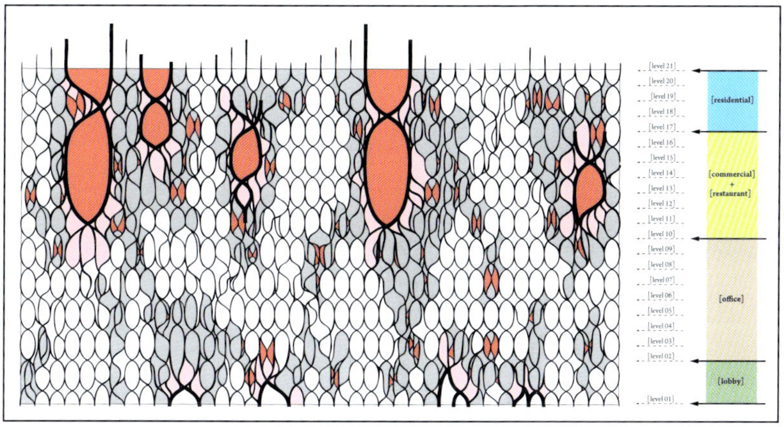

[crystal gradation façade - with implementation of wool thread technique + color technique by paul klee]

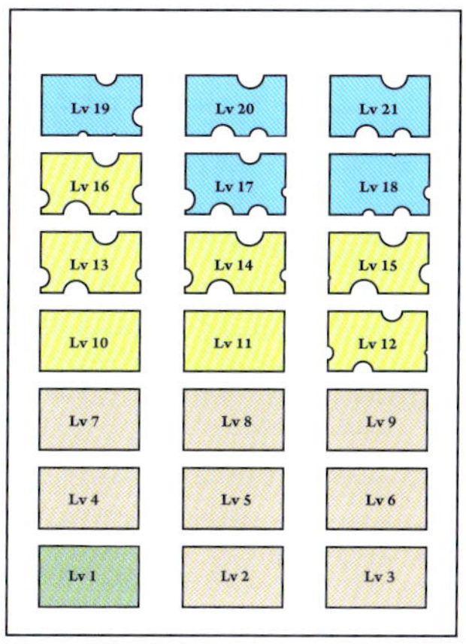

[diagrammatic floor plans]

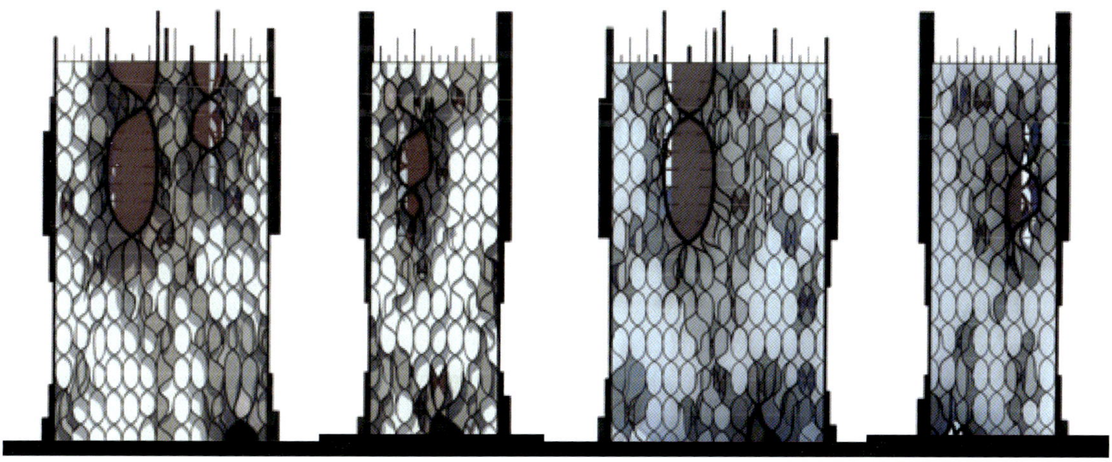

[south elevation]

[east elevation . s. michigan ave.]

[north elevation . e. adam st.]

[west elevation]

Tectonic Networking

Adrienne Froemelt & Paul Meyer

The concept of tectonic networking is developed from Frei Otto's well documented research of wool thread path-optimization systems. The self-organization of slacked wool thread, when submerged in water, creates a system in which flexibility and movement are used to develop a structural form. Within the system, loose figures of movement combine to generate networks of structure. It was from the desire to form a façade that depicts the values of flexibility and variation that we researched the following ideals of tectonic networking:

The first step in the process to develop a system of structural networking was to follow Otto's wool thread methodology and test the formation of networks within a series of analog models. Different amounts of slack were tested on the threads, ranging from 4% to 10%, with a conclusion that a slack of 8% yielded the tightest thread network. Through an objective analysis of the models, we classified three types of figures that appeared consistently within the networks: the Y-figure, the X-figure, and the Tangent-figure. These three figures were found within each analog model and are integral in the formation of a taut network.

Continued analysis of these wool thread networks led to a dissection of the three main figure typologies. Each analog model produced a unique thread configuration composed of a diverse range of figure variations. The figure variations are crucial to the formation of a tectonically networked system. From the analog models, we developed a catalog of figures that began with the three ideal figure types. By limiting the framework in which the figure variations could occur, we eliminated the possibility of an infinite data set.

Using our figure database, we constructed and analyzed a series of figure combinations. Four different classifications of configurations were determined: homogenous frameworks, homogeneous variations, heterogeneous frameworks, and composite variations. Homogenous frameworks consist of only ideal figures. Homogeneous variations attach a single varied figure type with itself, while heterogeneous frameworks bond multiple degrees of single-figure variations with each other; and composite variations include all three figure typologies using all ranges of variation.

Analogue Models

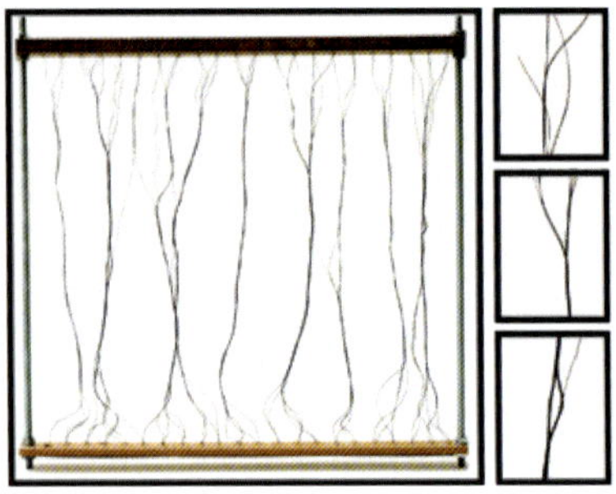

Prototype 1
8% overlength
A-A connection
1.00" spacing

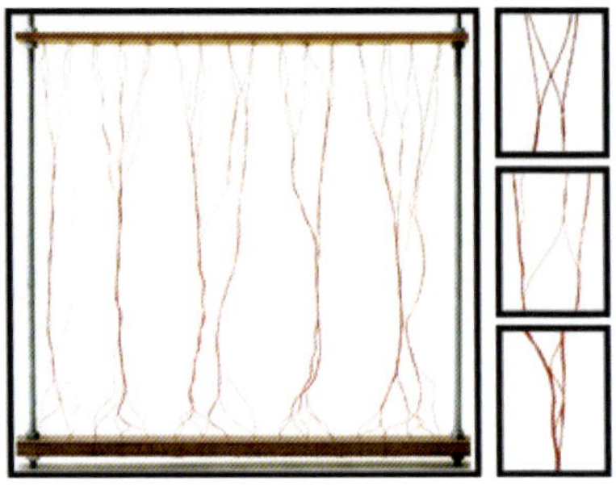

Prototype 2
8% overlength
A-A connection
0.75" spacing

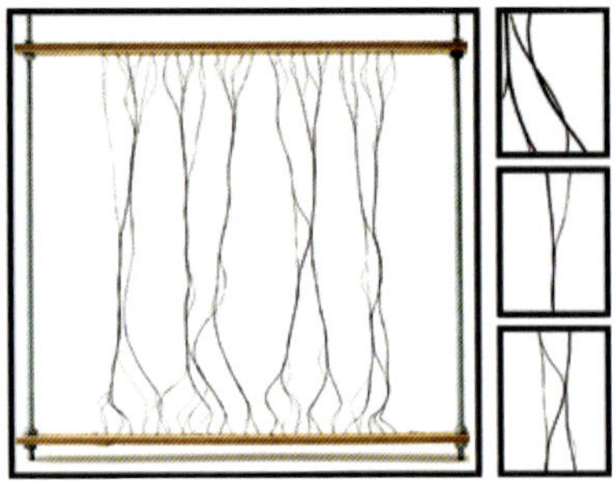

Prototype 3
8% overlength
A-A connection
0.50" spacing

Figure Variations

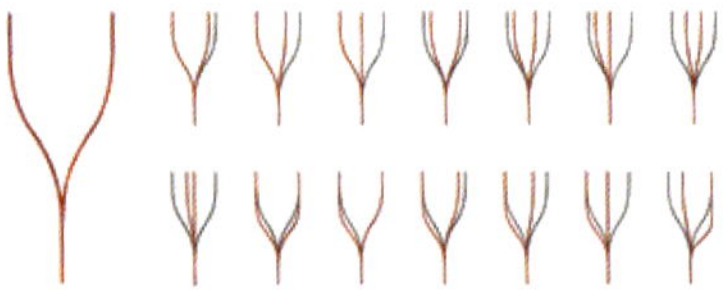

Ideal Y-Figure and Variations

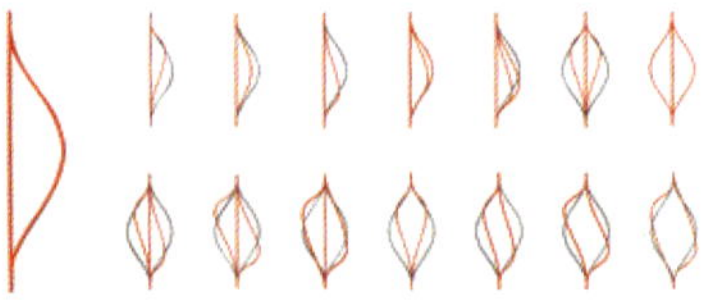

Ideal Tangent-Figure and Variations

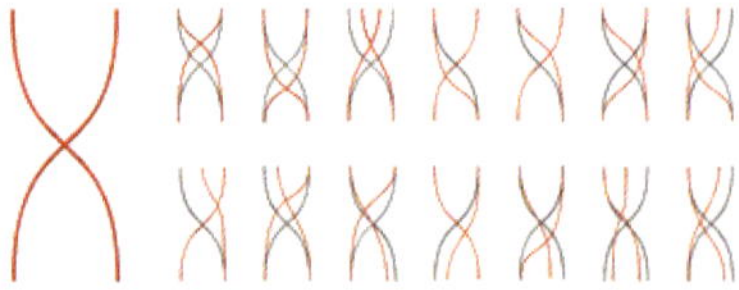

Ideal X-Figure and Variations

Tectonic Networking

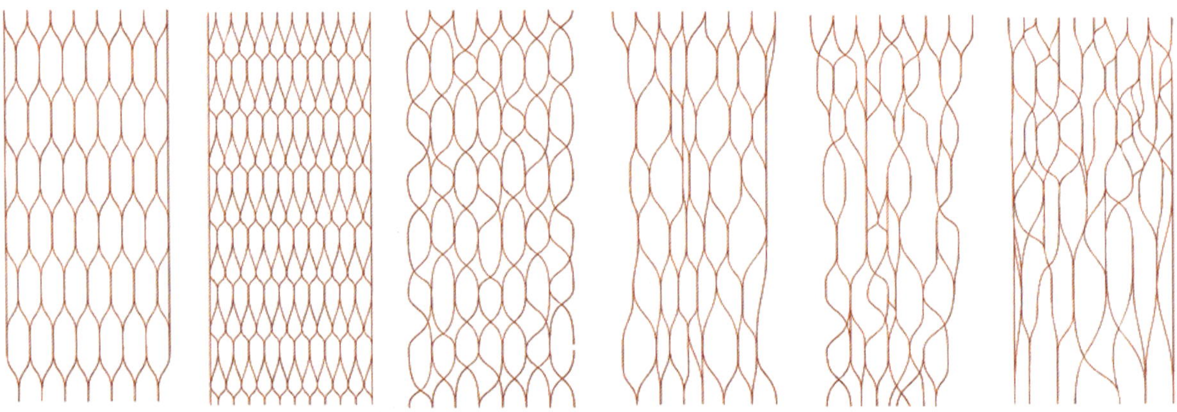

Left to Right: Homogenous Ideal Y Configuration, Homogenous Ideal Tangent Configuration, Heterogenous X Configuration, Heterogenous Y Configuration, Composite Configuration A, Composite Configuration B

Structural Mergings

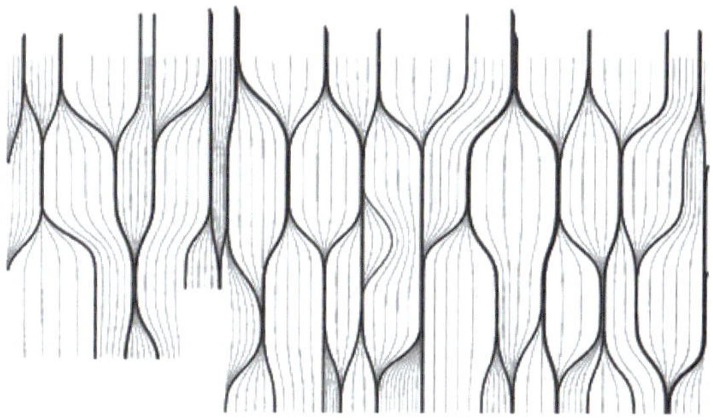

The type of tectonic networking depicted in this façade is based on degrees of mergings and splitting of the structural columns. The movement and fluidity of wool thread is displayed throughout the building in the form of mullions and cuts within the floor slab.

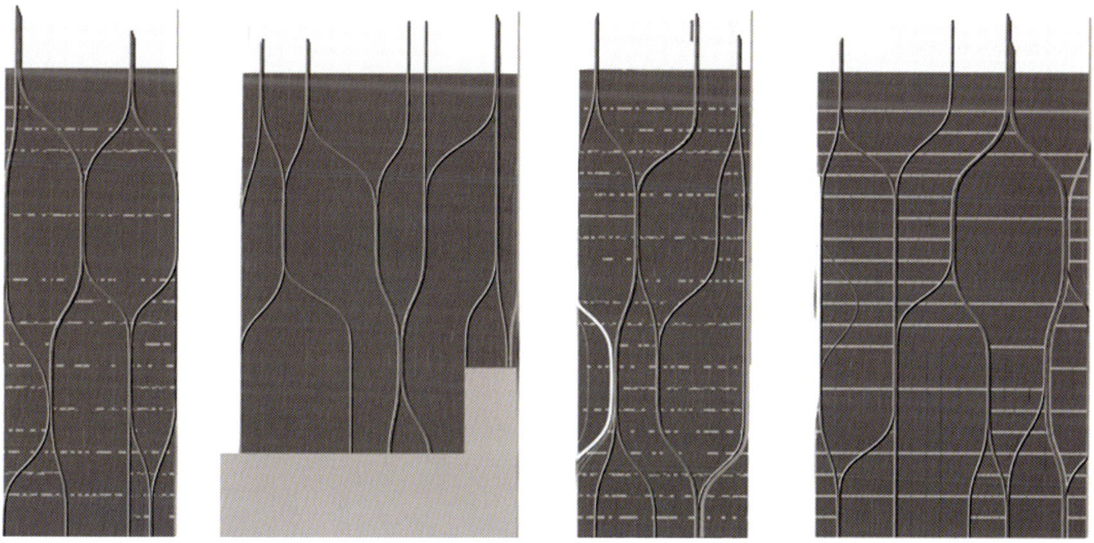

Floor Slab System

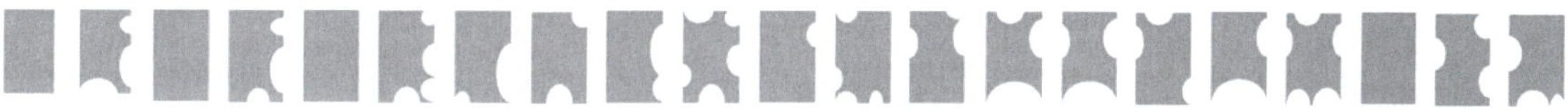

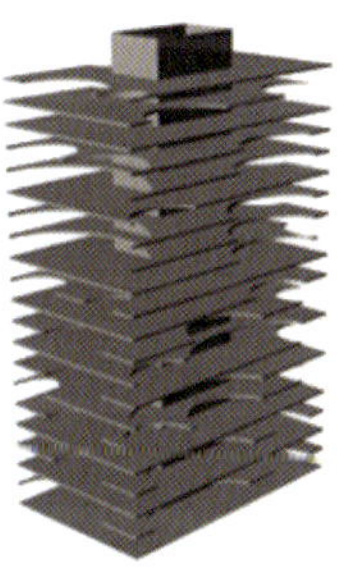

Cut Floor Slabs

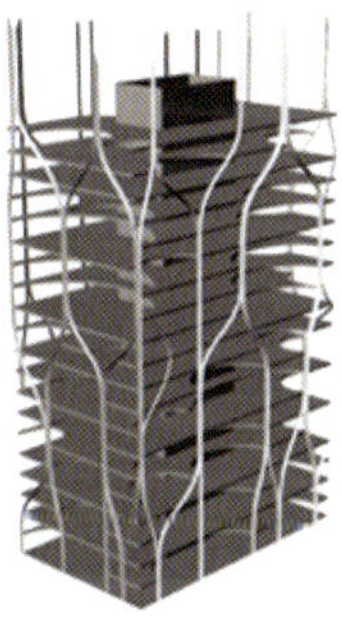

Column Span Guides Cut

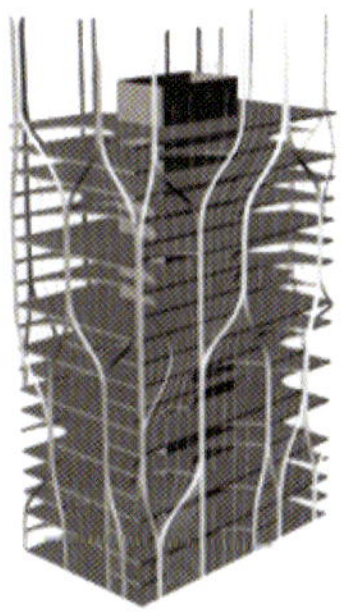

Mullions Depict Variation

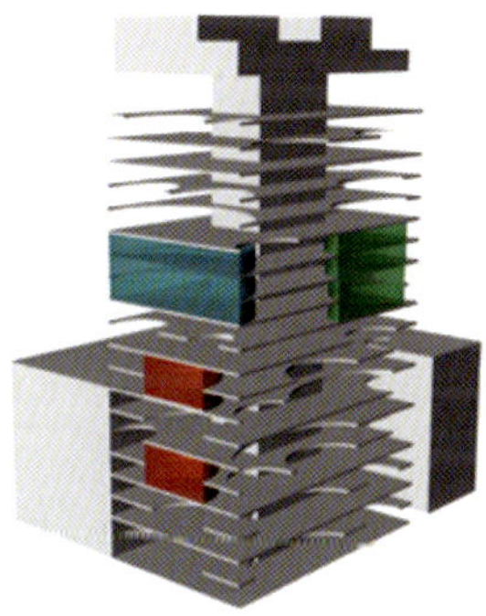

Gallery Spaces Created

Relational Network

The façade development originates from the wool thread configuration studies. The negative spaces that emerge from the areas in between the configurations become inspiration for façade elements that permeate the building's interior. On the east façade, a concave negative space extrudes into the interior to create a dominating alcove, allowing morning sunlight to reach the building's core. Two convex negative spaces on the north façade are expressed as balcony spaces. A series of roof top terraces is articulated by the gradation of the mullion endpoints.

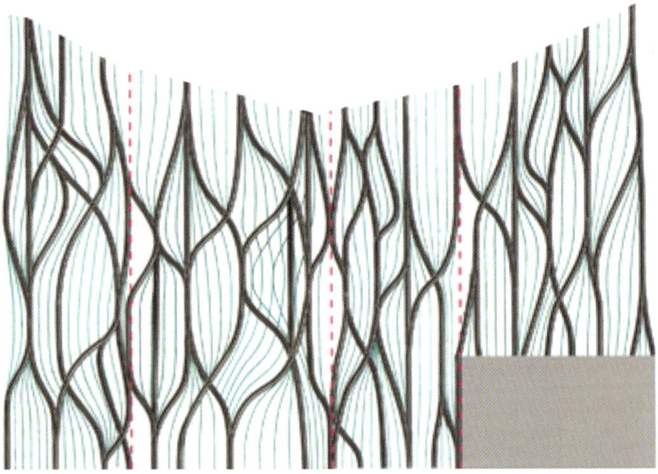

Negative Spaces

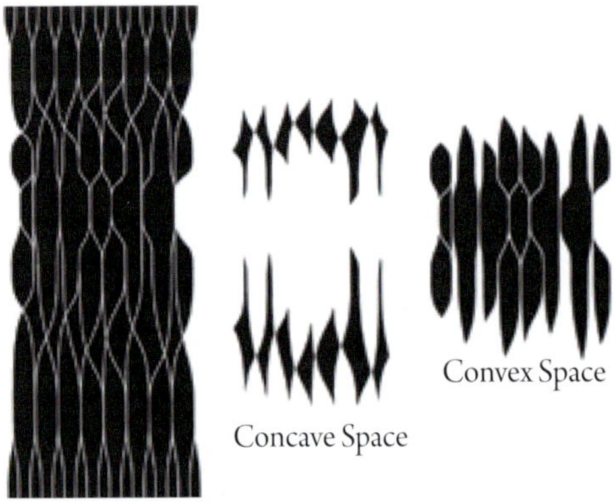

Figure Extraction and Mullion Development

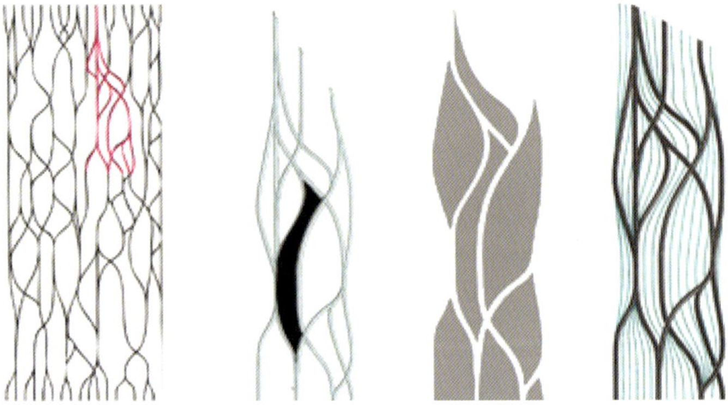

Interlaced

Katherine Giraldo & Atreya Safari & Be Thach

The technique of braiding has been apparent since ancient times, but may be studied to explore the possibilities and uses in the modern world. In the design studio, the main objective was to research this textile techniqe and analyze the various ways braiding patterns can be formed in order to create a skin or façade system. The façade would then be placed on the existing building located on 200 S. Michigan Avenue in Chicago, Illinois. The site is a highly dense, urban area where architectural influences from Burnham and Sullivan abound. Using the research and analysis found, the façade would reflect the intricate properties of braiding as well as fit within its modern location.

Originating in Peru, a braid is a complex structure or pattern formed by diagonally intertwining three or more strands of material. The strands pass in a diagonal direction until they reach a border, then they reverse directions and pass diagonally to the opposite border. The simplest of braids consists of three strands. Braiding systems can range from this simple three strands to an endless number of strands. From the research and analysis, local and global conditions were established that identified various attributes that occured in braids. Three types of braid families were recognized: the Simple Braid, the Curved Edge, and the Double Twist.

Braiding conditions were stressed in a façade pattern that consisted of important attributes from the established families. Dense, closed areas of the façades contained the tightly intertwining of simple braids. Windows were identfied by the curved edges that created a vertical border. Entrances were enhanced by the curvature of double twist braids that invited the flow of pedestrian movement. Overall, the braiding façade system reflected that which resulted in the program of a fashion department store; an abstract dress that wrapped around the body.

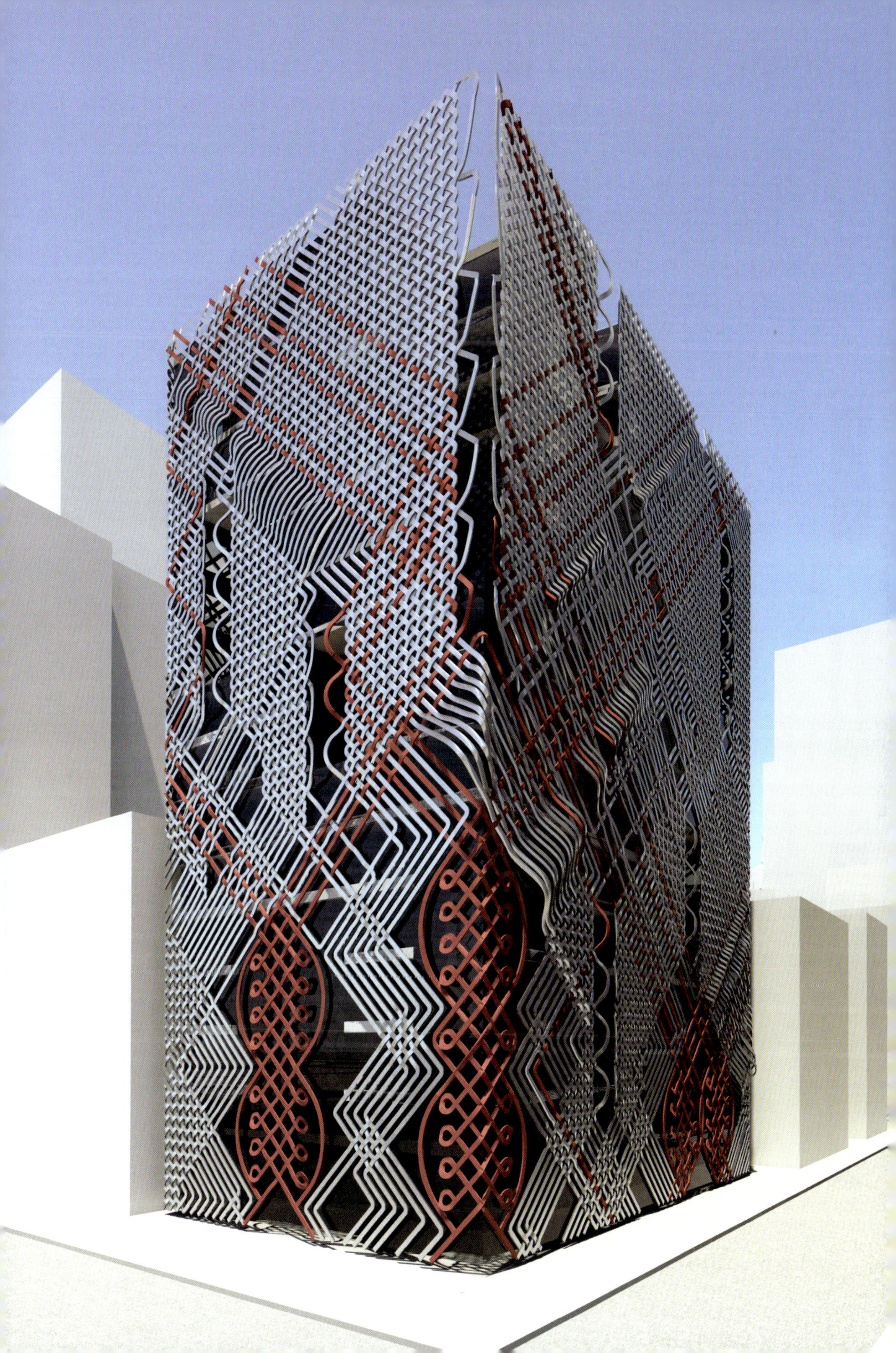

LOCAL CONDITIONS

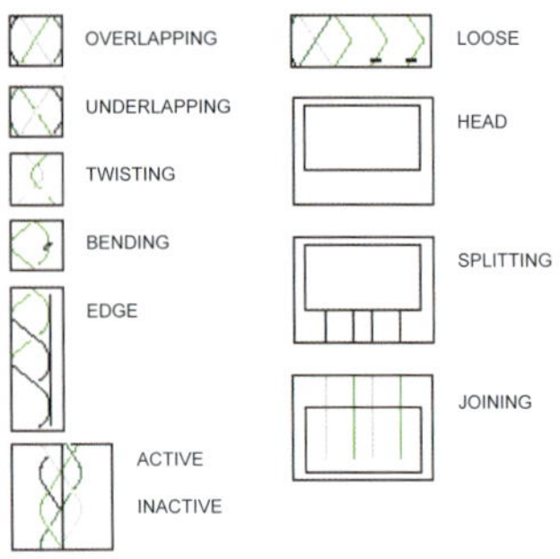

GLOBAL CONDITIONS

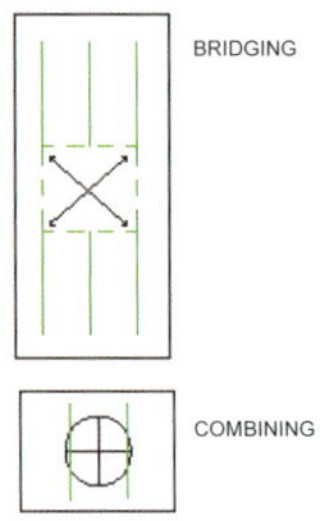

SYSTEMATICS

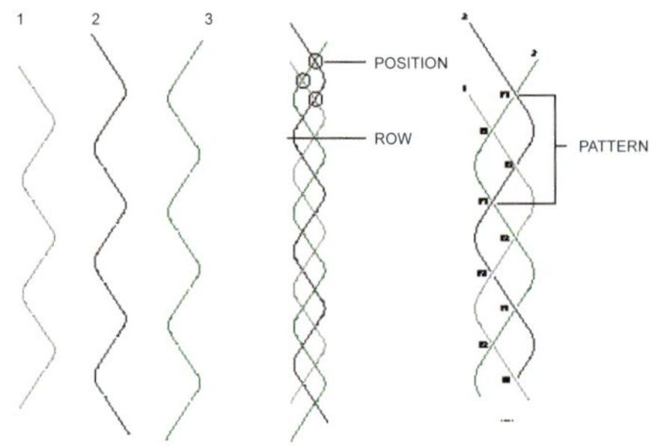

BRAID FUNCTIONS

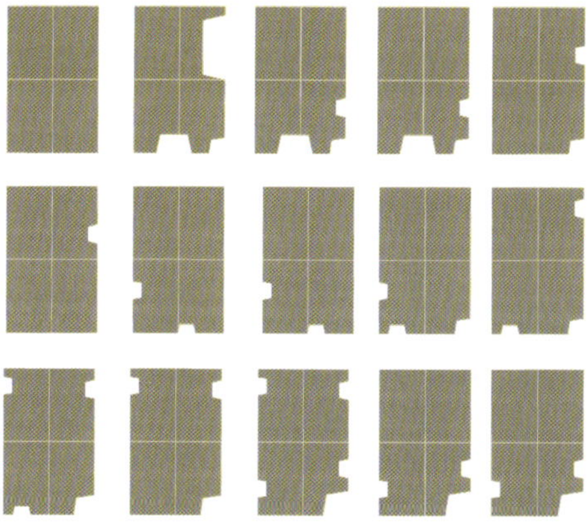

FLOOR SLAB CONFIGURATIONS

SITE PLAN

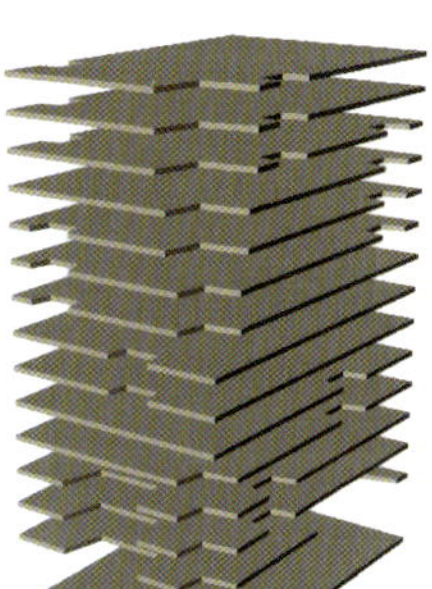

FLOOR SLABS

GLASS SURFACE

PATTERN APPLIED TO SURFACE

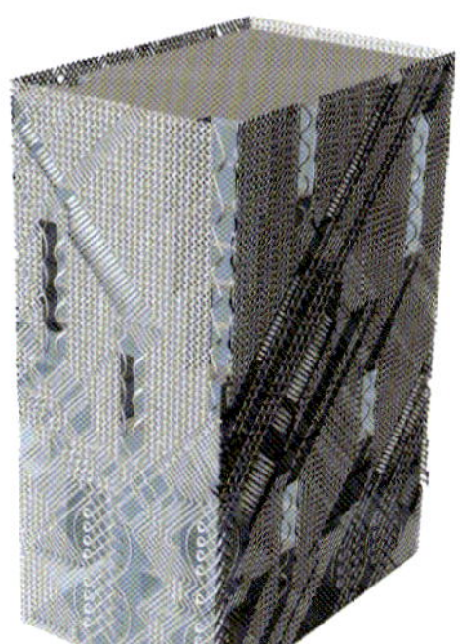

PATTERN LOFTED

Fissure

Jacob Porter & Darryl Zuk

We began this project examining the structure of foam. Foam is generally disordered and contains a variety of bubble sizes. Mathematics uses foam to solve problems of space-filling and minimal surfaces, but these fail to address that even within the most efficient packing lattices, anomlies occur naturally. We wanted to discover these anomalies, and after an exhaustive process of experimentation; we found two: triangulation and cracking. Triangulation is the base form of packing. Triangulation occurs when three congruent elements arrange themselves in a tight, rigid, triangular shape. These clusters combine to make much larger lattices, which resemble a honeycomb structure. Cracking is an irregularity that occurs in between two lattices of triangulation. Cracking is linear or radial in structure. Radial cracking has a definite epicenter with cracks radiating outward in various directions. Linear cracking has an explicit beginning point and ending point. Due to their dendritic nature, cracks can branch.

Our experiment showed cracking exists within a spectrum of fluidity that ranges from crystalline to liquid. A crystalline pattern is composed of relatively few patches of triangulation with straight edges. The cracks tend to be linear and don't branch out very much. A liquid pattern is composed of numerous smaller patches of triangulation with sharp, jagged edges. Liquid cracking patterns have multiple cracks branching throughout them in numerous directions. Liquid patterns tend to have less surface area of triangulated spheres. To apply these cracking patterns to our façades, we looked at our previous results and developed a library of crack typologies. Using this library, we were able to design cracking patterns for our building's façades.

By carving voids out from the floor plates where ever they met a crack in the façade, the cracks enter into the interior and become an experiential part of the building. The crack openings in the floors are used to enhance internal interaction via diagonal viewing and communication lines and vertical circulation spaces separate from the central service core. This arrangement system is a comment on normative office buildings. Instead of the relentless stacking of floors in contemporary office buildings that prohibits communication between floors, our system reorganizes the office tower as a more three dimensional system. The modern office building requires more interaction, and our system allows for that.

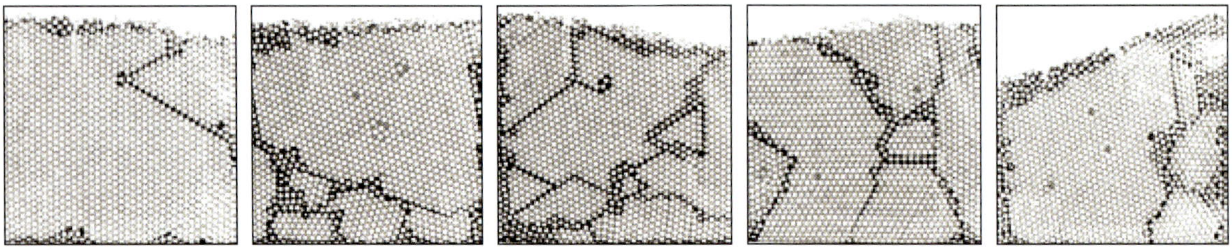

cracking

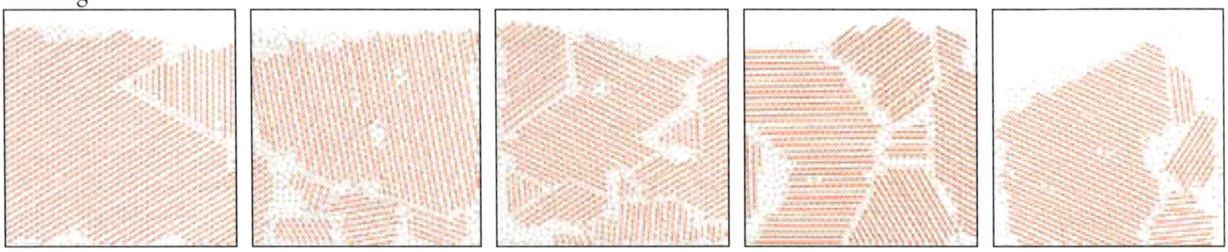

triangulation

generated cracking pattern

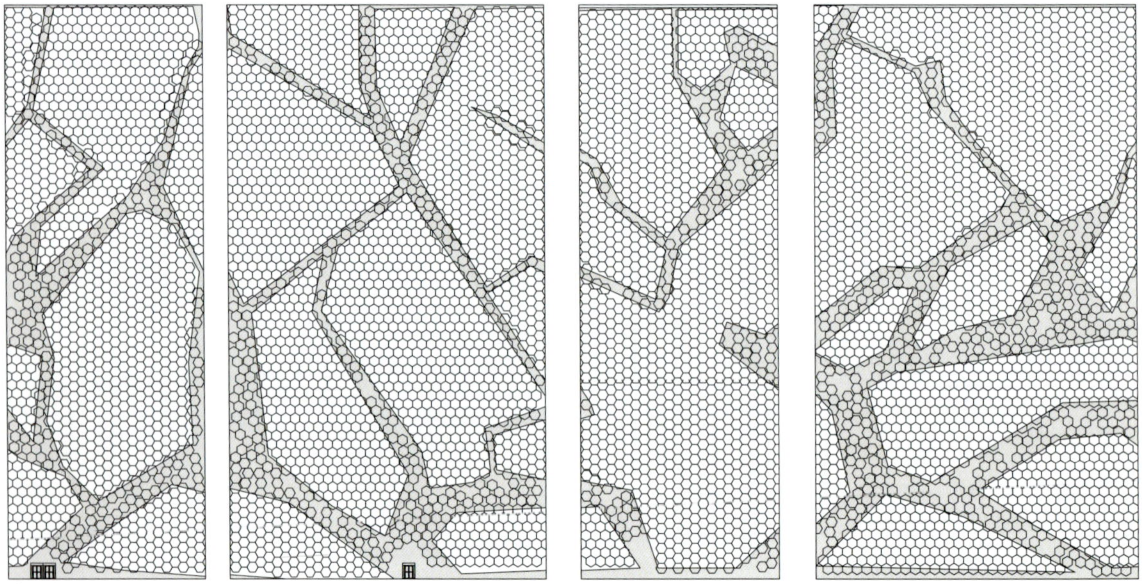

façade system

floorplan relationship to façade cracks

Radiolaria

Tasnouva Habib & Yasin Bulhan

Radiolaria who take their name from radial symmetry are protozoa living under water. At an initial stage they have an irregular double curvature shape which slowly starts to take a spherical form as they mature. The growth is contingent upon the flow of current as there is no gravitational pull under water and thus the force of the current pushes and pulls to form the shape of the organism. Depicting that characteristic, the shape of the building is formed depended upon the flow of traffic.

While analyzing the relationship between the perforations of radiolarian shapes, it was found that the penetrations are mere representation of pentagons, heptagons and hexagons at numerous scales and numbers each. To understand how the relationship between the shapes works, we started off with the parameters of having only one size of each pentagon, heptagon and hexagon and started to form agglomeration of those polygons to generate forms. This was more of a manual way of investigation to analyze the connections. But, in radiolarian, forms appear first and the perforations generate depended upon that. It is more of an involuntary action to fill the space and be structurally sound. Thus, more analysis led to Ansys, a 3D modeling program which allows one to produce tessellations in triangles which are structurally sound in a shell membrane, which, in our case, was the façade. This was coherent to the involuntary characteristics of radiolaria as we had limited control over the size of the triangles and no control over the pattern of the triangles.

A thorough investigation led to the understanding that the perforations are not quite as predictable in pattern. The tessellation of the same surface and with the some settings changed every time there was a push or pull. The global element size of the tessellation relied upon the complexity of the surface and the degree of curvature.

Radiolaria

Research

Radiolaria
who take their name from radial symmetry often marked by radial skeletal spines are protozoa distinguished :

1) by segregation of their soft anatomy into the central capsule, containing the endoplasm, and the surrounding ectoplasm (or calymma), and

2) by their siliceous (opaline) skeletons of the large majority of species.

Radiolaria - Zooplankton
-drift along water currents
-major controlling factors radiolaria distribution is water temperature and salinity.
-appear to be most abundant in warm waters of the equatorial zone. As a result of this trend, total Radiolaria diversity declines as latitude increases.

Individual radiolarians are normally in the size range of hundredths to tenths of millimeters, but some reach dimensions of a millimeter or more, large enough to be seen with the naked eye. Some species are amassed into colonies, which may reach sizes of centimeter and even meter scale.

Conspicuous features of the calymma are the frothy, bubble-like alveoli. The alveoli are presumably a floatation device, disappearing when agitated and reforming after the individual has sunk to a greater depth.

They are able to cling to and move the individual about surfaces of laboratory vessels, and may thus cling to foreign objects in nature.

The classification of Radiolaria recognizes two major extant groups:
1) the polycystines, with solid skeletal elements of simple opaline silica, and
2) the Phaeodarians, with hollow skeletal elements of a complex (and as yet poorly understood) siliceous composition that results in rapid dissolution in sea water and consequent rare preservation in sediments.

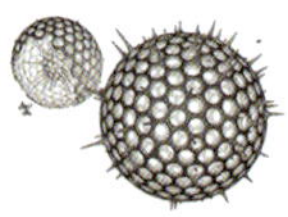

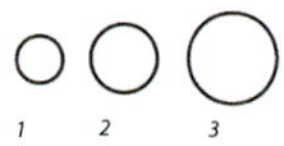

1. Pentagon
2. Hexagon
3. Haptagon

5 Hexagons fitting around one Pentagon

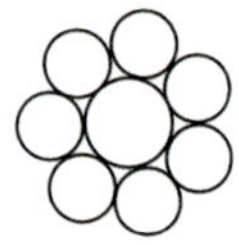

7 Hexagons fitting around one Heptagon

Analysis

A tessellation is created when a shape is repeated over and over again covering a plane without any gaps or overlaps. Another word for a tessellation is a tiling. The word "tessellate" means to form or arrange small squares in a checkered or mosaic pattern and is derived from the Ionic version of the Greek word "tesseres," which in English means "four." The first tilings were made from square tiles.

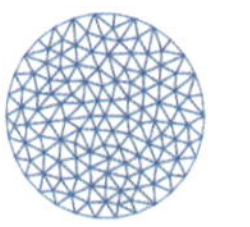

Tessellations and computer graphics
In the subject of computer graphics, tessellation techniques are often used to manage datasets of polygons and divide them into suitable structures for rendering. Normally, the data is tessellated into triangles, which is sometimes referred to as triangulation. In computer-aided design, arbitrary 3D shapes are divided (tessellated) into a mesh of small, easy-to-analyze pieces -- usually either irregular tetrahedrons, or irregular hexahedrons. The mesh is used for finite element analysis. Some geodesic domes are designed by tessellating the sphere with triangles that are as close to equilateral triangles as possible.

Transformation
1.To change in form, appearance, or structure; metamorphose.
2. to change in condition, nature, or character; convert.
3. to change into another substance; transmute.

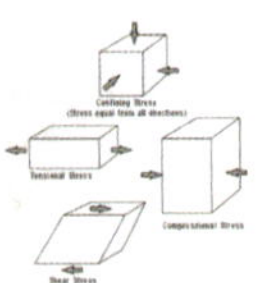

Deformation
1. the act of deforming; distortion; disfigurement.
2. the result of deforming; change of form, esp. for the worse.
3. an altered form.
4. Geology, Mechanics. a change in the shape or dimensions of a body, resulting from stress; strain.

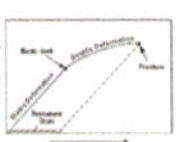

Elastic Deformation -- wherein the strain is reversible.
Ductile Deformation -- wherein the strain is irreversible.
Fracture - irreversible strain wherein the material breaks.

Uniform Flat Surface

Regular tessellation of the same sized circles (Hexagons), resulting in an uniform flat surface.

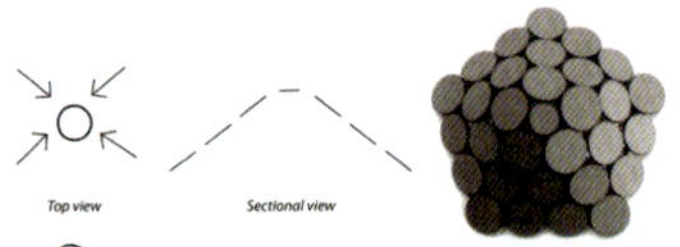

Pinch

Regular tessellation of the same sized circles (hexagons) and replacing the center circle by a smaller sized circle (pentagon) resulting in a pinch.

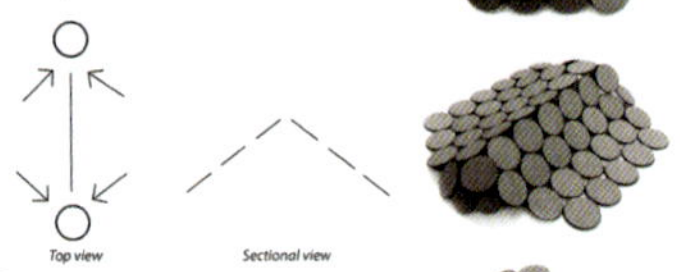

Ridge

Strain applied at two control points by inserting smaller sized circles (pentagons) resulting in a ridge formation in a flat plane composed of uniform tessellation of same sized circles (hexagons).

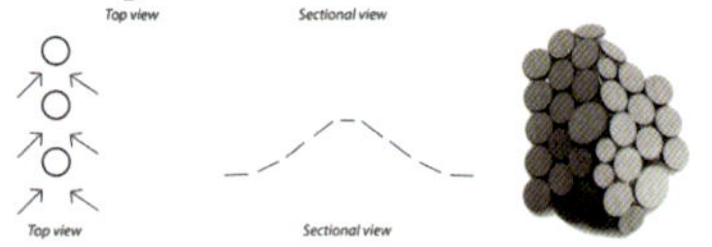

Fold

Arrangement of pinches in a series resulting in a fold.

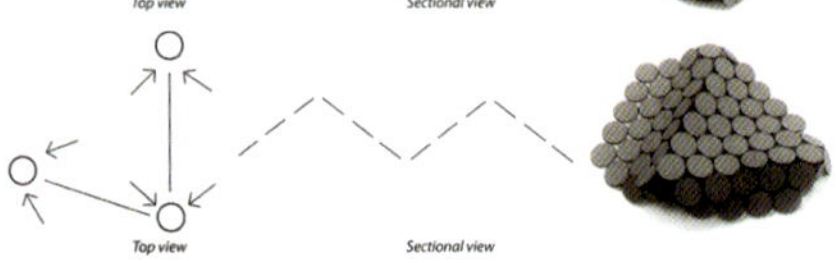

Double ridge

Strain applied at three control points with one common point by inserting smaller sized circles (pentagons) resulting in a ridge formation in a flat plane composed of uniform tessellation of same sized circles (hexagons).

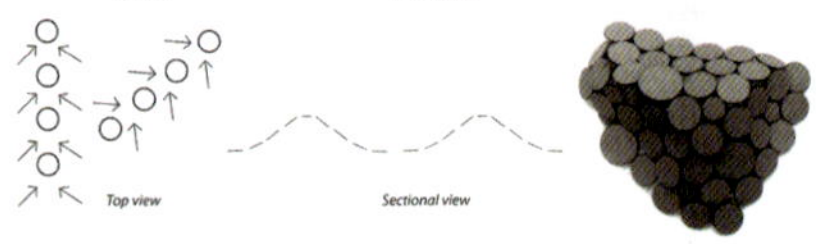

Double fold

Arrangement of pinches in a series in two different direction from one common starting point resulting in a double fold.

Combination of fold and ridge

An arrangement of pinches in a series resulting in a fold and an arrangement of two constrained points resulting in a ridge condition. Combining these two conditions into one linked plane creates a subtle curvature. Inserting a single pinch condition at any point in the plane results in a ridge formation.

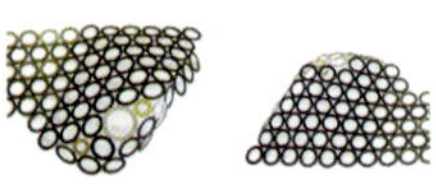

Fold Condition

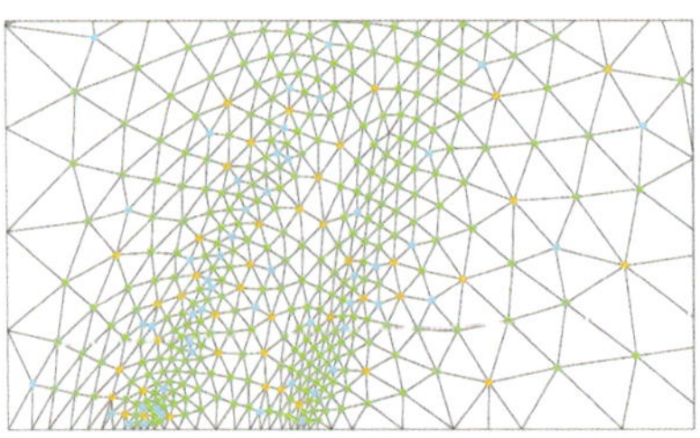

Segment of a fold condition

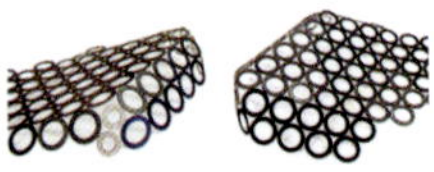

Ridge Condition

Analyzing the tessellation of polygons

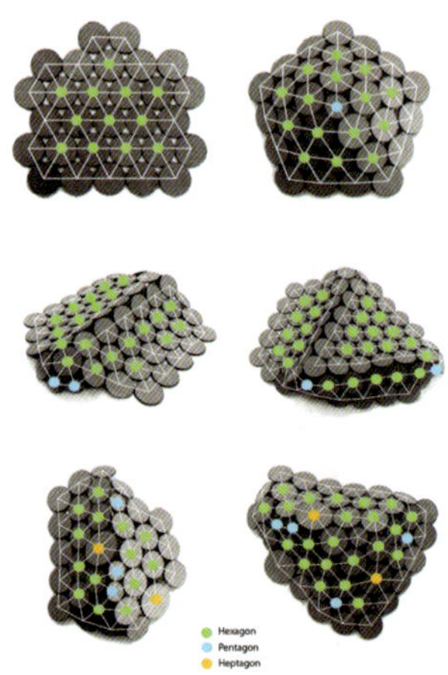

Radiolaria

Tessellation Analysis- Facades

Flat surface | Pinched surface | Pinch with lift | Pinch with lift and rounded corners

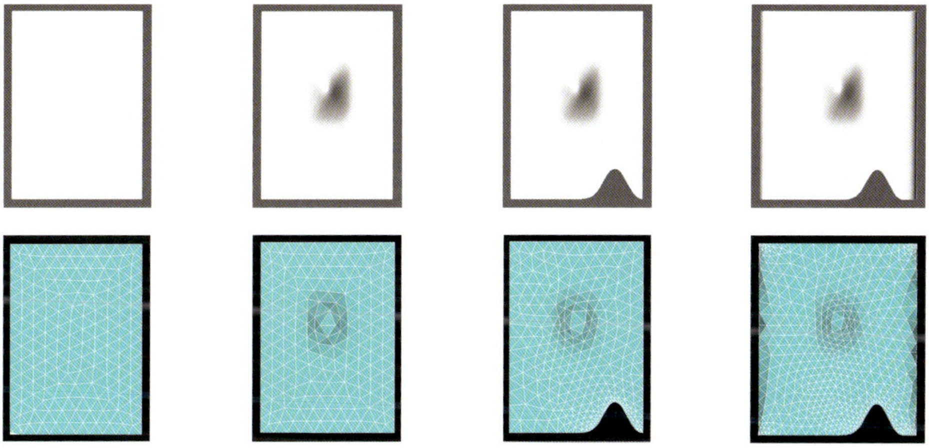

Tessellation Analysis- Corners

Flat surface | Pinched surface | Pinch with lift | Pinch with lift and rounded corners

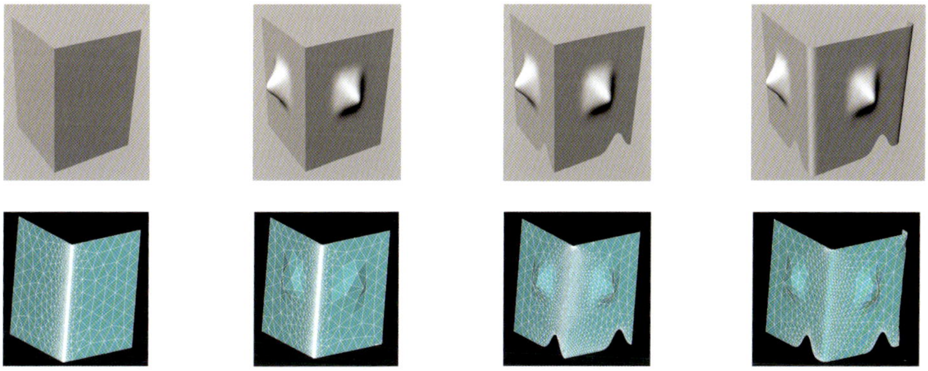

Form generation

Surfaces were created with the following conditions from a stable uniform plane. This was obtained by creating a flat plane and then control points were pushed and pulled to get a desired shape

Points were obtained with preferred options in Ansys from the surface created before and then the points were joined to form an agglomeration of triangles

The triangles were then transformed into meshes and then baked in Grasshopper to obtain the midpoints of the triangles from which the polygons would be derived

After connecting the midpoints, a pattern of polygons were formed from which the final penetration pattern was obtained. Then polygons were offset in Maya and then brought back to Rhino to ensure the normals of the faces

After the polygons were ensured of the normals, they were taken back in Maya where the offset polygons were converted to subdivision surfaces and then extruded to add thickness to the surfaces

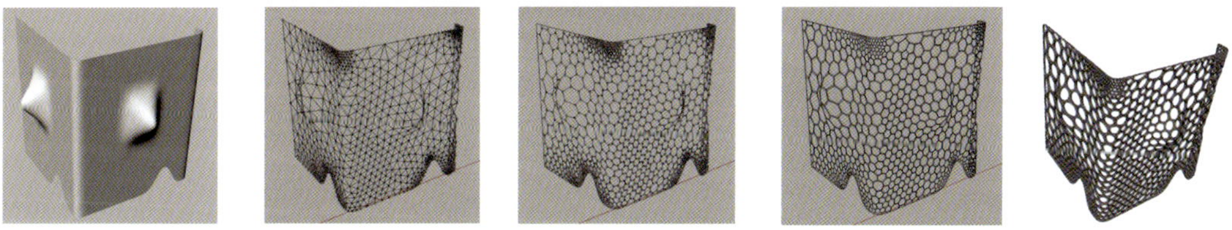

Floor distribution

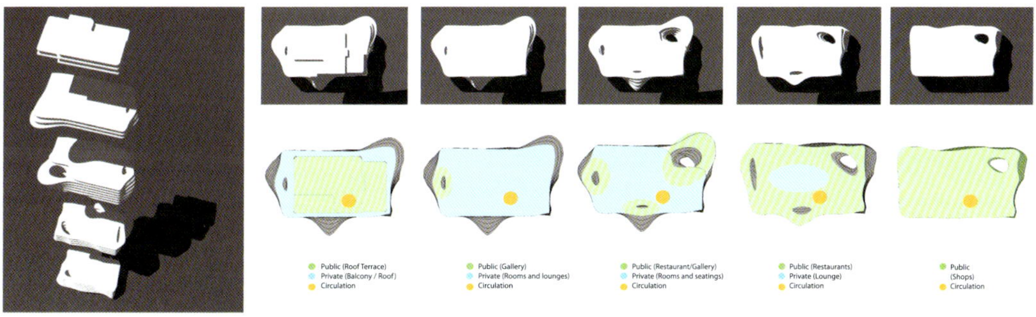

Gothic

Jennifer Reinhardt

Preliminary research on gothic figures was conducted by looking at rose window traceries, fan vaulted ceilings, and other decorative and structural elements found in gothic cathedrals and churches. From this extensive research, eight main figures were identified; s-curve, hook, claw, spade, asymmetrical curve, extended hook, double claw, and double hook. Each of these figures can be manipulated in various ways, however, the manipulations must follow certain rules. Once these rules were determined, different configurations of one, two, three, and four figures were created. From these permutations of figures, "carpets" of configurations were made. while some configurations have a horizontal or vertical direction to them, others created radial patterns. When the radial configurations were inserted into a horizontal or vertical configuration, a mesh of connections were made to create a fluid transition between them.

Once a carpet of configurations was chosen to transform into a facade system, its changes in pattern direction were translated into programmable spaces. Where radial configurations interrupted the carpet pattern, the façade emerged into a "stained glass" window, behind which could be a restaurant, a bar, an office workout room, etc.

The façade system was not only a pattern of configurations, but also a placement for glass. Research was conducted on different types of stained glass throughout past eras. the concept of silver staining from the early 14th century provided the color scheme. white, gold, and light yellow colors predominate the glass on the façade.

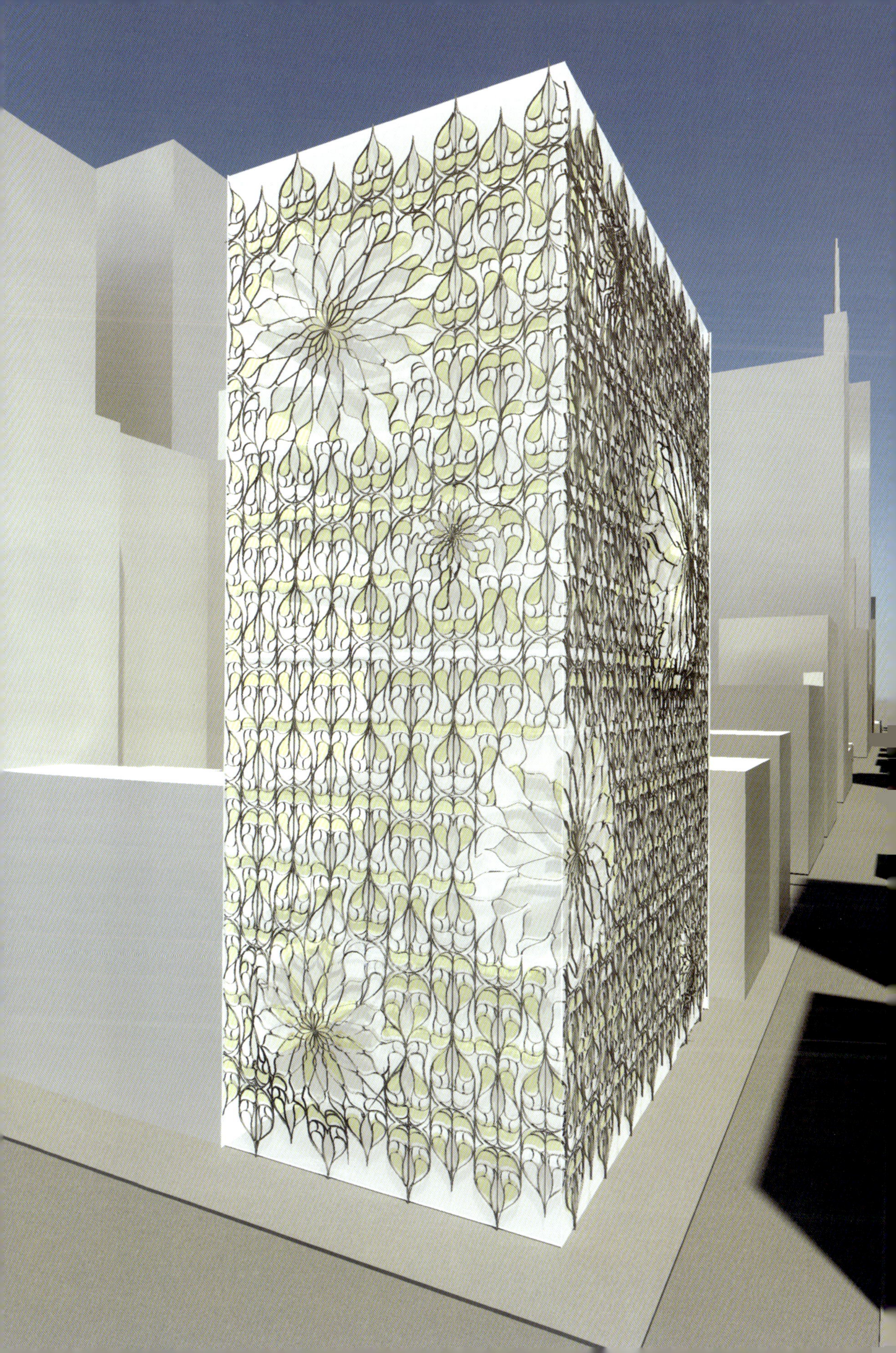

S-Curve

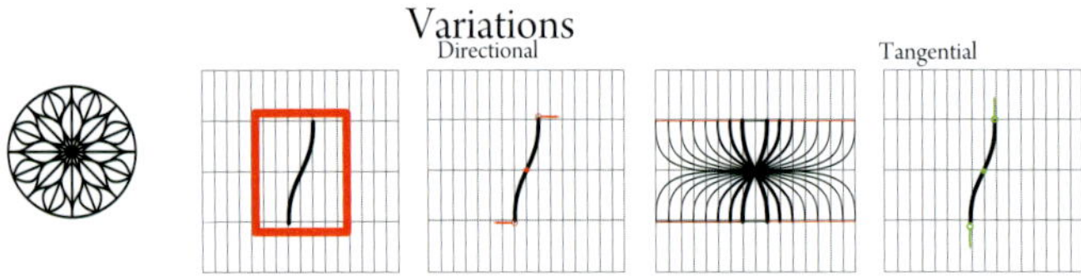

Hook

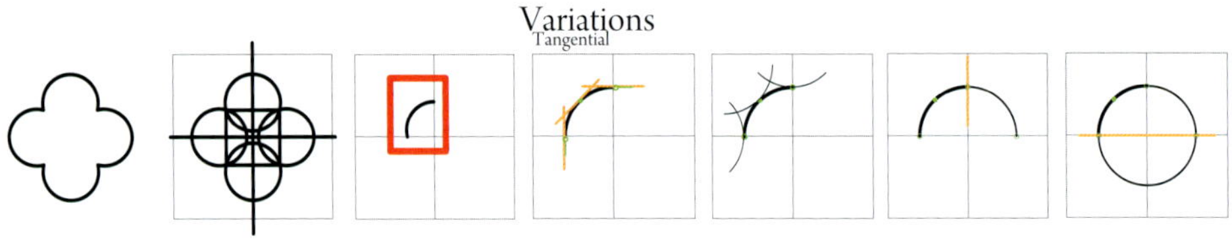

Claw

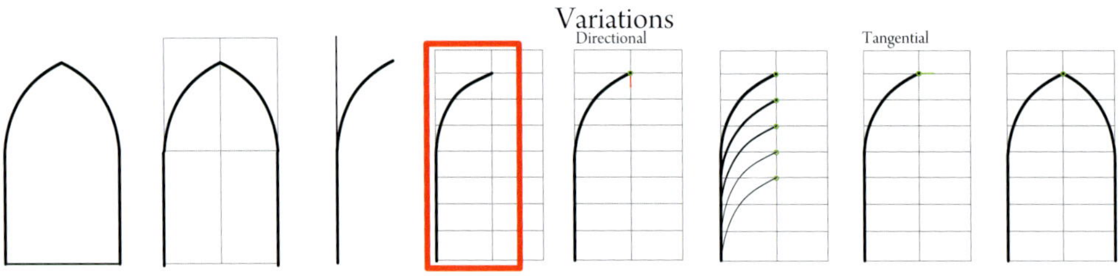

Spade

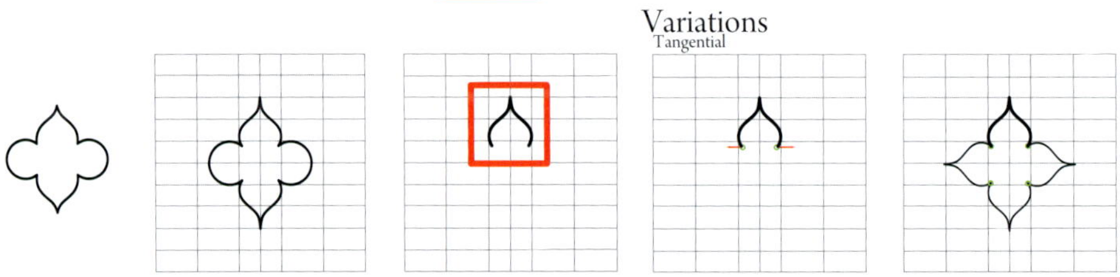

Asymmetrical Curve

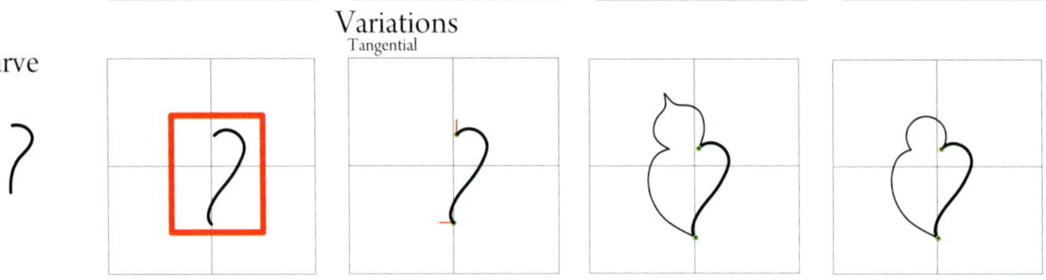

Extended Hook

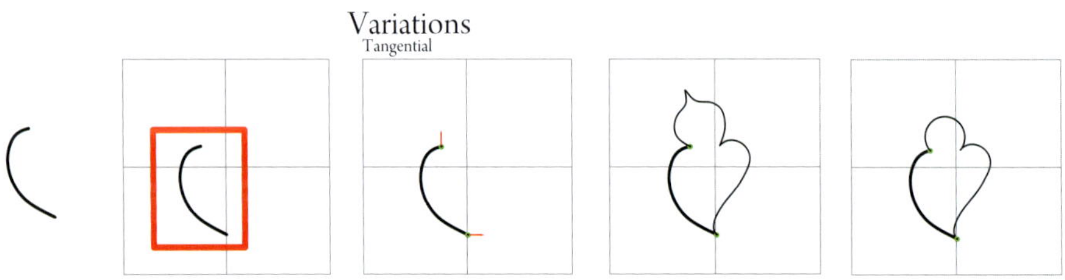

Double Claw

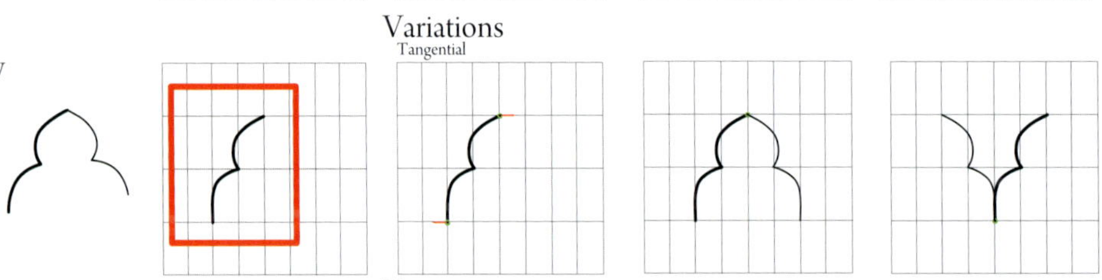

Double Hook

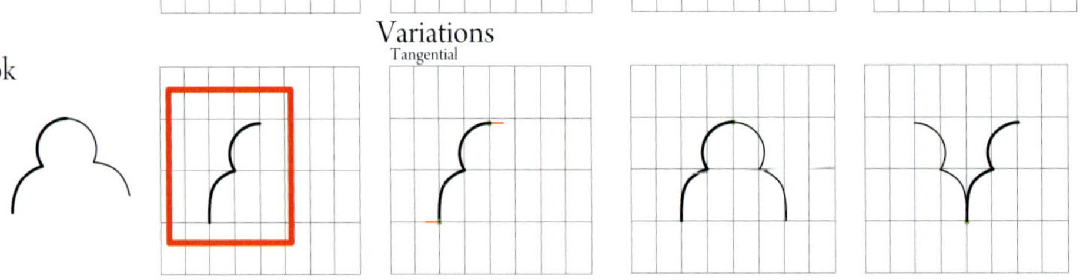

Three or More Figure Configurations

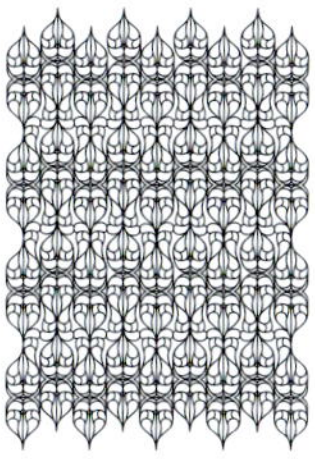
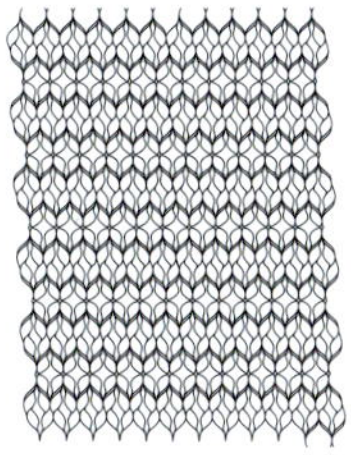
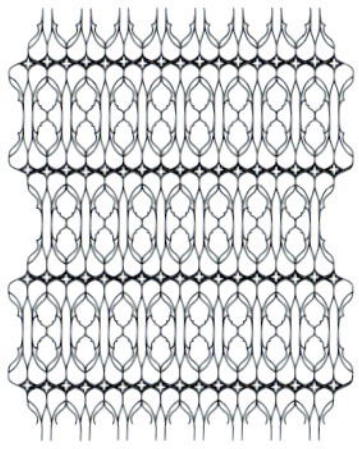
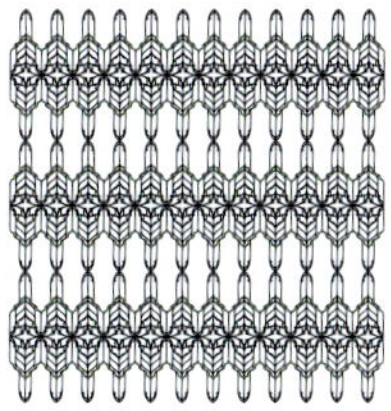
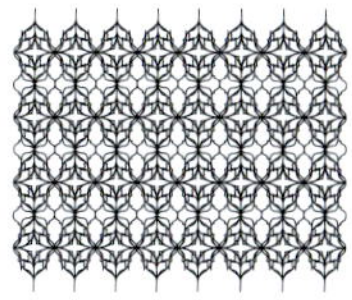

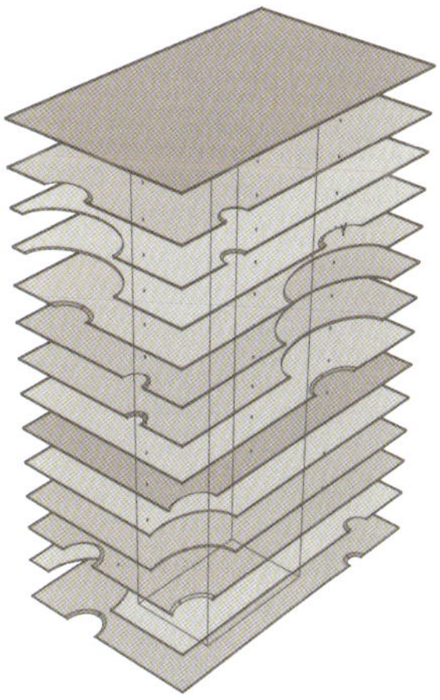

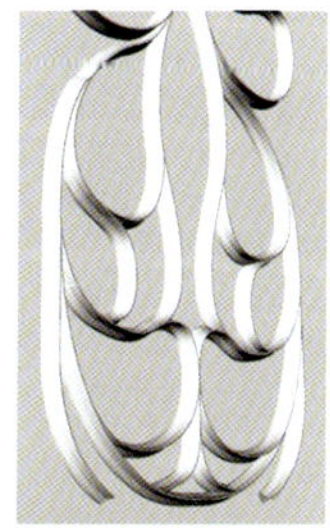

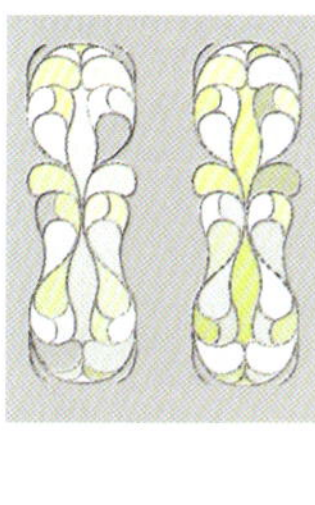

Acknowledgments

This book is the product of an intensive collaboration between teachers at the Georgia Institute of Technology and their students in 2008 and 2009.

First of all, I would like to thank our benefactors, Tom and Beth Ventulett, who have made possible the endowment of my Chair, and whose generosity has for years enabled me to work to connect architectural design with research. The strong ties that American universities maintain with their alumni never cease to amaze a European like me – not only the extensive barbecues and college football but most of all the way alumni, in accordance with the formula "learn, earn and return," feel the need to make significant contributions for the benefit of the school.

I must also thank the students who have contributed to this book, particularly Geoffrey Braiman, the assistant chief editor. The production of a book requires a complex organization; here we have followed the *Vogue* model: a chief editor with an assistant editor, copy editors, image editors, photographers, and designers and assistant designers. All these positions were filled by students, with occasional professional help. The creators of the recurring figure-configuration taxonomies definitely deserve special mention: Rae Smith (gothic rose windows and traceries), Matt Erwin (leaf venation), Dave Beil and Geoffrey Braiman (foam structures), Jacob Porter and Darryl Zuk (packing-cracking), Mara Neumann (hairdo's), Cameron Bishop (celtic knotwork), Valerie Bolen and Kim Wadelton (radiolaria). Thanks too to all my colleagues at Georgia Tech, who assist us with their feedback and criticism but also with the organization of our annual symposium. I also thank the speakers: Mark Burry, Cecil Balmond, Evan Douglis and Michael Hensel. And I thank Dean Alan Balfour for all the support he has given our program.

Finally, I wish to express my gratitude to Daniel Baerlecken for his tireless efforts, and for keeping our department organized every day and the students on track, producing our permanent exhibition, and answering impossible questions.

General editor: Lars Spuybroek
Production and design: Joke Brouwer, Bart Lans
Assistant chief editor: Geoffrey Braiman
Design assistants: Adam Sauer, Cameron Bishop
Text editing: Laura Martz, Dave Beil, Mara Neumann
Image editing: Matthew Erwin, Mara Neumann
Photography credits: Geoffrey Braiman, Sookie Kim

Illustration credits pages 108–220: Georgia Institute of Technology

© 2011 NAi Publishers, Rotterdam.
All rights reserved. No part of this publication may be reproduced, stored in a retrieval system, or transmitted in any form or by any means, electronic, mechanical, photocopying, recording or otherwise, without the prior written permission of the publisher.

Although every effort was made to find the copyright holders for the illustrations used, it has not been possible to trace them all. Interested parties are requested to contact NAi Publishers, Mauritsweg 23, 3012 JR Rotterdam, The Netherlands.

NAi Publishers is an internationally orientated publisher specialized in developing, producing and distributing books on architecture, visual arts and related disciplines.
www.naipublishers.nl

Available in North, South and Central America through D.A.P./Distributed Art Publishers Inc, 155 Sixth Avenue 2nd Floor, New York, NY 10013-1507, tel +1 212 627 1999, fax +1 212 627 9484, dap@dapinc.com

Available in the United Kingdom and Ireland through Art Data, 12 Bell Industrial Estate, 50 Cunnington Street, London W4 5HB, tel +44 208 747 1061, fax +44 208 742 2319, orders@artdata.co.uk

Printed and bound in Belgium

ISBN 978-90-5662-802-4

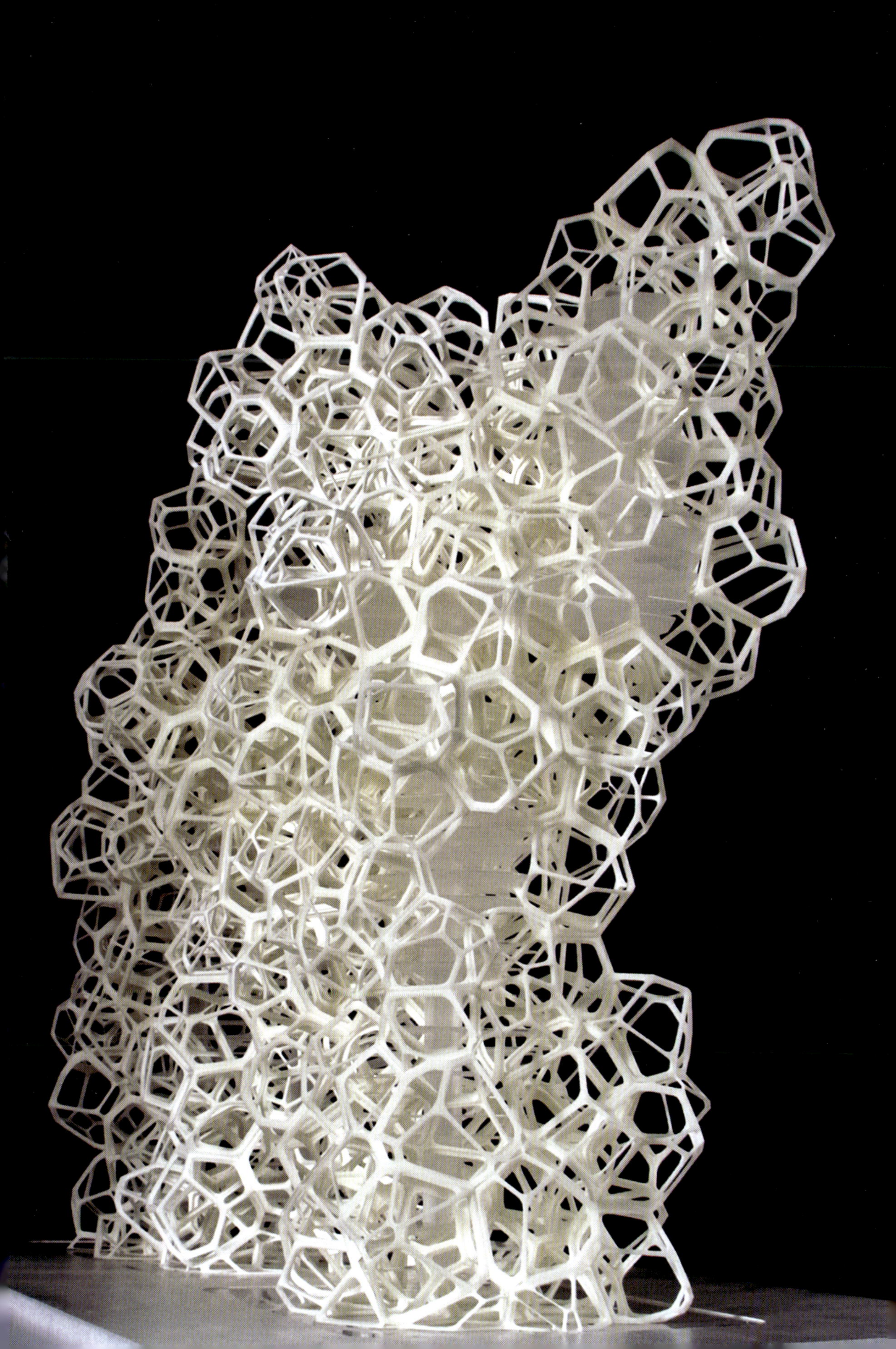